CW01394821

LITERATURE FOR
THE PEOPLE

Daniel Capron

Enjoy!

David Hoskresc
14 May 2024

ALSO BY SARAH HARKNESS

Nelly Erichsen: A Hidden Life

SARAH HARKNESS

LITERATURE FOR THE PEOPLE

How the Pioneering Macmillan Brothers
Built a Publishing Powerhouse

MACMILLAN

First published 2024 by Macmillan
an imprint of Pan Macmillan
The Smithson, 6 Briset Street, London EC1M 5NR
EU representative: Macmillan Publishers Ireland Ltd, 1st Floor,
The Liffey Trust Centre, 117–126 Sheriff Street Upper,
Dublin 1, DO1 YC43
Associated companies throughout the world
www.panmacmillan.com

ISBN 978-1-0350-0893-3

Copyright © Sarah Harkness 2024

The right of Sarah Harkness to be identified as the
author of this work has been asserted by her in accordance
with the Copyright, Designs and Patents Act 1988.

All rights reserved. No part of this publication may be reproduced,
stored in a retrieval system, or transmitted, in any form, or by any means
(electronic, mechanical, photocopying, recording or otherwise)
without the prior written permission of the publisher.

Pan Macmillan does not have any control over, or any responsibility for,
any author or third-party websites referred to in or on this book.

1 3 5 7 9 8 6 4 2

A CIP catalogue record for this book is available from the British Library.

Typeset in Dante by Jouve (UK), Milton Keynes
Printed and bound by CPI Group (UK) Ltd, Croydon, CR0 4YY

MIX
Paper | Supporting
responsible forestry
FSC
www.fsc.org
FSC® C116313

This book is sold subject to the condition that it shall not, by way of
trade or otherwise, be lent, hired out, or otherwise circulated without
the publisher's prior consent in any form of binding or cover other than
that in which it is published and without a similar condition including
this condition being imposed on the subsequent purchaser.

Visit **www.panmacmillan.com** to read more about all our books
and to buy them. You will also find features, author interviews and
news of any author events, and you can sign up for e-newsletters
so that you're always first to hear about our new releases.

In memory of my parents, Reg and Eileen Penney,
and of my dear brother Geoff, always missed.

Contents

Cast of Characters

AINGER, Alfred (1837–1904), cleric and critic, biographer of Charles Lamb. Chaplain to Queen Victoria.

ALEXANDER, Mrs Cecil (1818–95), writer of hymns, including 'All Things Bright and Beautiful', edited Macmillan's *Sunday Book of Poetry*.

ALLINGHAM, William (1824–89), Irish poet and friend of Tennyson, edited *The Ballad Book*, married Helen ALLINGHAM née Paterson (1848–1926), watercolour artist.

AMERY, William, partner in Pott and Amery, New York publishing house, partner in Macmillan & Co.

ARNOLD, Matthew (1828–88), poet and critic, son of Dr Thomas Arnold, headmaster of Rugby School, author of *Essays in Criticism*.

BAKER, Sir Samuel (1821–93) explorer of the Nile, naturalist, big game hunter and abolitionist. Author of *The Albert N'yanza*, etc.

BRIMLEY, George (1819–57), essayist and critic, brother of Caroline Macmillan, Librarian of Trinity College, Cambridge.

CARLYLE, Thomas (1795–1881), Scottish historian, biographer and philosopher, author of *Sartor Resartus* and *The French Revolution*.

COLENSO, John William (1814–83), Bishop of Natal, controversial theologian, disciple of F. D. Maurice.

CRAIK, George Lillie (1837–1905), partner in Macmillan & Co. from 1865, husband of Dinah MULOCK.

DAVIES, John Llewellyn (1826–1916), theologian and Christian Scientist, brother of Emily DAVIES (1830–1921), suffragist and founder of

Girton College, and grandfather of the boys who were the inspiration for *Peter Pan*.

DICEY, Edward (1832–1911), journalist, war correspondent for *Macmillan's Magazine*, cousin of Sir Leslie STEPHEN. Author of *Six Months in the Federal States*.

DODGSON, Charles (1832–98), Cambridge mathematician, better known as Lewis Carroll, author of *Alice in Wonderland* etc.

EVANS, Sebastian (1830–1909), poet, brother of Sir John Evans (and uncle of Sir Arthur Evans, excavator of Knossos).

FAWCETT, Henry (1833–84), statesman and economist, blinded in an accident in 1855, reforming Postmaster General under Gladstone who introduced the penny savings stamp, author of *Manual of Political Economy*, husband of Millicent GARRETT (1847–1929).

FIELDS, James T. (1817–81), publisher and poet based in Boston, Massachusetts, editor of *The Atlantic Monthly*, partner in Ticknor and Fields.

FORSTER, William E. (1818–86), Liberal MP, established 1870 Education Act, contributor to *Macmillan's Magazine*.

FRASER, Alexander Campbell (1819–1914), Professor of Logic and Metaphysics, Edinburgh University, biographer for the Clarendon Press of Bishop Berkeley.

FRASER, James, clerk to Alexander Macmillan, died 1865.

FREEMAN, Edward Augustus (1823–92), historian, Regius Professor of Modern History at Oxford University. Macmillan published more than twenty works by Freeman.

FURNIVALL, Frederick (1825–1910), philologist, co-creator of the *Oxford English Dictionary*, Christian Socialist and founding member of the Working Men's College.

GILCHRIST, Anne (1828–85) wife of Alexander (1828–61), biographers of William Blake. From 1876 to 1879 the widowed Anne took her children to live in Philadelphia to pursue a friendship with Walt Whitman.

GREEN, John Richard (1837–83), historian, married to GREEN, Alice Stopford (1847–1929), author and campaigner for Irish Independence. Macmillan published his *History of the English People* in four volumes.

GROVE, Sir George (1820–1900), engineer by training, editor of *Macmillan's Magazine* and of Grove's *Dictionary of Music*.

HARDY, Thomas (1840–1928), English novelist and poet. Despite rejecting several of his early works, Alexander Macmillan became a good friend of the author and published *The Woodlanders* and *Wessex Tales*.

HARE, Julius (1795–1855), theologian, Archdeacon of Lewes, brother-in-law of F. D. MAURICE, backer of the first Macmillan bookshop in Cambridge 1843. Author with his brother Augustus of *Guesses at Truth*.

HORT, Fenton J. A. (1828–92), Irish-born Christian Socialist and theologian, editor with Brooke FOSS WESTCOTT (1825–1901) of a *New Testament in Greek*.

HUGHES, Thomas (1822–96), author of *Tom Brown's School Days*, Radical reformer, Christian Socialist.

HUXLEY, Thomas Henry (1825–95), zoologist, known as Darwin's bulldog, contributor to *Macmillan's Magazine*, wrote the *Introductory Primer* to Macmillan's Science series.

JACK, William (1834–1924), Scottish mathematician and journalist. He was editor of the *Glasgow Herald* newspaper from 1870 to 1876, and Professor of Mathematics at the University of Glasgow from 1879 until 1909, briefly a partner in Macmillan & Co. from 1876.

JAMES, Henry (1843–1916), American novelist; Macmillan was his first significant publisher, including *The Portrait of a Lady* in 1881.

KINGSLEY, Charles (1819–75), Christian Socialist, novelist and natural scientist, author of *The Water Babies*.

KINGSLEY, Henry (1830–76), troubled brother of Charles, writer of Muscular Christianity novels drawing on his youthful experiences in Australia. Author of *Ravenshoe*.

LOCKYER, Sir Joseph Norman (1836–1920), physicist and astronomer, credited jointly with the discovery of helium. Founding editor of *Nature*.

LUDLOW, John M. F. (1821–1911), Founder with MAURICE of the Christian Socialist movement. Shared a house with Tom HUGHES.

MACLAREN, Rev. Alexander (1826–1910), Scottish Baptist minister, Pastor of the Union Chapel in Oxford Road, Manchester. Not related to:

MACLAREN, Archibald (1820–84), Scottish fencing master, gymnast, educator and author. His physical training scheme is the foundation of the British Royal Army Physical Training Corps. With his wife Gertrude (1833–96) he established Summerfield House School in Oxford in 1864.

MACLEHOSE, James (1811–95), Glasgow bookseller and publisher. His brother Robert was a printer. His son James John MACLEHOSE (1857–1943) followed him into the business and married Mary Macmillan, his oldest son Robert was a printer, and his third son Norman trained as a doctor and married Olive Macmillan.

MARTIN, Frances (1829–1922), pioneer of women's education, founder of the College for Working Women in 1874, of which Alexander Macmillan was treasurer, editor of Macmillan's *Sunday Library* series, shared a house with Dinah MULOCK in the 1850s.

MARTIN, Frederick (1830–83), Swiss-born founding editor of the *Statesman's Year-Book*, biographer of John Clare the poet.

MASSON, David (1822–1907), founding editor of *Macmillan's Magazine*, Scottish academic, supporter of women's suffrage, literary critic and historian. Author of a six-volume *Life of Milton* published by Macmillan.

MAURICE, Frederick Denison (1805–72), controversial theologian, founder of Queen's College for Women and of the Working Men's College, spiritual leader of the Christian Socialists.

MAYOR, Joseph B. (1828–1916), English professor, historian and theologian, father of Florence ('FM') Mayor the novelist.

MORLEY, John, Viscount (1838–1923), Liberal statesman and journalist, editor of the *Pall Mall Gazette*, biographer of Gladstone, Secretary of State for India and Lord President of the Council. Editor of the *English Men of Letters* series.

MULOCK CRAIK, Dinah (1826–87), popular novelist, author of *John Halifax, Gentleman*. In 1865 her husband George Lillie CRAIK became a partner in Macmillan & Co.

NORTON, Caroline (1808–77), author and campaigner for the rights of married women.

OLIPHANT, Margaret (1828–97), novelist, author of the *Carlingford Chronicles* and many books for Macmillan.

PRICE, Professor Bartholomew (1818–98), mathematician and clergyman, Secretary to the Clarendon Press.

ROSSETTI, Christina, (1830–94), sister of Dante Gabriel and William ROSSETTI, poet, author of *Goblin Market*.

RUSKIN, John (1818–1900), poet, artist, writer and critic.

SEELEY, Sir John R. (1834–95), Liberal historian and essayist, author of *Ecce Homo*, son of Robert Seeley, bookseller of The Strand, London. Appointed Regius Professor of Modern History at Cambridge in 1869.

SIDGWICK, Henry (1838–1900), Knightsbridge Professor of Modern Philosophy at Cambridge University, co-founder of Newnham College, married to Nora Balfour, sister of the Prime Minister Arthur Balfour. Macmillan published his *Methods of Ethics* and other texts.

SPENCER, Herbert (1820–1903), philosopher and sociologist, originator of the phrase 'survival of the fittest'. Contributed to Youmans' *Modern Culture*, published by Macmillan.

STANLEY, Arthur Penrhyn (1815–81), biographer of Dr Arnold, Regius Professor of Ecclesiastical History at Oxford, Dean of Westminster, liberal theologian. Macmillan published his sermons.

STEPHEN, Sir Leslie (1832–1904), literary critic and biographer, father of Vanessa Bell and Virginia Woolf. Contributed several volumes to the *English Men of Letters* series.

TENNYSON, Alfred, Lord (1809–92), Poet Laureate from 1850, author of *In Memoriam* and *Idylls of the King*. Macmillan & Co. became his publisher in 1884.

THRING, Edward (1821–87), headmaster of Uppingham, founder of the Headmasters' Conference, author of several textbooks published by Macmillan.

TODHUNTER, Isaac (1820–84), mathematician, college lecturer at Cambridge. Macmillan published more than twenty-five of his textbooks.

WALLACE, Alfred Russel (1823–1913), naturalist, explorer and anthropologist. Macmillan published nine of his books including *Darwinism*, and nearly two hundred articles in *Nature*.

WATT, David (1817–97), missionary to Benares, India, friend of David Livingstone, and of Daniel and Alexander Macmillan in the 1840s.

WILSON, Daniel (1816–92), Edinburgh-born archaeologist and ethnolo-
gist, President of University College, Toronto. Author of *Prehistoric
Man*. Brother of WILSON, George (1818–59), chemist and author, first
Director of the Industrial Museum of Scotland.

YONGE, Charlotte (1823–1901), prolific novelist, author of *The Heir of
Redclyffe*, one of the best-selling novels of the Victorian era. Devout
Anglo-Catholic and follower of John Keble. Macmillan became her
publisher in 1863.

MALCOLM MACMILLAN *m* JANET KERR

DUNCAN *m* KATHARINE CRAWFORD
(1770–1823)   (1771–1835)

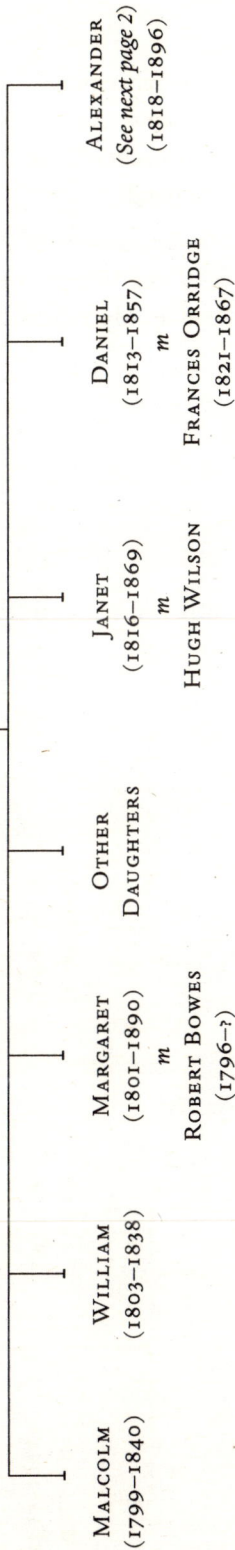

MALCOLM
(1799–1840)

WILLIAM
(1803–1838)

MARGARET
(1801–1890)
m
ROBERT BOWES
(1796–?)

OTHER
DAUGHTERS

JANET
(1816–1869)
m
HUGH WILSON

DANIEL
(1813–1857)
m
FRANCES ORRIDGE
(1821–1867)

ALEXANDER
(*See next page 2*)
(1818–1896)

ROBERT
(1835–1919)
m
FANNY BRIMLEY
(1831–1903)

FREDERICK ORRIDGE
(1851–1936)
m
GEORGIANA WARRIN
(1846–1943)

MAURICE CRAWFORD
(1853–1936)
m
HELEN ARTIE
TARLETON BELLES

KATHERINE
(1855–1910)

ARTHUR
(1857–1876)

3 CHILDREN

ELIZABETH
(*adopted*)

DANIEL DE MENDI
(1886–1965)

ARTHUR TARLETON
(1889–1968)

MAURICE HAROLD
(1894–1986)

THE MACMILLAN
FAMILY TREE

ALEXANDER
(1818–1896)
m
CAROLINE BRIMLEY
(1823–1871)

EMMA PIGNATEL
(1843–1935)

JOHN VICTOR
(1877–1956)
m
ANNIE MAURICE
(1879–1944)

PETER
(1913–1974)

JEAN
(1915–1982)

MARY
(1874–1959)
m
JAMES MACLEHOSE
(1857–1943)

(*See next page 3*)
WILLIAM ALEXANDER
(1856–1936)
(1864–1866)

MALCOLM KINGSLEY
(1852–1889)

GEORGE AUGUSTIN
(1855–1936)
m
MARGARET LUCUS
(1857–1939)

JAMES COLIN
(1897–1917)

ALEC
(1904–1989)

MURIEL
(1899–1987)

MARY ALISON
(1906–1991)

HELEN
(1883–1954)

WILLIAM
(1880–1954)

ALEXANDER
('ALISTER')
(1881–1892)

ALEXANDER
(1818–1896)
m
CAROLINE BRIMLEY

(MALCOLM)

(GEORGE)

MARGARET ANNE
(1857–1935)
m
LOUIS DYER
(1851–1908)

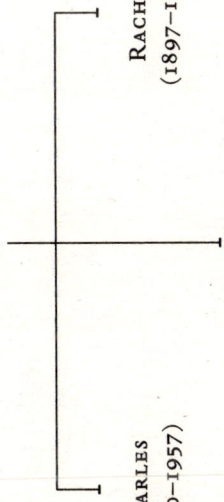

(WILLIAM)

OLIVE
(1859–1926)
m
NORMAN MACLEHOSE
(1859–1931)

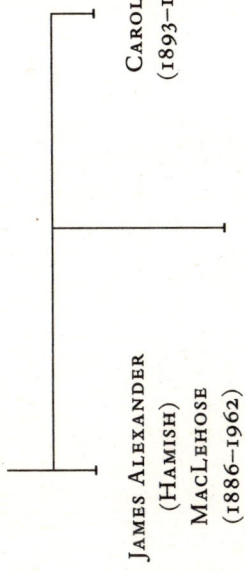

CHARLES
(1890–1957)

CECIL
(1894–1915)

RACHEL
(1897–1969)

JAMES ALEXANDER
(HAMISH)
MACLEHOSE
(1886–1962)

NORMAN
(1889–1915)

CAROLINE
(1893–1971)

List of Illustrations

Illustrations from *Alice's Adventures in Wonderland* and *Through the Looking-Glass* by John Tenniel, by permission of The Macmillan Archive, Macmillan Publishers International Ltd.

Illustrations from *Tom Brown's School Days* by A. Hughes and S. P. Hall, By permission of The Macmillan Archive, Macmillan Publishers International Ltd.

Integrated Illustrations

Alexander Macmillan's notice of death, by permission of The Macmillan Archive, Macmillan Publishers International Ltd.

Daniel Macmillan, by permission of The Macmillan Archive, Macmillan Publishers International Ltd.

Nineteenth-century printing press. M&N / Alamy

Fleet Street. Hulton Archive / Stringer

Aldersgate Street by Thomas Hosmer Shepherd / London Metropolitan Archives

Frederick Maurice. Hulton Archive / Stringer

Frontispiece to *Tom Brown's School Days*, by permission of The Macmillan Archive, Macmillan Publishers International Ltd.

Masthead of *Macmillan's Magazine*, by permission of The Macmillan Archive, Macmillan Publishers International Ltd.

The Water Babies illustration by Linley Sambourne, by permission of The Macmillan Archive, Macmillan Publishers International Ltd.

Goblin Market 1862 title page illustration by Dante Gabriel Rossetti, by permission of The Macmillan Archive, Macmillan Publishers International Ltd.

Matthew Arnold by Sandys, by permission of The Macmillan Archive, Macmillan Publishers International Ltd.

Alice's Adventures in Wonderland, Mad Hatter's Tea Party illustration by John Tenniel, by permission of The Macmillan Archive, Macmillan Publishers International Ltd.

William Alexander Macmillan by Lowes Dickinson

Henry Wadsworth Longfellow. Universal History Archive / Getty Images

Golden Treasury, 1861 title page, by permission of The Macmillan Archive, Macmillan Publishers International Ltd.

Nature cover, 4 November 1869, by permission of The Macmillan Archive, Macmillan Publishers International Ltd.

INTRODUCTION

DEATH OF MR. ALEXANDER MACMILLAN.

WE much regret to record the death of Mr. Alexander Macmillan, one of the founders of this journal. This is not the place to give a long account of his career. We may limit ourselves to the statement that outside the field of scientific workers there were few who possessed a greater sympathy with scientific aims, few who had a keener insight as to the place science should occupy in our national life and in our educational systems. It was the hope that a more favourable condition for the progress of science might be thereby secured that led him to enter warmly into the establishment of this journal in 1869. Mr. Macmillan was born in 1818, and died on Saturday last, at his residence in Portland Place.

Alexander Macmillan's notice of death

'Few men of our time have made a better use of a fortune of which they were the architects, or have been less spoilt by prosperity.'

Charles L. Graves

'I have lived among the Gods'

Alexander Macmillan

THE THIRD WEEK of January 1896 opened with blizzards across the east of Britain from Aberdeen to Kent, and drifts a foot high across Norfolk and Suffolk. But by Wednesday 29 January the snow had gone and the weather had turned surprisingly warm for the time of year, a glimpse of pale sunlight, with just the hint of spring. Early in the morning a heavily draped horse-drawn carriage halted outside 21 Portland Place, a grand terraced house near Regent's Park in central London, the central house in a symmetrical terrace designed by the Adam brothers, with a highly decorated front porch in the Doric style and ornamental white pilasters standing out against smoke-blackened London stock brick – the house of a wealthy gentleman. That day the windows were dark, with the curtains closed, a wreath of ivy and yew hanging on the front door. An unvarnished oak coffin was borne out of the house and loaded onto a hearse, and then the horses set off at a slow, dignified pace on the two-mile route across town to Waterloo Station. There, a small crowd of dark-suited and distinguished-looking mourners, alerted by a notice the previous day in the *Morning Post*, had gathered on Platform 1, waiting to meet the coffin and to board a specially chartered train bound for Liphook in Hampshire. For the deceased, punctuality was a virtue, and the train departed promptly at a quarter to eleven.

At Liphook Station the coffin, covered with elegant wreaths of white lilac, lilies of the valley, violets and Scottish heather, was transferred onto an open cart lined with more ivy and evergreens for the mile and a half journey down country lanes to St Mary's Church in the little village of Bramshott. One of the wreaths bore the inscription 'For Auld Lang Syne. A token of deep affection, for the dear master's memory, from his friends at Bedford Street.' The coffin-bearers were chosen from friends and retainers of the family and at the churchyard gate stood four high-ranking clergy, led by the

Bishop of Southwark. The opening part of the burial service was read in the church, where a large congregation joined in singing 'O God of Bethel, by whose hand, thy children still are fed'. A favourite hymn of the deceased, it had been sung at his father's deathbed in Scotland over seventy years earlier. Then the procession re-formed and passed out to the graveyard, through paths lined with yet more white and purple flowers, to the solemn organ notes of Chopin's Funeral March. The final hymn, 'Now the labourer's task is o'er', was sung as the coffin was lowered into the moss-lined grave, and the bishop pronounced a blessing.

The coffin bore the simple inscription: 'Alexander Macmillan. Born Oct 3 1818. Died Jan 25 1896.' He was laid to rest close to the grave of his ten-year-old grandson Alister, who had died of peritonitis just four years earlier. Yet for many of the mourners there was a darker shadow in the graveyard and a missing tomb – Alexander's eldest, unhappy and unconventional son Malcolm had last been seen on a mountainside in Turkey some eight years earlier and no one knew where he lay buried, or if he was even dead. The only certainty was that Alexander had never recovered from this loss.

The funeral party consisted of some eighty or ninety people, family and friends, including thirty or more representatives of the Macmillan publishing house in Bedford Street. Notable among the group of mourners were some of the heavyweight intellectuals of the day: John Morley, 'the last of the great late nineteenth century liberals'; Henry James, already a well-known and highly successful author; Professor Norman Lockyer, founding editor of the journal *Nature*; Sir George Grove, first Director of the Royal College of Music; and Sir Henry Roscoe, a chemist and Vice-Chancellor of the University of London. Around the grave stood the headmasters of Harrow and Westminster schools, honouring a man whose own schooling had finished at the age of fifteen. Some of the deceased's greatest friends were missing: at the age of seventy-seven, Alexander Macmillan had outlived many of the men who had shaped his life or helped him make his fortune. His heroes, Frederick Denison

Maurice, Charles Kingsley, Thomas Huxley, Matthew Arnold and Alfred, Lord Tennyson, were gone, and Tom Hughes, too frail to attend, would follow Macmillan into the grave two months later, the man known as Lewis Carroll two years after that. Chief among the long departed was Alexander's brother Daniel, his earliest partner in the founding of the firm, who had been dead nearly forty years. In his final decade, Alexander would still ask, in a puzzled tone, 'What would Daniel think of this?'

The funeral marked the passing of a man born in absolute poverty, with only the most rudimentary education, yet it celebrated a life of considerable achievement. Alexander's father had died in his early fifties, worn out by the toils of scraping a living amidst the harsh conditions of a small croft on the west coast of Scotland. He left his eight surviving children, including the two youngest boys, ten-year-old Daniel and five-year-old Alexander, to make their way in the world with nothing to shape their lives except the moral precepts that were drummed into them by their mother and the understanding that work was hard, even painful, but necessary. These boys' rise through apprenticeships and wretched servitude, as they described it, to become masters of their own business was not unprecedented in the Victorian Age – this was the era of Samuel Smiles's self-help handbooks. What makes their story so compelling and unusual is the humour and noble-heartedness of all their endeavours. Daniel and Alexander Macmillan were proud to call themselves Christian Socialists, being active philanthropists and loving family men, and between them they founded not just one of the great publishing houses of the Western world, but a dynasty that within two generations would leap across class boundaries to marry into the nobility and produce a British Prime Minister.

Alexander Macmillan once described himself as an 'advocate for the ignorant'.[1] Perhaps this phrase has lost its meaning, over the last century. Today we think of ignorance as a personal failing, a deliberate decision by an individual to avoid education, to turn one's back on the plethora of freely available sources of information and knowledge. To the philanthropic Victorians, however, it was seen as a want to be remedied, closer to hunger, thirst or ill-health, and signified a failing by society to nurture its members. To be ignorant was to be ignored. This was the cause that Alexander and his brother Daniel took to be their mission on earth – to be a conduit for cascading knowledge down to those who hungered for it, or whose salvation required it. They fervently believed that access to good and affordable literature would bring young people to God, would give them a moral code to live by, and might ameliorate the misunderstanding between the classes that led to political strife and unrest. Above all they thought everyone deserved the sheer pleasure and intellectual stimulation that books had given them.

Alexander Macmillan's four hundred and thirty mile journey from the bracken-covered hills of the west coast of Scotland to leafy Bramshott churchyard may have taken nearly eighty years, but it was nothing compared with the journey upon which the firm he and Daniel had created was embarked, from the first humble bookshop near St Paul's Cathedral to an international multimillion-pound business. The Macmillan brothers befriended, encouraged, shaped and published some of the greatest thinkers and writers of the nineteenth century: novelists, poets, historians and scientists – they were literary king-, and queen-, makers. The success of their firm was driven by their extraordinary appetite for hard work, and by the uncanny instinct they had for identifying those authors who had the most relevant messages for the reading public, and who expressed them best, whether the writing took the form of a philosophical tract, or of an adventure story for children. A deep moral purpose inspired their careers and their catalogue reflected their beliefs, as well as their intellectual curiosity.

Alexander always attributed his success to the way he had been raised, and it is fascinating to trace the links between the brothers' separate experiences as young men and their publishing choices. Not being Varsity men themselves, they had a knack for recognizing the depressing tendency of Victorian academics to produce dry, inaccessible tomes. They saw their role as moulding these works into material that would be attractive to the rapidly growing audience of enthusiastic, book-hungry amateurs such as they had been: from the self-made men, the John Thorntons of Mrs Gaskell's *North and South*, to the clerks and office boys, the Leonard Basts of *Howards End*, not forgetting the wives, the daughters and the sisters. In the same way that the Great Exhibition of 1851 opened the country's eyes and revealed cultural and scientific progress to a wider population than ever before, the Macmillans created a different version of literature, accessible to the common man.

In 1896, when Alexander died, the firm was still headquartered in premises he had acquired in Bedford Street, Covent Garden. The complete bibliographic catalogue of the books the brothers had published between 1843 and 1889 had taken two years to compile and ran to over seven hundred and forty pages. The firm was now publishing some hundred and fifty new titles every year. In addition to books, they owned enduring copyrights such as *Nature*, *The Statesman's Year-Book* and *Grove's Dictionary of Music and Musicians*. Writers whose works they were promoting that year included Henry James, Thomas Hardy and Rudyard Kipling. Annual sales had reached several hundred thousand pounds (over twenty million in today's money). The New York office alone, which would shortly be established as a separate entity, but still under Macmillan family ownership, was turning over fifty thousand dollars annually.

Although Alexander had been the driving force behind the firm for more than forty years, there was no concern that his death posed any threat to its future prosperity or direction, as it was already flourishing under the command of the next generation. The true signs of business achievement, today as much as then, are stability, longevity, and, a term that Alexander might not have recognized, scalability. By 1896 the house of Macmillan had firmly established itself as a scalable business, with representatives in New York and across the British Empire in India, Canada and Australia. Today Macmillan still flourishes in private hands but held since the late 1990s by the Holtzbrinck

Publishing Group, a large family-owned media company headquartered in Stuttgart, Germany. Its website records that it is one of the largest and best-known international publishers in the world, operating well-known imprints in over seventy countries around the globe. There are worldwide academic brands: Palgrave Macmillan and Macmillan Education, and in the United Kingdom, it publishes under the Pan Macmillan and Picador brands, among others.

Twenty-five years after Daniel Macmillan's death, he was commemorated with the publication of an affectionate 'memoir' edited by Tom Hughes, who was not just one of the firm's most successful early authors but also a great family friend. This was based on the correspondence between the brothers and on other family letters. When Alexander died, his son George edited a collection of letters interspersed with memories of his father, for private publication, and then a rather stuffy, one-dimensional memoir was commissioned from the biographer Charles Graves. Finally, in 1943, Charles Morgan, a fashionable novelist, was persuaded to shape and edit a history of the first hundred years of the house of Macmillan, written at very short notice. All of these works shed some light on the characters of the brothers and on the history of the firm but are written either in the stilted and reverential prose of the late Victorian era, or, as Morgan himself said, rushing to hit the centenary deadline, create 'a glancing impression, not a formal discourse.'[2] Some more recent biographies of Harold Macmillan have spared a chapter or two for his ancestors, with the brothers' lives confined to a prologue to the exploits of their illustrious grandson. Two hundred years after Daniel Macmillan joined the book trade, the brothers' incredible achievements are worthy of celebration.

– 1 –

THE BROTHERS
(1813–33)

Daniel Macmillan

'There were two springs which bubbled side by side
As if they had been made that they might be Companions for
each other'

William Wordsworth

DANIEL AND ALEXANDER Macmillan were born in distinctly unpromising surroundings, but they were always proud of their Scottish heritage and particularly of their upbringing. Indeed, they attributed much of their later commercial success to the lessons their parents had taught them by word and by example. They never sought to romanticize what were clearly the poorest of poor circumstances, but often spoke with humour and wistfulness of their youth and the struggles of their early life. Their reverence for these humble roots persisted through subsequent generations so that when Prime Minister, Harold Macmillan kept a photo of the family's croft on his desk.

The childhoods of the two boys were very different, although they were born only five years apart, and these different experiences shaped their characters and their outlook on life in complementary ways that would make them a well-matched and formidable team in business. For Daniel, the older boy, life was a serious, precarious and worrisome affair, only to be survived through hard work and strong religious faith. For Alexander, the baby of the family, life was an adventure, with some sadness along the way, but with many rewards to be gained from industry, from embracing friendships and from taking risks. It was a powerful combination of attributes with which to start, and sustain, a business.

Their parents, who they loved and admired deeply, were crofters, with a strict Calvinistic faith that ruled their lives. The Macmillan ancestors had dwelt for many generations on the south-west coast of Scotland, coming originally from the home of the Macmillan clan, North Knapdale, in Argyllshire, but in the many poisonous and violent disputes among the Scottish clans of the sixteenth and seventeenth centuries, the Macmillans seem to have lost out and been dispersed. Many years later, Alexander, in a characteristic burst of sentimentality, would name his first proper home in London 'Knapdale'. Alexander loved to spin tales of ancestors embroiled in feuds, fighting off the English, but he did not take any of it too seriously. The furthest back that he could reliably trace his branch of the family was to his great-grandfather Donald, also known as Daniel, whose ancestors had settled not far from Knapdale, but across the water on Arran.

The Isle of Arran today is an enchanting place, a hundred and sixty-seven square miles of peaty glens, purple-heathered hills and sparkling lochs, with a strip of little villages huddled along the coast-line, mostly attractive Victorian villas sitting with their backs to the moors. The geological fault that separates Highland and Lowland Scotland is replicated diagonally across the island, creating a miniature Scottish experience, but without the industrial belt. Tourists have been arriving since the first recorded day trip in 1829, appreciating the warmer climate, the wild and beautiful landscape, the sandy beaches and rocky headlands, the prehistoric monuments, the fascinating geology and the wildlife: red deer, golden eagles, wild orchids. Towards the north of the island sits the little ferry port of Lochranza, and just a few miles further along, at the northernmost tip, sits Cock of Arran, the farm which the Macmillans of Arran were calling home at the start of the nineteenth century.

For three hundred years the island had been owned by the family of the Duke of Hamilton, after an ancestor was given the castle at Brodick by King James III of Scotland in the fifteenth century. In the eighteenth century there were some six or seven thousand inhabitants, or a thousand families, making a living of sorts. They followed the common Scottish farming system known as 'runrig': strip-farming of crops (oats, flax, potatoes) in a three-yearly rotation, with some grazing land for a few cows, goats and sheep held in common, paying rent in kind. They heated their homes with peat, dug from the ground in April and left to dry into the summer months. The most usual habitation was the blackhouse – a long, low, narrow habitation of dry stone with rounded corners and a thatched roof. It had no windows or chimneys, just one central door, the smoke from the peat fire in the middle of the house blackening the thatch to control infestation – hence the name. The house was shared between families and their animals, who lived under the same roof for mutual warmth, in a byre separated by a wall.

By 1800, what was already a hard life had become much harder. The islanders were experiencing the devastating effects of enclosure, as the Duke's modernizing agent, John Burrel, slowly implemented plans intended to improve yields by rearranging and enclosing ancient smallholdings, giving the tenant farmers shorter leases and fixed rents. The higher ground would be given over to sheep. Almost immediately this left some eight hundred families with no access to land they could call their own: they had either to leave for the mainland to look for work or hire themselves out as casual labour on the island. Meanwhile, lack of capital prevented the new smallholders from investing to improve the soil, and to Burrel's disappointment, yields actually fell. In 1860, when Alexander visited Cock Farm, where his grandfather Malcolm had lived, the tenant told him that the land was too poor to raise crops, and could only support a few animals, but his aunt told him that when she was a girl, Malcolm was growing barley and oats for himself and for others.

Not surprisingly, beset by financial hardship and insecurity, some of the population turned to religion. The Church of Scotland, with its Presbyterian disciplines, was losing ground in the outlying regions of the country, and much of Arran had fallen back into superstition, with belief in ghosts and witches – 'turbulent, superstitious and otherwise degraded', as Alexander would later describe it.[1] But on the mainland a group of young men, led by two brothers, Robert and James Haldane, were inspired to revive the Christian faith and reach out as missionaries. In the late 1790s they began to tour the west coast of Scotland, drawing large crowds to hear them preach, often against the opposition of the Elders of the Established Church. By 1800 they had reached Arran.

One of the Elders on Arran was Malcolm Macmillan, Daniel and

Alexander's grandfather. Born in 1746, he had risen in seniority to be the tacksman of the farm at Cock of Arran, which meant that he was the senior tenant, with responsibilities to the Duke for collecting the rents from the other tenants, but also sharing out the corn and the peat fuel in winter and generally looking after the welfare of his neighbours. He was a man of stern character, though 'with a softer side to him to which illness or misfortune rarely appealed in vain'.[2] According to his grandchildren, he was often inclined to give extra-generous measures when he could see cases of need but hated to have any attention drawn to this. Census records are scarce and imperfect, however it seems that Malcolm and his wife, Janet Kerr, had at least ten children, and among these were a son, Duncan, and a daughter, Janet. The Macmillan family legend, as recorded by Thomas Hughes in his biography of Daniel Macmillan, was that Duncan attended a revival meeting, despite his orthodox father's misgivings, and there met Katharine Crawford, whose father farmed a little way further south down the coast at Sannox. If so, their meeting predated the well-documented 1800 visit by James Haldane, as other records suggest that they married in 1793, when Duncan was twenty-three and Katharine was twenty-two. Their first child, Mary, was born in 1794. (It is however true that Duncan's sister Janet met her future husband at a Revival meeting. Alexander Mackay had trained at the Haldanes' seminary and arrived on Arran to continue the mission in 1806: he married Janet in 1809 and remained as pastor of the Sannox congregation until his death in 1856. Alexander would visit his widowed aunt Janet on Arran shortly before her death in 1861.)

Meanwhile, with no space for Duncan, his wife and children at Cock of Arran, the family moved to a croft called Achog on land farmed by Katharine's father, William Crawford, and her brother Daniel. To our modern sensibilities, the stretch of land above the two little villages of Corrie and Sannox on the east coast of Arran is enchanting, the gentle slope of moorland rising over a three mile distance and nearly three thousand feet to the peak of Goat Fell, with its rippling streams, its heather and orchids. To the Crawford and Macmillan family it would become a place of acute suffering and eventual defeat. Achog, the farm above the granite boulder known as the Cat Stone between Corrie and Sannox, has long disappeared. Even in the 1960s a local historian tried to photograph the ruins but had trouble making them out. He thought there had been a traditional long blackhouse with two small cottages. Achog had been one of the larger farms on Arran with thirty-two acres of arable land, twenty-one of pasture and access to twenty-seven acres of open moorland for grazing cattle. 'A most humble house on the brow of a hill', as Daniel Macmillan later described his parents' home, overlooking the sea, and on clear days one could see the Ayrshire coast some forty miles away.[3] Behind the house were the mountains, sometimes covered in snow. It might have looked pretty, but the land was of little value – the soil was so poor that it could only barely support the grazing of cattle and sheep. The family often went hungry.

William Crawford died in 1803; he was buried in Sannox graveyard, and his son Daniel Crawford took over the tenancy. Around this time, the villages of Sannox and Corrie became the centre of the Haldane revival on the island, and by 1806 the group had some forty members. That was the year that Alexander Mackay arrived on the island to take charge of the congregation. Duncan and Katharine Macmillan lived at the centre of this group. The services were conducted in the open air, or in farmhouses in bad weather: the church was not built until 1822, on land leased from the Duke of Hamilton. Duncan preached in Gaelic and Katharine clung to her Bible. But the demands of their family became overwhelming: they would produce twelve children in all, over twenty-four years. The little cottage must have been a noisy place until suddenly stilled in the terrible year of 1814, when the couple's four youngest daughters, Janet, Bell, Ann and Lizzie, were carried off by some nameless epidemic within a few weeks. It is possible that the five older children only survived because they had already left to find work of some kind: certainly the two oldest boys, Malcolm and William, had settled on the mainland, although still young teenagers, and were working as carpenters in Irvine. The three daughters, Mary, Katherine and Margaret survived, as did little Daniel, born on 13 September 1813, the tenth child and the third son – possibly protected from infection by his mother's milk. This terrible loss seems if anything to have strengthened the parents' spirituality. Duncan and Katharine would need their faith to cope with the troubles ahead.

In later life, Daniel often spoke of his childhood – his Calvinist training, the morning and evening prayers, grace before and after meals, going to the kirk, the quiet solemnity of the Sabbath. Both brothers always spoke of their mother Katharine with reverence. 'She is gone from this world but her influence can never die' wrote Daniel to his fiancée Fanny in the summer of 1850: 'she helped to form my brothers and sisters: they have influenced others, and so the good works through all generations . . .'[4] Alexander wrote: 'My mother was a woman of very devout nature and habits, whose daily life was, as I believe, lived as in the conscious presence of God.'[5] From her father she inherited a surprising degree of religious tolerance, which would have a particular influence on her youngest sons. She had a fine voice and loved to sing the old Scottish ballads: Alexander learnt these by heart and in later life it took little persuasion for him to sing them at any social gathering. Perhaps most significantly of all, she was a voracious reader, still reading Dante in her old age.

In 1815 Daniel Crawford's lease came up for renewal and his landlord, the Duke of Hamilton, enforced new terms, which required enclosure of the arable land around the croft. The farm could no longer support Duncan and Katharine, and in 1816 they left for Irvine, a small harbour town directly across the sea from Sannox. However, the memories of Arran, and affection for its beauties, never left the family. In the 1860s Alexander visited several times, sometimes with family, sometimes with his friend David Masson, to walk the round trip between Sannox and Lochranza. After his death, the family made a pilgrimage to the sites of the ancestral home, placing a plaque in Alexander's memory on the wall of the little church at Lochranza. The pilgrimages continued into the twentieth century: Harold Macmillan was taken to the island as a small boy and returned in later years to shoot grouse on the moors. There were a few remaining Macmillan and Mackay relatives still living on the island in the 1980s, who called Harold their cousin and to whom Harold would pay a well-photographed visit – but most of the previous inhabitants of Corrie and Sannox had been evicted in 1829, with the Duke of Hamilton paying half the cost of their fare to emigrate to Canada. Among the eighty-six people who boarded the SS *Caledonian* en route for Quebec were eight Macmillans, including six children, and two Crawfords.

Irvine in the 1820s was very different from the isolated North Arran crofting community of Daniel's early years. There is a painting of the high street in 1819, just after the Macmillans had arrived, and it shows a wide paved road with elegant two-storey buildings stretching for some distance and, in the middle of the road, a large building with a tall steeple, which was the ancient tollbooth then in use as the Council chamber and prison cells combined. Irvine was an ancient royal burgh with a grammar school which dated back to the sixteenth century, undistinguished apart from the fact that Edgar Allan Poe had been a pupil there for a year in 1815 while living with his Scottish relations, the Allans. That same year the old school closed and a new building was commissioned – from now on the school was known as Irvine Academy, and in 1818 it was granted a Royal Charter. This was the school that both Daniel and Alexander attended.

Duncan Macmillan was a tall and strongly built man, according to his son Daniel, who thought that Alexander took after him, although he said that Duncan was more severe and stern-looking, yet he exhibited the family's good sense of humour, and had an ear for a good tale. On the mainland he found work as both a crofter and a coal carter, taking the coal from the new Ayrshire pits to the port at Irvine, but his cart was just as often full of children waiting to hear one of his stories. Perhaps the loss of his four daughters had made him particularly sympathetic and caring to other youngsters. He and Katharine had two more children after Daniel's birth: a girl, another Janet, born in the year that they moved to the mainland, and finally Alexander, born on 3 October 1818, nearly twenty years younger than his oldest brother Malcolm. The family settled at 25 Townhead, a one-storey thatched terraced cottage close to the parish church, and this is where Alexander was born. They continued to keep animals, a few cows on the burgh moor, and tried to grow crops – Daniel remembered as a little boy having to watch the cows to keep them from straying into the corn. Many years later, Alexander would tell his second wife Emma of the admiration and gratitude he had for his mother 'and the brave bringing up of his cottage home in Irvine.' He never forgot the devotion with which his mother 'rested the little tired feet of her boys by bathing them with oatmeal at night, before putting them to bed, while she kept their minds alive with Bible stories and with what she knew of Dante and Milton.'[6]

Marrying for love in his early twenties had required Duncan Macmillan to grow up fast and shoulder significant cares and responsibilities – as both a farmer of his own plot and a carter for others he was out in all weathers engaged in heavy labour. By 1823 his health had completely broken down, and he died, leaving Katharine with three children under the age of ten. Daniel remembered him as suffering from cold after cold 'so between one thing and another his vigorous, robust, manly frame was all too soon broken up and gave way. A braver more upright man never left this world . . . he was most truly a king and priest and true "man of God".'[7] He is buried in the graveyard of Irvine parish church, under a gravestone carefully repaired by his grandchildren in 1902.

On Duncan's death his son Malcolm, only in his twenties, found himself the head of the Macmillan family, with financial responsibility for his mother and the youngest children. Daniel, just ten years old and already a voracious reader like his mother, had been attending school for several years and was being coached and encouraged in his studies by his two older brothers, but there was no money for further education. As Tom Hughes put it: 'The marvellously few pounds which seem to be sufficient to maintain a Scotch lad at a Scotch University were not forthcoming in his case: and at the age when he should have been tramping to Glasgow to enter himself as a student, Daniel had already served his apprenticeship and was in full work in his trade.'[8]

Malcolm and William Macmillan were both working on the new Irvine Academy building as carpenters when an accident happened which broke Malcolm's arm so badly that he was never able to work in manual labour again. This must have seemed a further disaster to the family, but in fact it forced a change of career, into schoolmastering, which was to have a significant impact on the lives of both his younger brothers Daniel and Alexander. Somewhere along the way, Malcolm had gained sufficient grasp of the elements of a good education, including Latin, Greek, Hebrew and English, to find work as a teacher and then to rise to head of house. His brother William also became a schoolteacher and slowly the family began to climb up the ladder out of penury, and to mix with the professional classes of Irvine. They joined a Baptist community led by an inspirational preacher, George Barclay, which had grown rapidly in a few years from twelve to two hundred members. In May 1829 Malcolm Macmillan left Irvine to be pastor of the Baptist community in Stirling. Alexander's reverence and respect for these two older brothers can be judged in his naming his oldest son Malcolm, and his third son William. Both Daniel and Alexander would struggle with Baptist doctrines and ultimately find a happier home in the Church of England, but the determination to preach, to teach and to inspire, inherited from their father and their brothers, would lead them into publishing as a way to spread the Word of the Lord as efficiently as the late nineteenth century would allow.

Duncan Macmillan's death marked the end of Daniel's childhood. On 1 January 1824, at the tender age of ten, he was apprenticed to Maxwell Dick, bookseller and bookbinder of Irvine, for seven years – at one shilling and sixpence a week with a rise of one shilling a week for each of the remaining six years thereafter. If his brothers could not afford any more schooling for him, they could at least place him somewhere he might continue to educate himself, and keep warm. Maxwell Dick was quite a character, not just a bookseller but a town worthy, the publisher of a local newspaper, and an inventor and engineer. Mr Dick's enthusiasm for inventions was given a boost by the heavy snow that fell on Irvine in March 1827, which completely isolated the town from the rest of the county by road. It occurred to him that a suspended railway would be the best way of overcoming the problem of transporting goods and supplies. First he built a small scale model on his own premises and then, on farmland belonging to the Duke of Portland, he was given permission to erect a line of poles for two miles along which he hung heavy ropes and managed to propel a small carriage at the rate of thirty miles an hour, a system significantly cheaper than laying a rail track. Frustrated at the difficulty in getting any attention for his work, he recreated the original scale model, and hired a room near Charing Cross in London to display it. As the *Mechanics Magazine* of 1830 put it: 'The exhibition is well-deserving of a visit from the admirers of mechanical ingenuity for whatever may be said of the originality of the plan too much praise cannot be bestowed on the dexterity with which Mr Dick has managed to exhibit to the eye on a small scale all the details of its practical operation, or on the spirit and perseverance which has led him to take this rather expensive method of bringing it under the notice of the public.' Dick's enthusiasm for new ideas and inventions must have been inspirational to Daniel, and it lit a similar spark of ambition in the teenage boy. Twenty years later, as he started in business on his own account, Daniel would always be ready to try new ideas and to knock on doors.

Daniel's seven-year apprenticeship passed off very well, with the boy learning many new skills, including bookbinding, bookkeeping and, perhaps surprisingly, horse-riding. When Mr Dick went to London to show off his inventions, he left Daniel in charge, at the age of seventeen. But these two headstrong characters did not always see eye to eye, and after one incident when Dick had hastily accused Daniel of some 'small misfeasance' in the shop without evidence and followed it up with a blow around the head for insubordination, Daniel responded by grabbing his cap from the peg, hurling the daybook at his master's head and heading out of the door. He hitched a ride to Saltcoats some six miles away and then a passage on the fishing boat to see one of his sisters, still living on Arran, from where he could only be lured back by a fulsome apology from his master.

At the end of the seven years, Maxwell Dick wrote an endorsement on the indenture that 'the said Daniel has served me with diligence, honesty and sobriety, and it is with the utmost confidence I can recommend him as possessing these qualities in a very high degree.'[9] Daniel decided that Irvine had shown him all it had to offer and in 1830 he set off for Stirling, some sixty miles away, where his brother Malcolm had found him a job. In Daniel's view, Stirling was not a huge improvement on Irvine and whatever the job was 'I had not enough to do and felt the place dull. I wished to go to Glasgow or Edinburgh, or some large town, where there would be more room and better chances of rising . . . I felt "cribbed, cabined, and confined."' The result was a most violent brain-fever. 'The most scientific of the Stirling doctors was called in, and by lancing and leeching the fever was cut down and I soon recovered.'[10] This is the first of many occasions on which Daniel fell seriously ill and turned to physicians, suffering terribly at their hands from shockingly medieval methods: leeches, blisters and lancing.

Once recovered, he found a position with a bookseller in Glasgow, one Thomas Atkinson, where there was, if anything, too much to do. Atkinson, with his shop in Trongate, in the city centre, was known as a radical and intellectual who published poetry in his own right and edited anthologies. His shop set a pattern that the Macmillan brothers would repeat, making itself the social centre of literary life in the city, frequented by essayists and poets. For the first time Daniel was exposed to the world of radical politics. Atkinson himself edited and contributed regularly to a local magazine, *The Chameleon*. After the 1832 Reform Act, for which he had been an active campaigner, he stood as a candidate in the election in Stirling but was unsuccessful. The extra effort this entailed further damaged his already weak constitution. He became increasingly unwell and promised Daniel 'that if he found that he could leave the business in my hands while he went to the West Indies for the recovery of his health I should have a share in the business: and it was a first rate one.'[11] The young man set to work to earn himself this partnership in the business, starting at seven in the morning and often working fifteen-hour days. When he went back to his lodgings, feeling compelled to improve his education and get up to speed with current affairs, he would set to reading all the weekly, monthly and quarterly periodicals, and thus was often still poring over papers at three or four in the morning, as well as trying to keep a journal. The upshot was that his health and mental state deteriorated: '2nd December 1832: how ill I am. I feel as if I were dying. I have no one to sympathise with me; no one to mitigate my suffering; no comfort but what my paltry salary can procure.'[12]

For moral support the young man turned to religion and philosophy, reading sermons and tracts, falling under the spell of the charismatic Edward Irving, a controversial Scottish minister who had gained a huge following at his church in London preaching of an imminent second coming of Christ, for which the Church of Scotland expelled him. Unnerved by this embracing of heresy, and by his continued ill-health, Daniel's family tried to persuade the young man to slow down, after all he was only nineteen years old and carrying the weight of Atkinson's business on his shoulders. His brother Malcolm wrote to suggest that he was taking too much on himself – but this provoked a strong reaction from young Daniel:

> You seem rather to like twitting me about being ambitious, and this is the third or fourth time you have said 'What are you, or your father's house, that you should be ambitious?' . . . You must not think me angry though I should speak warmly . . . What am I? A very humble person who has no objection to raise himself if he could do it honourably. If all my relations were slaves, I should not feel bound therefore to be a slave, that is if I could purchase my freedom. I do not feel bound to follow in the footsteps of any of my relations. I am here to act for myself. None of them can stand in my stead in any very important matter. The most important things must be done by myself – alone.[13]

This was written in early June 1833, and would seem like a manifesto for commercial success, but just two weeks later Daniel received a diagnosis he must have dreaded – he was coughing blood and, like his master Atkinson, had contracted tuberculosis.

In the 1830s it was known that consumption, as they called it at this time, was eventually fatal, but it was not understood that it was contagious. Daniel may have caught the illness from Atkinson himself, as the two of them worked together in the shop. The disease was rife among the cramped and unsanitary living conditions of Glasgow. The symptoms were highly debilitating: apart from the cough, which eventually led to haemorrhages that could be fatal, there was breathlessness, fatigues, night sweats, fevers, chills and loss of appetite. There was no good way to treat it, and perhaps fifty thousand deaths a year in England were attributable to it. The most common and painful remedy in Daniel's lifetime was to apply a plaster impregnated with acid to the skin of the chest, which burnt a large blister. It was believed that as the blister subsided, the inflammation in the lungs would also be cured. Once blistered, the patient would be in severe pain and bed-bound until it had healed. If this painful remedy led to any improvement in the symptoms it was probably just a result of the enforced bedrest. Other remedies included taking calomel, a mercury-based purgative, or henbane, also now known to be poisonous, and applying leeches. It was decades before rest and a good diet in a warm climate became recognized as more effective, and of course, these were not options available to the poor. Antibiotics were not available for a century.

Daniel sent for his mother to come to Glasgow to nurse him and comfort him, but when she saw him she immediately determined to fetch him home 'to be blistered and all the rest'. He spent a month in Sannox with his aunt Janet Mackay and her husband Alexander, the minister, trying to recover his strength, hoping that he could fight the diagnosis: climbing the hills of Arran, visiting his sister Kate and riding his brother-in-law's horse. But the illness, and consciousness of its likely outcome, unsurprisingly caused Daniel to fall into despair. Furthermore, his reading of the books and periodicals of the day had made him aware that some of the bedrock beliefs of the family's Christian faith were being tested and shattered by scientific progress and philosophic enquiry, and Atkinson's passion for political reform caused him to question the social order. He wrote to a friend: 'I am now twenty and seem to be fast following my father . . . now when all things are uncertain and confused, when I can neither look steadily at myself nor at society without agony, it does cheer me to look back at my father's deathbed. Then my heart had no fear, my mind no doubt, no sceptical confusions . . . the only poetry I knew was the poetry of the Bible and a few old ballads.'[14]

Atkinson set off for Barbados to seek a cure but in October 1833 he died and was buried at sea. The opportunity to go into partnership with Glasgow's leading bookseller thus passed Daniel by, and he would have to find another town, another business, in which to flourish. Sometimes the failure of the best laid plans leads to much better opportunity. When he recovered some of his strength, he determined to set out for London, following in the footsteps of a good friend from the Glasgow book trade, James MacLehose. Daniel was now desperately devouring literature to make up for the deficiencies of his education and to keep up with his customers – reading Cowper, Scott, Byron and Shakespeare, hiding his piles of books from the doctors and his family. While he mastered the English classics, he was painfully aware that he had no Latin or Greek. In the 1830s book publishing was still predominantly aimed at the highly educated upper classes for whom these dead languages posed little difficulty – when the Macmillan brothers started their own imprint, they aimed to provide enough general material in English to keep the mainstream masses happy.

Letters from Daniel to James MacLehose were full of questions about the practicalities of London life – the young man's one ambition was to find work in 'The Row', being Paternoster Row, by St Paul's Cathedral, at that time the centre of the London book trade. Daniel wanted to join one of the publishing houses whose names he was beginning to recognize and admire. James sat up until two in the morning writing answers to his queries, presumably satisfactorily, as in September 1833, just turning twenty, Daniel took passage on a steamer from Leith to St Katharine's Dock in London. The journey itself was a terrible shock to his system, as he reported home, taking nearer three days than the two which had been advertised. The sights of the docks and the City, which so impressed Carlyle when he first arrived a few years earlier, did not get a mention in Daniel's letter home, perhaps because he was below deck in no fit state to appreciate 'the River and its ships in tens of thousands, its coal heavers, bargemen, mackerel men and variegated population from Purfleet (14 miles down) up to the London Dock . . . its dense mass of grim smoky buildings, its forests of masts, and the sound as of a million hammers.'[15]

Once arrived, Daniel took a hackney cab to MacLehose's lodgings, much to the surprise of James's 'little English' landladies who were astonished by his claim to half of MacLehose's bed. He then passed a highly stressful couple of days as he tried to find a position. Paternoster Row, 'the headquarters of English Literature', was already spilling out along Fleet Street and by 1818 there were some forty establishments in a square mile. Daniel tramped from bookseller and publisher to publisher and bookseller, backwards and forwards along Fleet Street from St Paul's to Pall Mall via The Strand, brandishing his references from Glasgow but with no joy, except for an offer of work at a place called Simpkin & Marshall. He gave it a brief trial, staying until ten at night writing invoices, but it seemed likely to kill him with overwork. 'I might learn a great deal about business, but my health, moral and physical, must suffer, must give way.'[16]

Just as he despaired of finding anything, word came of an opening with a Mr Johnson in Cambridge. By then Daniel had decided that London might not be his ideal place – he did not enjoy the life of the young men about town, and he certainly did not like living in lodgings and eating at London's chop houses. He hung on desperately for a couple of days hoping for a place to be offered at the firm of his dreams, Longmans, but there was nothing to be had, and after a short visit to the sights of London, the Zoo and St Paul's Cathedral, he packed up his few belongings and set off philosophically for Cambridge. 'On the whole, I really do think Cambridge is best for me – will be best for me ultimately. I did not wish to go there. God knows best. I ought to feel quite submissive, quite pleased, deeply grateful for all that He hath done for me, and cheerfully go where He leadeth me. It is strange how few things turn out as we design them . . .'[17]

Meanwhile, young Alexander was growing up in Irvine, going to school and making friends with whom he would stay in touch for the rest of his life. He was only five when his father died, so for him the principal influences in his life were his mother and his older brother Malcolm, head of the family, for whom Alexander had an enormous regard. Malcolm scraped together the fees to ensure the little boy could be educated at the Royal Academy, where he learnt English and the rudiments of the classics. Alexander later wrote that he had been particularly influenced by the master of the Commercial Department, James Connell, who taught maths. He wrote: 'The impression he made on me was such that even now, when I know most of the headmasters of the great public schools of England as personal friends, more or less, I am constantly thinking and comparing them with Connell . . . I think he was a common handloom weaver in early life and taught himself most of what he knew. And yet he was a perfect gentleman . . . with what keen intellect!'[18] This example of a man who could pass as a gentleman despite humble origins because of his behaviour and his love of learning set a pattern which Alexander lived by.

In 1870 Irvine honoured Alexander, by then a famous publisher, giving him the freedom of the borough, and the ensuing publicity triggered an exchange of letters and memories with old schoolfriends. The tales they swapped, combined with reminiscences published in the local paper, show Alexander as a typical naughty schoolboy, in rebellion against his life at home: 'I was brought up in the strictness of a Scotch Sabbath. I think their rules frivolous, tiresome, tyrannous.'[19] As soon as he could get out of the house and away from his mother and his older brothers, he would be running with a gang, lobbing stones at the boys from a rival school and snowballs at the weavers from Town-end, tearing down the street slamming all the window shutters on the houses they passed to frighten the housewives, teasing the schoolmasters and playing truant, and nearly killing himself by flinging himself in some wild backward somersault into the local river when dared to do so, forgetting that he could not swim. As the local paper commented in 1870: 'the characteristics of the boy, we believe, have not failed the man. A determination not to be beat, but pluckily to venture and to win, has no doubt helped materially to raise Alexander Macmillan to the high position he now occupies.'[20] Macmillan warmly welcomed these renewed contacts from his youth, saying, 'It may seem strange to other people, that I who really care intensely for the simple human being and his individual worth, and not very much for what is known as "position in society", "rank", "birth", and the like, have yet the most intense interest in, and love for old memories, old associations and old friends.'[21]

The contrast between the early years experience of the two brothers is striking and left a mark on their characters. Daniel's first ten years were marked by terrible hardship, the death of his sisters, the uprooting of the family from the isolation of an Arran croft to the bustle of a small town, watching his father struggling and failing, dying of exhaustion, he himself being sent out into the world of work aged just ten. For Daniel, life was frightening, full of illness, anxiety and care, with religion as the only source of stability. Alexander's experience was so very different – the death of his father when he was not even five would have marked him less, and the family was just that little bit more settled, able to afford to send him to a good school until he was fifteen, supported by his older brothers' salaries as teachers. He was the baby of the family, probably getting more attention from his mother, growing up with schoolmates whose friendship he would cherish all his life, less scarred by fear of poverty and destitution. Many years later Daniel remembered his childhood as 'wandering alone and thinking of the infinite, of space and time, of heaven and hell, good and evil, of angels and of devils. I remember Alexander's birth, and nursing him. I used to lie at the bottom of a very large cradle and rock him and myself to sleep.'[22] Alexander's childhood memories consisted of throwing stones, snowball fights and running wild through the streets of Irvine with his friends.

Daniel was driven to escape Scotland, to make money and buy security, to put as much distance as possible between himself and the hardships of his youth. From the age of twenty, he lived under the shadow of a death sentence, and it filled him with a determination to succeed as fast as possible. Alexander had the more relaxed confidence of the youngest child, of waiting to see what turns up and expecting to be rescued. 'He had known the pinch of poverty, but it had not crushed his spirit or embittered his heart.'[23]

– 2 –

THE
PUBLISHING INDUSTRY

Nineteenth-century printing press

'All that mankind has done, thought, gained, or been; it is lying as in magic preservation in the pages of books.'

Thomas Carlyle

'Make 'em laugh; make 'em cry; make 'em wait.'

Charles Reade

DANIEL MACMILLAN MAY have fallen into the book trade by accident, but once he was there, he was entranced. The industry was undergoing rapid growth and technological development, certainly in comparison with the declining agricultural life from which he and his family were struggling to escape, and the possibilities for advancement in such a fast-moving trade must have been intoxicating. For a young man with an enquiring mind but a weak constitution, to work in a bookshop and spend his day dealing with publishers and readers was the ideal environment.

To understand why the publishing industry was undergoing such rapid change, it is worth looking back briefly at its origins. Printed books, mostly scholarly and theological works written in Latin, had been bought and sold in Britain since the fifteenth century, initially as imports from the Continent. Then William Caxton, the first British printer, spotted an opportunity to satisfy the few wealthy customers looking for lighter reading in their own tongue – a gap in the market that he could supply with his own printing press, which he set up in London in 1476. Caxton selected classic titles that would appeal to the Royal Court at Westminster and to the aristocracy, such as Chaucer's *Canterbury Tales* and Malory's *Morte D'Arthur*. These were the sort of titles that would be bought to stock a private library and to demonstrate the educated and cultivated tastes of their owners. They needed to look beautiful as well as excite interest – hence the development of the bookbinding craft alongside the printing press.

Printing in England and Scotland was nearly always in the English language. The English Reformation, by creating an educated and curious English-speaking clergy and congregation, helped the domestic publishing market to grow rapidly. This demand for books was self-perpetuating. Once you teach someone to read, you create a never-ending demand for something else to read, and preferably something new. Endless reprints of the same few texts will not do the trick, so printers who had learnt a complex trade, employed expensive typesetters and invested capital in expensive machinery had to find and commission new works. Furthermore, the printer had an incentive to sell everything that came off his press as quickly and efficiently as possible. He had to learn to estimate the perfect print run for each title, as he did not want to be left with stock, nor to have unsatisfied customers. He had to create demand for new titles, which might or might not prove popular with the book-buying public, so each new book was a gamble. And once he had found and printed a book that sold well, he needed to protect his investment.

At first, the printers protected their right to print and sell a title by registering their copy with the Stationers' Company – once someone had registered a copy, no one else could print it. But slowly during the seventeenth century booksellers who were not printers themselves started to register copies, being the titles of books that they had commissioned to be written or which had been submitted to them by hopeful authors. Copyholding, the registering of a title, became the business of the booksellers, not the printers, who fell back to being merely part of the manufacturing process. Copyrights were items of value which could be traded, bought and sold, and a bookseller who acted in this way would thus become a publisher. The first recognized publisher in Britain was Henry Herringman at the end of the seventeenth century: originally a bookseller, he began to accumulate copyrights of the great English Renaissance and Restoration plays and poetry such as the works of Shakespeare, Milton, Donne, Jonson, Dryden and Vaughan. From 1680 onward he was living on the profits of these copyrights and after selling his retail business in 1684, he became, in effect, the first wholesale book publisher in England.

The next major development was for this new system to receive legal protection and acknowledgement. The 1710 Act for the Encouragement of Learning recognized the existence of copyrights and of the Stationers' Register. New copies were to be legally protected for fourteen years, and for another fourteen thereafter if the copyholder was still alive, which was good news for the publisher: but the Act also recognized for the first time that the book had been created by an author who must also have rights to his own copy, and therefore the publisher would have to negotiate a deal on each title. The two protagonists in the creation of the book – the author and the publisher – were now mutually dependent. Alexander Pope was the first author to make significant money from publishers by skilfully negotiating his rights to the works he was translating or editing.

The basic structure of the publishing industry had now been established, and the next hundred years was marked by steady growth in supply and demand. The eighteenth century saw the invention and development of the periodical magazine, such as *The Tatler* and *The Spectator*; and the newspaper: *The Daily Courant*, Britain's first newspaper, was selling eight hundred copies a day in London by 1704. The discipline of daily, weekly or monthly publishing and the distribution of these titles improved the management skills in the industry and created a market large enough to support professional writers.

The next major driver of demand for books was the novel, which came of age with the publication of Samuel Richardson's *Clarissa* in 1748. This was swiftly followed within just ten years by works from the literary giants Fielding, Smollett and Sterne. Not all novels were of this extraordinary standard: most were 'ephemeral productions to be read once and then forgotten'.[1] But the reading craze was gripping the nation and the creation of different styles fed the frenzy – from the Gothic horrors of Horace Walpole and William Beckford to the romantic sentiment of Fanny Burney. Reading for pleasure was becoming a widespread habit, as leisure and wealth increased, and literacy filtered down the classes. Circulating libraries and booksellers began to thrive outside London.

Despite the provisions of the 1710 Act, publishers continued to argue the right to perpetual copyrights, but 1774 saw the case of Donaldson v Becket, brought by a London copyright holder against an entrepreneurial Edinburgh publisher, Alexander Donaldson, who made a living out of cheap reprints. The case went all the way to the House of Lords, which ruled in Donaldson's favour – once the maximum twenty-eight-year term had expired, anyone could produce a reprint. This opened the floodgates for cheap editions of popular classics, and a whole new industry was born. In 1777 John Bell, owner of a bookshop in The Strand, began to publish his 109-volume series *The Poets of Great Britain* at a price designed to appeal to a far wider audience, and other publishers followed suit. This had two effects – it made it much easier for the masses to read good literature, obviously, but it also forced entrepreneurial publishers to seek out and commission new works that could be offered for sale on a protected basis.

Two of the early publishing pioneers in London were John Murray and Longman, and the firms they founded were still the major players when Daniel Macmillan began to learn his trade. John Murray, from Edinburgh, set up as a bookseller in The Strand in 1768, and by the 1790s was a recognized publisher of new literature. His son, also called John, took over in 1793, disposed of the retail business, bought out his partners, and concentrated on publishing books and periodicals including the highly influential Tory-supporting *Quarterly Review*. This second John Murray's authors included Sir Walter Scott, Jane Austen and Lord Byron. His home which doubled as his office at 50 Albemarle Street in Mayfair was the centre of a literary circle, fostered by Murray's tradition of 'Four o'clock friends', afternoon tea with his writers. This was an idea that would be further developed by Alexander Macmillan. Meanwhile Longmans had been operating in Paternoster Row, near St Paul's, since the 1720s, having taken over the premises and business of the original publisher of *Robinson Crusoe*. By the 1800s Longman was the publisher of Wordsworth, Coleridge and Southey and was the owner of the Whig-supporting *Edinburgh Review*, regarded by eminent writers such as Carlyle as the most important public journal of the day.

By the second decade of the nineteenth century the publishing industry as we know it today was fairly recognizable, with distinct classes of printers, binders, publishers, wholesalers, retailers and remainderers. There would be no major developments in book printing technology for the next fifty years, apart from useful changes in the way illustrations could be incorporated into the text, which fascinated and inspired Alexander Macmillan. Around 1820 the bookbinding industry did make a move which recognized the increasing demand for cheaper books: they changed from using flimsy paper covers for the cheaper editions to using cloth bindings, which were much harder wearing and a more acceptable substitute for the very expensive leather bindings still reserved for the wealthiest of customers.

One of the major decisions to be made by a publisher when placing an order to a printer was how many copies should be run off for the first edition and whether any precautions should be taken in case a second edition was needed – as once the first print run was complete, the printer would dismantle the blocks and reclaim the metal type for his next job. One way round this was to make a mould of each page of type, using papier mâché for instance, which could then be used to recreate a page of type for a subsequent print run without the expense of resetting the type. Hot metal was poured into the mould, to produce a negative image of the printed page. This process was called stereotyping and the metal plate which was cast from the papier-mâché mould could be re-used many times or sent to printers in other countries as necessary. The process had been invented in the eighteenth century: midway through the nineteenth century a rival process, electrotyping, was invented which was higher quality but more expensive. Macmillan used both systems.

Even though demand was growing exponentially, it was a tough market for a publisher. Between 1825 and 1850 the average price of a book halved, from around sixteen shillings a volume to eight

shillings, driven by the need to compete with much cheaper pamphlets and periodicals. Trying to reach this new hungry market was
expensive as well – to advertise publication lists in periodicals, the
most obvious means to reach a wide audience, was a major outlay,
because adverts were taxed at three shillings and sixpence each,
regardless of size. This duty fell to one and six in 1831 but was not
abolished completely until 1853. Publishers also had to absorb the
duty on paper, which made it more profitable to publish fewer copies
of a high-price well-produced volume than thousands of copies of
cheap books. The paper duty was not abolished until 1861.

There were three principal ways in which a book deal could
be struck – the author could bear all the publishing risk himself by
paying for the printing, or he could enter into a profit share, perhaps
50:50, with the publisher, or the publisher could purchase the copyright upfront, taking all the risk and all the profit but guaranteeing
the author a lump sum. Sometimes an agreement might be revisited
for the publishing of a second or subsequent edition, to allow a better
reward to the author. After all, it was in the publisher's interests to
keep a popular author sweet. In many cases the publisher would
open a list to encourage people to subscribe for a new book, which
allowed him to cover his initial outlay, the model used to this day by
publishers such as Unbound, but he would still have to take the risk
of collecting the subscription cash when the book was published. An
author had to decide whether or not to retain the copyright – there
was a suspicion among writers that although keeping the copyright
sounded like a good idea, those who did so would discover that
their books sold surprisingly badly in the hands of less motivated or
unscrupulous publishers.

When capital and ready cash were not available, a bookseller or
publisher might finance his business by issuing a bill to his creditor –
his printer, or his paper merchant, or his binder. These bills, by which
the publisher promised to pay the recipient the full amount owed
within say three months, were negotiable instruments – that is to
say, the printer, for example, could take one into the City and get

immediate cash for it, but at a discount. The discount house now owned the publisher's debt, and would be far more hard-nosed about collecting what was owed than the original creditor might have been. If the publisher could not repay the discount house the full amount at the required time, the discounter would swap it for another longer dated bill, probably at a higher rate of interest. This was the beginning of a publisher's slippery slope into debt and was the downfall of many businessmen, publishers being no exception. The smart publisher made it a rule never to embark on any enterprise that he could not finance in cash at the outset, but in the early days of the firm, the Macmillan brothers certainly relied on bill discounting.

With little capital in their businesses, and the necessity of offering credit to their retail customers, most booksellers carried only a limited stock of books. Much of the service they provided to customers consisted of sourcing particular books by enquiring of other booksellers in their network and then parcelling them up and sending them out. They would also arrange for books to be bound or re-bound to suit a customer's preference or decorating scheme. When Daniel Macmillan was building his relationship with Julius Hare in the 1840s much of his correspondence consisted of confirmations of orders to source books from other sellers and to get the old books from Hare's very extensive library re-bound.

The principal booksellers and publishers of London not only had a network to enable them to scour each other's catalogues on behalf of their customers, they had developed something much closer to a monopoly on the pricing of standard books. The rights to print editions of classic works long out of copyright – works by writers such as Gibbon, Smollett and Burns – were carved up among publishers with prices set at a level that would protect their profits. However, when new players arrived on the scene, they often sought to make a market by publishing these classic books at bargain prices. If they did so they risked incurring the wrath of the Trade, as the collective of older established firms such as Longmans and Murray was known, and could find themselves drummed out of business by being denied access to credit and supplies. Meetings of the Trade, usually in the committee room of the Chapter Coffee House on Paternoster Row, would be held to agree prices and determine who was sufficiently well-established to be admitted to the club. These were business-men solely interested in protecting their own positions; there was little apart from a love of money-making driving the ethics of the Trade, which often found itself viewed with scorn and disfavour, closely linked to the 'Grub Street' of hack writers, scurrilous gossip-mongers and scandalous infighting.

The Trade may have felt itself secure against competition, but it was slow to grasp the extraordinary opportunities offered by the rail-ways. When the Macmillan brothers came to England, the railway network was slowly spreading across the country, and by the 1840s it had had significant impact. Firstly, tangibly, it made distribution of books much easier. Books are relatively heavy to transport but the carriage charges on railways were low. Secondly, the travelling public would never have tried to read while being jolted around in a cart or carriage, or walking to work, but the relative smoothness of the railway journey, combined with waiting at stations, made it amusing to carry a book to while away the hours. New entrants spotted the opportunity: George Routledge made his fortune publishing a 'Rail-way Series' of popular classics, and W.H. Smith & Son provided retail outlets at stations. Smith not only sold books, but had a circulating or subscription library, putting it into direct competition with Mudie's, which since the 1840s had been the biggest circulating library in Brit-ain. Mudie's had begun in 1842, when Charles Mudie had started to lend the stock from his bookshop to students at the University of London for a subscription of one guinea a year.

All of this was the crucial information that Daniel had absorbed in his early years in Scotland and then at Johnsons in Cambridge. First, the basics: how a book was manufactured, the importance of the feel of a book, the quality of the paper and printing, the type-face, the illustrations, the binding (leather or cloth), the expense. Secondly, the structure of the industry: the different income streams of the printer and the publisher, the distribution network of wholesalers and retailers. Thirdly, how a book could be marketed and sold: advertising, catalogues, reviews, the second-hand and the remainder trade. What books sold well, what titles tempted customers into the shop but stayed on the shelves, how the prices were struck, the discounts that were allowed and those that were not. What was always in demand – the school textbook, the classic work – and what was a gamble on an unknown new author. Was it a one-, two- or three-volume set, had it appeared in a periodical first, how long had its copyright to run? What becomes very clear from Daniel's letters to his friends at home, however, is that more important to him than any of this was the intrinsic worth of the book itself. Daniel began to see the book trade as having a moral and social purpose and was determined to play a part in facilitating the dissemination of Christian values and intellectual enquiry to a wider audience than the traditional book trade had ever contemplated.

The 1830s and 1840s, the opening years of Victoria's reign, were a time of political, social and religious ferment, with new ideas abounding, shaking the foundations of British society. The 1832 Great Reform Act, for which Daniel Macmillan's employer Atkinson had campaigned, did not appear to have settled anything politically; if anything it had launched a myriad of new demands and campaigns as the recently enfranchised classes sought to flex their muscle, and those who were still excluded regrouped to start fighting again. It might have nearly doubled the size of the electorate to eight hundred thousand, but the adult male population alone was six million and growing fast on the back of rapid industrialization.

Meanwhile the Established Churches of England and Scotland, the principal source of education and authority for much of the population, had begun to lose their grip on men and women's minds and souls. There were not enough clergy or churches to keep pace with the growth of the urban population, and too many English clerics held their posts as sinecures, with no interest in doctrine, in salvation or even in the basic welfare of their parishioners. In

1833 John Keble's sermons in Oxford launched what would become known as the Tractarian Movement, an attempt to deal with the weakness of the Church of England by leading it back towards its English Catholic tradition, with an emphasis on mysticism and ritual. This was unlikely to appeal to the working classes. In the same year, Thomas Arnold, headmaster of Rugby School, published *Principles of Church Reform*, which became the rallying cry of the new 'Broad Church' movement, seeking to put a common morality rather than dogma at the centre of religious life, and thus to meet the needs of a wider population.

1833 also saw the publication of Charles Lyall's *The Principles of Geology*, which anticipated and influenced the works of Darwin and Wallace, leading many more to question the Bible in its entirety. At a time when society was being rocked by the impact of industrialization and urbanization, these disputes and doubts among academics, who were primarily men of the cloth and who might have been expected to give the lead to the nation in its spiritual and ethical life, were deeply disturbing. Daniel and Alexander Macmillan were members of a generation crying out for moral instruction, driven by a passion for intellectual debate and scientific curiosity. Robert Chambers' *Cyclopædia of English Literature*, which appeared in 1843, sold over a hundred thousand copies in its first few years. The Macmillan brothers could see that there was an enormous and growing market waiting to be tapped, and that the canny publisher who spotted the right opportunities would not only cater to the inner life of the working man, thus serving a social purpose, but might also make a fortune. They would not be the only publishers to launch a firm whose proclaimed purpose was to bring light to the masses, but they would be by far the most successful.

– 3 –

THE FOUNDING
of
THE PARTNERSHIP
(1833–43)

Fleet Street

'Wondrous indeed is the virtue of a true Book'

Thomas Carlyle

DANIEL'S FIRST THREE years in Cambridge, as a man in his early twenties, were chiefly important because they established his name and face in the city, and the friends and business contacts he made would remember him when he returned ten years later. He worked as a junior clerk in one of the smaller bookshops that served the university. His employer, Elijah Johnson, was a Baptist, which was a comforting thought for a young man who still hungered for religious certainties, and he offered Daniel £30 a year plus lodging and meals in his own home. Johnson was in his thirties, newly wed and with a growing family, which must have made the house a busy and noisy place. Daniel wrote that the Johnson family were 'nice folk, so pleasant, so kind, so pious, so everything I could wish.'[1] The good food and comfortable way of living improved his health and he prospered.

The shop was conveniently central at 30 Trinity Street, but there were at least half a dozen other bookshops along the same street, some even closer to Trinity College and the Senate House. However Elijah Johnson had smart premises, a red-brick Georgian terrace with a distinctive arched window. He was determined to develop a publishing business out of his shop and launched a weekly publication, *The Cambridge Review: A Journal of University Life*, which came out every Thursday in term time. In 1837 Johnson was the first publisher of the *Cambridge Mathematical Journal*, edited by two young Scottish mathematicians at Trinity College.

Daniel worked from 7.30am to 7pm or later, but he was not afraid of long hours. The greater difficulty for the Scot was that Johnson's shop, catering to the undergraduate market, mostly held classical stock, a problem for a shop assistant with no Latin or Greek. Daniel applied his mind and heart to the task and just one year later he claimed to know every book in the store. Johnson was keen to show Daniel the ropes and help him learn the business, and Daniel felt himself to be treated very well: 'I have breakfast with him at eight o'clock; dine (and fine dinners we have) at one PM; take tea at five PM; sup at nine: and then we have the pleasure of conversation at dinner and other meals, and of family worship. These are no small pleasures, I can assure you.'[2] The satisfaction was mutual; the Johnsons were delighted with him – and he rapidly made himself popular among the young undergraduates who came to the shop. There was pleasure to be had in chatting with this young and kindly enthusiast and sharing notes and reading lists with him. If these public school products noticed any gaps in Daniel's education, it clearly was not a handicap. The relationships he built were all good for business, although Daniel sometimes felt that Elijah envied his easy ways with the customers, who would walk past the owner to the back of the shop looking for Daniel.

His letters home to his brothers reveal how his tastes were changing as he grew – where he had once delighted in the romance of Byron, now he had read Moore's Life of the poet, containing excerpts from his letters and diaries, and had cast his work away in contempt: 'the everlasting tittering and smirking is most loathsome'. He was a bit of a prude – he preferred Shelley, who took a more moral view of life and gave his readers hope that Right would prevail. Daniel immersed himself in Voltaire, Hume, Gibbon, Paley, Sterne, Fielding and Swift: 'whatever came first to hand was greedily devoured. The result is a horrid chaos of the most undigested and contrary notions.'[3]

In particular, he found that the more reading he did, the more the Calvinist faith of his youth was tested. His brothers Malcolm and William, both now working as Baptist preachers, urged him to join a local church to find companionship, but he replied: 'I am not sure about what you said of my joining a church. I will think of it. I must say that at present I have no partiality for any sect of Christians. The very fact of there being sects confuses me. I hope God will direct me in the right way.'[4] However, whether at God's direction or driven by a need to conform, within a few months he was baptized into the

Johnsons' Baptist congregation, and his spiritual life became more satisfactory. He certainly had need of this community and support when in August 1835 he received news that his beloved mother had died. As far as he was concerned it cut once and for all his ties with Scotland, and there was no reason for him to call it home any more.

Meanwhile, his own career progression was one of his main concerns: when in the third year his salary rose to £35 he wrote home that it was 'less than I expected and I think less than I ought to have . . . I am a little in debt.'[5] Daniel, for all his careful ways, would always seem to spend more than he had. Twenty years later he was still dependent on the generosity of friends and family. Meanwhile, his determination to get to London, to join one of those famous Paternoster Row firms, had re-emerged. He wrote constantly to James MacLehose for news of any openings, and for advice along the way – sometimes the advice given was as basic as correcting his spelling – but mostly the young men discussed literature and philosophy. Daniel began to fill his notebook with rules to guide his studies, with paragraphs headed 'on study and reading', 'fixing the attention', 'improving the memory' and so on, interspersed with quotations from his favourite writers, and the beginnings of his own attempts at criticism.

After three years Daniel was convinced that Cambridge had nothing more to offer him and he and Johnson parted company on good terms. He was still ambitious to find a job in London, but first he returned to Scotland, suffering further ill-health following the sea journey to Leith. Yet again he had to be nursed back to health, this time by a Mrs Wilson in nearby Edinburgh, a woman well known to his old employer, Maxwell Dick. Archibald Wilson was a leader of the sect known in Scotland as the English Baptists and his family were to become some of the Macmillan brothers' closest and best friends. Daniel's correspondence with his only son George, an academic chemist, is one of the best-preserved records of his intellectual and commercial development.

Daniel spent a couple of months recovering his strength in

Edinburgh and found himself spending time with the poorer, struggling classes, the mechanics and weavers, but whereas he had previously enjoyed and been inspired by the countryfolk of his home neighbourhood on Arran, he found these men a disappointing group. 'They know nothing about duty, or faith, or God: they care only about their rights; they talk only about reform, universal suffrage, from which they look for justice and deliverance from oppression. They do not look up to God for help in the old-fashioned way. This may be a "progress of humanity" and all the rest of that jargon, but I, for one, cannot admire it.'[6] He might have stayed on as a bookseller in Leith, having secured a situation in a stationers' shop there on £50 per annum, but suddenly his prayers – and I suspect that they were actual prayers – were answered when, through James MacLehose's good offices, he was offered a position at Seeley's establishment in Fleet Street. He had finally made it to London, and on a decent enough starting salary of £60 a year. This was a significant increase over his Cambridge wage, but now he had to find, and to fund, his own board and lodging.

L. B. Seeley & Sons of Fleet Street was a third-generation bookseller by the time Daniel arrived in 1837. The firm was well known as a publisher of the Evangelical movement, and the Church Missionary Society met at their offices. Robert Seeley was a great philanthropist, a campaigner for education for the working man and the improvement of working conditions, a supporter of Lord Shaftesbury and the Factory Acts among others. The six years that Daniel spent at Seeley's, from 1837 to 1843, saw his salary more than double from £60 to £130, but despite the progress he was making professionally, he never managed to throw off the curse of consumption and twice had to return to Edinburgh to be nursed by Mrs Wilson. Despite these absences, Seeley's was a good employer, keeping his place open for him, but the worry to Daniel that he might lose the position was constant.

In Irvine, Alexander had been facing increasingly difficult circumstances. Even the modest fees charged by Irvine Academy were a problem to the fatherless family, and at the age of fifteen Alexander's formal education ended and he had to find a job. Following his brother Malcolm's example, he initially took up schoolmastering, first joining a small private school, Scotts, in Irvine as 'head of house' – the very school whose pupils he had previously pelted with stones. His next attempt at learning a trade was when he secured a role as assistant to George Gallie, a well-known Glasgow bookseller, where James MacLehose had also begun his career. Slowly but surely he was being pulled in the same direction that his brother Daniel had taken. As he wrote, 'there can be little doubt I was led into the line for which my natural gifts fitted me'.[7] Daniel was not the only brother who found it hard to keep his temper in a junior role. Alexander left Gallie's and returned to Irvine after the proprietor destroyed a trashy novel he found Alexander reading. The young man always had more of a taste for fiction than his brother, but Gallie may have been responsible for persuading him to be more selective in his choices.

Back in Irvine he managed to secure a role working for his brother William as a teaching assistant, in return for which he persuaded the masters to teach him some further rudiments of the classics. For a short time in 1834 he taught in Glasgow, then he tried working as an assistant in a pharmacy – but as his natural curiosity led him to start experimenting with the stock, including the nitrous oxide, it is fortunate that this job turned out not to suit him either. By 1836, bored with shop work, he wondered if a life at sea would suit him better, and tried a voyage to America 'before the mast' – a career move never repeated and seldom referred to. He rapidly found himself back in Glasgow, jobless and penniless. As he himself described it, he was in despair and forced to take a very poorly paid job as an usher at a school in Nitshill, looking after a hundred and thirty poor colliery boys. Here he lived on just five shillings a week for nine months, and it nearly killed him: 'I was then light-hearted, I suppose

what the English call plucky. I went at the job I got, did it as well as
I could, and so got on. It chanced to be in my line.' He was still only
eighteen, and seems to have packed a lifetime of experiences into
a very short time. This same letter, written to an old schoolfriend,
Spiers, in 1870, contains a telling couple of sentences which say much
of Alexander's view of life.

> I never had the least ambition to rise in the world, as it is called.
> I think that is the bane of life and action. Do the work that is
> given you, that seems to me the real law of life. Never mind
> whether you rise or not. It makes my heart ache often when
> young fellows call on me, as they often do, asking for situations
> or for work of a higher kind than they have. I have, I am thank-
> ful to say, often been able to help a man to work. I count it a
> great privilege when I can, but ambitious youths who want to
> rise in the world, and not simply do the little bit of work God
> gives them, are very hopeless.[8]

This is the philosophy of the self-made man who had nobody
to give him a leg up as he climbed the ladder and who believed
that promotions and rewards had to be hard won. The Macmillan
brothers were given financial help as they established their business,
but it was always given on commercial terms and repaid promptly
and with interest.

The six years between 1833, the year that Daniel first fell ill and
fifteen-year-old Alex started work, and 1839, when the two brothers
began to work together in London, were crucial in the formation
of Daniel's business ambitions. While Alexander was bouncing
from teaching to shop assistant, from pharmacy to ship and back
to school, Daniel was putting in the solitary hours learning the
book trade inside and out, at the same time as furthering his literary education. Alexander was always less widely read than his older
brother, sometimes failing to keep up academically, but he had seen
more of the world and had more physical and emotional energy for

socializing, as well as a better sense of fun. Even at Nitshill, when he was struggling to survive, he formed a small weekly literary and social club with the colliery owner's son, the colliery manager's son, the local minister and one or two others, where they read the novels of Dickens and consumed toddy and tobacco, such as they could afford. The differences in experience and outlook of the two brothers was a source of great strength to their future partnership.

1837 marked the start of a significant new era in Britain: the year that saw the accession of eighteen-year-old Victoria to the throne also saw the first publication of Dickens's *Oliver Twist*, overlapping with the last few monthly instalments of *The Pickwick Papers*. The age of the popular social comment novel, coinciding with a new era of nationalist sentiment, would develop over the next twenty years into the perfect climate for the launch of a British publishing house with a strong social conscience. Meanwhile Daniel found himself right in the heart of the London that the young Charles Dickens knew well – worried and malnourished clerks and shop boys scurrying from lodgings to dimly lit offices and warehouses, terrified of losing their positions. It was a violent and dirty city; every day Daniel walked past Newgate Gaol, where public hangings still took place regularly, drawing huge crowds. The streets were now lit by gas, but the light was poor and as Dickens wrote in *Nicholas Nickleby*, 'streams of people apparently without end poured on and on, jostling each other in the crowd and hurrying forward . . . life and death went hand in hand, wealth and poverty stood side by side; repletion and starvation laid them down together.'

Daniel had work, but conditions for lowly clerks and apprentices were hard. In February 1838 the back room at Seeley's bookshop was so cold that even the ink froze, and Daniel and his fellow shopmen huddled round two gas heaters in the warehouse for warmth. He began to keep a journal on and off – mostly full of prayers for strength and guidance in the face of poverty and ill-health. 'O Lord God, if it please Thee, release me from my present difficulties. While they last may they give strength and steadfastness to my principles. Keep me from cant and carelessness, haughtiness and sycophancy . . .'[9]

Slowly his expertise grew and his wages increased with added responsibility. But the more settled he became financially, the more his conscience pricked him when he thought of the struggles of his brothers and sisters still in Scotland. In theory his older brothers, at least, had settled employment within the Baptist Church, but William died suddenly in 1838 while at training college in Bradford, and Malcolm, a minister in Stirling, was suffering from ill-health and would not live beyond 1840, leaving Daniel as the head of the family. In 1839, after a visit back to Scotland, he wrote that he did not think he could ever return to Irvine, as he could not bear to see his nephews and nieces and yet feel that he had no ability to help them. His first action, appalled by Alexander's terrible situation working at the little school in Nitshill, was to speak to George Seeley, who made a generous offer to take Alexander on at the same salary they had paid Daniel, £60 per annum, to start at once. Alexander arrived on 3 October 1839, his twenty-first birthday, and from then on until Daniel's death the two brothers' careers were inextricably linked. Initially they shared lodgings in Hoxton, looked after by two spinster sisters, the Misses Nutter. The walk to Fleet Street every morning, down the Clerkenwell Road and Shoe Lane, would have taken an hour through rough crowded streets, plenty of time to shape their plans for the future.

Once Alexander had arrived, it struck Daniel that their youngest sister, Janet, who had been keeping house for Alexander, was now all alone in Glasgow, trying to make a living from a small sewing school. Daniel hoped that his landladies might be able to help her to learn to manage a household. But there was a need for cash to pay her fare and to set the three of them up in unfurnished lodgings together – and Daniel's savings amounted to a paltry £10. None of his friends had the wherewithal to help him out, so he turned to one of the partners in Seeley's, a Mr Burnside, who lent him £60 to set up home. Daniel's respect and gratitude to Burnside throughout this part of his career was such that he always after referred to him as 'The Patriarch'.

By March 1840 the brothers had borrowed and scraped enough money together to take smart rooms, gentlemen's lodgings indeed, at 26 Bartlett's Buildings, off Holborn Circus – a courtyard of dark red-brick houses with pedimented doorways and white window-frames, and with gardens behind them, notable for having been the London lodgings of the social climber Lucy Steele in *Sense and Sensibility*. Even with both brothers' salary coming in, Janet, who had failed to learn anything useful from the kindly Nutter sisters, was unable to make the housekeeping stretch. At one stage Daniel considered moving out, south of the river, to Camberwell, at that point still countryside, for the sake of his health. He had the idea of opening a small bookshop there which Janet could perhaps be left to manage. But the necessary investment was beyond his means and eventually he had to sell his cherished book collection to pay off his debts. It must have been an appalling blow, to give up these hard-earned and much-loved treasures. Janet returned to Scotland, eventually marrying a man named Wilson and living quietly until her death in 1869. She is buried with her parents in Irvine churchyard.

The two brothers gave up their fashionable address and moved back into lodgings, this time at 8 Charterhouse Square. This was a boarding house kept by a Mr and Mrs John Sewell, who also owned premises very nearby at 57 Aldersgate Street in the City, where they provided board and lodgings for young men who were training to be missionaries. Alexander, being the junior in the firm, had to be at Seeley's in Fleet Street to open up by eight in the morning, which required him to rise at six. Picture the two young men in their shared small room, no fire, relighting the candle that they had carefully conserved from the night before, breaking the ice in the shaving bowl, Daniel coughing and wheezing, Alexander cursing, hunting for his shoes, his muffler. While he dressed, Daniel read improving works to him – his favourite at that time being Thomas Carlyle's *Sartor Resartus*, a book he recommended to all his friends and was occasionally prepared to lend, but only on the understanding that it be promptly returned when finished with.

It is an illustration of how far the brothers had come in their reading, or perhaps of how far they aspired to go, that Carlyle's work meant so much to them. They might have recognized a common heritage with the author: like them, Carlyle had been born into some poverty in the Scottish countryside, but there the similarity ended. Carlyle's family had managed to scrape enough money to fund a university education for the boy and, with wealthy sponsors and a supportive wife, Jane, he was already making his name as a scholar and essayist when Daniel arrived in London. It was the publication of his three-volume masterpiece *The French Revolution* in 1837, at the age of forty-two, which was to cement his reputation as the foremost intellectual of his generation, and led to the re-publication of his earlier works, which the Macmillan brothers now fell upon with delight.

Sartor Resartus is hardly an easy read. Carlyle had struggled to find an audience for it until eventually, starting in 1833, it was published in instalments in *Fraser's Magazine*. However an American friend, Ralph Waldo Emerson, admired it so much that he arranged for it to be published as a complete book in Boston in 1836 and by 1838 it had found a publisher in England. It has been compared, in its peculiarity, to *Finnegans Wake*, published a hundred years later, and its influence on both British and American writers of the nineteenth century was immense. The title itself, translated from the Latin as 'The Tailor Retailored', must have been a challenge to Daniel and Alexander, the contents even more so. It takes the form of a long fictional review, by an unnamed and slightly cantankerous editor, of a work of philosophy by an imaginary German professor. The book is meant to be humorous and satirical – Carlyle was inspired by Sterne's *Tristram Shandy* and by Swift's *Tale of a Tub*, as well as by his extensive reading of German authors such as Goethe. The names given to characters and locations in the book are written in cod-German, designed to be amusing in translation: for example, the professor's name, Diogenes Teufelsdrockh, translates as 'God-born Devil dung'. But the underlying message is one of a deeply complex philosophy, derived from Carlyle's long study of German idealism. The work combines social criticism with spiritual enquiry, and tracks Teufelsdrockh's intellectual journey from a despairing, materialist atheism through religious doubt to an affirmation of faith: The Everlasting Yea. Daniel, who had been struggling to maintain and strengthen his own personal faith, now sought to inspire Alexander with uplifting texts to mull over on his way to work. Walking down from Holborn through Covent Garden, where the fruit and vegetable sellers had been up for hours, the young man turned over in his mind the phrases Daniel had intoned solemnly as he dressed: 'Silence is the element in which great things fashion themselves together . . . do thou thyself but hold thy tongue for one day: on the morrow, how much clearer are thy purposes and duties', or 'Even in the dullest existence there is a sheen either of Inspiration or of Madness' and 'Love not pleasure; love God. This is the EVERLASTING YEA, wherein all contradiction is solved.'

Carlyle counselled his readers to turn their backs on the frivolities of romantic writers such as Byron – and this was exactly the message that Daniel wanted to hear. The book became 'a necessity of life' to him.[10] Interestingly, in January 1840, shortly after Carlyle published his pamphlet on Chartism, the author wrote in a letter to Emerson of an unexpected visit he had received: 'Many applications have been made to me here: none more touching to me than one, the day before yesterday, by a fine innocent-looking Scotch lad, in the name of himself and certain other Booksellers' shopmen eastward in the City! I cannot get them out of my head. Poor fellows! they have nobody to say an honest word to them, in this articulate-speaking world, and they apply to me.'[11] Daniel was one of the group who had sent the messenger, hoping to persuade the author to meet them and talk freely to them.

Daniel's quest for a suitable spiritual home had led him to join a new church, the Weigh House Chapel in Fish Hill Street, led by Thomas Binney, a well-known Nonconformist minister and founder of the congregationalist Colonial Missionary Society. Among this congregation Daniel would have met another young man newly arrived in London who was similarly appalled by what he saw as moral degeneracy among his fellow drapers' assistants: George Williams, up from Somerset. In 1844, Williams decided to create a safe space for young men to preserve them from the temptations of the City. Initially based in the drapers' shop where he worked in St Paul's Churchyard, he called it the Young Men's Christian Association, and it would spread around the world. His view, which would have resonated with Daniel, was that 'the first twenty-four hours of a young man's life in London usually settled his eternity in heaven or hell.' This was an organizational mission dear to the hearts of the Macmillan brothers and when a branch opened in Cambridge in 1852, Alexander involved himself in the organizing committee.

Daniel wrote: 'I like Mr Binney's preaching so much. I should be very sorry indeed to leave him. I never met anyone whose sermons furnish so many materials for reflection. He has a noble mind: he is so very energetic and earnest: yet his manner is so simple and chaste; so free from all false glitter and show. I never hope to meet with his equal.'[12] It was not just that the preaching suited him, it was that Binney gave him food for thought – and Daniel's mind was desperate to be fed. Even when he was offered a well-paid job back in Glasgow, the circles he was moving in now gave him a reason not to leave London. To escape the drudgery of his work at Seeley's he took every opportunity to strike up friendships with the book-buying customers and through them he and his brother discovered further opportunities for education: attending evening classes and lecture series, of which those given by Carlyle were the most prized, of course.

He had found a small number of like-minded young Scotsmen to be his friends in London, particularly David Watt, an old schoolfriend of Alexander, later to be a missionary in India, and Watt's friend David Livingstone. These two young men shared lodgings owned by Mr and Mrs Sewell in Aldersgate Street, and their son Dr Charles Brodie Sewell later wrote: 'The men of most mark whom I then knew were David Livingstone and Daniel Macmillan, and although the former has since obtained the greatest celebrity . . . there was a quiet steady reserved thoughtfulness about Macmillan which made all he said worth hearing, and a general amiability of character which was very winning.'[13]

Daniel may have been tempted to join the foreign missionary life, but his health was against him. He consoled himself with the thought that the book trade was another honourable calling, writing to James MacLehose, who was now back in Glasgow and had established his own business:

> We booksellers, if we are faithful to our task, are trying to destroy and are helping to destroy, all kinds of confusion, and are aiding our great Taskmaster to reduce the world into order and beauty and harmony. Bread we must have, and gain it by the sweat of our brow, or of our brain, and that is noble because God-appointed. Yet that is not all. As truly as God is, we are His ministers, and help to minister to the wellbeing of the spirits of men. At the same time it is our duty to manage our affairs wisely, keep our minds easy and not trade beyond our means.[14]

With such high ideals and such aspirations, it is not surprising that Daniel, after nearly twenty years in the book trade, was keen to strike out on his own. He was tired of being at someone's beck and call, was longing for a time when 'no one can look over my shoulder and say Leave that and tie up this parcel'. By 1840 the two brothers' salaries combined were well over £200 per annum, and they began to feel that they should take a step forward towards independence in their professional lives. But how to get the capital to set up their own shop? Finding the means to do so was still beyond them – until a chance acquaintance, driven by another of Daniel's passions for a particular book, opened the doors of opportunity.

In the summer of 1840 Daniel fell in love with a new volume: *Guesses at Truth by Two Brothers*. The title must have caught his fancy, it would be something amusing for him and Alexander, being two brothers, to discuss in their evening walks over London Fields. It was a book of homilies, essays and sayings, collected from more than one source but primarily the work of the brothers Julius and Augustus Hare. The original version was published anonymously in 1827 but after Augustus died in 1833, Julius, rector of Herstmonceux in Sussex, re-issued the work in his brother's memory. It was perfectly pitched to appeal to the young men and women who were trying to educate themselves and make their way in the world: as Hare wrote, 'If then I am addressing one of that numerous class, who read to be told what to think, let me advise you to meddle with the book no further. You wish to buy a house ready furnished: do not come to look for it in a stone quarry. But if you are building up your opinions for yourself, and only want to be provided with materials, you may meet with many things in these pages to suit you.'[15]

Daniel loved the book, exalting it to all his friends, and in the way of many a true fan, became determined to communicate his enthusiasm to its author. His first letter to Julius Hare, written in September 1840, began: 'I feel so grateful to you for your volume of sermons that I cannot help breaking through the usages of society to express my thankfulness'. But Daniel wanted to do more than just express his feelings – he wanted to enlist the newly created Archdeacon of Lewes in a project to save men's souls. Passionately he wrote of his concerns for his fellow clerks and shop assistants in London and the other big cities, men who found themselves morally and spiritually adrift, in need of the sort of guidance to be found in Hare's work. He was particularly struck by a sermon on Self-Sacrifice and continued:

There are still large classes who have no sound foundation for their morality. In this London, for instance, I know a good deal of one class, a class very much overlooked, who very much stand in need of guidebooks to aid them in the formation of opinions on morality and religion; namely young men occupied in the different departments of commercial life. Hundreds of them are continually coming here, fresh from the country, with warm pure genial hearts, which soon become, one can hardly say what, for no expression can be too strong to indicate that which a few years produces.[16]

Daniel was very clear that these people, these men he had met and talked with at political, Chartist and Socialist meetings, would not read sermons, and despised the squabbling and humbug of the established Churches. What they needed was a simple book of advice aimed at their own intellectual level, perhaps taking the form of a calendar or almanac. The letter that begins as fan mail ends as an enthusiastic business proposition. But Hare, although he replied kindly, did not take the bait.

There was no further correspondence until 1842, by which time Daniel had found another hero: Alexander Scott, a preacher, teacher and writer of pamphlets. Daniel felt compelled firstly to introduce Scott's writings to the venerable Hare, and secondly, like a true disciple, to make it clear that he had spread the word about Hare among all his friends 'in various parts of England and Scotland, friends in India, in Africa, in New South Wales, who bought . . . *Guesses at Truth* because of my recommendation.'[17] And, explained Daniel, they were all eager for the next volume. A month later came the much longer reply that Daniel had been hoping for – Scott had been a hit! 'It is indeed a consolation under the grief for the loss of my noble-hearted friend Arnold, [Thomas Arnold of Rugby had died in June 1842] to find that there is another pure lover of truth like Mr Scott living among us.'[18] Hare now remembered Daniel's concerns for the spiritual welfare of the young men of London. He shared the letter with Frederick Maurice, the author of *The Kingdom of Christ* and soon to be his brother-in-law.

Greatly encouraged, Daniel wrote again, to remind Hare that his original purpose had been to interest him in taking up the cause of the Christian education of the 'class of London clerks'. 'It is certainly true that the Church, the God-ordained teacher of mankind, might make a much greater use of the Press than it generally does.' Every Sunday Daniel saw working men buying newspapers and reading them aloud to their illiterate friends, and yet nothing the press was saying was helping these men find God. 'As things go on at present there is no hope of a proper understanding between the different classes into which Society is divided. Those in the upper classes have no notion of what goes on in the minds of the lower and they give themselves no pains to learn'. He sent Hare examples of the periodicals found everywhere – with circulations of thirty to forty thousand – 'papers found on the tables of all small ale-houses, cigar shops, barbershops, coffeehouses . . . decidedly infidel in their tendencies and yet they are the real guides of great numbers'.[19]

Hare and Maurice considered the idea, and nervously responded that simply inserting religious teachings into articles in these papers would be casting pearls before swine: perhaps a better answer could be a newspaper or journal specifically targeted at this audience? Hare wondered if Daniel would like to become an editor. Or failing that perhaps he would like to consult with Maurice to see if any of his future writings could be suitably adapted to the readership. In any event, Daniel was warmly invited to discuss the problem and in September 1842 the Fleet Street shop assistant set off for Herstmonceux.

The impact on Daniel of this visit to Hare's beautiful and comfortable home, Buckwell Place, with some twelve thousand books lining every wall (and all of them, as he observed, read and annotated) can be judged by the lengthy letter he subsequently wrote to his friend David Watt, now a missionary in Benares. Daniel was starstruck, amazed to be so kindly treated by a family he considered almost god-like in achievement and grace, a family who had also entertained some of his idols, Thomas Arnold, De Quincey, Charles Lamb, Wordsworth, Coleridge, Thomas Carlyle and Walter Savage

Landor. Crucially, the family took him to an Anglican communion service on the Sunday, and the lifelong Nonconformist was an immediate convert: 'There one's heart really finds utterance. I know of nothing equal to it.'[20]

Daniel described Hare to Watt in great detail: his height, his hair, his expression 'that of a very thoughtful, kind-hearted, simple-minded man, quite free from all self-consciousness.'[21] The contrast between the two men would have been marked: Hare was forty-seven, public school educated, six feet tall, handsome, hale and hearty. Daniel was a much slighter man; his early poverty and ill health had not improved his physical appearance, leaving him frail. Portraits show him as thin faced, with smooth dark hair brushed back from a wide brow, strong nose and deep-set dark eyes. His Scottish accent would have been strong – this was a boy who had grown up in a household where his father spoke and preached in Gaelic. But the affection with which he was received by this cultivated English family was warm and genuine.

The stay in Sussex was swiftly followed by the development of a deep friendship with Frederick Maurice which had a profound effect on Daniel's life – he called his first two sons Frederick and Maurice in honour of the great man. Frederick Denison Maurice has been hailed by many as one of the greatest thinkers of the Victorian age – Tennyson would call him 'the greatest mind of them all', Hare called him 'The greatest mind since Plato'. He was not just a theologian and a writer, but an educationalist, who developed most of the philosophy that underlay the Christian Socialist movement while working in practice to promote the higher education of women and of the working classes. He is also the man of whom Matthew Arnold wrote that he 'passed his life beating about the bush with deep emotion and never starting the hare'. Daniel would not be the only young, impressionable disciple who would fall under his spell; his influence was far-reaching, but the practical impact was sometimes less easy to detect.

It took Daniel a while to track down a new edition of Maurice's

The Kingdom of Christ and, as he wrote to Watt, he at first picked it
up just to be polite 'imagining that it was some high Church Half-
Puseyite book which wood [sic] do very well for churchmen but
[be] of no value to one who has said goodbye to all parties . . . in a
very short time I found that [Maurice] was no common man: that
he dwelt in a higher purer clearer region than that of party. I found
it to be a book that I could not live without.'[22] In no time at all,
Daniel was offering to publish Maurice's works, either a collection
of translations, or perhaps a separate edition of an article Maurice
had prepared for an encyclopaedia, on the history of moral philosophy, which Daniel thought should be published as a standalone piece.
Here we see the entrepreneurial Daniel knocking at doors, hustling
for an idea – this time soliciting permission to reproduce the article
in question from the publishers of the encyclopaedia, who refused,
saying it would damage the sale of the larger volume. In his indig-
nation he wrote to Watt: 'these wretched men – these publishers!
What fools they are . . .'[23]

The added confidence that these new connections gave Daniel,
combined with the reassurance of a joint income of over £200 a
year, encouraged the two brothers to set up their own business.
They could not afford to rent premises in the fashionable West End,
but their friend and landlord Mr Sewell suggested they open a small
shop on the ground floor of his house at 57 Aldersgate Street, which
Alexander would run, leaving Daniel to work at Seeley's, securing
the better salary. The rent was £45 a year and they had to pay £100
for fixtures, but Mr Sewell took their credit until they were able to
pay him and the business was underway by February 1843.

Tucked into the correspondence folders at the British Library is
a copy of the letter posted out to announce the launch of the shop:

Sir (handwritten)

*We beg respectfully to inform you that we have commenced business
as BOOKSELLERS and STATIONERS: and to invite your*

*inspection of our stock, consisting of Theology, Poetry, Philosophy,
and General Literature, new and second-hand. Having had
considerable experience in old and modern Theological, Classical
and General Bookselling, and having every facility for procuring
new and second-hand books at our command, we can assure
you that any commissions with which you may favour us will be
executed with promptitude and care.*

*We shall always have on hand 'the Bible' and 'the Book of
Common Prayer', in every variety of size and binding; and
Stationery of every description at moderate prices.*

*We intend devoting much of our attention to the various styles of
Bookbinding: and we pledge ourselves the libraries, single volumes,
or music-books entrusted to us, shall be bound substantially and
elegantly, and at very moderate prices.*

We are, Sir, yours respectfully
Daniel and Alexander Macmillan

Hare was an immediate and loyal customer, ordering books and
bindings and introducing his friends. As Daniel wrote to him:

We are content to make the best of Aldersgate Street for the
present, hoping to move west by and by. We have a very neat
shop for a very small rent. It is within five minutes' walk of the
Post Office and Paternoster Row. Nowadays, with the penny
posts and Parcels Delivery Companies, it is an easy matter to
attend to orders from any part of town or country. We have
commenced in quite a small way. If a large tree grows from
this small seed we shall be grateful. If not we shall be content;
we shall feel that it is as it ought to be. We are determined that
it shall not fail through indolence or extravagance. If the business should prosper, we shall, both of us, do our best to realise
some of our ideals with regard to what should be done for the
craftsmen of our land. We feel, however, that the world can go

on without us or our ideals, and in the meantime we shall strive
to do the work that lies nearest us in the best manner we can.[24]

It was a brave statement, and laced with traces of the old Calvinist fatalism, and with Daniel's belief that he and his brother
were working out God's purpose on earth, in their own way. In fact
Aldersgate Street was not ideal, they were too close to the big and
established competition around St Paul's, nor were they in the up
and coming West End, they had little stock and no captive customer
base. However many books they parcelled off to friends such as
Archdeacon Hare and David Watt, the shop was not going to make
their fortune. And when the opportunity came to buy into an established business in Daniel's old stamping ground of Cambridge, he
could not resist stretching every sinew to get it.

– 4 –

'THIS SMALL SEED'

(1843–45)

Aldersgate Street

'Half the failures of this world arise from pulling in one's horse as he is leaping.'

Julius Hare

CAMBRIDGE IN THE 1840s was first and foremost a city of academics, an ideal place to own a bookshop. The university had already been in existence for over six hundred years, consisting of some seventeen colleges at that time, the largest being Trinity with a hundred and fifty freshmen arriving there in 1837 alone. The whole institution in the early nineteenth century had less than a thousand male students at any one time, studying principally the classics, theology and mathematics, many of them preparing to become clergymen. Tutors were drawn from the Fellows of the colleges; there were about three hundred and fifty, living off endowments, but only some seventy of these taught the students. There were two principal requirements for Fellows: that they had to take holy orders within the Church of England and they must remain unmarried. The conflicts of conscience that these requirements stirred in Cambridge's brightest men would regularly feature in the conversations and writings of the Macmillans' friends and customers. It also meant that some of the more interesting and rounded personalities, such as Charles Kingsley, left Cambridge on graduation, preferring the freedom of life in a parish with wife and family. College atmosphere became increasingly insular.

In the world outside the university, the demand for a better standard of higher education was growing rapidly, driven by the rise of the affluent and ambitious middle classes. By the time Daniel and Alexander set up shop, significant reforms were in contemplation. An honours school in Natural Sciences opened in Cambridge in 1848, as English scientists tried to dislodge the stranglehold the clergy had on university endowment funds, and to carve out for their discipline the space to compete with European geologists and naturalists. Another force for change was the utilitarian notion that education should have a purpose conducive to national economic and industrial success. Finally, there was real competition emerging, as the Nonconformist University College opened in London in 1828, followed swiftly by the Anglican King's College, and by the spread of universities and medical schools into the provinces.

Some of the internal struggle for reform in Cambridge was driven by Fellows interested in the values and ideas of the utilitarians and the Nonconformists, some by an evangelical desire to reinvigorate the old system and produce better citizens who might tackle some of the perceived ills of early Victorian society. Much of the pressure came from academics who wanted to be free to research their subjects and to improve their teaching, rather than spend all their time cramming students for exams. Undergraduates also found the experience unsatisfactory, as they felt themselves frustratingly close to so much knowledge but unable to unlock it. By the 1850s these pressures led to the creation of a Royal Commission and then in the 1860s to significant institutional reform. The Macmillan brothers were right in the centre of this debate, with the bookshop they owned, immediately opposite the Senate House, becoming a well-known meeting place for the younger, ambitious Fellows, and for students seeking help. Daniel and Alexander felt personally invested in the movement for academic reform – after all, a healthy debate in any subject was usually good for the book business.

Although the Aldersgate Street shop in London had seemed an answer to a prayer, there were reasons that made Daniel particularly anxious to improve his financial prospects: he was in love. He had fallen for a young woman called Hannah Budden, a sister of John Budden, one of the missionaries whom he had met in company with David Watt and David Livingstone. There was a clue in August 1842: in a letter to Watt, mostly full of his enthusiasm for the writings of Frederick Maurice, a final paragraph suggested there was more than one new interest on his mind, and that he was keen to check the lie of the land: 'I don't think I shall be able to write to Budden this time. But when you write pray tell him that I have not forgotten him, I have been twice out at his house. His brothers occasionally call on me . . . what a very superior family the Buddens are. Did you see much of them? If so I wonder you did not try to get one of his sisters to go out with you. But perhaps you did and failed, if so it would be rude to ask you.'[1]

The courtship progressed slowly, entangled with the fortunes of the business. On 29 April 1843 he wrote again to Watt:

I suppose you have heard of my being smitten. Do you remember Budden's sister Hannah? So it is. Well it is a most serious matter, but yet one of the most blessed and elevating things. But I must check myself lest you should laugh. Business moves on slowly. We have only commenced two months now so we can hardly tell how it will go. On the whole we have no reason to complain but it is uphill work commencing a business in London, but we must have patience. Being engaged and of course looking forward to getting married as soon as prudence permits, I cannot but feel anxious. If you can think of any way to give me a little help, that is to bring me some business, I am sure you will be glad to do so.[2]

The difficulty in making the London business pay when the shop was small and rather out of the way continued to bother him – only a month later he was writing: 'We are pushing hard to make a business and find it very uphill work. If the people had some sense they would come to us for books! We could sell them as cheaply as anyone & we could give good information on all points connected with books! People would be glad if only they knew! but alas! For their ignorance!'[3]

In August 1843 a couple of Daniel's old Cambridge friends tipped him off that a bookshop in Trinity Street, right in the centre of the city, was on the market. Daniel rather archly mentioned it in a letter to Julius Hare, saying that he had been to look at it, but regretted that acquiring it was beyond his means. In return he received a remarkable letter from the very kind archdeacon:

What sum of money would you want to enable you to take
Newby's business at Cambridge? And what chance do you think
there is of it proving a profitable one? My brother, whom you
saw here, on hearing what you said in your letter on the subject said that if it be so, means might perhaps be found to let
you have a moderate sum of money at moderate interest with
a reasonable security. But what are your prospects at present?
Every change must be attended with considerable loss and
would Cambridge be a place as well fitted as London for doing
anything with reference to your ultimate aim?[4]

Daniel seized his chance, never bashful about coming forward,
and his reply ran to nineteen closely written pages. He was per-
suasively excited about the opportunity. The two elements of his
proposal were to purchase the existing stock, possibly worth as
much as £750, and then to rent the premises for 80 guineas (£84)
per annum. Daniel did not think there would be any goodwill to
pay since the shop as it stood did little business, the books were too
expensive. He thought he could sublet the upper part of the premises for £30 or £40, which would help cover costs. In particular, the
situation was very good, being across the street from the gates of
Trinity College with only Stevenson's shop at 1 Trinity Street offering
any competition. Daniel understood the merits of being a big fish
in a small pool: 'I should give [it] close and careful attention, and
in Cambridge could get well-known quicker than in London.' He
explained to Hare that he knew the city from his time working at
Johnsons, mentioning how popular he had been with the customers,
and that he had two possible mentors and friends who would help, a
physician called Dr Cockle and a shoemaker called Mr Tupling, the
men who had encouraged him to look at the shop.

Daniel's proposal was that he himself would take responsibility
for running Cambridge until it was making profits, and meanwhile
Alexander would continue to manage the Aldersgate shop. There
was some commercial advantage to be got from this: London

booksellers got the best deals at trade fairs, so Alexander would be better placed for sourcing stock for both shops than any provincial agent, and the London shop could be an outlet to dispose of surplus Cambridge stock. Also, a London catalogue would have a wider circulation among other retailers and customers than a Cambridge catalogue. The downside of this arrangement which he glossed over was that neither brother would have a regular salary coming in. Daniel felt that he needed to be absolutely honest with the Hare brothers about his shortcomings: 'I have no learning, can read no language except English, speak none except a partly intelligible Scotch-English dialect.' A greater issue was the state of his health. After all, he himself had feared that he had consumption, particularly as he understood that it ran in families. However, when a post mortem had been performed on his brother Malcolm it showed healthy lungs, and recently a doctor (probably the newly qualified Charles Brodie Sewell, the son of Daniel's landlord at Aldersgate Street) had pronounced him healthy and said 'that if I lived to turn thirty I should in all probability live to be an old man'.[5] Nevertheless, he planned to take out a life insurance policy to provide cover of a thousand pounds. This would be a significant outlay for the brothers.

There was one final consideration which prompted Daniel to try to make a business in Cambridge. He feared that if he continued in London he would eventually be required to publicly support one political party or another, Tory, Whig or Radical, and to decide whether he was High Church or Low Church. He had no inclination to take sides and felt it would not suit his longer-term purpose. In Cambridge these things would not matter, he could be everybody's friend, and eventually, anybody's publisher.

The reply from Julius Hare was swift and very encouraging – his main concern was that Newby's shop would be too small to provide Daniel with a living. He offered to lend £500 if Daniel could raise the balance from Burnside, his old supporter from Seeley's, or other friends. He was particularly honest about his concerns for Daniel's health, saying: 'Your look when you were here led us to fear that you might have a consumptive tendency.'⁶ Hare happily assumed the role of mentor and advisor to Daniel, challenging him to justify his plans and think through his opportunities.

The next two months were particularly trying for Daniel, as Mr Newby was difficult to negotiate with, not surprisingly distrustful of this young man with the consumptive look, the strong Scottish accent and no assets of his own. But by 12 October he could write that with a great deal of help from Mr Tupling he had arrived at an agreed deal, a fourteen-year lease on the property at £83 per annum, with an obligation to keep the house in good repair, painting the outside every three years and the inside every six. Stock and fixtures were to be taken at independent valuation, with £300 paid upfront and interest accruing on the rest, fully secured. Hare lent £500 and Burnside, £250. The independent valuation when it came showed stock and fixtures at £634 2s 6d, about £100 more than Daniel had expected, so he accelerated his plans to mark down the stock and turn it quickly into cash. He wrote to Hare that the shop was small but that the room upstairs could be shelved and used – and added that 'if the thing grows so far beyond my expectations, the shop itself could be enlarged by striking backwards into one of the rooms of the Blue Boar Inn.'⁷ He set to work with extraordinary haste, in a mess of carpenters and painters, creating a catalogue, giving orders for fresh books and finding a great deal of rubbish to be dealt with and disposed of. The *Cambridge Chronicle* of January 1844 published a notice that the Macmillan brothers would be clearing out surplus stock soon, for cash only, to make space for 'more carefully selected books'.

In no time at all Daniel had overreached himself and the cold January weather and biting Cambridge winds brought on an extremely severe attack of his old illness, with, for the first time, a haemorrhage of blood from his lungs. Alexander was summoned by Tupling and took the first coach up to Cambridge – but in his haste, and to save money, he took an outside seat and by the time he arrived he was prostrated with the back pain that would plague his life. The pair did not seem to have been a good investment for Burnside and Hare. Alexander wrote to Hare in February 1844 about his brother: 'The doctor said that with very great care he would get over it in a month or two but that unless he was entirely relieved from all anxiety about business at once and for some time there was little hope of his recovery.'[8] Julius immediately took up his pen urging Daniel to keep Alexander with him and give up the London shop as soon as practicable: 'with your excitable temperament, constant care would be needed to prevent a relapse. Your plan was a prudent one but it seems rather ordained that the two brothers should work together in the same spot than divided'.[9] Very sadly, Daniel had to agree, writing to Hare against his doctor's orders: 'We have resolved to follow your kind suggestion. As soon as my brother can leave me he will go to London to get rid of the shop.'[10] He was particularly sad, for intellectual rather than financial reasons, to lose the Aldersgate Street link with the young missionaries, who he believed he had helped by introducing them to literature which widened their reading without weakening their faith. The good news was that the business was doing better than expected and everyone in Cambridge was being very kind. By the end of May, the London shop had closed and for the next thirteen years the brothers worked together to build a business in Cambridge. It was certainly a struggle. The account books for 1843 to 1846 show that they barely kept their head above water and were constantly in need of small loans from Tupling and Burnside to pay their bills. They relied on the London discounting houses to keep their creditors happy, but it was an expensive way to run a business. Their salvation came in the slow but steady creation of a publishing imprint, which in time overtook the bookshop.

The first book published by the house of Macmillan was lodged at the library in the British Museum on 10 November 1843, and it was a very simple piece, unsurprisingly considering everything else on the brothers' plate at that time. Nonetheless the very subject matter they chose was symbolic – they were as determined as their missionary friends to spread knowledge to all classes of men and women. If they could not find the books they thought were needed and wanted to sell, they would commission and publish them for themselves. Alexander had worked as a teacher, and the book was a manual for schoolmasters called *The Philosophy of Training*, by A. R. Craig, previously a Classics master in Glasgow and now teaching languages at the Barford Street Institution, Islington. It ran to just ninety-two pages, containing 'suggestions on the necessity of normal schools for teachers [the term used at the time for teacher-training colleges] to the wealthier classes, and strictures on the prevailing mode of teaching languages'. The first page declared that it was published by D and A Macmillan, 57 Aldersgate Street, and was to be sold through Thomas Varty of The Strand, K. J. Ford of Islington, Oliver and Boyd, Edinburgh, and James MacLehose, Glasgow – a primitive national distribution network had already been established. Throughout his career, Alexander focused on improving the quality of school textbooks, commissioning some of the best academic authorities to write primers and introductory texts aimed at the young.

The next volume Macmillan published still bore the London address as well as that of 17 Trinity Street, Cambridge and ran to 120 pages: *The Three Questions: What am I? Whence came I? Whither do I go?* by William Haig Miller, a bank clerk Alexander had got to know at the parish Sunday school. This religious text sold enough copies to justify a second edition.

For some time now, while he was forced to lie in bed recovering, Daniel's imagination had been full of publishing schemes, some of them extraordinarily ambitious. In May 1843 he wrote to George Wilson: 'I have been thinking for some time past of an Encyclopaedia much more complete than any we yet possess yet much shorter which would contain a short and complete account of anything which commonplace people could wish to know and furnish a guide to those who wished to follow out the several subjects. The whole thing should be done in three or four Imperial Octavo volumes. If I could only get the needful money I should commence making arrangements at once.'[11] It was probably fortunate that with so much on their plate, no one would give him this money. The labour of opening one new shop and closing down in London, coinciding with both brothers' ill-health, meant that the new venture into publishing began very slowly. Alexander was still suffering from sciatica, and the treatment, a course of mercury, nearly blinded him. Daniel wrote to George Wilson: 'He was very restless at first: but by the time it was over he was so much reduced that he was glad to lie still at last, for one or two days, he could not even get up. Now however his eyesight is saved: he has to go about with his eyes hemmed in from the light in every direction by means of smoked glass spectacles and though his strength is reduced more than expected we are glad to see him moving about again.' The treatment given to Daniel was hardly less harmful: 'In all my medicines there was a considerable quantity of henbane which really is a great help in quieting the nerves and lessening one's restlessness and sleeplessness and subduing the pain of the perpetual irruption which was kept up on my chest for three weeks by means of Croton Oil [a purgative] and Spirits of Wine.'[12]

The year 1844 saw the issue of a theological pamphlet by an anonymous writer and, more encouragingly, a new edition of an old text, *Remarks on the Fable of the Bees* by William Law, with an introduction by F. D. Maurice himself and printed at the University Press. As far as Daniel was concerned, the whole point of producing this book was to proclaim themselves as a publisher of the writings of Maurice, giving him great personal as well as professional satisfaction. The funds for the book had been provided by John Sterling, a Scottish author and friend of Carlyle and Hare. The relationship with Maurice deepened significantly at this time: the account books show that he advanced them £300 (now worth over £30,000) in December 1844.

Next, Daniel wrote to Archdeacon Hare wondering why the university was not publishing good editions of the major English theological works – instead allowing Oxford to get all the business and the glory, often on the back of Cambridge academics. 'If Cambridge were to republish the writings of the best of her sons, what a noble array of books we should have. It would be an easy matter to do it.' He had a plan to set up a subscription scheme – an annual amount of two guineas per subscriber would cover it, and the university authorities should do it not for the money, but for the honour of the institution and the advancement of sound learning. 'If such a thing could be set a-going I should be glad to take the management of it here.' He was also keen to get some tracts commissioned and published: 'The incendiarism in our neighbourhood and the discontent of the poor everywhere, call loudly for some mode of lessening the misunderstanding between rich and poor . . . One cannot read the papers day after day without agony of heart.'[13] If Daniel was hoping that Hare would sponsor these ideas, he was disappointed, the fish did not bite. Hare, not surprisingly, wanted Daniel to focus on the shop.

If the dreams and plans that Daniel spoke of seemed more urgent and vivid to him in 1844, they may have been as a distraction from bitter personal disappointment. The Budden family, when they heard of the return of his tuberculosis, had broken off his engagement to Hannah. As he later wrote, 'I was cast off with the greatest kindness on all hands, but still very distinctly. To a man so far away from all intimate friends as I was you can hardly tell how desolate my heart felt, or how much I endured; my health being so bad I felt my sorrows the more keenly and my sorrows increased my illness. When my brother came down and lived with me his society was most precious.'[14]

The only development which could lift Daniel's spirits was his increasing familiarity with the great and the good of the Cambridge academic and literary world. The young Scotsmen's charm and enthusiasm were making a significant impression on some of the serious intellects in the university. The brothers needed a stable of authors with recognition and selling power among the Victorian intelligentsia, and Julius Hare warmly introduced his protegees into his circle. His network of contacts soon became Daniel and Alexander's network too, assiduously cultivated, with reverential respect.

Daniel was always happy to acknowledge the impact Hare was having on his position in Cambridge: 'your kindness has gained me the Master of Trinity and the Master of Downing as customers.' The Master of Trinity, William Whewell, was a towering intellect in Cambridge and the wordsmith who coined the term 'scientist', a polymath, philosopher and theologian. 'I had the honour of a visit from Mr Stanley and from Mr Monckton Milnes, for which I feel indebted to you.' And the greatest introduction of all: 'I had a visit from the poet Wordsworth. The Master of Trinity, Whewell, called and introduced him to me. He came upstairs and stayed with me an hour and a half and discoursed with the greatest simplicity on all manner of subjects. He called again in the afternoon . . . and stayed half an hour. This I counted a great honour.'[15]

By 1845, with Daniel's strength and spirit much recovered, and Alexander working full-time alongside him, the publishing business could take off in earnest – issuing seven books that year which covered subjects as wide-ranging as law, theology, poetry, mathematics and mechanics. There was a strong bias in favour of Cambridge academics as authors. The brothers took every opportunity to improve footfall in the shop, and to reach out to a customer base that would be interested in the issues of the day; for instance they advertised in the local press that they held for signing a copy of a petition in favour of the Prime Minister Robert Peel's Maynooth Grant – a cash grant to a Catholic seminary in Ireland proposed by Peel as a way of improving Anglo-Irish relations. This was a hotly debated issue at the time, and the notice was designed to encourage those of a liberal or social-reformist persuasion to enter the shop. As Thomas Hughes put it, writing of Daniel:

The time was singularly fortunate for a man of his peculiar experience and wide sympathies to start as a bookseller in a University town. England has seldom been in a more electric state, intellectually and morally. The Anti-Corn Law agitation was stirring the nation to its depths, and the triumph of the middle class all but ensured. Behind and beneath it, the great movement of the working class was already making itself felt, in Chartism and half-blind attempts at association in one and another direction.[16]

The same year saw the brothers take a significant commercial risk – the death of their chief competitor, Stevenson, who operated out of 1 Trinity Street, offered them the chance to acquire his business for £650 plus the value of the stock. The acquisition necessitated them finding another investing partner in a hurry, this time a Mr Barclay, the owner of a well-known pharmacy in Farringdon Street, London – not a bookman at all, but an introduction from their old employer, Seeley. Barclay's lack of familiarity with the book trade would later cause them great frustration and concern, but for now they were delighted to relocate to the prime retail position in Cambridge, a corner house facing west towards the Senate House and with accommodation for the pair of them, looked after for the time being by a housekeeper called Ellen Stead: 'Kind, diligent and scoldy' as they described her.

Daniel and Alexander had stretched themselves to the limit of their finances and beyond, borrowing heavily, to take possession of such a perfect location for their trade. The rental alone was estimated in the Rate Books at £150 a year. The building (which survives to this day as the Cambridge University Press bookshop) is situated on the corner of Trinity Street and St Mary's Street, where the latter runs uphill to become Market Street. The shop faces towards the University Senate House and Tree Court, just across the road from St Mary's, the university church. Turning left out of the shop one reaches King's College, and in the other direction lies Trinity, the largest of the colleges, and the intellectual powerhouse of the university. The building consists of two storeys of brown brick with attractive wide sash windows above the ground-floor shopfront, and there are mansard windows in the attic facing front and side as well. The shopfront facing onto Trinity Street is just two windows wide, but the building reaches back up St Mary's at least three times as far. An inventory taken when the residential part of the building was sublet in 1863 shows a well-appointed house of eight bedrooms all heated by state-of-the-art 'Register' stoves, a system of bell pulls, hot and cold water in several rooms, two water closets and a cellar.[17] For now, when the two bachelors took up residence, Daniel occupied the warmer, south-facing bedroom with the views of St Mary's, while Alexander appropriated a little room on the third floor for smoking.

From this point on the brothers' relationship with Hare began to diminish in importance in comparison with the new responsibilities of the business. It is not clear whether the £500 debt was ever cleared, as interest was still being paid in 1849, and occasionally the relationship deteriorated into testy exchanges, such as when Hare criticized Macmillan for his choice of stock or for late payment of bills. However Daniel never forgot what he owed his first supporter. His direct approach to Hare in 1840 might have been an emotional reaction to a book he loved, but his second letter in 1842 appears calculated to elicit a response. Hare was flattered and impressed by the young man's perseverance, and by the style and content of his letters, and his curiosity provoked the invitation to visit. From that point on he was prepared to sponsor Daniel and to encourage him to improve his situation, and by supporting him with little commissions and introductions, Hare paved the way for the much bigger undertaking of renting a shop in Cambridge and the launch of a publishing house. Hare's contribution to Victorian intellectual life through his writings was seen as significant at the time of his death, but within a few decades it was almost forgotten.* It is the loan of £500 to Daniel Macmillan that should secure his place in any literary Hall of Fame.

---

* Not forgotten in the House of Macmillan, where a bust of Julius Hare stood in the main entrance hall until 1965, when it was reclaimed by the Macmillan family.

– 5 –

BUILDING A NETWORK

(1845–53)

Frederick Maurice

'The men whom I have seen succeed best in life have always been cheerful and hopeful men, who went about their business with a smile on their faces, and took the changes and chances of this mortal life like men, facing rough and smooth alike as it came.'

Charles Kingsley

FOR THE NEXT few years the brothers worked hard to build their Cambridge business, taking on apprentices and opening a small bookbinding business in the back of the shop, with at its peak seven men, two women and two boys at work. Producing beautiful bindings for their customers' treasured libraries was a good way to develop loyal relationships – but the takings needed to cover a weekly wage bill of nine pounds. The main focus of the bookselling business lay in cultivating clients, making new networks and thus developing a healthy list of potential authors. Charles Morgan writes: 'Now, partly through Hare, partly through Maurice, but much more by the brothers' power to win always the respect and nearly always the affection of those they met, they were making friends, and because in friendship, as in all else, they were unswerving and untiring, they did not lose them.'[1] Their customers became their guests, then their friends, and finally their authors.

Many undergraduates had only been sent to Cambridge as a prerequisite to taking holy orders, and struggled to make sense of their studies, finding no help from their tutors. To these young men, the guidance and wisdom of the friendly and accessible Macmillan brothers was invaluable. This would help to shape a whole generation of clergy. A particular friend from this time, Sebastian Evans, wrote that for many years afterwards when listening to a sermon he would often pick up a turn of phrase or thought that seemed to have come directly from the fireside conversations in the Macmillans' bookshop.

From one of these students we have a pen portrait of Daniel at that time: 'tall, but with a frame already somewhat wasted; pale face, aquiline nose, a large mouth with full lips, dark lustrous eyes with long lashes. He looked like one whom God loved, I mean one who might pass away from us while yet young.'[2] As for Alexander,

Evans notes 'the face of my friend as I first saw him, the black locks as yet unstreaked by grey, rippling outwards over a brow already perceptibly marked by lines of thought but as yet unfurrowed by deep sorrow – the joyous faithful eyes, the critic nose and sensitive nostril-wings – the dear lips parted to speak words of sympathy and encouragement.'[3]

Sadly, the more their business grew, the more Daniel's health deteriorated, and the more his face bore the signs of illness, as the worries did not go away. By the summer of 1847, book sales were running at £10,000 per annum but in February 1848 they had to repay £175 of the £250 they had borrowed from Burnside and trade was still slow. As Hare had warned them, customers in Cambridge, particularly the students, expected to be given lengthy credit, and they were constantly short of cash. To smooth cashflow the firm used the services of the London Protection Society, and when criticized by customers who objected to being chased to pay their debts, they were resolute: 'we are particularly anxious that everyone should know that we do not give long credit, and that we should much prefer being without the custom of those who wish for longer credit than a year's running account . . . Longstanding accounts eat away our profit and give us a great deal of trouble and oftener than we like end in bad debts.'[4]

Daniel needed to take regular holidays away from the stresses of running the shop and the bitter, damp Cambridge winters, seeking the warmth of Torquay in particular, just to restore his strength for term time. 1848 was the year that the railway reached Torquay, previously only accessible by coach from Newton Abbot, some seven miles away. The seaside town grew quickly into a fashionable resort, with a mild climate almost as lovely as the south of France, and wealthy families began to holiday there and build grand villas. The doctors had advised Daniel to visit Pau, in southern France, but as Alexander later confirmed, he never managed to get that far or to that warm a climate, instead spending three months in St Cloud, near Paris, which did him no good.

By necessity these absences forced Alexander to take a much more responsible position in the business, as the 'front of house', writing regularly, often daily, to Daniel with news of friends and the gossip of the university and the town, and for advice on business matters. Daniel's replies sometimes infuriated Alexander, as he would write long messages for other people embedded within his letters, which the already overworked Alexander then had to copy out again to send on. He begged Daniel to consider using separate sheets of paper, but to no avail. Nevertheless, the business continued to grow.

As Charles Morgan wrote:

When Daniel's health made it possible for him to be in the shop, they worked together in perfect balance, full of knowledge of their trade and of the love of books. The old principle of unity between bookselling and publishing had one of its last great exemplars in them, and the men who came into the shop to buy books stayed in the publishing house to write them. Thus they drew on the whole resources of the University and an upper room in Number One became a common-room where young men and old men assembled to discuss books or God or social reform – but chiefly it would appear, God – before going into four o'clock hall [dinner in college]. They drew on Cambridge, which was one world, and they drew on F. D. Maurice, which though the circles intersected and pretty fiercely on occasion, was another.[5]

To understand how the intellectual debates of mid-Victorian England lifted the publishing house of Macmillan from Cambridge obscurity to bestseller territory, we need a short detour into the political and religious concerns of the 1840s and 1850s. After many decades of increasing poverty and hardship among the working classes, to which neither the Reform Act of 1832 nor the repeal of the Corn Laws in 1846 had made any great difference, 1848 was the Year

of Revolutions. These began in France in February and by March
had spread to Berlin and Vienna. John Ludlow, a young and idealis-
tic lawyer who spoke fluent French, travelled to Paris in February to
witness the revolution at first hand. He firmly believed that appalling
violence and bloodshed between the classes in Britain could only be
averted if society put into practice the teachings of the New Testament, and tried to love and protect the interests of all men, not just
those of the wealthy capitalists and industrialists. The letters Ludlow
wrote from Paris to his friend Frederick Maurice, who had been
appointed chaplain of Lincoln's Inn in 1846, were seen by both men
as key in the development of Christian Socialism. This could be seen
as an Anglican response to the High Church spiritualism of Pusey,
Keble and Newman, but also as a counter to socially disruptive, atheistic socialism. It put a practical concern for one's fellow man, and
the importance of good works and charitable giving, ahead of doctrine and ritual, and took its enthusiasm for the language of the
contest and the fight from the writings of St Paul.

Against the backdrop of revolution across Europe, the authorities
in England observed the rise of the Chartist movement, combining
the voices of middle-class liberal intellectuals and the might of
working-class protestors, and thought they saw the writing on the
wall. Events came to a head on 10 April 1848, when a large demon-
stration was planned. The protestors would march through London
to Kennington Common and then present a petition to Parliament
supporting the Chartists' demands: the Government, in a panic, sent
the royal family to the Isle of Wight, put the army on standby and
swore in eighty-five thousand special constables, to stand alongside
the four thousand police and seven thousand soldiers.

Up from his rectory in Hampshire to observe the fray and hoping
to calm the violent tendencies of the crowd came a little-known
radical sympathizer, a twenty-nine-year-old parson and Cambridge
graduate, Charles Kingsley, determined to address the marchers at
Kennington Common. As a schoolboy at Clifton he had witnessed
the Bristol Riots of 1831 and had been scarred by the spectacle.

Kingsley was, like the Macmillan brothers, a disciple of Frederick Maurice, and had recently been appointed to teach literature and history at Maurice's Queen's College for young women in London. On his way to the Common he called on John Ludlow, back from Paris, holding a letter of introduction from Maurice. Torrential rain stopped the twenty thousand Chartists' march from gaining any traction, and when Kingsley and Ludlow, equally enthusiastic in their devotion to the radical cause, eventually set off for Kennington, they met the bedraggled protesters heading home. The two men returned to Maurice's house in Queen Square to continue their discussions, and thus began the grouping which was to be the spearhead of the Christian Socialist Movement in England for the next ten years.

Their passion for the cause was not dented by the sad turnout for the march, and the three men determined to wage the battle on behalf of the poor and disenfranchised through journalism and literature. Literacy and education for all must come before democracy could be achieved. Their first step, in less than a month, was to establish a weekly periodical, *Politics for the People*, published by J. W. Parker, with Ludlow as editor, and contributions from Maurice, Archdeacon Hare, Alexander Scott, another barrister called Frederick Furnivall, and Ludlow's great friend from Oxford, Tom Hughes. Its stated purpose was to set out the principles of what they termed Christian Socialism but, short of funds or sponsors, it ran for only seventeen weekly issues. Kingsley was determined to continue to use his pen, turning to fiction to promote his beliefs, and began a new career as a novelist of social purpose. He rallied his troops with the line 'Workers of England, be wise, and then you <u>must</u> be free, for you will be <u>fit</u> to be free.'

The Macmillan brothers' enthusiasm for the beliefs of Maurice and Hare drew them into this radical movement, and within a few years they became the group's chosen publishers. As early as May 1848, Archdeacon Hare was asking Daniel Macmillan to take an interest in the weekly paper as he was worried that Parker would give it up too easily. Until this time it is hard to be sure of the brothers' political leanings – press reports of Cambridge politics in the early 1840s suggest that they were supporters of the Conservative Prime Minister Robert Peel, attracted by his liberal attitudes to free trade and to religious tolerance for the Catholics in Ireland. Now they moved cautiously further left. Their desire to find solutions to the social problems of the day in Christian teachings made them open to the more politically driven thinking of men such as Kingsley and Ludlow. Daniel himself penned a letter to the editor of *Politics* which was included in the final edition, lamenting the demise of the publication. In it he made a plea for the clergy to speak more plainly to the common man, and less in riddles: 'If clergymen loved excellence for its own sake, we should have much wiser, more coherent and more beautiful sermons, and it is needless to say what the result would be.'[6]

Alexander, teased by his friends who called him 'The Red Radical', wrote to his friend Fenton Hort: 'About converting you to Socialism I am not solicitous. Believing in my deepest soul that the central principle is right, I am yet by no means cocksure about many details which I yet accept.'[7] Conscious that the main attack thrown at Socialism by the middle classes was its hostility to the teachings of the Church, Alexander found that writing helped him to clarify his thoughts, and he composed a lengthy, unpublished tract in the form of a dialogue which he entitled *British Industry and Socialism*. The participants were that mythical British hero, John Bull, described in this case as 'a city merchant', and a new character named Amos Yates, 'a small dealer from the country'. Yates, presumably representing Alexander, makes his political and theological sympathies, and his contempt for religious hypocrisy, very clear, drawing on his own experiences back in Glasgow.

> You accuse these Socialists of being infidels . . . Having met with several of the disciples of Robert Owen in this country I am bound to concede to you that in matters of opinion they are, as you say, infidels. At the same time it has often appeared

to me that the most serious obstacle to their conversion was the practical infidelity of men calling themselves Christian. And I can further say this, that if you felt inclined to try the experiment of acting out in Society more fully and simply Christian principles, you would find less hindrance from them than from many who claim to themselves to be peculiarly believers in Christ . . . It is easy enough for the wealthy orthodox enjoying every comfort, every luxury even, of life, to sit quietly at home and accuse these working-men of adopting infidel principles as a salve to their consciences . . . among these of whom you talk there are noble, earnest, self-denying, pure-living – why should I hesitate to say it? – Christ-like men who, in the deep shadow of <u>death of infidelity</u>, are yet struggling with a blind reliance on a God of love whom yet in name they deny, to raise their brethren in misery and poverty into something which seems to them to be a holy and saintly life.[8]

By 1851 Alexander was sufficiently confident in his views to contribute a further article, 'The Existence of Evil and The Existence of Good', under the same pseudonym, Amos Yates, to the *Christian Socialist* journal (the successor to the *Politics for the People*). It was a lengthy and learned response to a previous correspondent who had claimed that the belief in a loving God was incompatible with the acknowledgement of the existence of evil in the world. Alexander admitted that he had previously found it difficult to reconcile these issues, but now, after lengthy consideration, was convinced that man's free will would over time lead to evil being driven from the world. He became a regular correspondent in the pages of the journal, even submitting a sonnet: 'Why labour ye for that which is not bread?', and concluding:

> . . . our brother's misery
> Touches us not, though he be blind and weak:
> For vanity hath made our hearts like stone.[9]

Meanwhile, as Alexander grew in confidence and activism, his brother continued to fade. The winter of 1848 saw Daniel very unwell again and required a return to Devon to recuperate – in a letter to Watt he optimistically wrote, 'I am very stout and strong and never looked better – but off work staying at 2 Palk Street, Torquay. A great many people come here and recover. I have hardly had a cold since I came here and not the least hint of my old enemy the haemorrhage. I take good walks daily. My brother is here now, he has been a great sufferer with sciatica and has reduced almost to a skeleton. I hope a few weeks here will set him up.'[10] At first the two brothers were so disheartened by their various illnesses that they considered emigrating to warmer climes – South Africa, to open a bookshop, or even Australia, to try their hand at sheep-farming, the old family business. However, the house on the front at Torquay worked its limited magic and as 1849 rolled on, both brothers were sufficiently recovered in health and optimism to return to Cambridge. They had already strengthened the family participation in the business by bringing down from Scotland their eleven-year-old nephew, Robert Bowes, as an apprentice. In the years to come, Bowes took over the running of the Cambridge store and established his own publishing company. Ebenezer Budden, a brother of Daniel's lost fiancée Hannah, arrived from London to take over the operation of the bookbinding business. They offered employment to a Mr Robb, from Edinburgh, on a salary of £60, for which he was expected to start work punctually at 7am, to supervise the cleaning and tidying of the shop, to supervise the errand boys and stop them from gossiping together or wasting time generally, to 'do the day's work in the day', in other words to see that all post and commissions were answered on the day they were received, take an hour for breakfast, an hour for lunch and half an hour for tea, and to close the shop at eight in winter, seven in summer. The brothers minded the shop and concentrated on the clients, leaving the assistants to manage all the paperwork, including the quarterly customer accounts, which necessitated a great deal of writing. They offered good training and a chance to learn the trade from the bottom up. The offer letter ended with the encouragement: 'If you have no fear, if you don't shrink from the hours, if you would throw yourself heartily into the work, if you are resolved to do all you can to make yourself a thorough bookseller and man of business, we have no doubt you would get on very comfortably with us.'[11] It seems likely that Robb, having perused the job description, did not feel himself quite the man they were looking for, as he is never mentioned again.

There are no surviving diaries or letters of Alexander from this period, but the letters of his friend the Cambridge undergraduate Fenton Hort are instructive. Hort was a regular customer of the Macmillan bookshop and often cited Daniel's opinions or Alexander's gossip in letters home. In May 1850, Hort and Alexander spent two days together in London. They set off early on a Sunday, deposited their luggage at Woods, a family hotel situated in Furnival's Inn (advertising itself 'For Families and Gentlemen. Warm, Cold and Shower Baths Always Ready. Wine Merchant, etc.'), and sallied forth to Lincoln's Inn to hear Maurice preach. After the service they dined and then Macmillan took Hort to meet Ludovici, whom Hort describes as 'an odd Red Republican artist of some genius' at what Hort described as 'a curious foreign boarding house – truly a more strange Sunday evening I never passed.' The following day Alexander went to a sale of books at the shop owned by David Nutt, one of his old friends, while Hort spent time talking to the Christian Socialist group back at Lincoln's Inn – including Hughes and Ludlow.[12]

Back in Cambridge, Alexander was making a mark in society, among the great and the good of the town as well as of the university, and inspired by the teachings of the Christian Socialist movement to contribute in practical ways to improving the lot of the poor. He was chosen as an overseer of the Poor Law in the parish of St Mary the Great and a member of the Grand Jury for the Quarter Sessions. He joined the committee for the establishment of an Industrial School in Cambridge. This Church-supported institution on Victoria Road aimed to give solid moral and practical education to fifty teenage boys including such skills as shoemaking, tailoring and gardening. At a public meeting in November 1851, attended by the Mayor of Cambridge, Alexander spoke passionately and at length, as recorded in the press, saying the school 'met the very gangrene and ulcer that was eating into all society – it was an attempt to reform the dangerous classes otherwise than by the hangman and the policeman . . . mere physical want was not the grand evil we had to contend against, no it was vice, idleness and the want of self-command.' To much laughter, he remarked that idleness was not confined to the poorer classes, and that it was a shame there were no Industrial Schools for the rich as well as the poor. But he continued: 'if we did not pay greater attention to that festering mass of our population [it] would be likely to take the lead in political disturbances.'[13]

The start of this new decade felt like time to settle the brothers' personal lives and perhaps to secure some succession in the business. They discussed the idea of marriage, but Alexander thought it would be too hard to achieve, when they were so busy with everything: 'I cannot set my heart on anyone till I have had some opportunity of intercourse, and how that is to be brought about I know not, and taking a rush at a fancied good I don't think wholesome or safe, so I think I must e'en die a bachelor.'[14] And also 'my habits and in some degree my constitution . . . so totally vary from all that is required in married life that I never think of myself as a married man without something like trembling and fear.'[15] In his few spare hours, Alexander was happiest sitting with his feet on the fender in a fug of tobacco smoke and reading past midnight. Was this compatible with happy married life?

Daniel was the first to take the plunge. At the grand old age of thirty-seven, in September 1850, he married twenty-nine-year-old Frances, or Fanny, Orridge, the only daughter of a Cambridge chemist. Charles Orridge had premises on Market Hill, just round the corner from the Macmillans' shop, and was a well-known town worthy, being in his spare time a magistrate, the well-paid governor for twenty years of the county gaol, an official at Addenbrooke's

Hospital, and by way of trade, a purveyor of Orridge's widely advertised camphorated tooth powder and pure glycerine pomade.

The love letters that Daniel wrote to his darling Fanny following their engagement in June of that year detailed the trials of his early life, the disappointment of his courtship of Hannah Budden, and the growth of his religious beliefs and influences.

> I fear you will think I am very tiresome with these long letters. But the fact is that I am anxious that you should know all about me . . . It is strange that I have never been able to say to you what was at my heart and even on my tongue. It always seems as if I could not find utterance when in your presence; and yet there is more on my mind and more in my heart when I see you than at any other time; and perhaps it is because I have so much to say that I can utter next to nothing . . . You are more dear to me than words can utter. I love you with my whole heart, and wish you to know all my thoughts . . . when I met you and heard your dear voice, and looked into those most blessed eyes of yours, I waited and thought, and thought and waited, till I felt my heart say, as if it were the voice of God 'this is the right fair saint for you: there your heart and mind will find all you need.'[16]

They were married at St Bene't's Church, believed to be the oldest building in Cambridge, and then travelled north via the Lakes, hoping to visit Daniel's family and friends in Scotland. But by the time they reached Edinburgh the pain in Daniel's side, and the twinges in his bones, convinced the pair to travel straight back to Torquay to finish the honeymoon.

He was thus away from Cambridge again when the firm suffered an irritating setback. In February 1850 the Macmillans had approached a man called Batkin, then working in a stationery business in London, with an offer to join them in Cambridge and take on the management of their own stationery business. A written contract was drawn up, and Batkin was to be paid £70 per annum with three months' notice in writing. However after just a few months the brothers decided that the arrangement was not working out and at the beginning of June, Alexander spoke to Mr Batkin to tell him that they would no longer require his services, and that he should leave in three months. Naively he did not put this notice in writing, and although Batkin started looking around for other positions, he chose to believe that nothing was settled. When the subject was next discussed, in August, Batkin had said he would take three months' written notice from that date. Alexander, showing his quick temper, was enraged by what he thought was a breach of faith, called him 'Shylock' and asked him to leave at once. As reported at some length in the local press, Batkin took the brothers to court for lost income and breach of contract, and the judge ruled that whatever conversations Alexander and Batkin had had in June, Batkin was certainly entitled to his three months' written notice. Despite the best efforts of the Macmillans' lawyer, Mr Gotobed, the judge found against them. Alexander's inexperience in business, by not sticking to the written agreement, had cost the brothers £18, nearly £2,000 in today's money, and taught them a valuable lesson.

However, Alexander was sufficiently well-known and respected around the community now for this setback to be brushed off, and in August 1851 he followed his brother to the altar, having overcome his reservations and fallen for Caroline Brimley, five years his junior. She was the sister of his good friend George Brimley, the Librarian at Trinity College, and had been a witness at Daniel and Fanny's wedding. Caroline and George were the two oldest children of Augustine Gutteridge Brimley, a highly prosperous wholesale grocer, hop and provision merchant, a deacon at St Andrew's Baptist church, and soon to be the Mayor of Cambridge. By 1851 Augustine was for the second time a widower, having married in succession two sisters, first Hannah and then Harriet Gotobed, both of whom had died in their thirties. Marrying one's dead wife's sister had always been frowned upon under Church of England canon law: Augustine was a Baptist, but even so his second marriage just scraped through – he married Harriet in London in 1827, at St George's, Hanover Square, both claiming to be residents of the parish at the time. 1835 saw the passing of a law forbidding such marriages.

By 1850, the Brimley family were living at 13 Park Terrace, Cambridge, an elegant four-storey Georgian house. Caroline was only two when her mother died, and ten when she lost her stepmother, so the children had been brought up by their aunts Mary and Anne Gotobed, to whom they would always remain close. Caroline had two younger half-sisters: twenty-one-year-old Harriet, who was soon to marry William Henry Farthing Johnson, the headmaster of a small school, Llandaff House, in the centre of Cambridge, and twenty-year-old Fanny, who later cemented the Macmillan family relationship by marrying Robert Bowes, four years her junior. George Brimley, Caroline's only brother, had in his youth been a well-regarded scholar at Trinity College, but his ill-health, which led to an early death, meant that he could not take up a Fellowship. As Librarian of the college he was free to develop his skills as a literary critic, writing for *Fraser's* and *The Spectator* magazines, and became very well-known in particular for his lengthy essays on Tennyson and Wordsworth. Alexander's alliance with this family shows how easily he and his brother were now moving between the wealthy merchant circles of Cambridge and the academic elite, of which George was definitely part.

Alexander's wedding took place on 13 August 1851, in an Anglican church, with Thomas Hedley, a Fellow of Trinity College, officiating. The Macmillan brothers had now abandoned all connections with their Scottish Baptist roots, and if they wanted to get on in Cambridge academic circles, the parish church of St Andrew the Great was the place to be seen. George Wilson and his sister Jessie came down from Glasgow, and the other witnesses included George Brimley and Caroline's father Augustine, swallowing his own Baptist preferences.

As one of George Brimley's sisters, all 'highly educated girls of fine character', Caroline would become 'a wife whose intellectual, no less than her moral qualities, rendered her a true helpmeet.'[17] Her son George would write: 'The connexion [sic] was helpful in stimulating my father's keen interest in literature, philosophy and religion, for all such subjects were studied and discussed with no less zest in the Brimley family than by the two Macmillan brothers.'[18]

In October 1851, Caroline wrote to a friend, Frances.

Yes dear Frances this date convinces me that I have been married 2 months and yet have not written to you . . . Deep joy and deep sorrow seem to obliterate our sense of time, proving I think that time is only a circumstance, not the essence of our being. There, I shall begin, and how to convey to you any idea of what I have been doing. I don't feel inclined to describe scenery to you, to tell you how for five blessed weeks we were alone with each other in the very face of Nature. I feel rather inclined to dwell upon the 'humanside' – although it is very much connected with the mountains and valleys, the seas and lakes, Oh what a blessed change did it prove to all the turmoil, the bustle and anxiety of the weeks previous – you were witness to that.

Well from the first moment of the 13th, the worry even lasted to the very end of the Tuesday, about house furnishings – all was left behind and not a care, not one anxious thought remained . . . after three weeks at the English lakes I was permitted to have the high privilege of visiting Scotland – the very place of my dearest husband's birth, the scenes of his early youth and most sacred remembrances. I saw the grey peaks of Arran and the best scenery of the island, and the remembrance of the friends who welcomed me there, of the Sabbath spent among its quiet hills, when I had the privilege of attending a real Highland service and of hearing first a Gaelic, then an English sermon from such a dear Uncle of Alex . . . we sat together then with bare-footed women and children with nothing but the white mutch [cap] upon their heads and the kirtle or bedgowns upon their shoulders, but such a reverent such a thoughtful kind of people who thought unweary of a four hour service . . .

We saw Loch Lomond and the Trossacks and Edinburgh the Queen of the North.

We have now been home a month, and I may say with confidence that tho' travelling and taking pleasure together was exceedingly perfect enjoyment, settling down together to the serious duties of life, endeavouring to realise together the idea of a Christian family, is much more delightful. I think dear Frances if you were to see me now you would hardly know me, I sometimes hardly know myself. My fears are all given to the winds, Perfect love has indeed cast out Fear – you know my tremblings in looking forward to the future, although I had much faith, but all has turned out to be much better than my fears . . . I have found such a real helper in every good thought and action in my dearest husband . . . We are now in the very thick of business, today Trinity Lectures have begun – A has only just been up to meals and down again, but the glimpses are so precious . . .[19]

For the time being, both brothers and wives shared the accommodation over the shop, and Caroline found herself living once more with a seriously consumptive invalid, although now it was Fanny Macmillan's turn to be chief nurse, even though she had just given birth to her first baby, Frederick: 'Daniel has a son and heir, a little fellow who tho' only a fortnight old begins to have a character of his own. [Fanny] was up, the brave little thing stood over her husband for an hour to put on his leeches. He is quite well now, for him at least.'[20]

The next five years saw exponential growth in the publishing activities of Macmillan, Barclay and Macmillan, as the firm was known. They continued to experiment with new ways to build the business: in February 1851 the Cambridge press was full of advertisements for their newest venture, the Cambridge Reading Club, 'to afford to its subscribers the perusal of a higher class of Books than is usually to be found in Circulating Libraries, and at the same time offer a more extensive selection than private book clubs can furnish. Catalogues and Rules to be had GRATIS on application.' However, it was also time to enjoy the pleasures of family life, with five children born to the two brothers in just four years, and it is clear from the letters they shared with their closest friends, such as George Wilson, that these babies were an unexpected delight and joy. Daniel's first son, Frederick Orridge Macmillan, was born in October 1851, named in honour of F. D. Maurice. A second son, called Maurice Crawford, followed in 1853, with F. D. Maurice himself standing godfather, and then Daniel's only daughter, named after her grandmother Katharine Crawford, in 1855. Alexander's first son, Malcolm Kingsley Macmillan, was born in 1852, with Charles Kingsley and Daniel standing as his godfathers. George Augustin followed in 1855 and Margaret Ann, known as Maggie, in 1857.

A year or so after Daniel married, he left Trinity Street to rent a house half a mile away at 29 Regent Street (now number 88), leaving Alexander and Caroline living above the shop with Ebenezer Budden the bookbinder, Robert Bowes and another young apprentice, two lodgers (probably undergraduates) and the housekeeper Ellen. In May 1855, the freehold of 29 Regent Street came up for sale, and so we know that it was a well-built house of brick and slate, with stone steps leading up to the front door, iron railings enclosing an area at the front, with two kitchens, coal, wine and beer cellars, pantries, storerooms, six bedrooms and a dressing room, as well as a back garden and outbuildings. Daniel had come a long way from the shared room in Charterhouse Square. Later that year he swapped homes with his brother, taking him back to life above the shop, to save him from having to walk the streets in bad weather. Alexander however kept a room in Trinity Street where he could hide and smoke. The experience of the two young families growing up together, sharing these rooms in Cambridge, increasingly prosperous, must have often caused Daniel and Alexander to think how different their lives were from the Arran croft and the streets of Irvine.

By April 1851, Daniel was writing to Hare with encouraging news: 'our business seems to get more and more solid and we are now likely to get more publishing and to have the means of carrying it on. We find our partner [Barclay] a very satisfactory man to deal with and he has [the] means to undertake publishing when it offers.'[21] But in May 1852 he wrote, 'I am sorely tortured with an open blister and not allowed to move or speak or write.'[22] To add to his troubles, he was being dosed with cod-liver oil four times a day. Many years later, a family friend remembered that Daniel wore a respirator, a Victorian invention designed to protect consumptives from the dangers of cold air. It consisted of thin metal grilles covered in cloth and tied round the head. It must have been extremely uncomfortable and made communication difficult.

As the Macmillan brothers' life as booksellers became more settled, the industry shifted dramatically around them. The year 1852 saw the complete abandonment of any attempt by booksellers and publishers to impose fixed prices on the book-buying public, and the dissolution of the protectionist Booksellers' Association. It opened an era of unrestrained price discounting. Authors as prestigious as Dickens, Carlyle and Tennyson had all advocated reducing the price of books with the aim of encouraging more people to enter the market. Daniel was philosophical.

> If it leads to greater trade in books and speedier settlements than are usual here it will on the whole be a good thing. To get speedy settlements we shall require the help of the tutors. Our book debts are or have been for the last three years £8000. On many accounts the profit is swallowed up in interest and every now and then we make a serious bad debt and often small ones. So now in the hope that we shall not have to give such long credit in future and that we shall have no bad debts and that we

shall do more trade we shall throw ourselves heartily into the
cheap movement and sell as cheap as anyone. We shall publish
a catalogue of all our stock in early October.[23]

The Macmillan publishing list of 1852 is a mark of how strongly
the business was growing and the ambition the brothers had to
continue to publish works of spiritual and educational merit. The
list included the first edition of a translation of Plato's *Republic* by
John Llewellyn Davies and David J. Vaughan, which became well-
respected and went through many editions; F. D. Maurice's *Sermons
on the Prophets and Kings of the Old Testament*; and, stepping away
from theology into the world of mathematics, Isaac Todhunter's first
textbook, *A Treatise on the Differential Calculus*. The offer to Maurice
to publish his sermons is a good example of the way business was
being done: Daniel offered to publish an edition of 1,500 copies of
the *Sermons on the Prophets*: Macmillan would pay for the printing,
binding and advertising and would undertake to give away thirty-five
copies for review, to give the author twenty-five copies and to pay
him £125 in two instalments – £65 in January 1855 and £60 a year
later.

However, although the business appeared to be flourishing,
there were problems at the very heart of the partnership. Daniel's
incapacity meant that Alexander had to do the 1852 stocktake alone,
entailing more work than usual as they needed to reduce the prices
of all stock to match the shift in the terms of trade. This retail discounting, which seemed a positive development to Macmillan the
bookseller, became an increasing irritant in future years to Macmillan the publisher. Furthermore, although the Gotobed brothers, who
were Caroline's cousins and sons of a prosperous Cambridge brewer,
had bought out the previous partner, Edward Barclay, and should
have been ideal sleeping partners in the firm, no pun intended, the
relationship was far from ideal. Their father James Gotobed, Caroline's uncle, had provided the funds to buy out Barclay in 1850, but
two years later James died, and his share was divided evenly between

his sons Henry, who was a local solicitor, and James Vipan, a businessman who hoped to make his fortune in South Africa. These were men who knew nothing of the book trade, and certainly nothing of the ups and downs of publishing, and who seemed to care even less. They challenged Daniel and Alexander's investment decisions, down to the details of what to publish, and small differences of opinion became irritating grievances. Most importantly, the terms of the partnership agreement were that on the death of a partner his share was to be divided among the other partners, rather than passed on to his family. A fear was beginning to eat at Daniel's heart. This left his wife and children horribly exposed, dependent on the goodwill of Alexander to protect just half the value of their shareholding, and unlikely to see anything from the Gotobeds. This fear grew and became a trouble to both the brothers. Daniel wrote to Alexander: 'If I am to die in this year or the next, all my exertions will be for others, and really I feel no call to such work. I am sure you don't wish me to work myself to death for your sake.'[24] A harsh accusation, indicating just how despondent he must have felt.

Meanwhile, Julius Hare was also unwell, and would die in January 1855. Aware that neither of them had long to live, Daniel, who continued to feel enormous gratitude to his first sponsor and friend, wrote:

I have seldom ventured, when writing or speaking to you, to do more than allude to how much I feel that I owe to your great kindness and that of your brother Marcus. But I seldom forget it: my wife and my brother join with me: and our children will learn to love and reverence your name. If it had not been for your kind help and encouragement and friendly recommendations I should not have been here – I should never have been in a position to marry, nor would my brother . . . My life at Mr Seeley's had fewer cares and anxieties. I could think and read more continuously. My work had become so easy to me that I could do it without effort . . . but it would have been impossible for me to have retained any situation with such health as I have had for the last nine years . . . But both of us have always felt that we ought to work for the coming of Christ's kingdom . . .

My own home, though poor, seems to me noble and venerable now from the remembrance of the Godly kingly priestlike lives of our Father and Mother . . . they did not wish their children to be either rich or distinguished, but I am sure it was their constant prayer that they should be true Christians . . . the longer we live the more deeply we feel that we cannot live more nobly than by working in their spirit or striving after the same object. And here we feel we can do so, while quietly following our own calling and working for our own daily bread . . .[25]

For all these optimistic words, Daniel was not making enough to support his family and had to ask his father-in-law, who already paid their rent, for cash to clear his debts. Trying to make money in the publishing world while sticking to Daniel's ethical principles was proving hard work. Their catalogue was filling up with worthy but unprofitable titles. At times their focus on religious works led them into the deep waters of controversy: in June 1853, Macmillan published F. D. Maurice's *Theological Essays*, which opened a whole can of worms. Smuggled into these apparently harmless but well-written sermons was Maurice's belief that a God of Love could not be so harsh as to condemn a sinner to an eternity of punishment. He redefined Hell as a state of isolation from God, rather than burning fires and torment. Part of Maurice's appeal to his middle-class followers, and to Macmillan's customers, was that the idea of Hell was becoming increasingly unpleasant to the reading public, uncomfortably aware that the lives they lived might not be sufficiently wholesome to help them avoid damnation. The idea of a loving and forgiving God who had sent his Son as an example of how to live well was much more palatable.

This apparent abandonment of the established Christian conception of Hell caused such an uproar that Maurice was very publicly sacked, cancelled as we would say, from his position at King's College, London. Daniel spent an hour with him that day and wrote to Alexander: 'He is not even allowed to lecture today . . . He has lent me the correspondence and given me his whole defence. He has asked leave to print and publish the whole . . . It is sure to pay – most likely it would have a very large sale. I should be glad if it sold so well that we could give him £20 . . . He is a grand man! And must endure like other prophets'.[26] His dismissal from King's was accompanied by a prohibition on his books in some Cambridge colleges, which horrified Alexander to such an extent that he visited a leading Fellow at Gonville and Caius to argue the case. As he wrote to Daniel, 'I told him I wished him to know that we, in publishing the book and in continuing to help its circulation, were acting conscientiously.'[27] The Macmillan brothers clearly felt some responsibility for this turn of events but also saw that as publishers it was an opportunity to make profit while defending the freedom of the press and spreading the gospel of the man they called the Prophet. They negotiated with Maurice's previous publisher, Parker, to acquire the rights to all of his work, and he was happy to oblige, telling them there was no money in it. But as Daniel wrote to his friend David Watt: 'However Mr M has a higher task appointed him than to make money by his books for himself or his publishers'.[28] Alexander later said that he was prouder of publishing Maurice than of his appointment as Publisher to the University of Oxford, but also 'had we only such books as his we could not have lasted three years.'[29]

In the next two years, the brothers' close acquaintance with Maurice, Kingsley and their circle led them to considerable business success without needing to abandon their high-minded scruples: the publication of *Westward Ho!* and *Tom Brown's School Days* changed their fortunes dramatically.

6

WESTWARD HO!

and

TOM BROWN'S SCHOOL DAYS

(1854–57)

Frontispiece to Tom Brown's School Days

'I'm going to make your fortune!'

Thomas Hughes

CHARLES KINGSLEY, BORN in 1819, was a well-heeled, striking-looking Anglican cleric who had spent his years at Cambridge smoking and drinking, hunting, fencing, boxing, duck-shooting and rowing. Tom Hughes, born in 1822, was the son of a Berkshire squire of literary tastes, steeped in the traditions of the countryside, privately educated at one of the best schools in England and then as a student at Oxford, a vigorous sportsman and a practising barrister, in appearance rather like a young Mr Pickwick. These men had little in common with Daniel or Alexander Macmillan, poorly educated sons of an Arran crofter, but together the foursome created literature that became bestsellers and shaped children's literature for years to come.

Christian Socialism, and the Gospel according to F. D. Maurice, was the powerful force that united these men, but there had been one early advocate of a more strenuous, manly version of the Christian spiritual life – Dr Arnold, headmaster of Rugby School, whose teachings in turn inspired the writings of Maurice, Kingsley and of course Tom Hughes, one of his pupils at the school. Thomas Arnold arrived at Rugby in 1829 and over the next thirteen years completely transformed the public-school experience in England. Although he himself was a distinguished scholar, he believed that academic success was less important than moral progress within a strong Christian faith, and that character was formed through hard work and discipline. 'It is not necessary that this should be a school for 300 or even 100 boys, but it is necessary that it should be a school of Christian gentlemen.'[1] By the time he died suddenly in 1842, it was already possible to trace the impact he was having on the British public-school system, as ex-pupils and masters from Rugby spread his methods into other establishments. His disciples were determined to keep the flame burning.

Archdeacon Hare had spoken admiringly of Dr Arnold to Daniel

Macmillan at the same time that he introduced the brothers to both Maurice and Kingsley, forming friendships which would strengthen throughout the 1840s. The Continental revolutions of 1848, combined with the disappointing failure of the Chartist movement, galvanized Maurice's circle of academics, lawyers and clerics with a determination to improve the lot of the working classes, and to drive radical change across society. One key voice was that of Charles Kingsley, who addressed the working man, writing as Parson Lot, and declared: 'my only quarrel with the Charter is that it does not go far enough in reform. I want to set you free.' He believed in bold attack, that trying to change the social order just through Parliamentary means was missing the point, *trying* as he called it 'to do God's work with the Devil's tools'.[2] Like the Macmillans, Kingsley idolized Frederick Maurice, saying that reading *The Kingdom of Christ* had changed his life. Maurice taught Kingsley that the Church had social responsibilities, and that the attack on class structures, and the amelioration of conditions for the working poor, should be seen as key components of the Christian life.

In July 1850, Charles Kingsley visited the Macmillan brothers in Cambridge, much to Alexander's delight: 'even his finest writings are not up to the rich vigour and freshness of his conversation – especially when combined with the hearty, manly look of the man.' If they were impressed by Kingsley's forceful personality, there is a hint that their own characters, and their outlook on life, had made an impression on him. *Alton Locke* was Kingsley's first commercially successful novel, published by Chapman and Hall in 1850, and the presiding spirit of the book's philosophy is an old Scotsman called Sandy Mackaye, assumed to be based on Thomas Carlyle, and acknowledged as such by Carlyle himself. Mackaye is a bookseller, and one who takes a particular interest in the reading habits of the young men who frequent his shop, just as Daniel Macmillan did. Surely Kingsley had his new acquaintance in mind as he took up his pen. It is Mackaye who takes the young boy Alton Locke in hand, guides his reading and encourages him to tackle the classics. He says to Locke, 'Desultory reading is the bane o'lads. Ye maun begin with self-restraint and method, my man, gin ye intend to gie yoursel' a liberal education. So I'll just mak' you a present of an old Latin grammar, and you maun begin where your betters ha' begun before you.' Locke enquires as to who is to teach him Latin, and Mackaye replies: 'Hoot, man! Who'll teach a man anything except himsel'? . . . My father was a Hieland farmer, and yet he was a weel learned man: and "Sandy my lad," he used to say "a man kens just as much as he's taught himsel' and na mair. So get wisdom; and wi'all your getting, get understanding."'[3] This is more reminiscent of the philosophy of the Macmillan family than the Carlyles, who, although poor and ill-educated themselves, sent their son to university.[4]

That same year 1850, Kingsley, writing as Parson Lot, chose Macmillan to publish a pamphlet called *Cheap Clothes and Nasty*, which denounced the vile conditions in which the sweatshop workers in London's East End were labouring to produce clothes sold 'in plate glass palaces' in the West End. The pamphlet had a significant impact, with many of Mayfair's smart young men taking their custom away from the worst offenders and favouring the tailors of whom Kingsley approved. Furthermore, its publication coincided with the launch of a new periodical, *The Christian Socialist*, which would be the journal that promoted working-men's associations, the forerunners of the Co-operative movement.

The friendship between Kingsley and the brothers grew ever closer, Alexander even asking the parson to officiate at his wedding in 1851, although he had to decline as he was travelling abroad. It may have been that he had helped to bring Alexander and Caroline Brimley together, as in sending his best wishes for the forthcoming wedding he added that he felt himself 'a connoisseur in matrimonial matters and whose highest enjoyment is matchmaking'. He added that he hoped Alexander would 'go on as you have before, speaking the truth and fearing the face of no man and keeping yourself unspotted from the world.'[5] In 1852 Macmillan published Kingsley's brief philosophical work *Phaethon, or Loose Thoughts for*

Loose Thinkers, and in 1854 their friendship was more than rewarded when the author delivered the manuscript of a historical romance, *Westward Ho!*, to the firm.

The full title of the work is *Westward Ho! Or The Voyages and Adventures of Sir Amyas Leigh, Knight of Burrough, in the County of Devon, in the reign of Her Most Glorious Majesty, Queen Elizabeth, Rendered into Modern English by Charles Kingsley*. The social philosopher had changed tack, caught up in the increasing imperialist and military fervour that was gripping the nation in the summer of 1854 as it embarked upon the Crimean War. The original cause of the war, a dispute between France and Russia over who was to be the protector of Christians in the Holy Lands within the Turkish Empire, had long been forgotten by the British people, whose government's main aim was to safeguard the sea and land passage to imperial India and to limit Russian expansionism.

As an indication of where Kingsley's vigorous admiration for the heroic was taking him, he dedicated his novel to Sir James Brooke, the first white Rajah of Sarawak, a kingdom in Borneo. Brooke had only recently been cleared by a Court of Enquiry of the charge of using excessive force against the native peoples – Kingsley, who can easily and often be accused of racism, felt that Brooke had been badly treated. Now he was specifically aiming to produce a text that would put fighting spirit into his readers: he wrote to Daniel: 'we may make a book which people will read in these war times and learn what glorious fellows their forbears were.'[6] He had drifted away from the Christian Socialist movement – the passing of the 1852 Industrial and Provident Societies Act was enough of a victory to persuade him to look for a new cause, and he found it in a fever of hatred of the Tsar, and in a fury that the war was not being sufficiently well prosecuted. At first, he drafted a pamphlet of complaint against the government, blaming the influence of Prince Albert in particular, but his friends Hughes and Ludlow warned him it was treasonous and it was never published. Thwarted, he turned to historical fiction.

The book chronicled the fictional travels of a Devon adventurer sailing in the wakes of Sir Francis Drake and Sir Walter Raleigh. Much of the story concerned the kidnapping of Leigh's sweetheart Rose by Spanish pirates, led by the villainous Don Guzman, and was a chance for Kingsley to parade the anti-Catholic prejudices which landed him in serious trouble in the next decade. The novel was first mentioned in a letter to the Macmillans in February 1853, although Kingsley was trying to finish another novel at the same time (*Hypatia*, promised to Chapman and Hall, his previous publishers). By the summer of 1854 it was well enough developed for Daniel to send him a cheque for £100 as an advance, together with some tactful advice not to use too much archaic language: 'The style is now getting a bore. The free march of your own style will be much more Elizabethan in manner and tone than any you can assume. We feel sure it will be a right brave and noble book, and do good to England . . .'[7] At the end of July, Alexander read a first draft and reported to his brother 'it certainly has noble passages and will, I fancy, be a noble whole.'[8] This greatly cheered Daniel, who was recuperating in Cromer, Norfolk, from a very bad attack of haemorrhage and had come to realize that he would never be fit again.

Kingsley, perennially short of cash, was desperate to write a commercially successful book, and pleaded with Alexander to share the draft around anyone he thought would be a good sounding-board, particularly his brother-in-law, the critic George Brimley. 'Pray get everyone's opinion you can: I understand that both for the sake of success, and of putting into people's heads some brave thoughts about the present hour, I am aiming altogether at popularity and am willing to alter or expunge wherever ought is likely to hurt the sale of the book.' When Alexander wrote back with praise of some scenes, Kingsley was delighted. 'I shall be anxious to have Brimley's opinion: but (strictly between ourselves) I shall take it cum grano salis, thinking a more jolly man's opinion like yours on such a book quite as good as his.'[9] Kingsley also suggested that Daniel, unwell again, should join him in Bideford, north Devon, for his health – as good air as could be found in Torquay and a much cheaper place to stay.

On 26 February 1855 Kingsley acknowledged the receipt of £300 in connection with the production of the first edition of *Westward Ho!* – 1,250 copies in three volumes. By April he was despatching proofs of a natural history text, *Glaucus, or the Wonders of the Shore*, and trying to develop several more projects to pitch to the firm. 'But one thing I must say, both to you and your brother, that it is delightful to find in you not merely generous publishers but cordial and appreciating friends.'[10] By May, Kingsley's money worries were becoming pressing, and he wrote chasing a second edition of *Westward Ho!* – when would it be out and how many copies, he had heard that *The Times* was about to publish a review which would be 'very satisfactory, as far as it goes' . . . he needed the money from the sale of the second edition to pay his bills in Bideford before he could return to London. 'Thackeray sold 4,000 of Esmond, why should I not do as well – I am in a fix, I could scrape clear with £150'.[11] By August he was overdrawn at the bank and writing almost daily, wondering if the postman had stolen the cheque.

He need not have worried: the book was a rip-roaring swashbuckling, even bloodthirsty, success – the only work of fiction so successful that a holiday resort is named after it. Kingsley may have imagined that he was writing for adults, but in fact it was a fine book to capture the imagination of boys, with its battles with the Spanish treasure fleet, its South American jungles and its crushing defeat of the Armada. It had been long in the writing, and the contribution that its publishers made to the creative process was undeniable. Daniel and Kingsley were in correspondence throughout the final months of the writing process, as the manuscript got longer and longer (three volumes, 250,000 words). But its publication put the Macmillans on the map.

The financial success of *Westward Ho!* was not only a relief for the author – earlier in April 1855 Daniel in Torquay had become so despondent about the firm's finances that he had threatened to reduce his midday meal to a single chop. Alexander was having none of it.

> Now take two chops tomorrow or I shall think you a goose. I really am doing as well as I know how in every matter. Even though we have not a penny when we die, if we leave boys and girls who can do their work I don't think one need grumble about it – certainly anything is better than that foolish anxiety that could induce you to refrain from eating a chop on any other ground than that you could not digest it.

The next day he wrote again:

> Don't worry yourself and don't be too hard on me. For half an hour after reading your letter today I was under the impression that I was a terrible fool. I have been recovering my good opinion of myself by degrees, and at the moment I do seriously think I can get on without greatly damaging the business till your return next October.[12]

Alexander was adept at firmly but gently reassuring his worried older brother. Daniel fretted that he was useless and helpless – Alexander teased that he himself would have made the better invalid as being naturally lazy, he could have borne it with more fortitude.

Daniel's health continued to deteriorate. In October 1855 he wrote to his old friend David Watt from Torquay – his first letter for a year, he was ashamed to admit. The previous summer he and his wife had visited Cromer for some sun and sea air, but a cold wind had in fact made him worse and Alexander had had to fetch them home. Then he had spent the winter in Torquay again, returning to Cambridge in March, at which point he had contracted dysentery which 'brought me nearer death than I ever was before though I have had some frequent and narrow escapes.' Fanny was pregnant with Katherine so was not able to travel with him back to Torquay, but a month after the birth she took all the family to join him. He wrote, 'I have spent the chief part of my time in a wood under the shade of a tree enjoying the sea and land equally. Terrible cough . . . it is no wise the kind of life that I should have chosen for myself but it is given me and I am thankful . . . I have no hope of ever being well or having anything else than a constant stand up fight with Death'.[13] One can only pity Daniel, shuffling on draughty trains and coaches between boarding houses and rest cures in Torquay and Cromer, often parted from his wife and children, knowing that the end was inevitable and that his finances were not secure. It was no wonder that his letters to Alexander were so full of advice and reprimand – the future of the firm, and hence the livelihood of his wife and children, depended on his little brother making a success of the business once he himself had gone.

Alexander was now busy working with Kingsley on the proofs of *Glaucus*, taking immense trouble over the colourful illustrations and the design of the title page. His close relationship with James Burn, the bookbinder, and Harvey Orrinsmith, the woodcutter, began to pay dividends, as Alexander wanted the book to look pretty. From September onwards, the royalty cheques and advances for future work began to roll out to the mightily relieved cleric, £75 for *Glaucus*, and £150 for his next book, *The Heroes*, a collection of Greek myths for children. He wrote to Alexander: 'A thousand thanks for your obligingness. You certainly are a most pleasant person to deal with, and please God you will have no cause to regret it.'[14] His letters of 1856 are full of concern for Daniel's health but also of plans for many more publications, including the novel *Two Years Ago*. By 1857 his income from Macmillan had reached £1,500, and his literary success was getting him noticed in high circles: in 1859 he was asked to preach at Windsor Castle on Palm Sunday, and having passed the test, was appointed first as chaplain to Queen Victoria, and then as tutor to the Prince of Wales. The rebel parson was now a member of the Establishment.

As Kingsley slowly became disenchanted with the propaganda programme of the Christian Socialist movement, several of its members, including Tom Hughes, were looking for something practical they could do to further their goals. When Maurice was forced to resign his chair at King's College, London in 1853, he turned to the education of the working man as the way to counter the tempting atheism of the socialist movement. There had previously been many attempts to spread learning among the adult working classes, Mechanics' Institutes being a prime example. But these were focused on improving the working man's technical and scientific skills, and discussions of religion or politics were generally banned. Although popular, spreading rapidly throughout England and Scotland in the first half of the nineteenth century, these institutes were failing their audience – many working men wanted more than just technical skills, they craved answers to the questions that most influenced their lives, and better education should give them the tools they needed to develop political and spiritual understanding. Maurice wrote: 'We must aim in all our teaching of the working classes, at making them free.'[15]

The first Working Men's College was founded in Red Lion Square, London by Maurice, Hughes, Furnivall and other leaders of the Christian Socialist movement, and opened its doors in October 1854, with around a hundred and thirty students enrolled to study humanities (including theology, history and politics), mathematics and natural sciences – all to be taught by volunteers drawn from Maurice's circle. Tom Hughes, aware that sometimes more might be needed to encourage regular attendance, introduced social evenings of singing and sports, including boxing. Kingsley lectured there, as did Huxley and Dante Gabriel Rossetti, and in a tremendous publicity coup, even John Ruskin. Alexander Macmillan became determined to establish a second such college in Cambridge, where there would be no shortage of sympathetic scholars happy to lecture. Throughout 1854 and 1855 Alexander took advice, from Tom Hughes in particular, about the best way to set up the Cambridge college, and when the scheme was launched in March 1855, he was appointed Joint Honorary Secretary with Gerald Vesey, a Trinity graduate shortly to be ordained. This was a position Alexander took extremely seriously, often chairing the meetings, until 1859. The first meeting saw pledges of assistance from many academics and clerics who went on to hold high office in England.

Meanwhile, Tom Hughes was pondering how best to celebrate the life of his hero, Dr Arnold, and had come up with an idea for a semi-autobiographical novel aimed at boys. Arthur Stanley, a proud disciple of Arnold and the future Dean of Westminster, had already published a two-volume biography of the headmaster in 1844, which framed his life in mainly spiritual terms. Hughes wanted to highlight the effect the man had had on the pupils of Rugby School, but paid homage to Stanley's efforts by enshrining him within his novel as the saintly little boy, Arthur, whose life and near death have so much effect on the young Tom Brown. This new book was to be written with the express purpose of spreading Arnold's philosophies more widely across the population, particularly among the young, and so *Tom Brown's School Days* was born.

On 25 September 1856, Hughes, on holiday with his family in Deal, wrote to Alexander.

> Dear Mac. How's yourself and where's yourself? My chief reason for writing is, that, as I always told you, I'm going to make your fortune, and you'll be happy to hear that the feat is almost or at least more than half done. I've been and gone and

written or got in my head a one vol. novel, a novel for boys, to wit Rugby in Arnold's time. Ludlow is the only cove besides my wife who has seen a word of it, (and mind if you take it or don't I can't afford to have it known) and he thought it would particular do, and urged me to go on with it which I have this vacation and only want the kick on the breech that some cove's saying he would publish it would give me to finish it. Shall I send you three or four chapters as specimens or will you meet me in town . . . Do come up and we'll have a dinner and nox [night] together with baccy and toddy . . . Kindest regards to the frater. Ever yours fraternally.[16]

Alexander was in Brighton with his wife and family but replied at once to say that he would come to Wimbledon, where Hughes and Ludlow lived in adjoining houses, as soon as the author returned.

The idea of a novel that would bring Arnold to life delighted the brothers, and throughout the autumn of 1856 Daniel exchanged copious notes with Hughes on the subject, all of them extremely complimentary. The boy from the croft was the first to admit that he was no expert on life in an English public school, so when Hughes asked him for an opinion, he looked around for someone to help. Luckily in Cambridge there was no shortage of old Rugbeians, and he shared the manuscript with a Mr Mayor of St John's:[17]

who thinks it very fine indeed and sure to be a hit. He thinks the football business wonderfully done. I feel sure it must be – but as I know nothing of the way you played I cannot get up sufficient interest. Mr Mayor thought the peashooting stories would stand abridging. I am not sure that he is wrong. But of course you must be the ultimate authority on such matters . . . I cannot trust myself to tell you how much I like the other chapters . . . if the rest of the book is as good – and a man who could do these things could do anything of the kind he liked – there is no doubt of it being a hit.[18]

Mayor's other comments were that some of the speeches, especially from Brooke, the head of house whom Tom hero-worships, were 'too manly', his sentiments too much like the words of Maurice rather than Dr Arnold. Daniel warned Hughes against becoming too preachy. 'Boys w'd delight in it if care is taken not to let them the least see that you were trying to make them good.' The truth of this advice went to the core of the book's popularity. But Hughes was determined not to lose his moral purpose. In a preface to the sixth edition he wrote:

> Several persons, for whom I have the highest respect, while saying very kind things about the book, have added that the greatest fault of it is 'too much preaching'; but they hope I shall amend in this matter if I ever write again. Now this I most distinctly decline to do. Why, my whole object in writing at all was to get the chance of preaching! When a man comes to my time of life and has his bread to make, and very little time to spare, is it likely that he will spend almost the whole of his yearly vacation in writing a story just to amuse people? I think not. At any rate, I wouldn't do so myself . . . My sole object in writing was to preach to boys: if ever I write again it will be to preach to some other age.

Daniel's mind was already turning over the commercial possibilities, remembering what they had learned from the experience of *Westward Ho!*. His plan was to market Hughes' book initially into the circulating libraries and Book Clubs in one volume, and then as it became known, to publish a smaller cheaper version suitable for giving to boys as prizes or presents. He proposed an initial print run of 750 copies, enough for the libraries, and then to let it go out of print for a short while, sufficient for there to start a clamour for a second edition. Meanwhile Hughes' working title, 'Public School Life', needed revision. Daniel wrote 'please invent a title and as good a one as you can. A good deal depends on it. The shorter the better . . . Tom Brown's School Life? English School Life? School Life? School Life in England? These are all poor, most likely you have a genius for names.'[19] Hughes did not need to do much more work on this and *Tom Brown's School Days* was quickly agreed upon.

Hughes, whose profession was the law, was a nervous first-time author. 'Criticise, cut out, tell me to amplify anywhere . . . I haven't the smallest vanity in my composition and don't care three straws how it's knocked about . . . Show it to anybody you please, only don't give my name, as it might do me harm in this dirty hole, where people fancy you can't be worth a button if you've anything in your head but contradictory statutes and unprincipled decisions.'[20] This was not the usual type of language among Alexander's correspondents, and the freshness and humour was spilling into the novel as he wrote it, much to the brothers' delight. Hughes himself was showing excerpts to Maurice and to Kingsley and had a full chapter plan and a timetable worked out.

Suddenly all was thrown up in the air – Tom's children came down with scarlet fever and his eldest daughter Evie fell ill and died in December 1856. The writing ceased, and Ludlow suggested to Alexander that it might be best to find another author to finish it or publish just the fragment. But as Hughes wrote: 'I was very near giving up the book in disgust, but my wife is against that, and no doubt I should soon repent myself . . . '[21] In particular Hughes took comfort from his hero F. D. Maurice's teachings, that Death was just a river to cross, and that there was no reason to fear eternal hellfire or damnation, the family would all be reunited on the other side.

By January 1857 the Macmillans had begun typesetting and editing the work, perhaps keen to ensure that Hughes did not stop writing. Concerned that news of the project would leak out around the London market, they wanted it to be printed in Cambridge, and

they needed the language to be modified. In February Hughes had
to agree to let the 'damns' be taken out. He wrote to the brothers:

> I can't remember above two altogether. Only mind, boys then
> swore abominably: I did myself til I was in the fifth [form], I
> daresay they do still. Besides, if mamas won't buy for young
> hopefuls, young hopefuls will for themselves . . . But when you
> tell me that you have altered "beastly" into "inhumanly" drunk,
> I suppose I think really that it's time for me to give up in des-
> pair. However, my name's Easy: please yourself gentlemen, and
> you'll please me.[22]

The Dr Arnold shown in *Tom Brown's School Days* is a simplified version of the more complex original: Hughes was determined to make
clear the impact the headmaster had on his pupils, the archetype of
the wise but strong leader of men that the country needed. But if
Arnold was a simplified, hallowed version, Tom Brown is undoubtedly based on the real Tom Hughes with all his enthusiasms, and the
Rugby School of the book is the place that formed the man. Both
Toms come from typical English country gentry stock, where hunting, shooting, bird-nesting and fishing are the main entertainments,
and where the father's one care is that the school they choose will
produce a 'brave, helpful, truth-telling Englishman, and a gentleman, and a Christian . . . That's all I want.' As soon as Tom passes
through the gates he begins to be proud of being a Rugby boy: as
soon as he has heard Arnold preach, he resolves 'to stand by and
follow the Doctor'. Much of the early part of the book is taken up
with football and boxing matches, but gradually Tom faces a moral
struggle – should he cheat in his homework as many boys do, or
follow the example of the saintly Arthur, based on Dean Stanley, and
make the ethical choice of honest hard work and occasional failure.
Pleasing Dr Arnold means being honest, and gradually Tom realizes

that this is a parable for the Christian life. Where Tom Hughes's view of Rugby School diverges from the sermons of Dean Stanley is in the importance he places on team sports. Hughes was never an academic, but he was the captain of his house cricket and football teams, and his passion for sport, and his belief in the value of team games, shines through the book and makes it fun for a child to read. Tom says that cricket 'merges the individual in the eleven, he doesn't play that he may win but that his side may'. Dr Arnold had not been opposed to physical exercise, he understood that team spirit could be created on the playing field, but to Hughes it was more than that, almost part of religion itself. When Stanley, a less sporty individual, read Tom Hughes' book, he wrote that it was 'an absolute revelation . . . a world of which, though so near to me, I was utterly ignorant.'[23]

Tom Brown's School Days was published on 24 April 1857, with a second edition in July, a third in September, a fourth in October and a fifth in November. Initially it was Hughes' intention to publish the work anonymously, but by May he felt that the secret was out – he blamed Kingsley, who had told everyone in their circle. By August, with the book already into a second edition, he was writing, 'What an easy fool the public is! Had I known it sooner I would certainly have plucked the old goose to some tune before this.'[24] By January 1859, 11,000 copies had been sold, 28,000 copies by the end of 1862. Altogether they would print more than fifty editions in thirty years. Hughes had initially sold the copyright to the brothers for a £150 flat sum, but almost at once they offered to renegotiate – at first Hughes resisted, feeling duty bound as a lawyer to stick to his agreement, but under pressure from his friend Ludlow he repented. Thereafter the profits were shared 50:50 – in the first seven months, Hughes received £1,250. Charles Kingsley, who had loved it from the first, but in rather an envious way, wrote: 'From everyone, from the fine lady on her throne, to the redcoat on his cock-horse and the schoolboy on his form . . . I have heard but one word, and that is that this is the jolliest book they ever read.'[25]

Tom Brown's runaway sales were a massive boost to the Macmillans' business, showing that *Westward Ho!* had not been a one-off success. Furthermore, the publishing profits were theirs and theirs alone: the family was once again the sole owner of the business, trading in 1856 having been sufficiently strong to enable the brothers to buy out the last remaining investor, James Gotobed. This had been a constant source of worry and frustration, particularly to the dying Daniel, who was desperate to secure a legacy for his widow and four children. The 1856 balance sheet, the strongest yet boosted by the Kingsley profits, had given the brothers the firepower to take back control of their own destiny, and by Christmas of that year the deal was done, with the dissolution of the partnership with James Gotobed announced in the local press. Furthermore, the perception of their success in the market allowed them to secure better terms from paper merchants and printers. Daniel's business legacy was safe and Macmillan & Co. could operate unfettered. The fact that there had been these difficulties with the Gotobed brothers was glossed over in the official histories of the firm, the family preferring to give the impression that it was the unrelated Mr Barclay who had caused Daniel so much worry, but Daniel's letters to George Wilson tell a different story.[26]

In May 1857, Fanny gave birth to a little boy named Arthur, possibly named with Tom Brown's great friend Arthur in mind, and Daniel asked Tom Hughes to stand as godfather. Hughes loved to tease his publishers, revelling in his physical prowess and his skills in sports such as boxing and wrestling, where he felt on firmer ground than in spiritual matters. 'Dear Macmillan, I shall be glad to be godfather to your boy. I will teach him not only the church catechism set apart for that purpose but also the art of self-defence.'[27] But ten days after he wrote that letter, Daniel was dead. It was as if he had waited for two final events, the birth of this last child, and the buyout of the external investors, but now felt free to go. His last illness was very painful, and unpleasant for the family to witness – a large ulcer developed in his throat which made it impossible for him to swallow, to eat or drink anything at all, and he faded away in pain and in front of them over a two-week period. It may be that it was not the tuberculosis that killed him, but a cancer of the throat. According to Hughes, his last words to his wife were 'you will see so much of me come out in the children, dear. It will be a great comfort to you . . . but you will see the impetuosity.'[28] Within a few hours, the 'impetuous spirit' was at rest. He died, aged just forty-three, on 27 June 1857 and was buried in Mill Road Cemetery, Cambridge.

Daniel's death was hardly a surprise, he had been so weak for so long, and the probability had been weighing on his mind, and known to his closest friends, since before he was wed. Hughes wrote to comfort Alexander immediately: 'A nobler and purer soul didn't breathe . . . fatigue of mind and body in good honest work is the best break-grief, at least I have found it so . . . I shall consider the sponsorship of this child a sacred trust.' Twenty-five years later he would publish *A Memoir of Daniel Macmillan*, writing:

> there was something in this man's personal qualities and character, apart from his great business ability, which takes him out of the ordinary category – a touch in fact of the rare quality we call heroism. No man who ever sold books for a livelihood was more conscious of a vocation; more impressed with the dignity of his craft, and of its value to humanity . . . He was a genuine lover of books, regarding them not as mere articles of trade, to be bound artistically, deftly catalogued, and sold at a profit, but as acquaintances and friends, whom it was a joy as well as a duty to introduce to as wide a circle as possible.[29]

There is a sketch of Daniel, painted by Alexander's Christian Socialist friend Lowes Cato Dickinson, later used as the frontispiece of Tom Hughes's memoir of the publisher. It shows a thin serious man, with smooth dark hair parted at the side and framing his face, dark eyes, straight nose, thin lips, pale skin. It may have been done from memory after his death, as it looks lifeless and sad and does not

reflect the impression of vitality and enthusiasm that Daniel made
on his Cambridge customers and friends. But it echoes the words of
Archdeacon Hare, in that it showed the face of a man not long for
the world. Alexander would refer to his brother as 'the grave black
man'. His will, written in January 1854, bequeathed all his goods,
including his shares in the business and the proceeds of the life
insurance policy with London Life that he had taken out in 1843, to
his wife Fanny, with Alexander and James MacLehose as executors
of the will.

A good indication of Daniel's outlook on life came in a letter he
wrote to his nephew Robert Bowes two years before his death – he
was in Torquay, in reflective mood: 'As you were left under my care
a long time ago by your father and mother, I daresay you sometimes wonder that I don't sometimes give you formal advice. I have
not done so for several reasons. First because I am so very much in
need of it myself that it would look pretending to more wisdom and
goodness than I have . . . a second reason is that such things are considered a very great bore.' He went on to say that in his experience
there was no link between good behaviour and worldly success, or
why had his God-fearing parents and older brothers had such terrible
lives. 'It struck me that being noble and gentle, and just and true, and
meek and lowly of heart, and kind and generous, and pure of heart
and of life and speech were in themselves far greater things than
riches or high position could purchase.'[30]

Daniel Macmillan did not die a rich man, indeed for most of his
life he struggled to make ends meet, to support his young family and
to finance his business, but through his behaviour, his beliefs and his
ideals he had created a different sort of wealth, that of loyal friendships, strong connections and sound business practices, that laid the
seeds for the future prosperity of the next generation of Macmillans.
Whether they would enjoy the benefits of this prosperity would
depend upon the efforts of their uncle Alexander.

7

ALEXANDER ALONE

(1858–59)

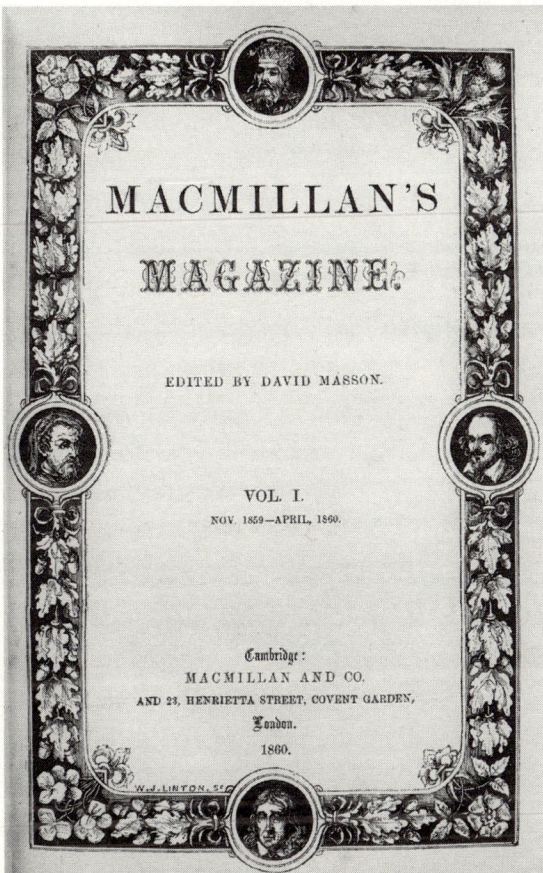

Masthead of Macmillan's Magazine

'Hope smiles from the threshold of the year to come,
Whispering "it will be happier" . . .'

Alfred, Lord Tennyson

As ALEXANDER MACMILLAN entered 1858, in his fortieth year, he felt himself alone and inadequate, beset by worries and griefs on all sides. The summer of 1857 had seen so much death: not just the loss of his only surviving brother and business partner, Daniel, but also of his brother-in-law George Brimley, within a few short weeks. Brimley had been one of Alexander's best friends, a man whose ency- clopaedic knowledge of literature had been a treasure trove for the poorly educated publisher's enquiring mind. Alexander's own health left much to be desired, with chronic sciatica and dyspepsia continu- ally aggravated by the miserable weather in Cambridge and by the long hours he worked. He had once had to apologize to Daniel for ill-temper: 'You can hardly realise – I don't wish you ever should – the utter unreasonableness of a man whose acrid stomach is always get- ting into his brain and crowding his heart.'[1] To support his brother's grieving widow Fanny, he moved back into the shop in Cambridge at 1 Trinity Street with his pregnant wife Caroline, creating a combined family of seven children under the age of eight. There were also an increasing number of household staff – the 1861 census shows a cook and four servants all sharing the same limited accommodation. This was a man under some domestic pressure.

With Daniel's death, Alexander lost the man whose vision and courage had driven the entire enterprise and who had brought him into the book business in the first place. It was Daniel who had nego- tiated the lease on the original Cambridge site, at 17 Trinity Street, and Daniel whose earnest character had persuaded Archdeacon Hare to lend them the capital (and the address book of future cus- tomers) that they needed to start a business. Alexander had always relied heavily on his brother's advice, even when Daniel had been too ill to be in the shop. Alexander may have complained about the extra work it gave him to correspond daily with Daniel, as the invalid shuffled between rest cures in Torquay or Cromer, but now it was up to him to make all the decisions. This was not just a busy shop, perhaps the largest bookstore in Cambridge turning over some six or seven thousand pounds every year, it was also a growing publishing firm. Alexander, determined not to let his brother down and unable to afford help, felt obliged to read every solicited or unsolicited manuscript, decide what to stock and what to publish, negotiate the contracts, supervise the printers and binders, and organize the publicity, alone. He greatly missed his brother.

The intellectual foundations that drove the publishing ethos of the Macmillan firm for decades to come were firmly laid by the brothers' admiration, bordering on hero-worship, for Carlyle, Maurice and Kingsley. But there was a fourth pillar to what can be termed Macmillanism, less political, less religious, but spiritual and romantic, and that was Alexander's passion for the poetry of Alfred Tennyson. Macmillan & Co. published the work of all four of these giants of Victorian literature, reverently in the case of the last three, rather nervously in the case of Carlyle, who by the time he was writing for *Macmillan's Magazine* in the 1860s had become a loose cannon, inclined to offend more than he inspired. To understand the community from which the brothers picked their authors, one has to see how tightly interlocked these circles of writers, poets, philosophers and essayists had become, and how the London–Cambridge nexus would allow the Macmillans to develop from a shop in Trinity Street to a publishing house in the heart of London's West End without losing their distinctive literary and ethical character.

Archdeacon Hare and F. D. Maurice had been early leading lights of the Apostles, a self-selecting intellectual debating society for Cambridge undergraduates founded in 1820, as had Alfred Tennyson and his friend Arthur Hallam. By the time that the Macmillans were ensconced in 1 Trinity Street, right at the heart of the university, the Apostles who became their friends and then their authors included Richard Jebb, later to be Regius Professor of Greek at Cambridge; Fenton Hort, whose life's work was to study the Greek

New Testament; Vernon Lushington, a senior civil servant and close friend of the pre-Raphaelites; James FitzJames Stephen, the noted jurist; Frederic Farrar, Headmaster of Marlborough College and later Dean of Canterbury Cathedral; and Henry Sidgwick, Knight-bridge Professor of Moral Philosophy at Cambridge. There was a thread that bound together these Cambridge men, mostly from Trinity College: they had been to the same public schools, they continued to socialize after they entered professional life, their families inter-married and they discussed each other's writings, whether political essays, theological comment, or poetry and novels. And slowly but surely Alexander Macmillan caught his finger in the thread that bound them and began to reel them in.

In the year of Daniel's death, the firm published fewer than forty separate titles, of which nine were new editions of works by F. D. Maurice, whose rights they had acquired from J. W. Parker in London. Aside from *Tom Brown* and *Westward Ho!*, their catalogue was dominated by textbooks, translations of classics, sermons, and occasional forays into the politics of Cambridge University. Once or twice they took a risk with collections of poetry, often devotional, and always sinking without trace. Apart from Hare, Maurice, Kingsley and Hughes, the only names on their list recognizable today are John Stevens Henslow, famous for teaching Darwin his botany, and Bishop Colenso, who would get into fearful trouble for his unorthodox religious views. Publishing no more than forty or fifty sermons and textbooks every year, at slender or non-existent margins, was a steady business but would not support a growing family. Most of the shop's customers were Cambridge undergraduates who were more than happy to patronize the store, chat with the owners and run up large debts, and less happy to settle them after they left town. If the business was to survive, Alexander would have to take some bold steps.

There is no doubt that Alexander felt the loss of Daniel very deeply; they had been through so much together and it was Daniel's drive and ambition, his determination to be independent, and his willingness to take risks, that had created the firm. However, as Daniel's health deteriorated, he had lost some of this entrepreneurial, risk-taking spirit, and had begun to hold the firm back. The death of his senior partner unleashed new creativity and enterprise in Alexander – ideas that he had nursed for years he rapidly brought to fruition, and the firm prospered. He set to work to honour his brother's memory and burnish the name of the firm he had founded. Sebastian Evans wrote that Daniel's death seemed 'to invest his life for years with something of the spirit of a kindly religious fanatic, who felt that he had a sacred mission laid upon him to perform'.[2]

The brothers' vision for the firm had always been inspired by their religious faith. They believed it was their vocation to spread education and enlightenment, moral and spiritual, among their fellow working men. Yet Alexander was more alive than Daniel had been to the rising tide of Victorian capitalism and entrepreneurship. Writing later in the century, the philosopher Herbert Spencer remarked that this was the age when wealth and respectability began to be seen as the necessary two sides of the same coin and men began to put 'the expenditure of all their energies into money-making.'[3] After all, one of the defining characteristics of the Victorian age was that money could now buy social acceptance, so that, for example, sending a boy to university was the approved and recognized method of converting a tradesman's son into a gentleman. Samuel Smiles published *Self-Help* in 1859, the 'do-it-yourself' guide to making a fortune, and sold twenty thousand copies in the first year. For Alexander Macmillan, with a family of ten to support, the need to improve his fortunes must have seemed imperative. It would require great reserves of courage and self-belief.

Alexander cut an impressive figure among the Cambridge merchant class. Taller and stronger than his invalid brother, he had a wide forehead, a long, narrow nose, centre-parted dark hair brushed smooth over his crown but curling over his ears, neat mutton-chop whiskers and a clean-shaven chin. A photograph taken in the 1860s shows him facing confidently into the camera, his hand in his trouser pocket, thumb in his waistband, and fob watch and chain on display, a typical Victorian businessman.[4] His strong Scottish accent, often heard ringing out in Town Hall meetings and dinners, distinguished him from the pack. Throughout the 1850s, despite regular bouts of crippling ill-health, Macmillan appeared to be a man of boundless energy, enthusiasm, and massive public spirit. In the years before his brother's death, as well as taking a role in founding the local Working Men's College, he was a leading light of the Cambridge Philo-Union Society, a debating social club for the townsmen to join; a member of the committee which ran the local Industrial School; and part of the town's committee to host 'Peace Rejoicings' for the end of the Crimean War. He was president of the local branch of the Young Men's Christian Association. The excess energy that in the 1850s was being channelled into this raft of local community projects and societies, while never weakening his efforts on behalf of his day job in publishing, would now be trained upon his main goal – the triumph of Macmillan & Co.

The first challenge he had to face was that now he, and he alone, would be the arbiter of the books he chose to publish. This was a heavy burden for a man with no formal education, reliant on his personal taste, and on his memory of Daniel's instinct for what would be morally, as well as commercially, worth publishing. He had employed a clerk, James Fraser, who could manage some of the day-to-day business, but that was not enough. Alexander had at times felt himself to be in Daniel's intellectual shadow: 'Recognising my own immense inferiority to him in every way, I feel that it is a wonder I have done so much.'[5] Needing someone off whom to bounce his publishing ideas, he began to turn to James MacLehose, an executor of Daniel's will and by this time a successful publisher in Glasgow. The correspondence shows that Alexander was tempted to offer MacLehose a formal partnership in the firm, which he never accepted, yet he was happy to act as coach and mentor as required. Alexander also relied heavily on the opinions of his sister-in-law, Daniel's widow Fanny, now the other partner in the business, until her declining health made this impossible.

Macmillan was focused on two crucial tasks: one was to open a London branch, the other was to launch a magazine. The brothers' first shop in London may have failed, but the logic of having a foothold in the capital remained compelling. As early as July 1852, Daniel had shared with MacLehose his vision for a London house 'where men might call and consult after leaving Cambridge'.[6] Daniel and Alexander often discussed the possibility of re-opening in London, indeed Daniel made it clear that he thought it was a safer bet than their other idea of launching a magazine, about which he was extremely nervous. Alexander had begun to travel regularly to London in the mid-1850s, both needing and enjoying the opportunity to meet and do business with printers, other booksellers, and crucially with potential authors. London was also the place where he could continue to develop his friendships with the leaders of the Christian Socialist movement. Sometimes he stayed with publishing friends in Surbiton, or visited F. D. Maurice in Russell Square, or saw Tom Hughes and John Ludlow at The Firs, the experiment in communal living they had built in Wimbledon, two houses with a shared living room. Or he went down to Eversley in Hampshire to stay with the Kingsleys. Ludlow urged him to re-open in London, in a location 'more West-endian than Bell's or Nutt's', in other words, further west than Fleet Street.[7] With Daniel gone, Alexander took the bull by the horns. The headquarters of the firm would remain in Cambridge until 1864, but in the summer of 1858, Alexander took premises in Covent Garden, at 23 Henrietta Street, and sent his nephew Robert Bowes to manage this shop.

Henrietta Street was largely rebuilt in the 1880s, so the original shop is lost from view. The street runs parallel with the Strand, and leads directly into Covent Garden market, making it a very convenient and increasingly respectable location in central London for retail, offices and residences. Paternoster Row by St Paul's, the home of the book trade at the beginning of the century, was no longer the place to be. Covent Garden itself was still the central London market for fruit and vegetables, and the streets around the shop will have been thronged with men pushing barrels and carts, and women selling flowers – the picturesque often overwhelmed by the smell of rotting vegetation. Yet in 1814 Jane Austen stayed at 10 Henrietta Street, in rooms above Tilson's Bank, where her brother Henry was a partner. It was here that she prepared the proofs of *Mansfield Park* for publication. The previous occupant of Macmillan's shop was Offley's Tavern, a smart eating place, and the coffee shop, Rawthmells, at number 25, had been the location for a meeting of artists which led to the founding of The Royal Society of Arts. Slowly the street was becoming a prime location for shops and tradesmen, jewellers, fruiterers, and the convenient Ashley's Hotel.

Robert Bowes was just twenty-three when he was sent to London to mind the new shop, but he had been working in the family firm since his parents emigrated to the States and he left Scotland as a boy of eleven. The lines between family, household and business were conveniently blurred. He took with him another even younger man, nineteen-year-old George Coxall, who would still be working for Macmillan in 1910. George was the younger brother of Mary Ann Coxall, a servant in the Trinity Street house, who was also still employed in the Macmillan household in the 1890s, working for them for over thirty years. Alexander set the London lads up with a 'trustworthy and motherly' Cambridgeshire housekeeper, Elizabeth Miles, to look after them. By the time of the 1861 census they also had hired a young girl, Jane Skarden, as a live-in servant.

The premises they leased had a shop on the ground floor, but also living quarters above for Robert and George, and on Thursday nights there was a bed for Alexander as well, when he would host an evening of 'tobacco and tipple'. Alexander would declare himself at home to all his literary acquaintances, serving a modest meal at six or six thirty, accompanied by tea, with pipes and stronger fluids from nine o'clock onwards as well. These Thursday evenings came to be known as the Tobacco Parliaments, attended by authors, clerics, poets, historians and men of science. Alexander played the inconspicuous host, making everyone at home, attending to the drinks, but never dominating the conversations. Sebastian Evans wrote of Alexander as the host of these gatherings: 'vividly as I recall the general outlines and colours of a few such ephemeral mosaic pictures, I do not remember any in which Alec figured as one of the more prominent personages represented. His inspiriting presence, indeed, was always felt, but it was rather as the indispensable but almost invisible cement in which the mosaic was set than as one of the tesserae forming the picture itself.'[8]

Tom Hughes loved these occasions and commissioned the construction of a round dining table by John Roebuck, a member of the London Working Men's College. For Macmillan, a devotee of Tennyson and sharing his fondness for Arthurian legend, the Round Table had special significance. The oak table survives to this day, in the possession of the Earl of Stockton, protected by a blanket of blue and red Macmillan tartan. It measures about four feet across, clearly not big enough to seat all the Tobacco Parliament members for a meal, but large enough for a collection of tobacco pouches, pipes, spills, glasses and bottles of beer and whisky. The names of the regular attendees were inked into the rim, and this engraved decoration illustrates the wide scope of the brotherhood Alexander was able to call his friends. According to Alexander's son George, at one time these names included F. D. Maurice, Tennyson, Herbert Spencer, John Ludlow, and an assortment of intellectual lawyers, poets, critics, academics and clerics, mostly bound together by admiration of Maurice and the ideals of Christian Socialism, or by friendship with Tennyson. The final name was David Masson, editor of *Macmillan's Magazine*. Sadly the names are now fading, the most visible being those of the founders, Macmillan, Hughes and Masson, as well as Thomas Huxley, Frederick Stephens, who was a member of the pre-Raphaelite Brotherhood, and one of the Rossetti brothers.

Alexander had two gifts to offer his visitors: there was his generous Scottish hospitality with tobacco, ale and whisky, but more tempting to some of the younger visitors and aspiring authors was the possibility of clinching a publishing deal. He was not the first publisher to recognize the potential of bringing writers together in a convivial atmosphere. In 1812, John Murray II, the publisher of Lord Byron, Jane Austen and Sir Walter Scott, took possession of smart new premises at 50 Albemarle Street, off Piccadilly, and began to play the host. Writers had always been in the habit of congregating in London coffee houses, to gossip and read the newspapers, but in Murray's morning room the coffee was free. Scott, a regular attendee, called it 'John Murray's Four O'clock Friends'. The idea caught on: from 1822 onwards, *Blackwood's Edinburgh Magazine* ran a series of articles entitled 'Noctes Ambrosianae', a fictional account of the lively meetings of contributors supposed to happen at the Ambrose Tavern in Edinburgh, and *Fraser's Magazine*, founded in 1830, chronicled noisy sessions in the backrooms of its offices in Regent Street, London. Perhaps the most formal of these gatherings was the one held every Wednesday at the offices of Bradbury and Evans, proprietors of *Punch*. Here the only invitations were to the writing staff of *Punch*, who enjoyed a splendid dinner with plenty of champagne and then set to work debating what should be the subject of the Large Cut, the full-page cartoon in each week's edition.

It was at Alexander's Tobacco Parliament gatherings, and in the correspondence that surrounded them, that Macmillan was encouraged to launch his magazine. Ludlow was persistent in the view that Macmillan & Co. needed a periodical of its own. He used Hughes's *Tom Brown's School Days* to illustrate his point: 'I suspect you will have some difficulty in getting for it all the success it deserves offhand, coming from an entirely new author. Now if that same *Tom Brown* had been published in a magazine, for which it is admirably adapted, not only would it have increased the sale of the magazine largely as it went on, but by the time it had got to the end it would no longer be a book by a new hand, – it would on being republished as a whole, just step into success, instead of having to fight its way into it.'[9] This, after all, was how *The Pickwick Papers* had made Dickens' name just twenty years earlier.

The launch of a magazine was not without substantial financial risk. A new publication would need to identify and occupy a niche in an already crowded marketplace. At the top end of the market were the long-established quarterlies, such as the *Edinburgh Review* and John Murray's *Quarterly Review*, aimed at an intellectual, academic audience, and priced at half a crown an issue. More popular was Dickens's weekly magazine, *Household Words*, launched in 1850 and priced at tuppence, but vulnerable to the regular fallings out between Dickens and his publishers; or *Blackwood's*, an Edinburgh-based periodical which specialized in serial fiction and had been going for some forty years. The bottom of the market was well-served by so-called 'penny dreadfuls' and by popular family magazines like *Cassells*, and *The London Journal*. There were some titles specifically aimed at women, such as Samuel Beeton's *The Englishwoman's Domestic Magazine*, made famous by the contributions on cookery and household management written by his wife, Isabella. But most educated women would have been secondary readers of the titles such as *Blackwood's*, bought by their husbands or fathers. Alexander Macmillan made sure that even the most learned articles in his magazine would be accessible in vocabulary and style to those who lacked a university education, and the advertisers of expensive fabric and servants' clothes who took space in the magazine were reaching out to a prosperous and educated female readership.

Macmillan, Ludlow and Hughes had been considering a launch in 1858, to coincide with the opening of the new London address. In May 1858 Hughes wrote to Austen Layard, the archaeologist who uncovered Nineveh and who had just returned from India, where he had gone to investigate the recent Indian 'Mutiny':

A number of men (Maurice, Kingsley, Forster (Goderich's friend) & many more, all good men) are going to start a quarterly in which the contributors are to sign their names – many men can't get heard in the present quarterlies because their opinions are unpopular, the editor is afraid, or for one reason or another equally futile. Our first number will come out towards the end of the year and will be a very strong one; no man need be ashamed of his companionship at any rate. Will you write us an article on India? The pay will be the best quarterly pay, a guinea a page.[10]

Originally the plan was that it would differentiate itself from the competition by being open and honest in its views, with contributors signing their names – many of the grander quarterlies were increasingly reliant on anonymous contributors, and Maurice for one disapproved of the habit. As Hughes put it, 'Everyone to sign his own name and no flippancy or abuse allowed.'[11]

All agreed that a monthly magazine was the perfect opportunity to showcase Macmillan's extensive network of writers, philosophers, scientists and educationalists. However, the news came that Richard Bentley, a publisher much admired by Alexander, was planning to launch his own periodical in April 1859 and it was thought wise, particularly by the cautious Maurice and Kingsley, to see how Bentley found the market. The publisher misjudged his audience, pricing the *Miscellany* at six shillings, and it failed. Alexander learnt from Bentley's disaster and continued to consult widely among his friends – should it be a quarterly or a monthly? Could he persuade Tom Hughes to be the editor? If all contributions were signed, would he still be able to attract authors beyond the cliquish Christian Socialist set? Should its name reflect the current fashion for things Arthurian: earlier that year Tennyson had begun to publish a series of poems under the title of *Idylls of the King*, which had flown off the shelves, selling ten thousand copies in a month.

By the time the publication finally reached fruition, Macmillan had determined that he would make it more than just a mouthpiece for the Christian Socialist movement, which had been Ludlow's plan. He wanted to call it 'The Round Table' and, abandoning the idealism

of Hughes and Ludlow, would allow authors to remain anonymous
if they preferred, as long as their contributions were 'popular, plain
and good.' In the spring of 1859, he took himself off to Scotland, to
clear his head, and to consult his friend MacLehose, bouncing his
ideas off other publishers such as David Douglas. Their feedback
determined him to proceed, but on his own terms. Cleverly, he laid
off the majority of the financial risk, taking £250 in a partnership
with Hughes and £250 each, contributed as goods and services
rather than cash, from the printer and paper merchant to whom he
gave exclusive contracts. He was keen to release the first instalment
in October, to give the magazine a good three months clear of the
rumoured launch of a competitive title, to be called the *Cornhill* and
to be edited by Thackeray. A further month's delay was necessary
to allow Hughes to cope with another appalling family tragedy,
the death by drowning of his young son, the boy for whom *Tom
Brown's School Days* had been written. Finally, the first issue was set
for November 1859 and the editorship was offered, at Hughes's suggestion, to a thirty-seven-year-old Scottish academic, David Masson.
This infuriated Ludlow, who had wanted the role for himself. It was
Masson, after a fierce struggle which Macmillan lost, who chose the
much simpler title, *Macmillan's Magazine*. Alexander may not have
felt that his surname was sufficiently well known to attract attention,
but on the other hand, if the magazine was a success, the firm would
benefit from the publicity.

David Masson was born in Aberdeen in 1822, the son of a stone-
cutter. In birth and early life he had much in common with his
future employer, but unlike Alexander he was fortunate to receive
a bursary to extend his education beyond the grammar school and
studied divinity at Edinburgh University, then returned to Aberdeen
to edit *The Banner*, a weekly newspaper. In 1843, while in London
staying with a schoolfriend, he was introduced into English literary
society, meeting and befriending both the Carlyles and John Stuart
Mill, and at their introduction he began to write for *Fraser's* and *The
Athenaeum*, while continuing to produce works of history for W&R

Chambers of Edinburgh. In 1847 he moved to live in London and joined a network of popular authors and journalists which would be highly complementary to Macmillan's more academic, Cambridge-centric circle. Among his new acquaintances were Douglas Jerrold, Shirley Brooks and Mark Lemon, the founders of *Punch*, as well as Thackeray and Dickens. Coventry Patmore, who was the librarian at the British Museum, introduced him to his brother-in-law Charles Orme, whose house in Regent's Park was a favourite meeting place for members of the Pre-Raphaelite Brotherhood, particularly Holman Hunt, the Rossettis and Thomas Woolner, the sculptor. In 1852, at the age of just thirty, Masson was appointed Professor of English at University College, London. The following year, Masson married the Ormes' eldest daughter, Emily, and moved into the Orme home.

Masson was intrigued by the Christian Socialist movement and through his friendship with the pre-Raphaelites he met the founders of the Working Men's College in London. The Brotherhood were sympathetic to the movement's social aims if not its theology. By February 1856 he had also met Alexander Macmillan, who was keen to reprint some of the literary biographical essays that Masson had published in Scottish periodicals such as *Fraser's* and the *North British Review*. The volume was to be published under the title *Essays: Critical and Biographical*, based on 50:50 profit share. When Daniel died Masson wrote to offer his condolences: 'I had not seen much of your brother, but all that I had seen had given me a high sense of his worth and manliness, moral and intellectual; and the half-hour I spent in talk with him last time I was in Cambridge has left an impression of his mind and manner upon me which I shall always cherish with respect.'[12] By November of that year Macmillan had commissioned a three volume *Life of Milton* from Masson, offering £150 for a first edition of 1,500 copies of the first volume. The relationship was going from strength to strength, and Masson and Alexander became personal friends, who went on walking holidays together in Scotland.

As Macmillan's reputation grew, the Tobacco Parliament evenings became a regular fixture on more people's calendars. One of
the defining features of the attendees was their comparative youth:
this was not a meeting of greybeards, but mostly of up-and-coming
men in their twenties and thirties still finding their way in the literary world. Regular guests included Franklin Lushington, poet and
judge, a close friend of Edward Lear and related by marriage to
Tennyson; George Stovin Venables, a journalist and barrister, mostly
remembered for having broken Thackeray's nose at school; Francis
Turner Palgrave, a critic and poet whose *The Golden Treasury of the
Best Songs and Lyrical Poems in the English Language* would be one of
Macmillan's great publishing successes of the 1860s; John Llewellyn
Davies, crusading cleric and alpinist who would be the grandfather
of the boy who inspired Peter Pan and brother of Emily Davies;
William Allingham, an Irish poet and friend of Tennyson; Coventry
Patmore, the author of a well-loved narrative poem, *The Angel in the
House*; and Alfred Ainger, a cleric, biographer and critic. They were
appreciative of the support Macmillan gave them, and of the freedom of the parliament to experiment with new ideas. From January
1860 onwards, Thomas Huxley was a frequent attendee, as well as a
contributor to the *Magazine*. Charles Kingsley and his brother Henry
came if they were in London.

Macmillan was so delighted with one particular party on the
night of 19 April 1860 that he proudly described it when writing to
his old friend James MacLehose.

On my last Thursday evening's gathering we had Tennyson,
Woolner, Hughes and a dozen other good fellows, and Sayers
and Heenan occupied one half the conversation. Tennyson
stayed till half past one, with only Francis Russell, an Edinburgh
Advocate, who is secretary to the Lord Advocate – after twelve,
and we had some nice chat on other subjects. He [Tennyson]
repeated a long poem in an impossible metre – the subject

Boadicea. Its roll was wonderful. It's not going into the *Maga-zine*. He is going to do no more of that sort of thing.[13]

It was not surprising that the conversation had turned to the American John C. Heenan and the Englishman Tom Sayers, who had just fought for the first ever unofficial world boxing title in a field in Farnborough. It had been a major talking point on both sides of the Atlantic. As Robert Colls writes, even though the fight was illegal, special trains had taken over fifteen hundred spectators to watch what became a bloody and indecisive brawl lasting over two hours. These were the conversations of men relaxed and enjoying each other's company, to Macmillan's great delight.

It was less than three years since Daniel had died, and Alexander had accomplished a great deal – he could now proclaim himself proudly as a London publisher first and foremost, and a Cambridge bookseller second. The speed with which Alexander was moving suggests enormous energy and self-confidence, but also reflects his frustration with the status quo. For a man in his early forties, lodging above a shop in Trinity Street, Cambridge, with eight chil-dren, the youngest, Olive, still a baby, the life that he was living was exhausting. He wrote to his old friend Fenton Hort that he rarely remembered to go to bed before two-thirty or three in the morning, so wrapped up was he in his reading pile, and rose by eight, unable to lie in bed, cursing his sciatica or pains in his shoulders. Other letters are full of complaint about the chill winds and rains in Cambridge, which aggravated his condition.

He worked in the shop from Monday to Wednesday, then every Thursday morning he walked the mile to Cambridge station and took the train to London, heading for Henrietta Street. He usually had a series of meetings planned during the day with authors, printers and wholesalers, as well as time to catch up and go through the orders with Bowes, and the plans for the *Magazine* with Masson. He dined at six thirty, often inviting favoured friends such as Hughes or Huxley to join him. Then at nine o'clock the office was cleared for the key gathering of the week. He slept above the shop, took more meetings in the morning, then caught the train home. The Cambridge shop was open on Saturdays, but Sunday was the day of rest, and a day when Daniel's presence was particularly felt and remembered across the household. The family were not strict Sabbatarians – both Daniel and Alexander had hated those Scottish Sundays of prayer and Bible study and silence – but they were days when everyone was together and the literature should at least be improving to young minds. However, it is hard to believe that Alexander was able to relax and forget about the business. Always there were manuscripts to read and endless letters to write. His mind raced on, with a ceaseless drive to extend his network, to cultivate new authors, to keep abreast of intellectual development, to launch new publishing ideas. He sought out clubs and societies to join which would give him greater access to possible authors and publishing initiatives: in November 1858, for example, he persuaded Thomas Hughes and others to nominate him for membership of the Society of Antiquaries of London – yet another call on his precious time in London.

The 1860s would be the busiest decade of Alexander's life, but also the most fulfilling and successful for his business. The risks that he had taken immediately following Daniel's death had more than paid off, and he could begin to enjoy the fruits of his labours.

8

MACMILLAN'S MAGAZINE

and

THE WATER BABIES

(1860–63)

The Water Babies *illustration*

'Did not learned men, too, hold, till within the last twenty-five years, that a flying dragon was an impossible monster? And do we not now know that there are hundreds of them found fossil up and down the world? People call them Pterodactyles: but that is only because they are ashamed to call them flying dragons, after denying so long that flying dragons could exist.'

Charles Kingsley, *The Water Babies*

ON ITS LAUNCH in November 1859, *Macmillan's Magazine* consisted of eighty closely typeset, double-columned pages, just six inches by eight and a half, and included eight lengthy, rather literary pieces. The principal draw was the eagerly awaited first instalment of Hughes's sequel, *Tom Brown at Oxford*, but there were also worthy essays on politics in Italy and a long poem by one of the Lushington brothers, prefaced by George Venables. Priced at one shilling, it was the first of the 'shilling monthly' periodicals, as the following year George Smith issued the *Cornhill*, which would be a friendly rival to *Macmillan's* for the next several decades. Many more followed suit, less successfully. But it was *Macmillan's* that set the pace, and its success must be attributed to the very great care that Alexander took with it – the publisher did far more to set the tone of any articles and contributions than the editors, usually by tactful negotiation and persuasion. He knew only too well as publisher to F. D. Maurice that most of Maurice's books remained unread. His plan in launching this magazine was to make the philosophy of the man he called the Prophet accessible and attractive to a wider audience, by slipping Christian Socialist propaganda in among a limited amount of popular fiction and articles designed to have middlebrow appeal. Specifically, he asked authors not to use technical or over-complex language, or too much Latin or Greek, ensuring that his *Magazine* was as accessible as possible. Over the early years, for the duration of the first two editors, he coaxed and flattered contributions out of his contacts and their friends and relations, honing them into a team with a single purpose. Within four months the *Magazine* was achieving sales of over 10,000, heading towards 12,000, which, while never on a par with the more light-weight, illustrated *Cornhill*, was a good business proposition. It also achieved its aim of publicizing the Macmillan brand around the world. Five hundred copies of the first edition went to a bookseller in Melbourne, Australia, and Ticknor and Fields in Boston had a licence to republish much of the material for an American audience.

It was always part of Macmillan's vision for the *Magazine*, shared with Masson, that it would derive strength from the increasingly well-respected network of contributors being developed at the Tobacco Parliament. However, Macmillan was still a newcomer on the London scene and his circle was heavily weighted towards Cambridge. The *Magazine* was launched with a celebratory dinner on 1 November 1859, and Macmillan had great plans, inviting Tennyson, Nathaniel Hawthorne, currently living in England and known to Hughes, and other worthies. However, the only guests listed in Alexander's biography as attending are Maurice, Hughes and Ludlow, FitzJames Stephen, the jurist, Lord Ripon, a radical campaigner and friend of Hughes, and Charles Bowen, a barrister later credited with being the first to use the phrase 'the man on the Clapham Omnibus'. Macmillan had not yet achieved the pulling power he desired.

The failure to lure Alfred Tennyson as his principal guest would have been particularly disappointing, and not for want of trying. Macmillan first met his favourite poet earlier that year when Tennyson visited Cambridge. Alexander was already known by name to Emily Tennyson since the previous year, when he had been helpful to her in organizing for Thomas Woolner's bust of the poet to be put on display at Trinity College. This had required a certain amount of tactful lobbying of the college authorities by Macmillan, and Emily, prompted by Woolner, had written to Macmillan to thank him and invited him to stay at Farringford, their house on the Isle of Wight. Masson and Macmillan, in hopes of obtaining a poem from the Laureate for the *Magazine*, were quick to follow up on this invitation when repeated by her husband.

Macmillan was too respectful of long-term publishing partnerships to attempt to dislodge Moxon, Tennyson's principal publisher, but a poem for the *Magazine* seemed achievable. Emily, who regularly acted as her husband's literary agent, was very nervous about breaching the contract with Moxon, and was juggling competing requests from other periodicals. Alexander's thank you letter of 11 October 1859 to the poet shows the extent to which he was prepared to promote his cause: 'I can now say unreservedly that we shall be most glad to have your Idyll for our *Magazine* . . . I hope Mrs Tennyson will feel satisfied that a poem of this length will be more appropriate to our graver monthly than to the lighter weekly, which I trust you will find able also to gratify with some smaller piece.'[1] Enclosed with this letter were gifts of three small books for the Tennyson boys, and copies of the latest works from Maurice and Henry Kingsley. He also wrote to Emily: 'It will be an inexpressible delight for me to be in any way connected as a publisher with Mr Tennyson – gratifying to my vanity I fear I must honestly admit – perhaps a little of some better feeling mingles with it, and commercially I think it will do our magazine a great deal of good.'[2]

Macmillan and Masson offered the extremely generous sum of one pound a line to Tennyson, and ended up paying £300 for the poem, *Sea Dreams*, which was featured in the January issue, timed to act as a distraction from the launch of the *Cornhill*. Macmillan, keen to get maximum public notice for this coup, asked Tennyson if he could add as subtitle 'An Idyll', as the public were waiting with bated breath for more Arthurian Idylls from the Poet Laureate.[3]

By the spring of 1860, Macmillan knew the *Magazine* would pay its way. Its circulation was regularly reaching 12,000 or 15,000, twice what he needed for break-even, and was seen to be sufficiently different from the *Cornhill* to hold its own place in the market. The timing was perfect, for there was plenty of controversial subject matter to inspire political or theological debate in Britain. Just three weeks after the launch of the *Magazine*, John Murray published *On the Origin of Species* by Charles Darwin. Eight days after that, the abolitionist John Brown was hanged in Virginia for his part in leading the raid on the Harper's Ferry armoury. Although these two historically significant events were unconnected, they marked points at which controversial currents of thought burst into the daylight of public consciousness and triggered chain reactions. Scientific and theological disputes over the problems of creation and evolution, which had been bubbling quietly within academic circles for decades, now surfaced. They provoked a flood of articles and editorials in response, posing an increasing challenge to Christian orthodoxy. Meanwhile the deep divisions in the United States over slavery and secession pointed towards civil war. The more liberal-minded commentators began to articulate a link between the speculations of scientists regarding the ascent of man and the aspirations of those who argued for the emancipation of the slaves. The waves of doubt and controversy which were crashing against the foundations of Victorian institutions were becoming more violent. Macmillan and Masson shared a set of clear moral and ethical principles, founded in Christian Socialism and radical politics, which would enable them to tackle these controversies. The stances they took in *Macmillan's Magazine*, being supportive of scientific enquiry, hostile to the Establishment where it held back intellectual and democratic progress, and optimistic about the powers of cooperation and brotherhood, created clear water between their position and the rest of the Victorian literary press.

Setting a high standard for the topicality of its content, the December issue of *Macmillan's Magazine*, published one week after *Origin*, contained an article by Thomas Huxley which concluded with a highly supportive commentary on Darwin's thesis. This was the opening salvo in Huxley's lifelong campaign to ensure that Darwin's work would get the recognition he believed it deserved. With hindsight, it was an extraordinary coup for Macmillan – that the man who later described himself as Darwin's Bulldog, and was certainly his loudest and most belligerent disciple, should grace such a newly fledged periodical with his thoughts. It also demonstrated to his audience that Alexander, through his chosen editor David Masson, would not be afraid of covering the topics that raised serious questions for Christian theologians, however uncomfortable some of these theories may have personally made him feel.

Alexander Macmillan had always intended that his *Magazine* would include scientific material. After all, he had learnt his trade and established his principal network of authors and customers at the heart of Cambridge University, arguably the main centre of scientific enquiry and debate in England in the first half of the nineteenth century. Science was increasingly fascinating, and sometimes alarming, to a middle-class audience disenchanted with the Church of England and looking for alternative sources of certainty. If the discoveries of scientists, geologists and naturalists all contradicted the biblical creation story, why should anything in the Bible be true? And if not true, what was the source of its moral authority? Did God even exist?

A layman's guide to issues of topical scientific discovery, *Vestiges of the Natural History of Creation*, published anonymously in 1843, had sold twenty thousand copies by 1860. The author was eventually revealed as Robert Chambers, an Edinburgh publisher, and his work anticipated many of the concerns that Darwin sought to address, but the scientific community rejected his book, pouring scorn on the work of an amateur enthusiast. This had not stopped the general public from lapping it up and hoping for more. John Murray only ordered a print run of 1,250 copies for the first edition of Darwin's *Origin*, but Mudie's Circulating Library bought 500 of those and demand was such that the publisher had to order a reprint of 3,000 copies in December. By January 1860 Darwin was working on a second edition.

The Macmillan House was already a significant publisher of mathematical and scientific works emanating from Cambridge; by 1859 its catalogue included textbooks by the mathematicians George Boole and Isaac Todhunter, which sold to schools in huge numbers, and, for the scientifically curious, texts by the botanist John Henslow, the geologist Adam Sedgwick and the astronomer George

Airy. For the less academically minded, Charles Kingsley's *Glaucus, or the Wonders of the Shore* was highly popular as a handbook for the amateur naturalist. With an office in London, Macmillan was now able to increase his network, notably to include the ambitious up-and-coming Thomas Huxley, whom he and Masson had both come across earlier in the decade through the Working Men's College.

Thomas Huxley, born in 1825, did not have the advantages of a university education and had taken medical training in London before joining HMS *Rattlesnake* for a voyage round the world. In 1850 he arrived back in London determined to make a career for himself as a scientist, desperate to earn enough money to bring his fiancée home from Australia. By 1854 he had begun to supplement a very meagre living as a professional scientist by writing articles for John Chapman's *Westminster Review*. In the same year he was introduced through a mutual friend to Maurice and his set, and they encouraged him to try his hand at teaching the working man. In February 1855 he wrote to this friend, 'I am sick of the dilettante middle class and mean to try what I can do with these hard-handed fellows who live among facts.'[4] In 1857 he gave his first lecture at the Working Men's College to an audience of fifty, including Maurice himself. Alexander heard him lecture and was impressed by his easy style and delivery.

In 1853 Huxley had been introduced to Charles Darwin at a meeting of the Geological Society, and they began corresponding and sharing specimens – such as Darwin's sea-squirts (unusual animals that resemble coral) from his voyage on the *Beagle*. Throughout the 1850s Darwin shied away from publicity and preferred to test his theories quietly by sharing them with other men of science whom he admired, principally Huxley, the botanist Joseph Hooker and Sir Charles Lyall, the geologist. Darwin's theory of evolution by natural selection only reached a wider audience when Hooker and Lyall presented a paper from Darwin alongside one from Alfred Russel Wallace at the Linnaean Society in July 1858, but this received little coverage. The first edition of *Origin* arrived on Huxley's desk a week or so before its publication in November 1859, as Darwin was particularly keen to garner support from the new generation of scientists. Huxley was initially overwhelmed by a book with no references, no illustrations, just five hundred or more pages of facts, theories and deductions. But he worked his way slowly through it and picked up his pen. He had a standing invitation from Alexander Macmillan to contribute to the new *Magazine*; this seemed the ideal subject.

Huxley's article 'Time and Life: Mr Darwin's *"Origin of Species"*' summarised the key points of Darwin's thesis, cautiously making it clear that his own supportive conclusions were based on the sheer quantity of the evidence presented, on his high opinion of the author's intellect, and on the years of work demonstrated within the text. He argued that Darwin's theory appeared to be the best available explanation given to date of a question that was puzzling scientists:

> If it can be proved that the process of natural selection, operating upon any species, can give rise to varieties of species so different from one another that none of our tests will distinguish them from true species, Mr Darwin's hypothesis of the origin of species will take its place among the established theories of science, be its consequences whatever they may.

He went on to confront those who would criticize from ignorance or theological panic.

> In either case the question is one to be settled only by the painstaking, truth-loving investigation of skilled naturalists. It is the duty of the general public to await the result in patience; and above all things, to discourage, as they would any other crimes, the attempt to enlist the prejudices of the ignorant, or the uncharitableness of the bigoted, on either side of the controversy.[5]

Macmillan was proud to be publishing this piece. He wrote to Tennyson, unable to resist a sly tribute to *In Memoriam*, 'Pray look specially at Huxley's article, *Time and Life*. Darwin's book, which it mentions, is remarkable certainly. I thought of "Nature acts in tooth and claw" as I was glancing over it. I wish someone could bring out the other side. But surely the scientific men ought on no account to be hindered from saying what they find are facts.'[6] These new disruptive theories continued to excite intellectuals of all disciplines and to dominate discussions: on 12 January 1860 Macmillan hosted a Tobacco Parliament at Henrietta Street attended by Thomas Huxley, Charles Kingsley, F. D. Maurice, Tom Hughes, David Masson and Henry Kingsley, 'and had much fine talk, chiefly about this species question. It seems of great importance. I hope it won't swallow all other interests in earnest men's minds.'[7]

There is no doubt that, living among the older generation of Cambridge academics who felt themselves discomfited by Darwin's disruptive theories, Macmillan found himself conflicted. Add to this the commercial concern that if they were not careful, he and Masson would find their colours nailed too firmly to a mast that turned out to be on the wrong ship. Alexander was extremely cautious about becoming embroiled in any wider debate about the origins of Man and the implications for religion. 'There seems to me a great danger of our popular theologians tying us down to a position where science in its advance will leave our Protestantism alongside Popery in its dishonest and impudent treatment of fact and nature.'[8] Even before *Origin* was published, he had been concerned about the fate of a society with no religious certainties. He wrote to Sebastian Evans, who had submitted poetry for publication which had an atheistic tone:

I have too much reason to fear that you are right in thinking that a large and intelligent class of Englishmen is fast drifting away from the old moorings and steerings too, and don't appear either to have or to care to possess any in their stead. A kind of

hopeless, aimless philosophy – somewhat of the Topsy order* –
is all that remains. I don't like it in any way as you know.'[9]

In the early months of 1860, Macmillan took soundings among
his Cambridge friends of what might be a reasonable response to
Darwin, but always tried to ground any argument on scientific
fact rather than emotional or religious response. In March he was
writing on the subject to his friend Fenton Hort. 'With Sedgwick,
Hopkins and Clark the opinion of Darwin is pretty uniform – they
think his premises too narrow for his theories. Hopkins said "Darwin
would never have ventured on such argument if he had had a thorough mathematical training" . . . Henslow by the by too disagrees
with Darwin.'[10] These were significant names for Macmillan to
be canvassing – John Henslow had been Darwin's tutor in botany,
Adam Sedgwick was Cambridge's Professor of Geology, William
Hopkins, a mathematician and geologist, was a former President of
the Geological Society. However dismissive these gentlemen were,
Macmillan seems to have taken the view, which he said he shared
with 'the more thoughtful' that 'opposition or notes of alarm on the
production of scientific theories are false in policy and fruitless of
any real good even in the view in which they are made.'[11]

Macmillan saw Huxley several times in the early months of 1860
and tried to persuade him to write for the *Magazine* again. In the
letter that accompanied the cheque for Huxley's first article, he suggested that next time Huxley might use the simpler style that he had
heard him use when lecturing at the Working Men's College, as it
might be more suitable for Macmillan's readership. When this fell on
stony ground, he tried to tempt him with further Darwinian debate.
On 30 April he wrote: 'Do you see that Hopkins is going to deal
with the questions in *Fraser's Magazine*? What have you to say to it?

---

* Topsy, a character in the anti-slavery classic *Uncle Tom's Cabin*, when asked if
she knew who made her, replied, 'I s'pect I growed. Don't think nobody never
made me.'

Can you come and take a bit of mutton with Masson and myself on Thursday?' In June he wrote again, inviting him to dine with Charles Kingsley and lamenting 'all these months without a scratch of your pen in the Mag!'[12] But by now Huxley was in great demand from newspapers and periodicals of all kind, having had notable pieces in *The Times* and the *Westminster Review*, among others. Macmillan was never able to claim a monopoly on Huxley's writings, but one of the scientist's most famous essays, 'On a Piece of Chalk', delivered as a lecture to the working men of Norwich in 1868, was first printed in *Macmillan's Magazine*. It was Macmillan & Co. which published Huxley's *Collected Essays* in the 1890s, and subsequently Leonard Huxley's biography of his father in 1900.

In December 1860, the *Magazine* contained the simple, informative article that Macmillan and Masson had been hoping to coax out of Huxley. The author was a young Cambridge don, whom Alexander would take under his wing. Henry Fawcett had arrived as an undergraduate in Cambridge in 1852, and in 1856, aged twenty-three, became a Fellow at Trinity Hall. Tragically, in September 1858 Fawcett was blinded in a shooting accident, but continued with his studies, employing the young son of a college servant as his companion and amanuensis. He now turned his attention to politics, economics and social affairs. Macmillan recognized him as a man of intellectual talent and radical politics, an ideal candidate to join his circle of associates. In his 1880s biography of Fawcett, Leslie Stephen wrote: 'Amongst our friends of those days were Mr Alexander Macmillan, already rising as a publisher, though his business was still confined to Cambridge . . . Macmillan was often in our rooms, trying rather fruitlessly to stimulate Fawcett's interest in the writings of Carlyle, Maurice and Kingsley.'[13] In 1862, when a parliamentary election was held in Cambridge, Macmillan persuaded Fawcett to stand as a Liberal candidate, and acted as chair at the campaign meetings. Fawcett was quoted by Stephen as saying, 'If I am anyone's candidate, I am Macmillan's candidate'.[14] He failed to win the seat on this occasion, but in 1865 he was returned as MP for Brighton, and served in the

House of Commons for the next twenty years, latterly as Postmaster General under Gladstone. His politics, which we can assume were shared with Macmillan, were strongly influenced by the writings of John Stuart Mill. This would explain his antipathy to Maurice and Carlyle, opponents of Mill's Utilitarian philosophies. According to Stephen, it was Macmillan who persuaded Fawcett to write his first great textbook, *A Manual of Political Economy*, published in 1863. This work was key, later that year, in positioning him to win the election for the next Professor of Political Economy in Cambridge.

The immediate furore over *Origins* began to die away, as scientists around the world busied themselves gathering evidence either to support or to disprove the Darwin hypothesis. But one of Macmillan's closest friends continued to work through the implications for his Christian faith: this was the Reverend Charles Kingsley, now Regius Professor of History at Cambridge. Kingsley had already been pulled into the debate when Darwin sent him an advanced copy of his book in November 1859. Kingsley, an amateur naturalist, had written offering enthusiastic support and quoting St Paul: ' "Let God be true and every man a liar" . . . I have gradually learnt to see that it is just as noble a conception of Deity, to believe that He created primal forms capable of self-development into all forms needful . . . as to believe that He required a fresh act of intervention to supply the lacunas which he himself had made. I question whether the former be not the loftier thought.'[15] Darwin paraphrased this sentence from Kingsley's letter of thanks in the second edition of *Origins*, published in 1860. Generally speaking, Kingsley was happy to accept that Darwin might have disproved many theories on which he himself had previously relied, but to his way of thinking, the discoveries of science could only be to the glory of God, not a challenge.

Kingsley had an even closer relationship with Thomas Huxley, whom he had first met in 1855 through the Christian Socialist set. They bonded over their shared passion for natural history and met several times at Macmillan's Tobacco Parliament evenings. If Huxley, who was becoming ever more fervent in his rejection of Christian certainties and liked nothing better than a good fight with a clergy-man, expected to find a conventional sparring partner in this man who was now also Chaplain in Ordinary to the Queen, he found instead an open-minded yet deeply spiritual friend. Having read Huxley's review in *Macmillan's Magazine*, he wrote to congratulate him, it 'said what ought to be said' and would 'keep the curs from barking'. Kingsley would continue to follow Darwin's 'villainous shifty fox of an argument into whatsoever unexpected bog and brakes he may lead us.'[16] The letters they exchanged late in 1860 after the death of Huxley's little boy, Noel, are masterpieces of tolerance and respect for each other's views. Kingsley offered consolation that Huxley would meet his son again. Huxley replied that as he could not see any proof of eternal life, he could not accept it as fact. He went on, 'I don't profess to understand the logic of yourself, Maurice and the rest of your school, but I have always said I would swear by your truthfulness and sincerity, and that good must come of your efforts.'[17] Their correspondence continued and their friendship deepened.

In June 1862 Macmillan was staying at Eversley, Charles Kings-ley's parsonage in Hampshire, and wrote to James MacLehose: 'We are to have such a story from him for the *Magazine* . . . It is to be called "The Water Babies". I have read a great deal of it, and it is the most charming piece of grotesquery,* with flashes of tenderness and poetry playing over all, that I have ever seen.'[18] Its composition was closely tied to the debates on evolution: when the British Association met in Cambridge in October 1862, Kingsley held open house for Huxley and his associates, and wrote the final instalments of the tale in the evenings after they had gone. The serial ran for eight months from August 1862 and was then published as a book for children in 1863. By now, Macmillan's own children were old enough to be guinea-pig listeners. Daniel's oldest boy, Fred, was ten years old, and Alexander's youngest daughter little Olive had just turned three; the

---

*　　Grotesquery here simply means the absurd or ludicrous.

eight children listened entranced as Alexander read them the story. Many years later his daughter Margaret set down her private reminiscences of her childhood and this is the one book she particularly mentions.

> The greatest excitement in the nursery world that I remember in the Cambridge days was caused by my father reading us *The Water Babies* . . . the fresh wonder of those opening chapters, surely the most charming part of the book . . . how we all sat spellbound . . . That nursery scene is still vivid, and the keen joyousness of my father's face and voice as he read. It is typical of the delight that lay for him in his work and which was imparted to the atmosphere of his home.

Margaret also describes Kingsley at this time.

> The keen eagle-like face lighted up by those wonderful blue eyes, the elaborate courtliness of his manner, his boyish spirits, his delightful talk of outdoor things, the impetuosity of his utterance, which was emphasised by his stammer; all deeply impressed the childish mind.[19]

The Water-Babies: A Fairy Tale for a Land Baby was an immediate success, quite unlike anything Kingsley had written before, or indeed, with its excursions into fantasy, any previous children's literature. As Humphrey Carpenter wrote, 'like all Kingsley's work it was both brilliant and a failure, self-contradictory, muddled, inspiring, sentimental, powerfully argumentative, irrationally prejudiced, superbly readable. In a small space it managed to discover and explore almost all the directions that children's books would take over the next hundred years. And in exploring them it usually fell flat on its face.'[20] When Kingsley revised the serial for publication as a book he tried to make it more child-friendly, softening some of the language and omitting some of the more frightening passages.

He tempered some of his anti-Americanism and hid his antagonism towards the North in the Civil War then raging. Above all, he tried to bring out more clearly his underlying themes: the importance of the Moral Law, the consequences of Sin, and the need for spiritual growth. Kingsley was dismayed that the leaders of the Church of England appeared so eager to deny Darwin's theories. As with his previous campaigning fiction, Kingsley believed he was most persuasive when he took up his pen to tell a story. He wrote to his friend Maurice that he was trying 'to make children and grown folks understand that there is a quite miraculous and divine element underlying all physical nature . . . And if I have wrapped up my parable in seeming Tomfooleries, it is because so only could I get the pill swallowed by a generation who are not believing with anything like their whole heart in the Living God.'[21] Tucked within these theological messages were more topical concerns: specifically, his horror at the working conditions of chimney sweep boys. This certainly had the desired effect on the voting public, as the Chimney Sweepers' Regulation Act, forbidding the use of children under the age of sixteen in sweeping chimneys, was passed the following year. The book has been in print ever since publication, and for two years would be the best-selling British children's book, until Macmillan published *Alice's Adventures in Wonderland*.

The first year of *Macmillan's Magazine* saw Macmillan and Masson not only testing their market and honing their product but learning to work together. In most areas of his business, Macmillan exhibited some of the tendencies of a control-freak, but in this case, he was determined to leave Masson with editorial freedom, as can be seen in various tactful letters prompting or querying editorial decisions, but never over-ruling. Together they found a way to steer through the perils caused by the provocative writings of Darwin and Huxley without alienating their core middle-class audience. The strength of their relationship stood them in good stead when a conflict arose that was so controversial that it eventually split Macmillan's closest friends into factions, turning Hughes, Maurice and Ludlow against

Kingsley and Tennyson, and almost everyone against Carlyle. This was the impact of the American Civil War. The position taken by *Macmillan's Magazine*'s contributors was one of the ways in which it stood out against the British press pack.

Thomas Hughes and his friend John Ludlow, with other Christian Socialists, were fierce opponents of slavery, and in the prelude to hostilities had become friendly with leading American abolitionists such as James Russell Lowell. They followed the 1860 American presidential election campaign closely, hoping that the newly formed Republican party would be victorious and would move swiftly to abolish slavery across the country. This might have seemed a topic on which all British churchgoers and liberals would agree; after all, it was the British who had led the world in suppressing the Atlantic slave trade as long ago as 1807. When Harriet Beecher Stowe published *Uncle Tom's Cabin* in 1852, it sold more copies in Britain than in America, a million in its first year. However Macmillan and Masson, with a *Magazine* to run, were well aware of the complexity of Anglo-American relationships: the British public viewed American politicians, especially those from the industrial North, with great suspicion – irritated that America still professed territorial ambitions in Canada, and had not supported Britain in the Crimean War. To further complicate matters, there were very strong trading links between the north of England and the southern States: according to the *New York Times* in 1861, the annual value of cotton exported from the States to Britain was £28 million (£3.4 billion in today's values), and more than a million people, principally in Lancashire and the north-west, were employed in the cotton industry. To take a bold stand in support of the North, which was blockading Southern ports, would risk alienating readers and advertisers. For most British papers, the easiest position to take was non-interventionist, with pronounced sympathy towards the Southerners, who seemed to be better friends and active trading partners. In return, the Unionist press attacked the British for sitting on the fence.

Macmillan was as firmly abolitionist as any other disciple of

Maurice. He wrote to a new acquaintance, Mrs Gaskell, 'No one can feel more the iniquity of slavery than I do.'[22] However he had a businessman's nervousness of the impact of a commercial crisis on the British economy, fearing financial disruption to Macmillan & Co. as well as its potential to cause social unrest. In December 1860, shortly after the election of President Lincoln, he wrote to George Kingsley, brother of Charles, 'if we have commercial distress this winter, I should not wonder if we had worse things at the back of it.'[23] In the early years of the war, when Lincoln was afraid that he might alienate the border states by too early a declaration of emancipation, supporters such as Macmillan in Britain found the North's position hard to justify, and were further distressed by the antagonism against the British seen in the American press.

The mainstream British press took the line that the Northern cause was cynical, with politicians in pursuit solely of economic domination and not sufficiently committed to emancipation. This was accompanied by charges of hypocrisy, as there seemed to be much evidence of unpleasant racism in the Northern states. Nevertheless, as the war began, *Macmillan's Magazine* stuck fast to its principles, with regular contributions supporting the Federal cause, while urging Lincoln to make the abolition of slavery an avowed war aim. In June 1861 Macmillan wrote, perhaps optimistically, to his friend J. T. Fields, the Boston publisher: 'I don't quite understand the furious speeches that are being made by your statesmen against England. They should know us better than this ere now. You may know where the sympathy of England really lies.'[24] Two months later he wrote again, lamenting that Fields' journal, *The Atlantic Monthly*, had published an article which again criticized the British in a way that Macmillan thought would increase the mutual bitterness: 'Surely the task of feeding the fuel of strife between the two great free nations of the world ought to be left to the vulgarer prints who grow on excitement regardless of the claims of humanity and justice.'[25] However, when writing to Westcott, an old Cambridge friend, his tone was significantly less conciliatory, as he described 'a long series of insults and mad wicked braggadocio by the Yankees' which he feared might lead to war between the two countries.[26]

The September 1861 issue of *Macmillan's Magazine* saw Thomas Hughes contributing an article in the form of a letter to the editor, written in the aftermath of the North's first major defeat at Manassas, when British support for the South was gathering pace. He wrote that 'the tone of all our leading journals . . . has with the single exception of *The Spectator*, been ungenerous and unfair, and has not represented the better mind of England.' He acknowledged that as yet the North had not made an avowed aim of abolishing slavery, but concluded: 'It is the battle of human freedom which the North are fighting . . . If the North is beaten it will be a misfortune such has not come on the world since Christendom arose.'[27] Throughout 1862 and 1863, and frequently thereafter, an article on the subject of the war, which echoed Hughes's thoughts, if not his style, ran in every issue. Contributors included the well-known abolitionist Harriet Martineau, the novelist Elizabeth Gaskell (who contributed a poem mourning the loss of Robert Gould Shaw, the commanding officer of the Union's first all-black regiment), and the author and critic Leslie Stephen.

Not content with printing contributions from armchair commentators, Macmillan enterprisingly commissioned Edward Dicey, who was sailing to America to observe the war on behalf of *The Spectator*, to send back an additional series of articles for the *Magazine* 'the great aim of which will be wisely to remove the misunderstandings between the Northern states and this country.'[28] Dicey was a young professional author and journalist, whom Macmillan knew from his time as an undergraduate at Trinity College, Cambridge, when he was President of the Union. In 1860 Dicey had travelled to Rome to experience some of the revolutionary activity underway in Italy, and the following year published two books detailing his experiences.

He was well connected in English literary circles, as the nephew of Sir James Stephen the jurist, and he was an enthusiastic follower of the politics, if not the theology, of F. D. Maurice and the Christian Socialists. His initial commission had come from Richard Hutton, newly appointed editor of *The Spectator*, a friend of Maurice and another supporter of the Northern cause. It appears that Masson was less enthusiastic about the project than Macmillan, so it was left to Alexander to finalize arrangements: 'I do not know whether Masson would like to commit himself to having so much space occupied every month for four months. I think if we can arrange it, it would be well worthwhile myself.'[29]

The role of the modern war correspondent had first been developed in the British press by William Howard Russell in the previous decade when he sent regular dispatches to *The Times* from the Crimean campaign and then the Indian 'Mutiny'. Russell arrived in Washington in March 1861, shortly after Lincoln's inauguration. Dicey, who arrived a year later, has been described as 'a comically incompetent war correspondent, but the most sophisticated and sympathetic European traveller in America since Tocqueville'.[30] He was also a committed abolitionist, a grand-nephew of William Wilberforce, and was appalled at the attitude of much of the British press: 'I remember as a child having learnt that England was the home of the free, and that the slave and the oppressed looked to her for succour. It seems that now the roles are changed, and that it is the slave-owner and the oppressor who look to England for succour.'[31] Unlike Russell, he did not attempt to follow either army into battle, admitting that he had no understanding of military matters. His pieces for Hutton and Macmillan, designed to be read in weekly or monthly journals, were more reflective, as he spent his time travelling the country by train, observing the countryside and talking to the civilian population. A subscriber hoping for tales of swashbuckling bravado and cavalry charges would be disappointed – the titles of the articles in the *Magazine* suggest a more impressionistic style than that of the usual war correspondent: 'Three Weeks in New York', 'Washington During the

War', 'Notes of a Tour through the Border States'. But Macmillan was more than happy for his *Magazine* to be a conduit to promote the better understanding of two nations which seemed to rub each other up the wrong way with alarming regularity.

After the war had ended, in 1866, William Rossetti, brother of Christina and Dante Gabriel, and an occasional guest at the Tobacco Parliament, wrote a long piece for an American periodical, *The Atlantic Monthly*, analysing the British response to the war. He wrote: 'Among the magazines, the *"Quarterly"* and *"Blackwood,"* with various others, not all of them colleagues of these two in strict Conservatism, were for the South; *"Macmillan's Magazine,"* again an organ of the advanced and theoretic Liberalism, consistently for the North, so far as it could be considered to express aggregate, and not merely individual, views.'[32] However, there had been one notable exception to the stream of pro-Northern articles, which caused considerable personal embarrassment to Alexander Macmillan. Masson had been a regular visitor to the Carlyle house in Chelsea since he had first arrived in London, and at some point around 1860 had introduced Alexander Macmillan and his wife Caroline to Thomas and Jane Carlyle. This must have ranked as a highlight of Macmillan's career. Both he and Masson had begged the master for a contribution to the *Magazine*. Eventually something arrived, fewer than two hundred words, and causing a huge headache to the liberal owner and his editor, which they held for several months before publishing.

Ilias (Americana) in Nuce[33]

Peter of the North (to Paul of the South). 'Paul, you unaccountable scoundrel, I find you hire your servants for life, not by the month or year as I do! You are going straight to Hell, you——!'

Paul. 'Good words, Peter! The risk is my own; I am willing to take the risk. Hire you your servants by the month or the day, and get straight to Heaven; leave me to my own method.'

Peter. 'No, I won't. I will beat your brains out first!' (And is trying dreadfully ever since, but cannot yet manage it).[34]

It was not the first time that Carlyle had expressed views that were shocking to emancipationists, equating slavery with any other form of employment contract: an article he contributed to *Fraser's* in 1849 had caused a quarrel with John Stuart Mill which had never been mended. Masson and Macmillan must have hoped for a contribution on a less controversial subject, although the publicity the actual piece aroused would not have damaged that month's circulation figures. Most newspapers commented that the piece would never have made its way into the pages of the *Magazine* if it had not been by such a famous author. But Macmillan believed strongly in freedom of expression and was prepared to take the consequences.

John Ludlow, a founding contributor to the *Magazine*, exploded with rage in a letter to Macmillan: 'I did not think your *Magazine* would ever fall so low as to insert that thing signed TC in the new Number. It is a lie and the bad old man who wrote it knows it to be such, as well as you or I. That you should have chosen for circulating it a moment like this, when Secession is on its last legs . . . is a piece of unwisdom which fortunately serves as its own punishment. Yours truly, JML.'[35]

Macmillan responded that same day:

My firm conviction that Thomas Carlyle is wrong in thinking that slavery and service from man to man for life are synonymous, does not render me unjust towards him. He is not a 'bad old man' but a very noble and useful one, and even his wrong sayings have wisdom and significance in them which are wanting in the rabid vapid utterance of deepest truths. Instead of writing such a letter to me, which is valueless for all conceivable human uses, why don't you sit down and calmly expose the fallacy of the application of permanent relationships – which relationships, with your theories, you ought to value more highly than true Thomas himself – which has been made in slavery? I am sure you could do it if you would keep your temper and your head cool. And you know very well that the pages of the *Magazine* are opener to you than to Carlyle. Wherein does the value of a theory of human freedom consist that permits no divergence of opinion, no freedom of discussion? . . . I am for freedom, my most excellent and well-beloved friend John, and mean to have it against all tyrannies over others, even in thought.[36]

Ludlow's next, rather sulky broadside came just three days later.

My dear Macmillan, I hold by what I have written. I have never yet tracked Carlyle on any subject but what I have found him dishonest. In this instance he has lied and he knows he has. You say that the columns of *Macmillan* are opener to me than to him. The last article of mine published was kept in hand a year and a half. The last two sent were declined. The staple of the *Magazine* has been for a long time such as I care little to be mixed up with. However I send you herewith what you can certainly find room for and what I should wish to see published in your next number. I have shown it to Hughes. Pray hand it over to Masson when you have looked at it. Yours very truly JML.[37]

Ludlow's brief response was included in the September issue. This was not the end of the personal difficulty for Macmillan. Frederick Maurice himself was sufficiently incensed to write a response to Carlyle in *The Spectator*, although as it was written in his usual verbose style it was very hard to follow his argument. Macmillan's next letter to Maurice, although making uncomfortable reading today, indicates the growing confidence he had in his ability to defend the positions he took: 'I did not agree with Carlyle, as you know, and think your retort in *The Spectator* merited. But I do not feel that it was open to the charge of being mere folly. There is a root of wisdom in what he said. It is an element of good in slavery that the connection has a certain permanency in it. He ignores – no doubt with a humorous wilfulness – the other side. But I do not think the grand old man is the fool you say.' It is worth noting that Alexander would have been well aware of the terrible hardships being suffered by the unemployed, subject to sudden appalling layoffs, in the Manchester cotton mills at that time. Other parts of this letter make clear that Macmillan himself was increasingly unhappy with the progress of the war and nervous of giving unconditional support to the North, still perhaps suspicious of the 'Yankees': 'God knows I hate and abominate slavery in every shape with my whole heart, but there are really worse forms of it than the planter form.'[38]

Hostility to Carlyle among Maurice's supporters was now rife but hidden from public view. Just as upsetting to loyalists such as Hughes and Ludlow was the position taken by Charles Kingsley, once one of the most prominent members of their group. Kingsley was one of the few leading English literary men identified with the Confederate cause – his family had included West Indies plantation owners, who blamed the emancipation of West Indian slaves in 1833 for their financial ruin. There are many unhappy traces of racism in Kingsley's published works, including in sermons published by Macmillan in 1863.[39] But the lectures that Kingsley gave in Cambridge in 1862, which Macmillan will have heard about, if he did not actually attend, and which seemed full of anti-Northern rhetoric, were never published. Kingsley offered them to Macmillan, but he tactfully demurred, sidetracking Kingsley with a proposal for more stirring history books for boys. This undercurrent of racism led to a complete rupture within the Christian Socialist movement in the years following the American Civil War over the reception of Edward Eyre, the Governor of Jamaica who had brutally suppressed a rising by the black population in 1865 and been dismissed from his post. Back in England, Tom Hughes and John Stuart Mill formed the Jamaica Committee, to campaign for his prosecution for murder, while Charles Kingsley and Carlyle were leaders of what became the

Eyre Defence Committee. Huxley and Darwin rushed to support Hughes and Mill, while Ruskin, Dickens and Tennyson lent their weight to the Eyre team. The Defence Committee supporters were a mixed bunch: some, including Carlyle and Professor Tyndall, held openly racist views; others, such as Dickens, seemed to be more concerned that a government official should not face prosecution for upholding law and order at a time of potential civil unrest across England as well as its Empire. In the end, no prosecution succeeded and the controversy faded from view. The argument seems to have passed *Macmillan's Magazine* by: with unlucky timing, just as the story of the uprising broke in London, Masson published a two-part article by Henry Kingsley which lauded Eyre's previous career as an explorer in Australia.[40] Had Masson and Macmillan finally come across an issue which they could not handle without offence to some of their best friends? The letters collected and published by Macmillan's son George contain no references to this crisis among the brotherhood.

Controversies sell newspapers and magazines, and Macmillan and Masson were not afraid to wade into troubled waters from the very first year of the publication of their *Magazine*. The content that they published, the writers they commissioned, and the editorial lines taken were often controversial: when the topic was evolution, the *Magazine* followed the science; when the issue was politics and foreign affairs, their stance, with the notable exception of anything from the pen of Carlyle, was liberal. The overriding rule for the publisher was that his *Magazine* should promote free speech and the search for truth wherever it led his readers. If any article he published might have shaken his faith, Macmillan rose above it. His daughter Margaret wrote: 'The quality of his mind was essentially mystical . . . he took refuge from disturbing controversies in the light of his own spiritual imagination . . . my sister . . . remembers him exclaiming "Suppose Christ was never born and never died, Christ is." '[41]

Macmillan wanted his *Magazine* to reach the men who were

making their living through professions, or in industry or commerce, who might not have gone to public school, let alone to university, and whose wives certainly had not. This was the class that Alexander recognized well, being himself a prime example. Although the *Magazine* deliberately avoided becoming solely a mouthpiece for the Christian Socialists, under David Masson's editorship readers were gently instructed in many liberal and progressive views: the debate on evolution, the Northern cause in the American Civil War, the importance of improving education, and the rights of women. If Macmillan had an explicit desire to educate his readership with serious editorial, the content was leavened with lighter pieces, poetry and fiction. But even the fiction was carefully chosen to be acceptable to a genteel family audience.

After its first few years *Macmillan's Magazine* became less radical, particularly when David Masson moved back to Edinburgh in 1865 and George Grove gradually took over as editor. There may have been a subtext to his old friend John Ludlow's bitter complaints about Carlyle's article in 1864, that he felt the *Magazine* was already drifting away from his initial conception – but there again, it was not Ludlow's magazine nor his commercial risk. By the mid-1860s, the publication was proving profitable for Macmillan beyond its value as a promotional tool and when Macmillan bought Tom Hughes out in 1865 his capital value had nearly trebled to £700. *Macmillan's Magazine* ran for forty-eight years, under four different editors, publishing authors as influential and diverse as Tennyson, Stevenson, Trevelyan, Conan Doyle and Kipling, R. D. Blackmore, Sir Winston Churchill, Walter Pater and Matthew Arnold. As its fiction improved in quality it carried the serialization of novels as ground-breaking and prestigious as *The Woodlanders* and *The Portrait of a Lady*. By the time it was finally abandoned in 1907 it had more than proved its worth.

9

BUILDING THE BRAND

(1860–63)

Goblin Market *1862 title page*

'Uncommon things must be said in common words, if you would have them to be received in less than a century.'

Coventry Patmore

THE 1860S WERE a watershed decade for the Macmillan publishing house. Alexander could be congratulated on his achievements since 1857: he had continued to build on his brother's legacy and had proved that although it was often lonely, he could drive the business forward single-handed. Yet there would be no resting on his laurels – if anything, the pace would accelerate, with each success giving him the confidence to push harder and faster. Within the next four years alone he consolidated the success of his *Magazine*, published a couple of bestselling novels, launched a new publishing format that would underpin the company's income for years to come, relocated both his headquarters and his family to London, became part of the capital's literary set, and to crown his achievements, was appointed Publisher to the University of Oxford.

With the London shop thriving and the *Magazine* flourishing, Macmillan could turn his attention to other new publishing avenues. He was still a very reluctant publisher of fiction, unless he could be sure of the market. Apart from Hughes and Kingsley with *Tom Brown at Oxford* and *The Water-Babies*, the only other novelist he promoted was Charles Kingsley's brother, Henry, who produced adventure stories, such as *The Recollections of Geoffrey Hamlyn* and *Ravenshoe*, which were reasonably successful, having been first serialized in the *Magazine*. He developed niches, such as school textbooks, and exploited them carefully – commissioning the best academics in the country to write them. Cambridge academics such as Isaac Todhunter and Barnard Smith, both acclaimed mathematicians, gave him a ready supply of material that ran to annual reprints and new editions. He was similarly successful in sourcing Latin and Greek primers. The education market was buoyant and Macmillan, by pin-sharp focus on quality, prospered with it.

There is increasing evidence in Macmillan's correspondence that he was becoming as confident in handling scientific writers as he was essayists, novelists and poets. One of the longest letters in the outgoing correspondence files for January 1861 is to Professor Daniel Wilson of Toronto University. Wilson was an old family friend of the Macmillans, a son of the Mrs Wilson who had nursed Daniel Macmillan through so many of his early illnesses in Edinburgh, and brother of the George Wilson who became a great friend to both Macmillan brothers but who had died in 1859. Daniel, born in 1816, had initially trained as an engraver, working in London in the studio of J. M. W. Turner. On his return to Scotland he was appointed Secretary to the Society of Antiquaries of Scotland and began his lifelong study of archaeology and anthropology. In 1851 he published *The Archaeology and Prehistoric Annals of Scotland*, an early use of the word 'prehistoric'.

In 1853 Wilson emigrated to Canada, taking the position of Professor of History and English Literature at the University of Toronto. But he kept up his correspondence with Alexander Macmillan and 1861 he proposed a new book which Alexander was keen to publish. Wilson, who was fascinated by the archaeological and anthropological discoveries he was making in North America, suggested calling the book 'Prehistoric Glimpses': Macmillan suggested that 'Prehistoric Man' would be a much more memorable and striking title. '. . . it is a great matter to have a title which catches and sticks in the memory. No one would mistake 'Wilson's Prehistoric Man' for any other book or misunderstand the nature of your book.'[1] The year 1861 saw a great deal of advice and counsel passing from Alexander to Daniel as the manuscript began to arrive in Cambridge. It was as if Wilson in Canada was unaware of the last twenty years of scientific discovery and debate. On 22 January 1861, Alexander wrote to Daniel:

One point still appears to me to deserve very serious reconsideration . . . you appear to pledge yourself to the so-called biblical chronology, and here and there as I fancied you felt it rather hampering. I believe that quite as many thoughtful and devout believers in the essential Revelation contained in the Bible begin to feel that it is not pledged to any distinct chronological, any more than to a distinct cosmogenic, theory . . . you feel too much reverence for the spiritual revelation of the Book of Books to permit of your binding up the reception of it with uncertain and vaguely deductive chronologies, as much as theories of Astronomy or Geology supposed to be found in it . . . I am quite sure you would not hesitate to modify anything that seemed to rest on a narrow uncertain basis, prejudicial alike to science and revelation.

In other words, he offered Wilson the chance to rescue his work from certain derision among the British scientific community by allowing him to follow the new science and not the Bible in his explanations of pre-history. But he allowed Wilson the final decision, saying 'A Publisher's judgement is right in his own eyes but his author cometh after and findeth him out'.[2] Macmillan was never able completely to loosen the Bible's grip on Wilson's theories, but the most important point that Wilson wished to make was the common ancestry of Man across continents, and this liberal attitude, particularly at the time of the American Civil War, was something that Macmillan was only too happy to promote.

The money being earned from textbooks and scientific publishing gave Macmillan freedom to invest in his private passion for poetry. His wooing of Tennyson continued for many years until he became the Poet Laureate's last publisher in 1884. Among his regular guests in Henrietta Street were various characters with aspirations to be published poets, including William Allingham, Coventry Patmore and Francis Turner Palgrave. Masson introduced the Rossetti brothers, Dante Gabriel and William, to the party. When Patmore finally completed the fourth part of his most famous work, *The Angel in the House*, it was Macmillan who collected the pieces into one volume, published in 1864. However, it was a woman who would never have felt able to attend these Tobacco Parliaments, or to take the role of angel in the house, who was Macmillan's greatest and most successful poetic gamble of the 1860s: Christina Rossetti.

Rossetti, sister of Dante Gabriel Rossetti, had first offered her poems to *Macmillan's Magazine* in January 1861. She wrote modestly to David Masson, whom she had met through his wife's family, the Ormes, 'Bored as you are with contributions, many of them doubtless being poems good or bad by unknown authors, I feel ashamed to add the enclosed to the heap: the more so as personal acquaintanceship might make it more unpleasant for you to decline them.'[3] Masson showed them to Macmillan who was delighted with them, and the first, 'Up-hill', was included in the February issue, with two more to follow in April and August. At a subsequent Tobacco Parliament gathering, Alexander approached Christina's brother, enquiring about further publishable material. By this time Christina had several notebooks full of poems including a longer work, *Goblin Market*. Dante Gabriel had previously shared this with John Ruskin, who advised that it was unpublishable because of its 'quaintness and other offences', but now he wrote to his sister: 'I saw Macmillan last night who has been congratulated by some of his contributors on having got a poet at last in your person . . . He is anxious to see something else of yours and is a man able to judge for himself; so I think you might probably do at least as well with him as with Masson.'[4]

Christina agreed to show her notebooks, after some revisions, directly to Macmillan. In late October 1861 Alexander approached Dante Gabriel again. The publisher was a great believer in reading out loud to gauge effect; he regularly tried poetry out on Caroline and Fanny. Back in October 1855 Macmillan had advertised a public reading of Tennyson's *Maud*, with explanatory remarks, to be held at the Alderman's Parlour in Cambridge, concerned that the newest work by his favourite poet had been badly received in much of the press. One audience member wrote: 'All who were present did not fail to appreciate the grand aim of the poem, and as a work of art worthy of much earnest study. We trust Mr Macmillan will be induced to give another public reading, when we can promise our readers an evening of rich and choice instruction.'[5] Now he had taken the brave step of reading *Goblin Market* aloud at one of the evening sessions of the Cambridge Working Men's College: 'They seemed at first to wonder whether I was making fun of them; by degrees they got as still as death, and when I finished there was a tremendous burst of applause. I wish Miss Rossetti could have heard it.'[6] It is hardly surprising that the initial reaction was surprise, and one has to wonder what Macmillan himself made of this extraordinary poem with its vivid imagery and erotic undertones. At its simplest interpretation, it is a poem of temptation, resistance and redemption, presented as a fairy tale. When she wrote it, Christina was working at a refuge for fallen women in Highgate. The conclusion to be drawn from her parable seems obvious to us today, but may not have been either to Alexander, or even to Christina. But the language must surely have raised a smirk among the working men of Cambridge:

> She suck'd and suck'd and suck'd the more
> Fruits which that unknown orchard bore;
> She suck'd until her lips were sore.

Goblin Market finally appeared with Dante Gabriel Rossetti's woodcut illustrations in March 1862, to enthusiastic reviews. The risk that Alexander took in publishing it was mitigated by the commercial attractions of her well-known brother's illustrations, and by the renown of the family name. Thereafter, with further encouragement and flattery from Macmillan, Christina Rossetti regularly supplied poems to the *Magazine*, more than twenty in all over the same number of years.

Poetry became increasingly important to the firm. Alexander commissioned a series of books offering his readership the best selections of various types of poetry chosen by experts. The editor he alighted on for the first in the series was Francis Turner Palgrave, Fellow of Exeter College, Oxford, and eldest son of a famous historian, and the book they produced, known as Palgrave's *Golden Treasury*, created a steady stream of income to the firm for years to come. Palgrave worked on it throughout 1860, regularly consulting Tennyson on its contents, and when Alexander published it cautiously in July 1861, printing at first only 2,000 copies, the attractive, green-bound volume was so well reviewed that it sold 10,000 copies in six months.[7] Its well-publicized association with the Poet Laureate was an enormous boost to the sales figures, as was its neat appearance in a format specially designed to fit into a pocket.

The first edition now appears rather odd, as Palgrave and Tennyson took a strongly moral view of what would be suitable for a family audience, omitting anything by Blake, Donne, the Brontë sisters or Coleridge. The title had been suggested by the artist Thomas Woolner, and Macmillan himself designed the symbol, or colophon, for the series: a saltire cross, with three stars in the upper quadrant 'for heavenly glory and light', a bee in the right quadrant 'for useful industry', a butterfly on the left 'for beauty pure and aimless' and at the base three acorns 'for earthly growth and strength'.[8] The original poetry selection was quickly followed by other volumes in the series: Roundell's *Book of Praise*, Coventry Patmore's *The Children's Garland*, Allingham's *Book of Ballads* and Mark Lemon's *The Jest Book*, Dinah Mulock's *The Fairy Book*, and Mrs Alexander's *Sunday Book of Poetry for the Young*.

1860 saw the beginning of another project which was potentially even more risky than the *Magazine*, when William George Clark, a Fellow of Trinity College and Public Orator of the University of Cambridge, raised the idea of a Cambridge edition of Shakespeare, to be given the same careful treatment as any Greek or Latin classic, and using the early Folios in Trinity Library. Assisted in this project by John Glover and Aldis Wright, this was an astonishing editorial feat, with nine volumes completed in just three years. Apart from the glory of the work itself, Alexander had spotted a much bigger commercial opportunity: in 1865 he was able to launch an attractively priced one volume *Globe* edition of the *Complete Works of Shakespeare*, which remained a standard school text until the middle of the next century. From this sprang the whole *Globe* library of popular classics, attractively produced and sold very cheaply across international markets. This series continued to be published until 1976. Macmillan's aim to capture international sales was clearly stated in the introduction to the *Globe Shakespeare*:

> It seems indeed safe to predict that any volume which presents in a convenient form with clear type and at a moderate cost, the complete works of the foremost man in all literature, the greatest master of the language most widely spoken among men, will make its way to the remotest corners of the habitable globe.[9]

Moving beyond the confines of Cambridge colleges and their academics, Alexander found a whole world of women writers working hard at their occupation and eager to find new outlets and sources of regular income. One of these, Dinah Mulock, became a close family friend and eventually, through her husband, part of the business. Dinah Mulock's life reads like one of those melodramatic three-volume Victorian novels with which her more gentle romances competed. Born in 1826, she was the eldest child and only daughter of an impecunious and thoroughly disreputable, occasionally insane, itinerant preacher, Thomas Mulock, who had had the good fortune to marry a woman with a little independent wealth. Luckily his wife's family had the sense to tie her money up in trust for her three children, which did not stop Thomas spending a great deal of time and energy trying to get his hands on it. Dinah's mother died when she was just nineteen, at which point her father deserted her completely, leaving her to care for her two younger brothers, Ben and Tom. At this point the writing of poems and short stories which had been a hobby became her means of survival, as she would not inherit until she turned twenty-one. It must have been a joy and a relief as well, as life did not become any less sad. Her younger brother Tom went to sea but died in 1847 after falling from the mast into a dry dock on just his second ship. Ben, who was training to be an engineer, set off for Australia, leaving Dinah alone writing and publishing from her cottage in Hampstead. When he finally returned it was clear that something was wrong – whether it was alcohol, opium or mental illness is not clear, but he could not or would not settle to anything.

In 1850 Dinah began to share her house with another independent young woman, Frances Martin, and this led her into the world of the Christian Socialists as Martin had been one of the first students at Maurice's school for girls, Queen's College in Harley Street. She was already a well-known author when she met Alexander Macmillan, having written her first novel in 1846 at the age of twenty-three. Her output of novels, poems and articles for periodicals such as *Chambers' Edinburgh Journal* continued at an impressive rate and in 1856 she produced her most famous work, *John Halifax, Gentleman*. Her fame grew, with sales in the United States as well as Britain, but the pressure to keep turning out bestsellers was wearing her down. By 1859 she and Ben were living in a cottage called Wildwood near Hampstead Heath and, looking for more regular income with less strain than novel writing, she made a direct approach to Macmillan: 'My health has rather given way with over-work – If it were possible to get any mechanical literary work, such as being a "publisher's reader" or the like, which would give me a settled income without need to write for a year or two, it would be a great blessing to me.'[10] Alexander and Dinah met and struck up a very close friendship, which was rapidly extended to include his family. Dinah spent two weeks with them in Cambridge in November 1859, and then hosted Fanny Macmillan and the three oldest boys (Frederick, Maurice and Malcolm) at her cottage in Hampstead. The timing of her offer was good, Alexander had just launched *Macmillan's Magazine* and needed all the help he could get as the unsolicited manuscripts began to flood in.

Mulock became Macmillan's first paid manuscript reader, earning £100 a year for three years from 1860. Macmillan mostly asked her opinion on the lighter fiction manuscripts and poetry, and she was an assiduous correspondent, often working directly as an editor with authors to improve their style or plotting. She was also partly responsible for Macmillan's 1860 move into books for younger children, recommending Georgiana Craik's *My First Journal* and herself writing *Our Year: A Child's Book in Verse and Prose*. She was the first female contributor to *Macmillan's Magazine*, and over the first fifteen years of the *Magazine* she was the most prolific of the female contributors, with sixteen articles, thirteen poems, and one serialized novel.

The growth in the business was being achieved through an almost superhuman level of exertion by Alexander. Close analysis of the outgoing letterbooks in the British Library, all written in Alexander's clear flowing script, show his phenomenal work rate. To take one example, between the beginning of May 1861 and the end of October that year, there are 800 pages of letters in the Cambridge volume. These range from polite notes to authors chasing their corrected proofs or organizing the despatch of complimentary copies to reviewers, to closely argued responses to explain his decision on unsolicited manuscripts, all of which he had read. For instance, the Reverend Fremantle, later to be Dean of Ripon but at that stage just the newly appointed vicar of Lewknor in Oxfordshire and a former student of Benjamin Jowett, Master of Balliol, was treated to four closely argued pages of theological material to support Macmillan's decision not to publish his work.

However, while the firm began to prosper, the strains it placed on Alexander were beginning to take their toll. His worries included the frequent sickness of James Fraser, his principal clerk, as well as the very poor health of both his wife Caroline and his sister-in-law, Fanny. Both women were clearly suffering from the difficulties of handling a growing family (eight children under the age of eight) in the uncomfortable Cambridge accommodation above the shop. A few years earlier, in December 1858, all the children had fallen ill with measles, a potentially lethal illness, and as Caroline was six months pregnant, the stress was considerable. Olive was safely born on 23 March, but her mother took time to recover. In the summer of 1859, Caroline went to take the air at Great Yarmouth with her ailing father: meanwhile Fanny was complaining of headaches. Alexander arranged for the whole family to have a summer holiday in Lowestoft, where he would join them for a few days at a time.

The following year Alexander took Fanny to Arran for a change of scenery, but the winter of 1860 saw the household in further trouble, as the children were all ill again and Fanny was dosing herself for some unspecified complaint with chloride of potash. As the business prospered, more domestic help could be hired: the census of 1861 listed four maids and a cook living above the shop in Trinity Street. But the strain was telling. In May 1861 Caroline was again away for her health, this time in Brighton. At one point in June Caroline's health deteriorated so badly that Alexander was called to leave the office at midday to rush to join her. It may have been the onset of the heart disease that would kill her. Deciding that she could not be brought home, he took a house in nearby Eastbourne for the summer and shipped his children and their nurses down to join their mother and aunt by the sea. He himself was suffering from what he referred to as 'gout in his fingers' and by the summer of 1862 he was crippled by a fierce bout of his old trouble, sciatica, which required him to spend several weeks taking the waters in Malvern and then

Whitby. He wrote to Charles Kingsley that he was attempting to cure himself by inflicting burns on his leg, which became infected. The stay in Whitby was cut short by Caroline's increasing ill-health, which required a return home.

Initially, Alexander found support in the business from Daniel's widow. When Daniel died, Alexander tried to involve Fanny as much as he could in the business in which she was now his partner. She was often mentioned in his letters as 'Mrs Daniel', as someone who helped him in his work, reading manuscripts and suggesting new publishing projects. His letters from 1858 onwards often refer to his sister-in-law: 'I find Mrs Daniel a help to me in this as in other matters. Her taste is excellent in most things and I always listen carefully to what she says.'[11] In among the letters to Macmillan from Alexander Gilchrist, who was working on a biography of William Blake, there is a handwritten note from the publisher forwarding the first manuscript to Fanny for her comment. This was before he had even looked at it himself. In particular, at a time when the public seemed to be fascinated by a stream of self-help books, Fanny suggested that it might be a good idea to remind the public of the value of self-sacrifice: this was rapidly taken up by Alexander and emerged in 1864 as *A Book of Golden Deeds of All Times and All Lands*, edited by the well-known author Charlotte Yonge.

> The idea of the little book I spoke to your brother about was suggested by my sister-in-law (who is also my partner) Mrs Daniel Macmillan. She was struck with the large attention that seemed to be drawn to the idea of getting on, as depicted in such works as *Self-Help*. And noble and good and important as this idea is, it seemed to her and to me that another aspect of human effort should be brought out – help of others. She suggested to me some months since that a little book of the *Golden Treasury* series should be made of it and the title we hit on for it was 'the Golden Deeds of all Ages and Nations'. Our notion was that the greatest instances of self-sacrifice of all

182   LITERATURE FOR THE PEOPLE

times should be selected and told in as simple, terse, beautiful language as possible.[12]

Alexander encouraged Fanny to mix socially with his female authors, cementing relationships in a way that he was unable to do. But there were limits to what Alexander could expect from Fanny, domestically, let alone commercially. While Daniel was alive she had given birth to four children in quick succession, Frederick, Maurice, Katherine, and Arthur, despite the illness which necessitated her husband spending many months away from Cambridge in Torquay and Norfolk: Arthur was born just two months before his father's death. In January 1862 her physician Dr Reynolds diagnosed shattered nerves and exhaustion. In the autumn of 1863, Alexander took her again on a visit to Scotland where unfortunately she was slightly injured and badly shaken in a nasty accident when the coach in which they were both travelling ran away. Over the next three years her mental health deteriorated in a truly alarming manner.

It was becoming clear that something had to give. Alexander's life needed a dramatic re-organization if he was to continue working at this frenetic pace. In March 1863 the sensible solution came with a move for the whole family, as Alexander signed a lease on a house in Tooting, South London. After five years of weekly commuting to London, diligently building his network, he was confident that he could shift the centre of gravity of the firm. His circle of authors, friends, and associates had widened so that he was no longer dependent on Cambridge academics for new titles or publishing ideas, and he was regularly declining more manuscripts than he printed.

The house Alexander leased and later bought was on Tooting Bec Road and called The Elms – a large and comfortable house in its own grounds, described by his son George as 'old-fashioned but commodious.'[13] It took the form of an H-shaped, substantial three-storey gentleman's residence constructed in brown London brick with an 'in and out' carriageway from the main road. The brick of the house covered what in the eighteenth century was a timbered black and white house, with mahogany doors added, and delicately carved Adam-style mantelpieces in the reception rooms and the large bedroom. The attics were large and airy. On the ground floor, beside Alexander's library, there was a good sized entrance hall with a broad staircase, and dining and drawing rooms. The nursery and night nursery were on the first floor corner facing the street, and Maggie and Olive, as they grew up, were given the next two front bedrooms. Alexander and his wife slept at the back overlooking the garden, and there was a gallery that ran from their room to the top of the staircase, along which the children built toy villages and roads on wet days.[14] Today the house survives as part of a Catholic College and from the outside looks very little changed since Alexander's day.

In the 1860s, Tooting was still a largely rural area with orchards and farmland as well as the Common, a place where many wealthy Londoners had chosen to build comfortable villas with gardens. However, the opening of Balham Station in 1856 was leading to rapid urban development. The house was highly convenient for Alexander, being only a fifteen-minute walk from Balham Station and its trains to Victoria Station. It allowed Alexander to dispense family hospitality, home-cooked meals supervised and hosted by his wife and his sister-in-law, gardens to enjoy and the offer of a bed for the night. The Tobacco Parliaments of Henrietta Street were replaced by open invitations to visit the publisher at his home. *Macmillan's Magazine* was already showcasing female talent, now he had somewhere he could host these contributors. Christina Rossetti wrote accepting an invitation from Caroline Macmillan to spend a night in June 1864. Jane Carlyle stayed in Tooting on several occasions in June 1865 while her husband was travelling: she wrote that she had been entertained by Alexander singing Scotch songs, accompanied on the piano by the governess, but had been kept awake all night by the family dog (a gift from Henry Kingsley) under her window. When she returned the following week the dog had been confined to the washhouse, and Alexander gave her a toddy of whisky to ensure she slept better. Alexander's daughter Margaret recalled how Mrs Carlyle loved 'the little attentions bestowed upon her by my mother, saying "Make of me, my dear, I love to be made of." '[15] Margaret wrote a memoir of her father at this time. The family's day started with prayers at eight o'clock, followed by breakfast and then 'the departure for the station, bag in hand. A short cut to Balham station led across a field belonging to a neighbour, and my sister and I often stood and watched him at the garden gate. I can see him now, his broad figure of average height, the shoulders a little rounded, and a rather peculiar walk, the toes turned outwards. Always a leisurely walk, for he gave himself plenty of time to catch the train.'[16]

Not all the necessary entertaining could be done in Tooting. Membership of the Garrick Club in Covent Garden played a crucial role in Macmillan's ambitions for the firm. Founded in 1831, the first clubhouse was situated in King Street but in 1864 a new home was built for it in Garrick Street, less than two minutes' walk from Macmillan's offices. The entrance fee was twenty guineas, the annual subscription eight guineas, and it marked a very significant step up in class from the type of social gatherings that Alexander had enjoyed in Cambridge. For a start, it was highly selective. To become a member, Alexander had to identify a proposer and a seconder to enter his name on the candidate's page in a book kept in the club sitting room, but entry would depend on at least seven members putting their names to signify agreement. Alexander was proposed on 25 October 1863 by one of the most highly respected authors in London, William Makepeace Thackeray, and seconded by Mark Lemon, the founding editor of *Punch* and *The Field*. However, on Christmas Eve, Thackeray was found dead in bed by his valet, a sudden and very unexpected loss. Amidst the general shock and grief of literary society, Alexander had a particular worry: what would happen to his application. On 8 January he penned a letter to Tom Taylor, ostensibly regarding some instructions for an engraving, but with a short postscript: 'Poor Thackeray proposed me for the Garrick. I am told that a good show of names in the paper would probably ensure my early election. Can you help me? I shall feel grateful.'[17] He was duly elected in April, with some twenty support-ers including Tom Taylor, Shirley Brooks the journalist and novelist, William Clowes the printer, John Everett Millais, Charles Reade the novelist and Frederick Mullett Evans, publisher and printer. Evans was the brother-in-law of Charles Dickens Jr and of Fanny Macmil-lan through her brother Robert, who had married Margaret Moule Evans. Macmillan began using the Garrick for strictly male dinners – his All Fools' Day dinners on 1 April became regular events, either in Tooting or at the Garrick, with several signed menu cards preserved by the family.

Another significant addition to the Macmillan catalogue occurred in 1863, when the publisher John Parker dissolved his company. Mac-millan had already been slowly picking up new authors as Parker's wound down, including Maurice, Kingsley, and Archbishop Trench, all of whom he was proud to publish but who would make him little money, even though Macmillan planned extensive re-issues of these authors' works. The best pick in the rummy pack was Charlotte Yonge, and Parker in a rather high-handed manner had proposed to transfer all her titles to Longmans. Yonge was not just a prolific and very popular author of children's tales, but an astute busi-nesswoman, and she chose to negotiate her own transaction with Macmillan, feeling that his reputation for moral seriousness would suit her well. In his turn, Macmillan was delighted to take on works as successful as *The Daisy Chain* and *The Heir of Redclyffe*. Their cor-respondence and relationship quickly became close: as he had done with Miss Mulock, he rolled out his wife and sister-in-law to cement the relationship, and Yonge was invited to spend time with his family in their new home in Tooting, and to collaborate with Fanny on the *Golden Deeds* project.

However, the real game-changer in 1863 was Macmillan's appointment as Publisher to Cambridge's academic rival. The Oxford University Press had been substantially modernized as a manufacturing facility in the first half of the nineteenth cen-tury, with the latest printing and paper-making technology, but its business model was too dependent on the printing of Bibles and the publication of a few scholarly works, known as Learned Texts, to suit current market conditions. To compete successfully, the Press would have to learn how to address the large and rapidly growing secular textbook market. The Delegates who supervised the Press, comprising some of the most senior Oxford academics and Heads of Houses, chaired by the University Vice-Chancellor, recognized that they needed outside help. Their initial approach in early March 1863 was to John Murray, one of the best-known and well-respected London publishers, who swiftly turned them down. By the end of the month they were talking to Macmillan and just a few weeks later, on 24 April 1863, the Delegates agreed to offer the role of 'Publisher to the University' to Alexander. The proposition was that Macmillan, recognized as a modern publisher of scale, particularly of educational works, would advise and guide them in their new project, to launch a series of school textbooks to be known as The Clarendon Press series. They had also held discussions with Longmans, a firm with a hundred and fifty years of history behind it, so the decision to work with the twenty-year-old newcomer firm was a commercial risk and speaks to Macmillan's growing reputation as an ethical and financially sound firm. Above all, 'his educational mission chimed in with the Delegates' new concerns.'[18] It is possible that Alexander had been preparing the ground – as early as May 1860 he had begun paying visits to Oxford, meeting with the highly influential Arthur (later, Dean) Stanley, Regius Professor of Ecclesiastical History, and his friend Benjamin Jowett, Regius Professor of Greek.

Negotiations continued until the Articles of Agreement were signed on 12 June 1863: for Macmillan's part, he had to offer security in the form of a bond for £4,000 and to undertake to open and manage a bookshop in Oxford. (This he never did, although he did approach his friend James MacLehose in Glasgow to see if the latter's brother Robert might be interested in managing such a shop.) The guarantors of the bond executed a year later were his old friend Tom Hughes, and the printer, Richard Clay. Neither the archives of the

Press nor of Macmillan & Co. currently contain a copy of this bond, but it can be seen in the British Library among the correspondence from Hughes.[19] Macmillan's role was to commission new educational books on behalf of the Press, to negotiate with authors and to advise on pricing and advertising, in return for 10 per cent commission on everything he sold. However, his greatest success was to persuade the Delegates to lend him a thousand guineas (£1,050) at four per cent to fund more spacious business premises in London.

In 1862 he had become aware that a large site was being cleared for redevelopment just around the corner from Henrietta Street, in Bedford Street, which ran down from Covent Garden to the Strand. The site was owned by the Duke of Bedford, and Alexander negotiated an eighty-year lease, which was granted to him in December 1863. Alexander wanted to build something grand, which would indicate how far his firm had progressed in its five years in London. He chose for the project Samuel Teulon, a well-respected and prestigious architect, better known for spectacular country houses and Gothic style churches. Number 16 Bedford Street, of which the facade survives to this day, is five storeys high and three windows wide, with a shop front on the ground floor, and designed in a more traditional Italianate style than Teulon was known for. Alexander enjoyed the prestige of employing the famous architect but required a building in a classical style in keeping with his surroundings. The premises would demonstrate quality and good taste, without being a slave to fashion or upsetting the neighbours – a reflection of the firm's ethos. Here Alexander took charge, relocating the publishing business, and his nephew Robert Bowes went back to manage the Cambridge shop. Robert spent the rest of his career in Cambridge, with the retail business being carried on under the name Bowes and Bowes after Alexander's death, until it was eventually sold in 1953.

Macmillan spent seventeen years working with Oxford University Press. The relationship was not perfect, his advice was not always taken and the accounts he produced were scrutinized and challenged, yet he is credited with refashioning the Press as a modern publisher of mostly secular and educational books. He repeatedly warned the Delegates that they were paying too much to their authors: 'It is easy for the wealthy University to lose – it has got into a habit of losing, perhaps rather likes it than not. But it is a game I could not afford to play.'[20] On several occasions, he offered to negotiate on their behalf as it would be easier for him to play 'bad cop' and keep the authors' fees under control.

What Macmillan gained from the relationship financially is hard to quantify, but the benefit to his reputation and the expansion of his publishing catalogue was worth the enormous amount of time and trouble it demanded.

10

CONTROVERSIES
and
PARTNERSHIPS
(1862–67)

Matthew Arnold

'The free-thinking of one age is the common sense of the next.'

Matthew Arnold

IN THE SIX years since his brother had died, Alexander's position in society had changed a great deal. From the humblest beginnings he had become a prime example of the Victorian self-made entrepreneur. He and his family were the sole owners of a successful and rapidly expanding publishing company. He was publisher to the great and the good of the Anglican Church, to a prestigious university, to several famous names on the Victorian literary scene, and to the up-and-coming scientific brotherhood: even if he was not the latter's exclusive publisher, he was in a position to command their articles and essays. He had become an extremely assured and confident businessman, rapidly throwing off new publishing ideas, creating exponential growth. Sometimes the sheer pace of expansion brought lapses in judgement, or maybe he was missing Daniel's perspective, and Macmillan found himself deep in controversial waters, particularly with the debates and disputes that divided and threatened the Anglican congregation, at a time when what had been solid ground seemed increasingly treacherous. In 1867, Macmillan published Matthew Arnold's 'Dover Beach', but he was already well aware, through bitter personal experience, of the 'darkling plain, Swept with confused alarms of struggle and flight, Where ignorant armies clash by night'.

His first clash with public opinion was particularly galling, as he had taken great care to be sure of his ground before publishing. The book in question was a novel, *Out of the Depths*, written by a young clergyman, Henry Gladwyn Jebb. It purported to be the life story of a young woman seduced and ruined. Beginning life as a respectable lady's maid, she is impregnated and abandoned by an Oxford student, falling by degrees to the depths of depravity: from mistress of a young lord, to mistress of a rich barrister, to eventually a street-walker in London, finally seeking redemption. The manuscript had come to Alexander in the summer of 1858, and it was he who came up with the title. Both Caroline and Fanny Mac-millan read and approved of it, Alexander himself thought it 'a very remarkable book' which he was happy to publish at his own risk. He sent it for review to Tom Hughes, whose wife read it and liked it, and to Charles Kingsley, explaining that it was a 'story on the Social Evil ably and purely written – the interest almost wholly centring on the attempt to rise'.[1] Even F. D. Maurice had approved its pub-lication. However, as Alexander began to read the proof sheets, he lost confidence, asking Jebb to tone down or omit entirely several of the more explicit passages. In March 1859, Alexander wrote to Jebb that the amendments to the love scenes seemed to have made them worse: 'all the pulling about and the violent language', warning that they must 'on no account increase the hazard'.[2]

The book hit the shelves in June and was generally well received, although the *Saturday Review* was unpleasant, warning that it was not suitable family reading, and causing Alexander to remark that he had 'never meant or wished the book to go into families'.[3] At that stage he was still happy to assure Jebb that he did not regret publish-ing the book. But within the month he completely backed down, writing to Charles Kingsley that he had withdrawn the book from both his own shop counters and the lists of current sales.

If it goes out of print, which as there was not a large edition, it may, I would never reprint it because as I said an opinion such as you give and which is echoed by Hort and George Wilson is too emphatic to be disregarded, though I have frequent testi-mony that the book is likely to do good. Of course I don't think it should be put in the way of young ladies and never thought but that its title would warn those concerned of its nature and prevent this happening, I don't feel the less now that its publi-cation is a mistake on the whole which I would gladly remedy if I saw how.[4]

The book never again featured in any Macmillan catalogue, and Macmillan never published anything else by Jebb. The book survives only because it was pirated in the United States and then reissued by another British publisher in 1873. George Eliot published *Adam Bede*, with her own tale of a woman seduced, to great acclaim in the same year 1859, and Jebb might have felt that Macmillan should have held his ground. Of course, in *Adam Bede* Hetty the fallen woman meets a terrible, retributive end, whereas Jebb's poor repentant Mary Smith survives and hopes for rehabilitation. That is what made the book unpalatable to polite Victorian society, at least as defined by the Reverend Charles Kingsley.

As Macmillan's circle of authors widened, he found himself forced to choose between competing philosophies, suffering personal discomfort when old friends had to be sacrificed to changing fashions in expression. One such friend was John Colenso, who was a regular customer in the Cambridge shop in the 1840s. In 1846 the brothers published Colenso's *Cottage Family Prayers* and in 1853 his *Village Sermons*, dedicated to F. D. Maurice at a time when Maurice was under attack from the Church Establishment. In that same year Colenso was created Bishop of Natal and set off for South Africa on missionary business. In 1855 Macmillan published *Ten Weeks in Natal*, a journal of his first impressions, which ruffled a few feathers among the Establishment for raising questions about the way the mission was being conducted, Unfortunately, the longer the bishop remained among the South African native people, trying to spread the Word of the Lord, the more sceptical he became about the Church's teachings. He became particularly uncomfortable with the Church's condemnation of polygamy, a policy which caused real economic suffering among the families of the newly converted: he felt it wrong that the price of a man's conversion to Christianity should be the dissolution of a household and the abandonment of wives and children. In early 1862 he addressed the issue directly in a *Letter to the Archbishop of Canterbury*, which Macmillan published through two editions, as he had previously published Colenso's translation of

St Paul's Epistle to the Romans. Alexander was prepared to publish what were seen as controversial opinions, and recognized that they were good for sales, writing to Colenso:

> On the whole the reception has been calmer than one expected. There would have been advantage commercially had it been attacked more fiercely . . . there seems to be much wakefulness to heresy. Would there were as much to truth . . . If any proceedings are taken you will get cordial support from not a few in England . . . there is a large body of real earnest men coming for the truth more than applause or success.[5]

However, Colenso had only just begun his attack on the Church Establishment. He returned to England in the summer of 1862 determined to publish a new commentary on the Pentateuch, which would demonstrate, mathematically and in great detail, that the stories of the first five books of the Old Testament could not be true, and should not be taught as such. This was his response to the difficulties he was having in persuading a sceptical Zulu people to accept the stories of Creation and the Flood and was, he believed, in keeping with much recent scientific questioning of biblical truths. The problem was that his many calculations, such as the amount of water required to cover Mount Ararat, and the number of sheep taken by the Israelites into the desert, seemed to make the whole Bible a joke.

Colenso showed his draft to Maurice who was appalled and begged him not to print it, threatening to resign his post at St Peter's, Vere Street as he would be shamed by his known association with the author. It is not clear if Colenso offered the book to Macmillan to publish, but Macmillan never published the bishop's writings again. Alexander wrote to his friend Vaughan 'it is perfectly amazing that a good and apparently sensible man should have thought it worth disturbing men's minds on grounds like these.'[6] Nevertheless the book was published in October by Longman, and flew off the shelves, ten thousand copies in two weeks. Colenso would probably have forgiven his old friend Alexander for being so squeamish, but it was what happened next that caused a permanent rupture between the two men.

The December edition of *Macmillan's Magazine* carried a review of the book from the pen of Matthew Arnold, son of Dr Arnold, an author who the firm was extremely keen to cultivate and who became a significant contributor to the catalogue thereafter. In an article approved by Masson, Arnold poured scorn on Colenso's arithmetical methods. Alexander wrote hastily to his old friend to warn him that he might not think the article quite fair. If he had been the editor, he said, he might have asked Arnold to tone down the language in some places. However, he bravely told Colenso, he had himself now read the book in question and 'am obliged to agree in the main with the estimate [Arnold] has made of it.' Macmillan thought that the bishop's style was 'fitted to offend the weak believer needlessly and unsettle and pain him and then furnish the vulgar unbeliever with obvious and debasing means of hardening him in his unbelief.'[7] Colenso fired back a reply that he had expected better of Macmillan. The tone of the letter annoyed and upset Alexander a great deal, but he was corresponding with a man who was already in great pain from the reception the book had received, including facing deposition and excommunication in South Africa.

Alexander sent the letter on to Arnold with a covering note.

I am writing to him as civilly and inoffensively as I can to say that I quite accept the responsibility of your article, so far as it concerns him. It is very painful for me to say this as he has always been kind and friendly to us. But he had no reason to say that he 'didn't expect it of me', for I told him here, months since, what I thought of this sort of thing and in as plain terms as I could.[8]

In January Alexander wrote again to the bishop, offering him space to reply in the *Magazine*. Nevertheless, his position had hardened: 'You are wrong utterly in the road you are going.'[9] The verdict of history is that it was Arnold's review, with its flippant tone, that led many to disregard Colenso's work, laughing at his pedantic calculations, without addressing the real questions that it posed. Alexander was always prepared to give scientific questioning of the Bible a fair hearing, but Colenso was no scientist and his work did not stand up to the high editorial standards by which the firm abided.

Scarcely had the dust settled when, yet again, a review in *Macmillan's Magazine* that Alexander had not read in advance stirred up a furore between two of the great Christian commentators of the Victorian world, John Henry Newman and Charles Kingsley. Newman, a distinguished theologian and cleric, had rocked Victorian England on its heels when in 1845 he left the Church of England and became a Roman Catholic priest. The occasion of the quarrel was Kingsley's review of James Antony Froude's latest volume in his *History of England*. Kingsley and Froude, who was his brother-in-law, were both fervently anti-Catholic and becoming more so with the passing years – a sentiment that put Kingsley on a collision course with Maurice and the other more tolerant and inclusive Christian Socialists. In the January 1864 edition of the *Magazine*, Kingsley wrote:

> Truth for its own sake had never been a virtue with the Roman clergy. Father Newman informs us that it need not, and on the whole ought not to be; that cunning is the weapon which Heaven has given to the saints wherewith to withstand the brute male force of the wicked world which marries and is given in marriage.[10]

This suggestion, that Newman was happy to tell lies to further the work of the Catholic Church, seems to have been a wilful misinterpretation of some of the cleric's writings from 1844, in which he had actually said that the Catholic Church defended itself with holiness and innocence, which the material world found so incomprehensible that they assumed it must be 'craft and hypocrisy'. To accuse Newman of being a supporter of lies and falsehoods was to throw down a massive challenge which would be unlikely to go unanswered.

Newman was at this point living quietly at the Birmingham Oratory he had founded, but some helpful busybody sent him a copy of the *Magazine* with the paragraph carefully marked, and Newman wrote a gentle letter to Macmillan with a protest at the 'grave and gratuitous slander'. Macmillan, who was upset and embarrassed, did not fully share Kingsley's horror of the Catholic Church, although in that same week he appeared to refer to Newman as 'the great pervert' in a letter to Maurice (perversion in this context meaning the adoption of Catholicism).[11] Using his many years of experience of editorial diplomacy, he tried to pour oil on troubled waters, writing back to Newman on 6 January 1864: 'Precious memories of more than twenty years since when your sermons were a delight and blessing shared (and thereby increased) with a dear brother no longer living'. Invoking Daniel's memory made it easier to hide his own instinct to side with Kingsley and, more importantly, to defend his publication. His letter, although naive in its honesty, was an apology, and was accepted as such by Newman, who never mentioned Macmillan's name in any of the later public quarrels.

I cannot separate myself in this case from whatever injustice – and your letter convinces me that there was injustice – there may have been in Mr Kingsley's charge against you personally. I had read the passage, and I will confess to you plainly that I did not even think at the time that you or any of your communion would think it unjust . . . A man who like myself is brought into near contact with very various phases of human thought in men equally noble has often occasion to mourn over harsh, unjust words spoken by men who would not consciously wrong any. I really ought in no way to aid, even by carelessness, increase of wrong like this.[12]

Kingsley also wrote to Newman, but it was not enough of an apology to end the quarrel, which continued in print between the two antagonists and their various supporters and ended in April 1864 when Newman wrote his *Apologia Pro Vita Sua*, an autobiography which did a great deal to rehabilitate him among the British middle classes, and to leave Kingsley, beaten in debate, looking like a bad-tempered bigot. The fact that F. D. Maurice had also written to Macmillan exhibiting severe disapproval of Kingsley's conduct drove a further wedge into the former unity of the Christian Socialist brotherhood.

All of these difficulties and embarrassments weighed heavily on Alexander, who was increasingly suffering from stress and overwork. In March 1865, his long-standing clerk James Fraser died. The following month he wrote to James MacLehose:

The sense of the sole responsibility of this large and growing business is weighing on me terribly. I have had it on me really ever since Daniel left me, for though poor Fraser was most helpful in many ways, yet the ultimate decision of everything lay on me, and latterly – for the last two years – even in the matter of accounts and calculations, I had to watch and look after, else things did get overlooked. Even as it is I find a good many things have been overlooked, and are left in a state that will need a good deal of work and skill to extricate. I have had various small monitions in the shape of swimmings in the head, a sense of faintness, fits of distressing and as far as I know, causeless anxiety, so that at times in the night I wake with a feeling as if everything were going to crack around and leave me sinking into horrid abysses. As I said, I believe that if I can go on I have no ground for anxiety, for things are going on as prosperously as ever, and on the whole I believe that no house stands firmer than I do, or has a career before it brighter or more hopeful. But these things mean in plain English that I have too much on me. My life has always been a hard one, as you know. Even at Nitshill I worked at pressure – it's my way. In my early years too, as you know, I had a somewhat pinched life. When I lived the nine months in Glasgow on 5s. a week, paying lodging and washing out of it, the very poor food and confinement, I am sure, told on me. Now I eat and drink well enough, and I have no doubt it helps me get on. But as I said the tension is too high. In order to have the sense that I am going on prudently, I ought to have a partner who would have a complete mastery of all details of the past and a clear knowledge of what our calculations for the future are, and how day by day's experience justifies them. To watch each book, and each class of book, whether it requires special attention and of what kind. I know perfectly how all these things are to be done, and to a great extent I get them done . . . But I have to see all done. An intelligent partner would also be of the highest value in helping me to decide on what books I should take, and in consulting and helping me to carry out my various plans. I have no power of making use of the usual publisher's taster [reader] – two attempts I made turned out failures.

I don't in the least want anyone to bring grist to the mill in the way of new ideas or new connections. I have far more of both than I can avail myself of now and can get both any time I want. What I do want is an intelligent, able man who would consult with me on what of several things we should undertake, on the mode of undertaking them, and who would see to the details being carried out. I would of course help him in this, as he would me in the other, but I would wish to be head in one department and he in the other.[13]

Luckily, help was on hand from an unexpected quarter. On 29 April 1865, a very quiet wedding was performed at Trinity Church, Bath, the couple choosing to marry by special licence, which meant that no banns were required and publicity could be kept to a minimum. The bride was Dinah Maria Mulock, the celebrity novelist and Alexander's great friend, aged thirty-nine. Her husband was a one-legged Scottish accountant, George Lillie Craik, aged twenty-eight. If they had been hoping to slip into matrimony unnoticed, they would have been frustrated by the news article that was rapidly syndicated across Great Britain and which wrongly identified the groom as George's father, the sixty-four-year-old cleric James Craik. Dinah and George were forced to publish a correction, which only served to emphasize the unusual discrepancy in their ages.

Four years earlier the thrifty George was travelling in the second-class compartment of a night train to London when the carriage was derailed outside Harrow in the early hours of the morning. George was the only serious casualty – the railway company had him carried to a London hotel where it rapidly became clear that his badly fractured leg would need to be amputated. With all his family four hundred miles away in Glasgow, the only person he could think of in London to support him was a friend of his uncle George, a woman he had met at various literary and Christian Socialist gatherings, Dinah Mulock. Dinah rushed to help and, after supporting him through the operation, took him back to recuperate at her cottage in Hampstead, Wildwood, where she hosted him, joined by his mother and sister for several months, then accompanying him and his family to Scotland. At some stage their relationship became romantic.

She had not been looking to change her life – in October 1860 she wrote to her brother Ben: 'For me, I shall never marry, it would be simply impossible. I'd rather live as a friend and sister to Joe and Maggie and aunt to their children than I'd marry any man alive.' But somehow Craik's situation, and the love she experienced within his family, touched her deeply; just eight months later she wrote: 'they say they can't do without me . . . It may be a weakness but it goes to my heart their all being so fond of me – besides I have such an intense respect for them all and the more I find out of them the more I respect them.'[14] It was after all a huge contrast to her own experience of family life.

In the spring of 1865, Dinah told Alexander that she intended to marry and move to Scotland with George, and it spurred him into making an unusually rapid decision, concerned by the potential loss of a woman whom he had come to depend upon for literary counsel and contributions. He made enquiries through MacLehose in Glasgow into George's business abilities, and two months later offered to make him a partner in Macmillan & Co., if the couple would stay in London. It says a great deal for Macmillan's respect and affection for Mulock, as George was so little known to Macmillan, and had no experience in the publishing trade. In July 1865 the newly-weds moved into the Macmillan family home in Tooting while a nearby house, Arran Cottage, was prepared for them.

Once the word was out, the marriage was discussed across literary London. Jane Carlyle wrote bitchily to her husband that they 'did not look at all ill-matched. His physical sufferings have made up in looks the ten years of difference. He has got an excellent imitation leg.'[15] The marriage was apparently happy and successful, as was George's lifelong partnership with Alexander. Craik stayed at the firm for forty years until his death in 1905, and was known and loved, stomping up and down the stairs in the Macmillan offices in Bedford Street, asking the hard-pressed staff 'Is your hearrt in your worrk?'[16] Craik was primarily interested in the financial side of the publishing business, leaving Alexander to cultivate authors and dream up new schemes. They exploited the 'good cop, bad cop' opportunity, allowing Alexander to flatter and cajole the talent, while Craik could be relied upon to deliver any bad news. One author in particular found this irritating, but nothing about Macmillan's relationship with the first editor of the Statesman's Year-Book would be simple.

Frederick Martin was probably born in Geneva, Switzerland in 1830 and educated in Heidelberg, although there is some dispute about his early life, which he did little to elucidate. He settled in England at an early age and in 1856 found work as secretary to Thomas Carlyle, at that time immersed in his research for Frederick the Great. However the appointment did not last long – although Carlyle described him as a 'desolate little German with a good hand of writing', and willing and industrious, in March 1857 he sacked him for incompetence. Apparently he had driven Carlyle mad with 'hysterical futilities' and annoyed Jane with 'whistling through the nose' in cold weather. He helped Martin find a post as a copyist at the British Museum, but told Martin in firm terms that he was not recommending him as either editor or translator.

It is not clear how Martin met Macmillan, or where the idea for the *Statesman's Year-Book* originated, although Martin had earlier tried to write a biography of Carlyle to be entitled 'The Statesman'. The project of an almanac was first discussed between Frederick Martin and Macmillan in the autumn of 1862. On 25 November, Alexander wrote to Martin thanking him for a draft prospectus he had prepared, and suggesting titles: The Statesman's Annual? Or The Political Annual – the first sounded better, the second 'rather dry'. Alexander mocked up a title page and printed the prospectus with some alterations. He suggested that they could include advertisements to help defray the costs – these would be a source of constant irritation to Martin as he complained that the 'ugly things' were always supplied too late to the printer and held up the publication. By December Macmillan had settled on the title, *The Statesman's Year-Book*, and was encouraging Martin to use contacts such as Carlyle and Lord Ashburton to open doors. The key was to persuade the various civil servants and embassy staff to provide the information they required. The two men signed a simple agreement in the Henrietta Street offices on 11 December, giving Martin the copyright and a half-share of the profits.

As might have been predicted, it all took much longer than anticipated, and the first volume was not published until January 1864: *The Statesman's Year-Book: a statistical, genealogical and historical account of the states and sovereigns of the civilised world for the year 1864*, offered at ten shillings and sixpence. It comprised nearly 700 pages, but only two advertisements had been sold. Martin had by now persuaded Macmillan that half-profits would not compensate him for the labour involved, and Macmillan paid him a £100 editing fee as well.

Daniel Macmillan.

Alexander Macmillan,
photographed by
O. J. Rejlander.

Alexander Macmillan in
old age, in 1889: by Sir Hubert
von Herkomer (*left*) and
Lowes Dickinson (*below*).

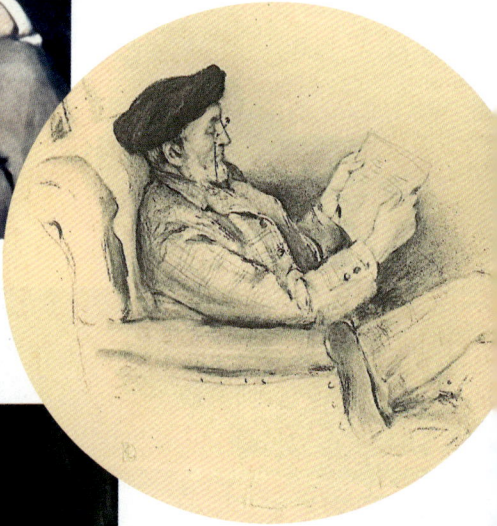

Frederick Macmillan by
Sir Hubert von Herkomer.

George Macmillan by
John Singer Sargent in 1925.

Maurice Crawford
Macmillan by Sargent.

Malcolm Macmillan. The frontispiece of *Selected Letters of Malcolm Kingsley Macmillan*, 1893.

John Victor Macmillan, photographed by Walter Stoneman.

Emma in old age.

lexander Macmillan's office,
Bedford Street.

John Tenniel's illustrations for the first edition of *Alice's Adventures in Wonderland* (1865).

John Tenniel's illustrations for the first edition
of *Through the Looking-Glass* (1871).

Illustrations from
Tom Brown's School Days (1882)
by A. Hughes and S. P. Hall.

The Statesman's Year-Book is still published today by part of the group that owns Macmillan. Martin continued as editor until December 1882, when he was compelled by ill-health to sell his copyright back to Macmillan, and the editorship was taken over by John Scott Keltie. However, the files of correspondence received from Martin make it clear that he was difficult to deal with, demanding and emotional, as he and his ever-expanding family struggled to make ends meet. In 1864 he complained to his publisher that he 'had been fighting the battle of life in rather a rough manner and, often wounded and trod underfoot, [was] sore all over.'[17] A year later, as the second volume went to press, he wrote:

In the circular respecting my book which you had the kindness to hand me this morning, I miss my name. I miss it likewise in various advertisements in *The Times, Publishers' Circular* and other papers – not to mention its absence in the book itself, which is noticed by many friends who have spoken to me on the subject. You will not accuse me of vanity, I trust, if I tell you I am sorry to see my name thus ignored. It is simply that I have given a vast amount of labour to the book and continue to give it in the hope that the outlay will not only bring me a small return in money but lead to my name becoming more known than it is at present so as to lift me from that dreary sphere of labour, paid by the day or week, in which literature is a mere trade and the right to live must be purchased by never-ending anxiety.[18]

The strangest item in this list of complaints is the suggestion that his name was not mentioned in the *Year-Book* itself, as the title page very clearly identifies him as its author.

The *Year-Book* remained Martin's major occupation: 'to give the greatest mass of information, to give the newest and to give it absolutely correct, has been and will be my constant endeavour and though we have hitherto failed in achieving all we might wish,

I think we are getting hopefully nearer and nearer the aim'.[19] Macmillan provided Martin with other sources of income, publishing his well-received *The Life of John Clare*, in 1866, and in the same year *Stories of Banks and Bankers*. The editor also wrote for various newspapers, edited other almanacs, and was an occasional contributor to the *Athenaeum*. 1870 saw the publication of a *Handbook of Contemporary Biography* but its production led to a nasty fight between Martin and Macmillan. The issue, according to Martin, was that the original agreement for the *Handbook* had been made back in 1866, when Macmillan had offered Martin £200 for the work, promising that all the proof-reading and corrections would be done by 'gentlemen of [Macmillan's] acquaintance in Oxford and Cambridge'. Martin said that he had delivered the manuscript on time to Clay's the printers where it had lain untouched for several years despite repeated reminders from Martin and 'remarks by Mr Craik that in his opinion the book would never pay.' When the proof sheets eventually were returned to Martin they needed completely updating, and he approached Macmillan for more money to complete the task, whereupon, according to Martin, Alexander 'addressed me in a way I consider utterly cruel and unjust – it came upon me like thunder from a blue sky. In all my dealings with you I have been the very opposite from mercenary and it is on this account mainly that I deeply feel the injustice of your reproaches.' Martin demanded that Macmillan issue him with a new contract for the *Year-Book*, as he felt that the original agreement signed in 1862, a document he had 'scarcely glanced at', had been superseded by many verbal concessions, and as he wanted to draw up his will, he needed the precise state of copyright to be documented. Alexander seems to have decided that this letter was better left ignored, and a few days later Martin backtracked . . . 'not a line from you? Are you displeased with my previous letter . . . life is short and memory shorter. If I valued your friendship less than I do, I would not press for the written agreement . . . I am truly anxious to be on the old friendly terms with you.'[20]

The agreement was re-drawn, but it did nothing to improve the financial position. In November 1870, Martin wrote 'I hoped the tide of ill-success of my Year-Book had turned last year and hearing that there is again nothing to divide I feel more miserable than I can tell you . . . ten years . . . it has ruined me in income and ruined me in health and I can go no further.' He complained that he was losing his eyesight and now had seven children to support. He wondered if another publisher like Murray or Longmans would take it: 'I should be glad to cede my copyright and whole interest in [it] on reimbursement of the "time-capital" and continue the editorship on an annual salary of £200 plus office expenses.'[21] Nothing came of this. The revised written agreement between Martin and his publisher did not bring their acrimonious disputes to an end. Martin was drawing £150 a year and entitled to half profits, and Craik advised that the calculation of profits must include the salary cost. Martin disagreed furiously, and was in the wrong. The following year he lost his temper again, writing to Alexander 'will you kindly inform me whether it is with your consent that Mr Craik is withholding from me the share of profits usually paid over to me at this time of year.'[22] In 1879 the Prime Minister, Benjamin Disraeli, who found The Statesman's Year-Book useful, awarded Martin a pension of £100 a year. But that would not be the end of the sorry tale.

Macmillan may have dodged the Colenso controversy and extricated himself tactfully from the Kingsley–Newman argument, but he was not afraid to contribute to the debates rocking the Anglican Church, and in November 1865 he published anonymously a work which set everyone talking. The author, whose identity remained hidden for nearly a year after publication, was John Seeley, the son of the brothers' old employer, the bookseller Robert Benton Seeley. Robert had taken his boy to visit the Macmillan shop in Cambridge in 1852 when he became a student at Christ's College. On graduating in 1859 John took a job teaching Classics at City of London School, and in 1863 was appointed Professor of Latin at University College London. Alexander and John were thus old friends with several decades of mutual history. The book which Alexander agreed to publish was *Ecce Homo: A Survey of the Life and Work of Jesus Christ*. John Seeley had taught at the Working Men's College alongside Maurice and the other Christian Socialists and had been influenced by the Positivist movement. His book focused primarily on Christ as a man and a moral philosopher, leaving for a later date the discussion of what this meant spiritually or theologically. Seeley's Jesus was a man fitted for Victorian times, a man whose love of humanity and moral character would provide an example that all could follow. Jesus was brought to life as a real person, within a recognizable nineteenth-century political context.

Seeley wished to remain anonymous as he knew his views would hurt his family; their evangelical beliefs were strong, and they took the Bible literally. He also wanted to avoid the appalling treatment that had been meted out to Colenso, and to the authors of *Essays and Reviews*, some of whom had been dragged into the courts and charged with heresy. Macmillan was happy to keep Seeley's name secret, and used the mystery cynically as a marketing strategy; it created the false impression that the author was concealing his identity because he was better known than he actually was. Slowly the reviews began to appear, and sure enough there were some extremely damaging comments made. But the more intemperate the reviewers, the more sales increased. The book went through six editions in its first year and by March 1867 had sold nearly 20,000 copies, earning royalties of over £1,000 for Seeley (around £100,000 in today's values). Fans included Dean Stanley, Goldwin Smith and Charles Kingsley and his wife and daughters. The review in *The Guardian* (not to be confused with *The Manchester Guardian*: this one was the leading weekly newspaper of the Church of England) could not have been more enthusiastic, and did much to reassure a more conservative audience: it may have been written by William Gladstone, at that time Chancellor of the Exchequer. On the other hand, the article in the *Quarterly Review*, probably by Bishop 'Soapy Sam' Wilberforce, was so rude that even more copies were bought in sympathy. When Lord Shaftesbury, the well-known social campaigner and evangelical Anglican, was heard at a public meeting to call it 'the most pestilential book ever vomited from the jaws of Hell', its success was assured, with another 9,000 copies sold in the next ten months. Macmillan advertised it as 'A Dangerous Book' and continued to stir the pot regarding the authorship. His son George claimed that his father once organized a party 'to come and meet the author of *Ecce Homo*', invited all the obvious candidates including Seeley, but let them all go home again none the wiser.

However, Seeley's cover was blown by the Cambridge academic clique at the end of 1866, and his identity was revealed in *The Spectator* and *The Athenaeum* in November and December, causing much distress to Seeley's relations. The controversy did his career no harm at all, as in 1869 both Gladstone and Kingsley supported his appointment as Regius Professor of History at Cambridge. J. R. Seeley is today recognized as a significant historian, especially of British imperialism, yet another man who owed much of his career to the care Macmillan had taken with him in his first publishing endeavours.

The story of Macmillan and Seeley's relationship during the first year or so of *Ecce Homo*'s publication is so illustrative of Alexander's character at this time that it is worth looking at some of their exchanges more carefully. First of all, Alexander took a chance on the book because he genuinely loved it, he thought it was well written, but more importantly, he thought it was important and valuable in the struggle against atheism which was sweeping the land. Seeley had struggled through a personal crisis of faith and had emerged revitalized and determined to reach out to other non-believers. He made it clear time and again in letters to his friends and family that he had not written the book for steadfast Christians, but for the doubters. He wrote to his sister Ann: 'Tell me dear Ann, what is to be done for the poor sceptics . . . as you do not meet them, you probably think there are not many of them, but I tell you there are so many that I sometimes wonder whether the Church and Christianity in England can last another twenty years . . . one book that establishes something and gives people something to stand upon may make a great difference.'[23] This chimed with Alexander's own concerns: that was why he had been so angry with Colenso, who had only given more ammunition to the doubters by bringing the Old Testament into ridicule. There must be a better way to bring the teachings of the Bible into harmony with the Victorian quest for scientific and historic truth, and Seeley's fact-based analysis of the Gospels tried to do just that.

After the book was published, Alexander's best hopes for it were more than realized. Its sales were well beyond expectations and it brought very welcome publicity to the firm. He was particularly thrilled that it brought him into close correspondence with William Gladstone, who wrote to him on Christmas Day 1865 expressing extraordinary enthusiasm.

> I have sometimes had tokens of your kind remembrance, in the receipt of new publications, where I had felt ashamed to send you a merely formal acknowledgement – now my acknowledgment must be more than formal I still feel ashamed because it will be wholly insufficient. It is very rare with me, under the pressure of office, to read a book of the nature of *Ecce Homo* . . . but from the moment when I opened that volume, I felt the touch of a powerful heart drawing me on . . . I will not attempt to draw out the long catalogue of its praises: but I will venture to say I know of, or recollect, no production of equal force that recent years can boast of . . . this noble book.[24]

Alexander had started a correspondence with Gladstone only a few months earlier, in July of that year, wondering whether the statesman could be persuaded to revise his University Press published translation of Homer, but 'I cannot honestly say that I would like to see the country deprived of your service in her financial affairs.' Now he felt able to share his thoughts on Seeley's work with Gladstone himself. He claimed that he had received the manuscript anonymously, which was probably not true, and as he read it:

The reality of the Temptation, and the Victory over it, the force of this example, His human love and righteousness and purity, came to me with a power I had never felt before, so that I was almost overwhelmed with a sense of shame at the poverty and feebleness of our Christian life. Can this be our King, whom we have bound ourselves to follow and can we be content to live as we do live. A new meaning seemed to flash on me from the familiar words of our Lord "if you will do my will ye shall know of my doctrine" . . . I seemed to see the true road to a unity of Christendom.[25]

Macmillan suggested that a really good review piece in *The Guardian* might help to spread the word, and it seems likely that Gladstone did indeed contribute the review in that magazine the following month: in March Macmillan was forwarding a new work on economics to the Chancellor, adding 'The author and publisher of *Ecce Homo* owe you much gratitude and they feel it.'[26]

Already Macmillan's religious delight in the message of the book was multiplied by his delight as a publisher in the sales figures. But his mischievous sense of humour threatened to mar his relationship with Seeley: it is clear from Seeley's letters that his concern to preserve anonymity was genuinely based on fear of upsetting his deeply religious family. On the other hand, Alexander was put under enormous pressure by his circle of authors and the academics he was cultivating to reveal the name. At times he was happy to play along because the anonymity helped make sales to curious readers, but he also stirred things up, dropping clues and half-hints, half-denials. For instance, after Tom Hughes expressed a view that the book was written by Shairp, a professor of poetry at St Andrews, Alexander told Seeley that he had written to Shairp asking if it was him. None of this was amusing to Seeley. When eventually his name came out, Seeley was furious, writing to his old friend Joseph Mayor: 'I am angry with people for their reckless curiosity and with some of my friends Abbott, Macmillan, Gimson, for their utter inability to hold their tongues . . . I receive now – from relatives and others – letters classing me with Judas Iscariot.'[27] Even though it was now common knowledge, Seeley refused to let Macmillan acknowledge it publicly, and the book was never published under Seeley's name until after his death in 1895, suggesting that Macmillan was shamed by his failure to play his part in keeping the secret. When Seeley wrote a slightly disappointing sequel, *Natural Religion*, in the 1870s, Macmillan published it as 'by the author of *Ecce Homo*', again refusing to name Seeley, although by now everyone knew. Whatever his irritation with Alexander, he still admitted 'No other publisher would have done for the book what you have done.'[28]

Alexander's relationship with Gladstone flourished. The Chancellor, who lived at 11 Carlton Gardens, was known for hosting weekly 'Thursday Breakfasts', and Alexander became a regular attendee. In 1869 the firm published Gladstone's work *Juventus Mundi: The Gods and Men of the Heroic Age*, and in 1876 *Homeric Synchronism: An Enquiry into the Time and Place of Homer* (with Alexander unable to persuade the author that 'Homer in History' would be a more attractive title). The greatest coup was that Gladstone contributed a volume to J. R. Green's series of school primers, again on the subject of Homer. This relationship was one of Alexander's great prides.

There is one more controversialist whom Macmillan was delighted to add to his roster of writers: Matthew Arnold. He would have been thrilled to add any member of Dr Thomas Arnold's family to the catalogue, especially after the success of *Tom Brown's School Days*, but Matthew was already proving himself a noteworthy essayist, poet and critic, and the ablest of the Arnold family. In 1857 he had been elected Professor of Poetry at Oxford. His relationship with Macmillan had only just begun when his review of Colenso's *Commentary on the Pentateuch* launched him more firmly into the public's consciousness. He became an occasional guest at the Tobacco Parliaments, and later a regular guest at Alexander's All Fools' Day dinners. In 1864 his brief work, *A French Eton*, attacked the English public school system, suggesting that by keeping fees so high, the

English public schools were failing the aspirational middle classes, to the detriment of the men who would be required to govern an ever-expanding empire. Arnold knew what he was talking about, as he mainly drew his living as an inspector of schools, and he dreamt of a great future of subsidized education. Macmillan had helped him with the research for this piece, gathering information from Edward Thring, reforming headmaster of Uppingham, on the economics of a small public school.

Arnold's poetry was some of the best-loved of late Victorian England, and Macmillan was proud to publish it, including his best-known piece, 'Dover Beach'. The returns were not great; Macmillan earned less than £10 per year from the *Collected Poems*, but it never dinted Alexander's pride. He was not Arnold's only publisher: George Smith of Smith, Elder seems to have had a more convivial relationship with his author, but Arnold's letters to and from Macmillan discussed the content of his writings rather than just matters of business. In 1862 Macmillan wrote to Arnold:

> The stuff that passes for criticism in our common English press is, as a rule, at present the dreariest stuff – barren platitudes or stupid and impertinent witticisms. I don't read all of course but I see none that have an approach to the honest pains which Brimley used to take with his work . . . too often it is about how to say a clever thing. Not really how to make clear the character of the book you are handling.[29]

It was with the enthusiasm of the genuine admirer that Alexander encouraged Arnold to pull together his *Essays in Criticism* in 1865: the volume went through many editions and reprints, although the most famous essay, 'Culture and Anarchy', went to George Smith.

Alexander was confident enough to tell authors, even well-known and respected authors, exactly what he thought of their work. In 1864 *Macmillan's Magazine* published anonymously a serialized novel, *A Son of the Soil*, the author of which, Mrs Oliphant, was at that time enjoying great success with her *Carlingford* series. Macmillan had known Margaret Oliphant for a decade or more, having been introduced to her by her cousin George Wilson. It may be true, as John Sutherland writes, that it was 'one of the more depressing and Calvinistic of Oliphant's novels',[30] and when the next year it came to the end of the serialization and Alexander had to consider publishing it in book form, he did not hold back, even though another publisher was prepared to take it off his hands.

> I am disinclined to part with a pet child, even though he has taken to private ways of his own. The last chapter is beautiful – very, and shows what might have been: 'The Not Impossible Book'. If you could eliminate the polemic which is an artistic mistake and dreadfully weakens the general interest, and make [the hero's] Oxford career a little more probable, it would do. I daresay you will see all that as you look [it] over yourself . . . with all its faults it is a very excellent story and has very high qualities. I am always hoping some day however that you will do a thorough work of art, painfully and carefully worked out. Forgive my preaching, I was a schoolmaster many years.[31]

Mrs Oliphant took the criticism in good heart: Macmillan published this novel and several more, as well as commissioning her to produce travel writings on Italian cities and a *Literary History of England*.

A year later Macmillan found himself wrestling, in correspondence at least, with Caroline Norton, who had famously fought her way through the divorce courts and campaigned for significant improvements in the rights of married women. This well-connected and strongly opinionated woman had been writing poetry and fiction since her youth and had contributed to the *Magazine* on and off over several years, much to Alexander's pride and delight. In 1866, Masson had started to serialize her final novel, *Old Sir Douglas*. However he and Alexander agreed, when they saw her chapter for the April issue, that she had let her pen run away with her. As Alexander politely put it in his first letter on the subject, 'I think you can hardly have duly considered this chapter, as it has an air of personal pique that would be liable to very severe strictures, and I think most hurtful to yourself.'[32] The issue was the implied criticism of Queen and Court. If he had been expecting compliance and regret, he got the opposite. Norton had been a close friend of Lord Melbourne in Queen Victoria's early days, and, feeling sure of her ground, not only refused to alter her words, but insisted on withdrawing the whole book. 'Each of my novels has been written, not as a mere story but with a distinct purpose, and I cannot unweave my book because those who differ from me are startled at what one of the personages in it is made to say.'[33]

Losing a serial halfway through its publication would have been highly embarrassing to Masson and Macmillan. The debate rumbled on with neither side giving way. Mrs Norton expressed surprise that the publisher of *Ecce Homo* was being so squeamish. In June, Macmillan wrote again: 'I would repeat that the point we object to is the personal reflection on the Queen. You have been kind enough to refer to my inconsistency in regard to the story and the attacks made on *Ecce Homo*. But the cases have this great difference – that the one is dealing with principles, not with persons. As I have said before, I have not the slightest objection to any dealing with mean craving after Court favour, or social follies of the kind. Personal scandal of any kind, or reflections of a personal kind regarding the Queen, do not appear to me needful to the maintenance of great principles.'[34] It appears that Mrs Norton finally gave way, as the serialization was resumed in the September issue, without containing anything that could offend the royal family.

By the mid-1860s, Alexander was presiding over a profitable and well-respected publishing concern. Even so, the brushes with controversy and the occasional disapproval of his old friends continued to shake his confidence and caused him distress and worry. He wrote to an old friend, a clergyman who had commented on the many debates which seemed to accompany Macmillan's progress:

> Our controversies go out in God's Providence. They have their value I do not doubt but how they pale in colour and [fade] like spectres of the night before the <u>Fact</u> of human and divine Love, as seen in flesh and blood and as cherished in living memory, equally precious as when it was visible. I daresay that I who am in the middle of it all get a little more tired of controversy than you who see it from a distance.[35]

Bringing George Lillie Craik into the business took a weight of administrative burden off his shoulders, and a piece of publishing good fortune, in the shape of a little girl called Alice, would give him even more financial stability.

– 11 –

ALICE IN WONDERLAND

and

OTHER SURPRISING ADVENTURES

Alice in Wonderland, *Mad Hatter's Tea Party illustration*

'My dear, here we must run as fast as we can, just to stay in place. And if you wish to go anywhere you must run twice as fast as that.'

Lewis Carroll

An unexpected bonus of Macmillan's position as the Publisher to Oxford University Press was the introduction made by the University Printer, Thomas Combe, to Charles Dodgson, a tutor in mathematics at Christ Church, in the autumn of 1863. Dodgson had spent the previous year working on a manuscript of the children's tale which was to be published as *Alice's Adventures in Wonderland*, and was paying Combe to have it printed, with illustrations commissioned at his own expense from John Tenniel, the famous *Punch* cartoonist. Dodgson gave Combe £140 to print 2,000 copies on the University presses, and now arranged for the books to be distributed by Macmillan on 10 per cent commission. This was the beginning of an extraordinarily fruitful publishing relationship which lasted through to Dodgson's death in 1898 – there are over two thousand letters in existence between the author and the firm, with many more missing. It was also extremely unusual, in that throughout his life, Dodgson retained the copyright of his works, paid the expenses of printing and took all the publishing risk: Macmillan received the same 10 per cent commission on every book sold.

Charles Lutwidge Dodgson was born in 1832, the eldest son of a Cheshire cleric, and was educated at Rugby and Oxford. By his mid-thirties he had established himself as a senior member of the academic staff at Christ Church, and was a formidable scholar in mathematics. But his fame has been built on what he achieved under the 'Lewis Carroll' pseudonym; his second life began when he promised ten-year-old Alice Liddell, daughter of the Dean of his College, to write down a story he had made up for her and her sisters one afternoon while rowing them on the Thames. The original manuscript for *Alice's Adventures under Ground*, in Dodgson's own handwriting, is held by the British Library.

Alexander held Dodgson's hand throughout the initial printing contract with Combe, advising on details such as the weight of the paper, the dimensions of the book, the list of the recipients for review copies, even the title. In October 1864 he wrote to Dodgson: 'I think all the experiments in the title which you propose will be most effectively made in the sheet by Mr Combe. You will never be able to judge absolutely till you see it there. I should certainly incline to put the dedication in one size smaller type . . .'[1] By February 1865 Macmillan was becoming nervous that Combe might not be up to the job: 'We agreed if you remember that the book should be the same size as Kingsley's *Water Babies* . . . if Mr Combe has any doubt about it he can easily borrow a copy . . . I hope he won't make any mistake about this, it is perfectly simple . . . paper of 60lb weight would be the thing.'[2] In May he wrote again:

> I quite agree with you that a slight increase of the outer and diminution of the inner margin will be an improvement . . . you had better measure it and not with your eye and mark it with a pen or pencil so that no mistake can occur. When this is done I think we can go ahead. The devices [engravings to go on the cover] are being cut. But they are much more elaborate than is usual with cloth blocks and I fear will take some time. Had you been content with puss, we could have done it quicker. The young lady and all her surroundings will take some time and labour.[3]

By this point they had already missed the Easter publishing season, but at the end of June 1865 Combe sent the first sheets to Macmillan for binding, and on 15 July Dodgson was at Macmillan's offices signing early hand-bound copies for despatch to his friends. But on 19 July, Tenniel, who had a reputation to maintain, saw a copy and complained to Dodgson about the reproduction of his illustrations. In a panic, Dodgson asked Macmillan to get a quotation for printing the whole thing again, this time from Macmillan's preferred printer, Richard Clay in Cambridge. Even though this new outlay represented a very significant financial setback for Dodgson, who was after all bearing the costs himself, he pressed on, and in November 1865 received the first bound copies from Macmillan, just in time for Christmas. Sales crept steadily upwards; in August 1866 Macmillan ordered another 3,000 copies, in February 1867 they had sold more than 6,000. The flawed original Oxford copies, nearly 2,000 of them, were despatched to Appletons in New York, as Dodgson was less interested in the book's reception among the Americans. Today, surviving copies sell for $50,000. By 1869, *Alice* had been through five editions and has never been out of print. Translations into French and German, published in 1869, marked Macmillan's first venture into European 'own language' markets. Alexander had originally advised Dodgson to find a foreign publisher for these editions, but the author persuaded him to publish under the Macmillan name. In 1871, when Macmillan published *Through the Looking-Glass*, they sold 9,000 copies in two weeks.

The 1889 *Catalogue* lists over a dozen children's books by Lewis Carroll, as well as six mathematical textbooks published under his real name. Dodgson was a perfectionist when it came to the look of the books he wrote, and in Macmillan he found a publisher both sympathetic to his ambitions and patient in the extreme. His relationship with the firm was not without its ups and downs, but Alexander took all Dodgson's letters and complaints in his stride. Dodgson was certainly more demanding than any other of Macmillan's authors, but he was also the client and picking up the bills, and Alexander recognized that both men were driven by the same goal of perfection in publishing, which took time and endless patience. The publisher was perfectly capable of giving as good as he got, being firm when he needed to be and offering valuable counsel. When Dodgson asked if he should spend more money on promotion, Alexander advised against it: 'Each copy of your book that is sold is an advertisement.'[4]

Alexander had accommodated many of Dodgson's ideas to connect with his young readers, such as binding *Alice in Wonderland* in red leather and typesetting 'The Mouse's Tale' poem, which appears in the book, in the shape of a tail. He let Dodgson add Easter and Christmas messages as the reprints happened. However, when Dodgson asked whether it was possible to insert a slip into the books requesting all his little girl fans to send in photographs, his publisher put his foot down. Alexander must have been alarmed at the prospect, but he wrote teasingly:

> Did you ever take a shower bath? Or do you remember your first? To appeal to all your young admirers for their photographs! If your shower bath were filled a-top with bricks instead of water it would be about the fate you court. But if you will do it – there is no help for it, and as in duty bound we will help you to the self-immolation. Cartes! I should think so indeed! – cartloads of them. Think of the postmen, open an office for relief at the North Pole and another at the Equator. Ask President Grant, the Emperor of China, the Governor General of India, the whatever do you call him of Melbourne, if they won't help you. But it's no use remonstrating with you. I am resigned. I return from Scotland next Monday week. I shall be braced for encountering the awful idea.[5]

Dodgson got the message and dropped the plan. And when in 1871 he asked Macmillan what he thought about delaying the publication of *Through the Looking-Glass* until after Christmas, to be sure of receiving Tenniel's illustrations in plenty of time, Alexander replied:

> What do I think! That your proposal is worse than the cruellest ogre ever conceived in darkest and most malignant moods. What do I think! Why half the children will be laid up with pure vexation and anguish of spirit. Plum pudding of the delicatest, toys the most elaborate, will have no charm. Darkness will come over all hearths, gloom will hover over the brightest board. Don't think of it for a moment. The book must come out for Christmas, or I don't know what will be the consequence.[6]

Alexander got his way: although the first edition is marked 1872, the copies were flying off the press well before Christmas.

The two men became good friends. Dodgson became well known to the whole family; he entertained Macmillan in his rooms in Oxford, he stayed with him in Tooting, he dined at the Garrick with Alexander and his son George and went to the theatre with them. At times he asked Alexander to gauge his children's opinion on items of literary style. Sadly, although Dodgson was a keen photographer of children, Alexander's seem to be the only boys and girls in his social circle that he did not photograph, not even little Mary (born in 1874). Alexander's oldest daughter Margaret's reminiscences speak lovingly of Charles Kingsley and other authors, but never mention the other Charles, the Reverend Dodgson.

Dodgson's relationship with the firm went far beyond what was normal for an author: Alexander was happy to get his clerks to run London errands for Dodgson, such as buying his theatre tickets for him; copying out all the speeches from *Alice* so that they could be registered as dramas; even replying to the correspondence which arrived in Bedford Street addressed to Lewis Carroll. In return, Dodgson was happy to pay tribute to the service he received from Macmillan – at one point when he was embroiled in public controversy over the profits being made by the retailers, he wrote:

The publisher contributes about as much as the bookseller in time and bodily labour, but in mental toil and trouble a great deal more. I speak, with some personal knowledge of the matter, having myself, for some twenty years, inflicted on that most patient and painstaking firm, Messrs. Macmillan and Co., about as much wear and worry as ever publishers have lived through. The day when they undertake a book for me is a *dies nefastus* [an unlucky day] for them. From that day till the book is out – an interval of some two or three years on an average – there is no pause in 'the pelting of the pitiless storm' of directions and questions on every conceivable detail. To say that every question gets a courteous and thoughtful reply – that they are still outside a lunatic asylum – and that they still regard me with some degree of charity – is to speak volumes in praise of their good temper and of their health, bodily and mental.[7]

The respect was mutual.

1866 was a golden year for Macmillan's publishing ventures: the sales of *Ecce Homo* and *Alice* were rising daily, and waiting in the wings were Yonge's *The Dove in the Eagle's Nest*, Huxley's *Lessons in Elementary Physiology*, Kingsley's *Hereward the Wake*, and Oliphant's *A Son of the Soil*, as well as numerous mathematical and classical textbooks and primers, further volumes of the *Globe* Shakespeare, and the *Globe* edition of the *Works of Sir Walter Scott*. With Craik at his side, Alexander was no longer so overwhelmed by the material pouring in on him, and could take the time to initiate new projects, and to continue to improve the material at his disposal. Looking through his voluminous correspondence one can see that some of his major commercial successes, such as William Allingham's *Ballad Book* and Mark Lemon's *Jest Book* were his own initiatives; and that it was Alexander who outlined the arrangement and treatment of Alexander Smith's edition of Robert Burns, collating the material himself.

One of the titles being prepared for publication the following year was neither fiction, nor politics nor textbook, and Alexander was delighted with it. Sir Samuel White Baker's *The Albert N'Yanza, Great Basin of the Nile, and Explorations of the Nile Sources*, a weighty tome of nearly six hundred pages including two maps, twenty-four full-page illustrations and vignette portraits of the author and his wife, would run through four editions and four reprints in the next ten years.

Macmillan had begun to take an interest in travel writing at the start of the decade, working with a polymath and scholar by the name of Francis Galton, half-cousin to Charles Darwin. Galton may have known the Macmillan brothers in Cambridge in the early 1840s as yet another Trinity man, but had since made a reputation for himself as an explorer in Africa. On his return he joined the Royal Geographical Society as Secretary and acted as editor of three collections of travel writings published by Macmillan between 1860 and 1863 under the title *Vacation Tourists and Notes of Travel*. These had been well received, if hard to collate, and had contained gems such as Leslie Stephen's account of ascending the Allelein-Horn, Roden Noel's 'Syrian Travels', Archibald Geikie's 'Geological Notes on the Auvergne', and 'Christmas in Montenegro' by 'IM'.

It was rare for these travel essays to be anonymized, but this last essay was particularly unusual, as 'IM' stood for Irby and Mackenzie – Miss Adeline Pauline Irby and Miss Georgina Mary Muir Mackenzie, to be precise. These intrepid women may have met when Pauline started giving classes for women at F. D. Maurice's Working Men's College. Bored at home, they began in their twenties to travel to Europe, unaccompanied except by a maid, visiting the spa towns of Germany and Austria. Their lives changed for ever in 1858, when they were arrested as spies in the Carpathian Mountains on the grounds that they had been spreading 'pan-Slavistic tendencies'. If ever an arrest was counter-productive, this was it, for although they were released after consular pressure, they became fascinated by the issues raised, and deeply sympathetic to the cause of the Serbian nationalists under the yoke of the Ottoman Empire. In particular they were appalled by the plight of Serbian Orthodox women and girls who had poor access to education or work. In 1862, Macmillan published *Across the Carpathians*, a 300-page account of their travels, which they promoted with lectures and a fund-raising campaign. Eventually Muir Mackenzie opted for respectable married life, but Irby, after many struggles, opened a chain of schools for girls in Sarajevo, which she managed to protect even during the Bulgarian atrocities of the 1870s. Irby is buried in Sarajevo, and her name is still revered by its citizens, with one of the main streets named Mis Irbina.

Adventures such as these sold books, and fascinated Alexander

Macmillan, who was bitten by the armchair travel bug; the catalogue began to feature regular accounts of exploration and vacation. 1862 saw Seemann's book on Fiji, followed by Edward Wilton's account of the Negev in 1863 and Anderson's *Seven Months in Poland* in 1864. 1865 saw two highly popular works: Lady Duff Gordon's *Letters from Egypt* and William Gifford Palgrave's *Arabia* in 1865. These were all interesting books and did well enough for the firm, but Alexander was determined to find a category-killing bestseller, at a time when all anyone in England seemed to care about was the search for the source of the Nile. As Samuel Baker was to put it, in the preface to his book:

> In the history of the Nile there was a void: its Sources were a mystery. The Ancients devoted much attention to this problem: but in vain. The Emperor Nero sent an expedition under the command of two centurions, as described by Seneca. Even Roman energy failed to break the spell that guarded these secret fountains. The expedition sent by Mehemet Ali Pasha, the celebrated Viceroy of Egypt, closed a long term of unsuccessful search. The work has now been accomplished. Three English parties, and only three, have at various periods started upon this obscure mission: each has gained its end. Bruce won the source of the Blue Nile; Speke and Grant won the Victoria, source of the great White Nile, and I have been permitted to succeed in completing the Nile Sources by the discovery of the great reservoir of the equatorial waters, the ALBERT NYANZA, from which the river issues as the entire White Nile.[8]

Alexander had tried to make some African capital out of his previous acquaintance with David Livingstone, but despite several letters had not been able to squeeze so much as an article for the *Magazine* out of the great explorer. But late in 1865, as the newspapers thrilled to the exploits of Samuel Baker, who had discovered and named Lake Albert as a previously unknown source of the Nile,

Macmillan was contacted by Baker's family and offered the chance to bid for Baker's memoir. Fortuitously, he had published a couple of pamphlets concerned with the military volunteer movement in the early 1860s written by Samuel's younger brother James. His negotiations with Colonel Valentine Baker, another of Samuel's brothers, show that he was prepared to risk a truly significant amount of money to capture the prize. In November 1865, Macmillan wrote to the Colonel offering an advance of £4,500 plus half-profits, or £2,000 up front and two-thirds profits to the author, assuming the book would be comparable in size to those of Livingstone and Speke. For comparison, Alexander had only paid £500 up front and two-thirds profits to Palgrave for *Travels in Arabia*. After some brinkmanship on the part of the Baker brothers, Macmillan was pushed to £2,500 up front and two-thirds profits.

The negotiations are interesting, but the truly fascinating letter in the files is from Alexander to Samuel in early May 1866, as he started to read the manuscript.

> There is a terrible defect in your summing up. You should say something about Mrs Baker. It may be as slight as you please, very little more than your most tender and delicate allusion at starting, but indeed something should be said. You mention Richarn [one of the bearers] and his wife and your man. It struck me as strange to a degree. Of course I understand your feeling of not wearing your heart upon your sleeve, but I do think people would wonder.[9]

Had Alexander heard the rumours that might have explained Baker's reticence about his wife, Florence? Or was this an extremely tactless suggestion? Baker was indeed very nervous about discussing the role played by Florence, who had been with him throughout his appalling and dangerous trek across Africa, had nearly died on more than one occasion, and had saved his life on others with bravery and skilled nursing, and she is seldom mentioned in the book.

The truth that would have shocked his Victorian readership to the core was that Florence was not his wife at any stage in their African adventures, and they were only married on their return to England in November 1865. Samuel had found nineteen-year-old Florence in 1859 at an auction of white slaves in a Turkish-administered town in Bulgaria. Her parents had been killed in the 1848 uprising in Hungary, and Baker bought her, and subsequently fell in love with her. They became inseparable, but the longer they were together, the worse Samuel's problem became: how was he to explain this relationship to his four daughters at home, who he had left with their aunt after his first wife died?

The final paragraph of the book as published does pay tribute to Florence. 'Had I really come from the Nile Sources? It was no dream. A witness sat before me; a face still young, but bronzed like an Arab by years of exposure to a burning sun; haggard and worn with toil and sickness, and shaded with cares, happily now past; the devoted companion of my pilgrimage, to whom I owed success and life – my wife.'[10] Baker had taken Alexander's advice to heart, realizing that it was the presence of a woman on this journey which differentiated it from competitor titles. The public loved Florence and thrilled to the dangers undergone by a white woman in darkest Africa, as they saw it. Samuel was knighted in August 1866 and Florence became Lady Baker, but the rumours about her origins continued to rumble: Queen Victoria refused to receive her at Court, despite her delight that Samuel had named his great lake after her beloved Prince Albert.

Macmillan published nearly all of Baker's subsequent works, although the negotiations for the second book, on Baker's travels through Abyssinia, suggest that he was slightly nervous that he might have overpaid for the first. In March 1867 they were discussing the second edition of *Albert-Nyanza*, and the first edition of *Abyssinia*. They had agreed that Baker would receive £400 for the second edition of 3,000 copies of the first book, and for the second, Alexander suggested £1,000 for 500 copies and two-thirds profits. When Baker protested how much less this was than he had commanded for the first book, Macmillan replied, 'though one may venture now and then to do a plucky and unprofitable thing, but . . . we cannot do all our business on such terms, even when we are doing it for one we honour so much as we do . . . my calculation is that you will have received £3,900 and we have £700 . . . our general overhead stands at about 5 per cent of sales – were I to take this into account our actual profits would I am afraid be less than nothing.'[11] He need not have been too concerned: over the next few years *Nyanza* sold some 25,000 copies, and even *Abyssinia* sold 18,000.

It seemed that the publishing business had reached a golden period, as bestsellers fell into Alexander's lap. Yet just as he felt he had reached clear smooth waters, his family life, which had seemed so promising when they settled in London, was about to undergo some terrible shocks and losses.

DEATH COMES TO
THE ELMS

William Alexander Macmillan

'That loss is common would not make
My own less bitter, rather more:
Too common! Never morning wore
To evening, but some heart did break.'

Alfred, Lord Tennyson

THE MOVE TO Tooting was a massive relief for the Macmillan family, not just for the simplification of Alexander's business life, but in terms of the space it gave the children, who 'tumbled about in the grass' all day long. He remarked that it was funny that they had moved to London to find themselves living in the countryside. 'I never knew what the blessing of a country life was before.'[1] Alexander had always valued the limited time he was able to spend with the children, taking them on holidays as early as 1861 to the south coast, where Malcolm was nearly washed away by a big wave, and where two-year-old Olive, or Toodles, walked 'about four miles on her own private and personal legs, a great part of it being on a shingle beach.'[2] The house began to be filled with animals – a pair of parakeets or love birds, called Major and Mrs Buckley in honour of two characters in a Henry Kingsley novel; a pony, a cat, and a dog, a gift from Henry Kingsley himself, called Viola: 'she gets well pulled about by the childers and don't bite them. Her chief love is the stable boy whom she follows after at night till he has to scold her home. I think I am next in her love.'[3]

Alexander discovered an interest in the garden, asking Kingsley to send him seeds, employing a couple of gardeners, and begging R. D. Blackmore, who alternated between writing novels and running a successful market garden, for trees and advice on how and where to plant them. Sitting in the garden after work in the evenings, or at the weekends with his friends and authors, was a huge pleasure to him. At first it seemed that the stress that had been affecting the health of both his wife and his sister-in-law, living in cramped conditions in Cambridge, might be eased by this new life, and in February 1864, Caroline bore a fifth child, William Alexander, generally called Winks.

The eight children who had been born in Cambridge were

growing up fast. Having created a strong foundation for the business, Alexander began to focus on the need to protect the family's legacy and secure a smooth succession. Some big decisions were required about education, and he was faced with the same problem as many newly rich middle-class businessmen of the time: how best to educate the next generation, who were growing up in such different conditions from those which had shaped their parents, and whose expectations would be very different.

The challenge for Macmillan and his publishing contemporaries was to rise above their origins without losing their entrepreneurial drive. Financial success alone did not entitle a Victorian family to be treated as gentlemen and ladies. Shopkeeping and bookselling were trades, with money changing hands over the counter, and a tradesman could not be a gentleman – commerce was perceived to be an unattractive source of income, often downright grubby. The Victorian era saw the blooming of a prosperous middle class which needed new definitions to distinguish itself from trade. Professional groups such as doctors and lawyers were able to create barriers of training and qualifications, supervised by bodies such as Royal Colleges. This route was not open to the men of letters, but Macmillan and his like nevertheless sought to distinguish themselves from the retail trade – the bookselling part of their business was slowly relegated in importance to the publishing. In the 1861 census, Alexander described himself as a bookseller and publisher: by 1871 he had dropped the first descriptor. He wished to be seen as a gentleman, and his children as young ladies and gentlemen.

The recognized route to achieving acceptance and to cementing connections with other gentlemen and their families lay primarily through the public schools, and occasionally through society marriages. This sometimes frustrated the merchant classes: the masters at the great schools still believed their duty was to build character and moral fibre, rather than useful academic or commercial skills. In the 1860s, boys at Rugby, a trendsetter in modern public school education, were still spending seventeen hours a week on classics, three on maths and only two on either modern languages or science. 'Rugby was exceptionally advanced in teaching science at all'.[4] The Clarendon Commission on Schools (1861–64) noted that there was a paucity of specialist science teachers and textbooks. (Macmillan was doing his best to plug this gap.)

Nevertheless, the Macmillan boys were all sent to establishments that would impart some public-school gloss. Financing their schooling represented a challenge for Alexander, and not everything turned out quite as he had hoped. In Cambridge, things had been easy to arrange – Caroline Macmillan's half-sister Harriet was married to William Henry Farthing Johnson, the proprietor and headmaster of a very well-regarded school for boys, Llandaff House Academy in the centre of town, and Frederick and Maurice were sent there as day boys. Caroline and Fanny probably felt able to teach the little ones and the older girls themselves: they were both well-read and capable women, and Caroline was particularly loved for her reading voice. But their prolonged periods of ill-health caused disruption and put a strain on the household. In 1864 a governess was hired, twenty-year-old Louisa Cassell. She rapidly became part of the family, and even when the children grew up and she left to take on the job of Matron at the Working Women's College, she remained a friend and was a witness at Olive's wedding in 1886.

The older boys began to outgrow what Llandaff House had to offer, and even before he made the decision to quit Cambridge, Alexander was weighing his options. The most prestigious schools were Eton and Harrow, but Daniel Macmillan had always been particularly admiring of a Cambridge graduate called Edward Thring, who had obtained his Fellowship at King's College in 1844, just as the Macmillans were making their mark across the road in Trinity Street. In 1853 Thring accepted the challenge of a lifetime, taking the headship of a poor provincial grammar school in Uppingham. Within ten years he had turned it into one of the top English public schools. The Uppingham School archives hold the letters that Alexander wrote to his old friend. Among several business letters relating to the publication of the school song book, there are letters in which Alexander talks more freely about his family worries than to anyone else. The first is dated 25 February 1861.

You know that I have a great many – five that is – boys. They are of course very young as yet but one of them, my eldest nephew . . . will be 10 next October. He went to a town school as day boarder six months since. But I have always had an idea of sending him to a public school. His father always wished it, and was often talking of where he would send him. Your own school and Rugby were the two he spoke most of. I understand that a boy must be entered years in advance if he goes to Rugby and I suppose with your present prosperity you will be coming into this condition yourself soon. His mother and I have been talking the matter over a good deal lately and your letter this morning has determined me to write you and ask what you thought would be the proper age, in case we decide on sending him to Uppingham. I also wanted to learn what the subjects are in which you examine for the scholarships you give. I had an idea that you had two ages but I have not one of your circulars by me at present. I fancy the boy has ability and could work well. He does a little Latin Grammar and is tolerably well up in the earlier parts of arithmetic.

The next boy too, my eldest son who is a year younger – he was 8 in December, is at the same school with his cousin and is in the same class. Perhaps he is a little sharper, but not so steady as Frederick, the eldest. I shall feel anxious about him too, to know if anything can be done to prepare them for entering creditably at such a school as yours. The scholarships if they could get them would be a matter of consequence to us of course, with so many of them. The mothers know your little tract well, and often wish you ever came to Cambridge that they might have a talk with you. Have you had any men coming up to Cambridge of late? I am asking your advice and

information rather vaguely I fear, but you can perhaps understand that at present I am rather uncertain about the whole
matter. Any light from you I shall be grateful for.[5]

Not surprisingly, it was a matter of loyalty for Fanny Macmillan
to send her eldest boy to the school of her husband's old friend – in
April 1862 Alexander took her and ten-year-old Frederick to Uppingham so that he could sit the scholarship exams. Whether because
Llandaff House had not prepared him properly, or because he was
not the brightest of the Macmillan boys, he did not achieve the
scholarship that his brother Maurice would win five years later, but
nevertheless he started at Uppingham that very month, a boarder
at Thring's house. In June Alexander wrote to Thring: 'I hope my
nephew will do better next term. We are very glad to get so candid
reports of him. I am afraid he is a little inattentive in his studies and
does not throw his mind with his work.'[6]

The next boy to leave the nest was Alexander's oldest, the
'dreamy and wayward' Malcolm. He had always presented Alexander with a challenge, having a character markedly different from
that of his younger brother George and from Daniel's sons. Dinah
Mulock wrote to her brother Ben in 1860, when the boys had all been
staying with her in Hampstead, that Malcolm, then aged seven, 'was
a queer solitary boy' who held long conversations with Dinah on
everything from insanity to chemistry to astronomy. His brothers
would make fun of him 'and tease and hit him and then he howls!'[7]
Alexander entered him for the Uppingham examinations in March
1864, but possibly feared that the boy would not do well enough, as
he had already been sounding out another old friend, George Bradley, headmaster of Marlborough College, for the fallback he would
need. 'I hardly know what to do if he does not get [the Uppingham
scholarship]. I think he will be clever – what father doesn't of his
boy?'[8]

Marlborough was a new public school, having been founded in
1843 to cater for the sons of the clergy. It got off to a poor start, but

in 1858 the governors appointed Bradley, a former pupil of Arnold at Rugby, as Headmaster and for the next decade Bradley established the school as an academic hothouse with a reputation for 'godliness and good learning'. The year after Malcolm went up, having failed to get into Uppingham, Tennyson sent his sons Lionel and Hallam to join him, saying that he sent his sons to Bradley, not to Marlborough. However, Malcolm did not settle at the school. In the sweet letters preserved for many years by his little sister Margaret, there are traces of homesickness. 'In nine weeks I shall see you again. While I am writing I am looking at your photograph and thinking that I am talking to you . . . I am very sorry that I can say no more, but I am for ever your loving brother.' Even when he had been there a year, in March 1865:

> Dear Maggy, I will now begin to write to you after parting from you for six weeks, since that time I saw you running along the Balham Road. I think I see those fat rosy little cheeks of yours; and I think I see you standing on Papa and looking in the glass to examine them. I suppose you have been happy this week, and I suppose Olive has been happy, and it has been very nice to have a birthday, and I suppose you remember Olive's last. Was it not a nice one? I think you remember the musical box, and the see-saw, and the oranges . . . yes it is nice to be at home, and of course you know nothing about what it is to be away; still it is quite necessary that I must go from you, dear little Margy.[9]

These are the words of a young boy whistling to keep his spirits up, repeating the words he had been told, rather than entering wholeheartedly into the spirit of things. And sure enough, for whatever reason, maybe the bullying for which Marlborough was known at that time, maybe just incurable homesickness, he left early, and it would appear in circumstances that Alexander found upsetting. In comparison with the deprivations of his own childhood, he must have found it hard to empathize with the young, sensitive boy. In April 1867 Macmillan again consulted Thring.

I am still uncertain what to do with Malcolm. He has grown greatly in all ways during the last year, is far more thoughtful and manly and I feel far more hope of his growing a really good man. I have now gained his full confidence and he writes me very open-hearted and very sensible letters. I told him recently of two schemes I had as alternatives for him. One is to go to Uppingham and the other is to send him to King's College School, under my excellent friend Maclear. He would greatly like to go to Uppingham for many reasons but shrinks from a public school life, and rather leans to a course where he would be more at home and more in contact with his mother and me. Mr Paul, whose judgement, though he is a really excellent fellow in many ways I only partially trust – pray consider that very confidential – takes the same view and may have to some extent influenced the boy's judgement. I naturally have a great dread of another change, after whatever step we now take, for the boy. One scheme as a kind of compromise I had thought of, that was to bring him home at Easter and let him go, profess-edly as a temporary arrangement, to King's College School and then after midsummer decide what to do. I rather think that it would be better, in case of his going to Uppingham, that he should not be there while Fred was [Fred would leave in June 1867]. There are certain slight juvenile antagonisms apt to arise between the two boys though substantially very loving friends, that might not be good for either. With Maurice he always has, and certainly would get on well. Now I am talking on the assumption that you would still be willing to take the boy as you kindly said you would when you were here last. Could you arrange so that he would be either in your own house or Rose's? Or could you take him at all?

You see how much I am relying on your friendship. And I do rely on it. Whatever your advice or action may be I cannot after all these years of experience doubt it, Would I were worthier of what I value so much.[10]

The Mr Paul referred to in this letter is Charles Kegan Paul, previously a master at Eton and a disciple of Kingsley and Maurice, now the vicar of Sturminster Marshall near Wimborne in Dorset. Kegan Paul was supplementing a very meagre income by taking in boys at the vicarage, a thatched house known as Bailie Gate, and tutoring them. In May 1865 a very reluctant Emily Tennyson had been persuaded to send her boys Hallam and Lionel there as a preparation for starting at Marlborough the following year, and this must have been a great recommendation for Alexander, looking for somewhere quiet to lodge Malcolm while they decided what to do next. Kegan Paul later became a publisher himself, acquiring the publishing business of Henry S. King in the 1870s. Malcolm never attended a boarding school again. Alexander paid the fee for him to enter King's College School on the Strand at the end of April 1867 and he joined in the summer term that year, staying until the end of the summer term 1870, when he was nearly eighteen years old. His time there seems to have been successful, academically, at least, as he won the annual prize for verse ('Edward, The Black Prince') and for English literature (essays on Shakespeare and Milton).

In October 1863, now resident in London, Alexander entered his ten-year-old nephew Maurice into Westminster School, but by the summer of 1864 a much more adventurous choice had become available. Alexander took Maurice out of Westminster and sent him and his cousin George to Summer Fields School, which had opened in Oxford that year. The school had its home in a picturesque house in the middle of a large and beautiful orchard garden in the Summertown district, the property of Archibald and Gertrude Maclaren. Archibald, Scottish by birth, had visited France as a teenager where he had studied fencing, gymnastics and medicine. By the 1850s he had settled in Oxford to teach fencing, and married Gertrude Talboys, the daughter of a local radical bookseller and publisher, making friends with Edward Burne-Jones and William Morris. In 1858 he had a gymnasium erected in central Oxford, and this led to his being asked to develop a new system of physical training for the British army, and army gyms built to his design were erected at Aldershot Barracks and elsewhere.

Maclaren had already been introduced to Macmillan in 1860, and by 1861 the Macmillan and Maclaren families were friends, with Maclaren contributing to *Macmillan's Magazine*. One of the first articles in the *Magazine* to tackle the education of young women was written not by any of the female authors who Macmillan and Masson were cultivating, but by Archibald Maclaren. 'Girls' Schools', in 1864, was an impassioned plea for improvements in exercise, in clothing, in ventilation and in diet to improve the mental and physical wellbeing of girls in education.[11] Much of the theory might have been shocking to Victorian parents, but Maclaren had his standing with the British army to recommend him. In the spring of 1863, Shirley Brooks, a *Punch* journalist, came to consult Gertrude Maclaren about the health of his two young sons, Reginald and Cecil, aged nine and seven, and then asked her to take charge of them. Alexander Macmillan suggested that she make a little business of it in her parlour, taking also his boys George and Maurice; the two sons of his good friend the South African clergyman John William Hoets; and Robert and John Hughes, sons of Tom. Schoolrooms and bedrooms were added year by year and the establishment grew and grew. Archibald became the headmaster until ill-health overtook him while Gertrude, a classical scholar, taught the fifth form and scholarship classes herself.

The couple were pioneers of a different sort of preparatory school education, with a liberal approach in advance of the times. Physical health was deemed as important as educational progress; the pupils' letters are full of trips to the gymnasium, hockey, cricket and races. The Macmillan boys both thrived, becoming the first to win scholarships from Summer Fields: Maurice followed his brother Frederick to Uppingham in 1866, and George even more prestigiously took an Eton scholarship in 1868. Further Macmillan generations attended this preparatory school, not the least of whom was Harold Macmillan, Maurice's son. Alexander developed an enormous respect for both Mr and Mrs Maclaren, writing in 1869: 'He is my special friend, and a man of very noble nature, fine natural gifts of head and heart – not omitting the body. But she is the scholar and maker of scholars . . . some writers, if they were dealing with the question of the function of women in Education, would submit that they . . . could not lay any solid basis for science. This is not the only, but it is the strongest, disproof of this notion that has come under my notice.'[12]

In term time at least, the Tooting house must have felt much quieter by 1866, but just as life began to settle into these new routines, tragedy struck not once but twice. The year began badly, with Fanny in mourning for her younger brother Robert, a barrister, who died suddenly of heart failure just after Christmas 1865. Robert had wed Margaret Evans, the daughter of Frederick Mullett Evans, publisher of Charles Dickens, and they had only been married for five years when he died. The next and more terrible loss was Alexander's youngest lad, William or Winks, on 22 June 1866. The little boy was not much more than two and had been the delight of the family. Alexander wrote to James MacLehose: 'I had looked forward to his life with peculiar hope. His temper was so good, and his intelligence, without any unnatural precocity, so clear and bright. He was as full of life and fun and playfulness as he could hold.' His death was quite sudden, resulting from convulsions, but he may have been suffering from a more serious but undiagnosed ailment for some months; Alexander spoke of congestion of the lungs, followed by slight gastric fever that 'pulled him down very much', then an 'inflammation of the membrane of the brain', with convulsions.[13]

Losing a child was tragically very common among Victorian families: in the last ten years alone, Tom Hughes had buried two of his offspring and Huxley had lost a four-year-old son. Mrs Oliphant had lost four children, including her darling daughter Maggie. Nothing had prepared Alexander for it being his own. On the day that William died, Alexander scribbled a note to MacLehose with the news: 'God knows best what is good for us. I have only time for this much, but was unwilling you should learn it from anyone but myself.'[14] He buried himself in his work. The letterbook of the time shows only the slightest gap in the pace of correspondence, taking a day off for the funeral, and apologizing to Samuel Baker that he had not been able to attend the meeting of the Royal Geographical Society on 25 June: 'my wife has felt the loss so sudden of our dear child that I could not well be away. We bury him tomorrow so I shall not be here but will on Thursday all day.'[15] He was buried in West Norwood Cemetery, the service conducted by the same minister, Edward Cree, who had baptized the little boy just two years earlier.

A few years later Alexander tried to make more sense of his loss, writing a meditation on what it meant for him spiritually. He clearly intended the essay for publication, as he refers in the text to a frontispiece drawing of the boy by Lowes Dickinson, but sadly only a fragment of 'The Child in the Midst' remains, published with a collection of his letters by his son George after his death. The tone is rather typical Victorian sentimentality: the first ten paragraphs tell the story of the baby who brought joy to the household, who became a little boy with 'flaxen ringlets and sunny brow':

> On the father's return from the bustle and worry of business in the city, to see the boy surrounded with his sisters, and the household servants kneeling round him, and listening to grave wise speech – prattle we call it – or to merry laughter, mixed with the ineffable sweet serenity of the playful sparkle of the intense blue eye, was in itself a well-spring of rest and refreshment. What king ever ruled by sternest will with a sway so complete as child Willie ruled over the affection of all the inmates of the house, by the mere fact that he was a sweet

gentle child set in the midst of our household, as one was set in the midst of His disciples by the Master?[16]

The fragment then moves on to consider the symbol of the baby and the child within the teachings and stories of the Old Testament. Alexander may have been happy to publish *Ecce Homo*, with its emphasis on facts rather than mystery, but it is clear that the old Bible stories were a source of infinite meaning and comfort to him.

The death of the little boy came at a time when there was already grief and trouble within the family home. Increasingly Alexander had written of his dear sister-in-law Fanny's headaches, giddiness and insomnia, and now she was struggling with depression. Within seven months of William's death, Fanny Macmillan was also dead, at the age of forty-five. The official biography of Alexander gave no explanation of her death, which was dismissed as occurring after a period of illness.[17] Her death certificate revealed to me that she had died in York, and in fact, the story was shocking, reflected in lurid headlines in the York newspapers: 'Melancholy Death of a Lady by Burning', and 'Melancholy Death of an Insane Lady in York'. Fanny Macmillan had committed suicide by throwing herself into the burning coals of a fireplace while under the care of a York physician.[18] At the inquest it emerged that the family had been sufficiently alarmed earlier in 1866 to engage a full-time nurse for her, after she attempted suicide by cutting her wrists. When William died, Alexander felt that he and Caroline could no longer cope, and reluctantly he contacted Dr Tetley in Torquay, who had cared for Daniel and knew Fanny well. Through him they were eventually introduced to Dr Kitching, the Medical Superintendent at The Retreat in York. This was a well-known establishment run by the Quakers and known to take a much more sympathetic approach to mental illness than any other asylum in England. Alexander's letters to Dr Kitching are preserved in the archives of

The Retreat. He wrote first on 14 August 1866 explaining that Fanny had been 'under mental disturbances for the last three months'. He and his wife were going to take her to Eastbourne for a holiday, 'to try the effect of the society of her old friends', but her current doctors thought it likely that she would need 'systematic care' in an institution.[19] Kitching and Alexander initially agreed that Fanny would be admitted to the asylum as a first-class patient at three guineas a week, and he and Caroline would call in on the way to a holiday in Scotland to inspect the building, leaving Fanny at home with her nurse, Mrs Turner, and Caroline's sister, Fanny Brimley. Following their visit it seems to have been decided that Fanny would not be admitted to The Retreat itself, but that she and Mrs Turner would take lodgings in York and be attended privately by Dr Kitching. The family were trying to make her life as comfortable as possible. Fanny's surviving brother, William Orridge, installed Fanny and her nurse in a house in October, and there is no further information about her progress in Kitching's files.

When news of the incident reached Tooting, Alexander rushed north to be with her, but Fanny died on 21 January 1867, three days after suffering terrible self-inflicted burns to her face and neck. She left four children under the age of sixteen, the youngest, Arthur, being just ten. To Alexander's probable relief, although the story was picked up by many local newspapers and even some London press including the *Morning Post*, none of the articles made the connection with the Macmillan publishing concern.[20] Alexander was not a witness at the inquest, the family being represented by William Orridge. She was buried in Mill Road Cemetery in Cambridge beside her husband Daniel, F. D. Maurice having come down from London to officiate.

In a strikingly honest letter to Thring in April 1867, Alexander wrote:

When I look at the date of your letter, Feb 27, and remember how gratefully it came to me while our great sorrow was fresh on us, like the words of a brother, and how on reading it again and again it still has to me the flavour of the Divine, became truly human sympathy, I feel rather ashamed of myself that I have not earlier written to thank you for having so truly struck the true chord of consolation in my heart, that the memory of those we have lost is by one of those strange anomalies to the intellect which yet in our deepest heart we feel to be the deepest harmony, the very best comfort that God gives "if I go not away the spirit (the comforter) will not come to you". In the mid most heart of grief this wonderful God-given joy comes. Not that we can always feel sad, indeed I often feel very much otherwise, and it would be mere hypocrisy to pretend to be always in that high mood, perhaps it is neither necessary nor good for one that we should be always so. A feeling akin to resentment often comes across my mind, when all the burden, blessed as it is in its way, comes over one and the work to be done, and which she and he who went so long before her would so gladly and so wisely have shared with me: "how is it when our life's work, both as regards the business and to us far more important the rearing of the young human creatures, our children and God's children, was becoming day by day of so much more importance, and so far more difficult, how is it that I am left without their help who would have done it so infinitely better than I can hope to do it?"[21]

It is possible that Fanny's children were never told exactly what had happened to their mother (at the time both her elder boys were boarding at Uppingham School, and Arthur was at Summer Fields). Alexander told Thring that he tried not to make their loss seem any heavier than it was. Some of Fanny's ill-health may have been unwittingly self-inflicted. In a letter to Miss Mulock in November 1860, Alexander wrote: 'Has Fanny M told you of the wonderful Chloride of Potash which has been getting them all right? I hope she will.'[22] This compound was taken to alleviate sore throats, but in large quantities over time it can be toxic and can cause confusion and anxiety.

If watching his beloved sister-in-law sink into depression, despair and mental collapse had been upsetting, the circumstances of her death were appalling. The letter Alexander wrote to Charlotte Yonge after Fanny's death reveals some of the horror of the situation, but also his usual coping mechanism: 'The events of the past month are scarcely realizable to me, and on the whole the best healer, or at least anodyne is one's daily work.'[23] Yet again, Alexander coped with deep grief by working harder, and the business took another huge leap. Within two years, it would become a truly international concern, with the opening of a New York office.

− 13 −

MACMILLAN CROSSES
THE ATLANTIC
(1867)

Henry Wadsworth Longfellow

'Go forth to meet the shadowy future without fear and with a manly heart.'

Henry Wadsworth Longfellow

IN MAY 1867 the London correspondent of *The Tennessean*, an American regional paper, filed a piece entitled 'Some Notions of an English Publishing House and Book Publisher' which included the following paragraph:

The best example of the thorough British book publisher of the modern school is undoubtedly the publisher for Oxford and Cambridge. In person Mr Alexander Macmillan realises that agreeable cross between the man of business and the man of books – the practical scholar and critic whose opinions mean something and are therefore worth having, for they never appear in reviews, are not paid for by the sheet and are beautifully curt and to the point. The dreamy and somewhat lazy, antique notion of the lettered magnate – that power behind the throne of genius – would hardly apply to this bright-eyed, vigorous, sagacious, genial, enthusiastic, plain and simple Scotchman, who came to London . . . got among scholars, wits and statesmen, and now leads the most illustrious coterie that gathers round any of his compeers of Pall Mall, the Strand or Piccadilly . . . The personal influence of a publisher too, his character for integrity, culture and liberality, go a long way . . .[1]

And so the article continues, emphasizing the weight of the Oxford and Cambridge connections (although Macmillan was never the Cambridge University publisher), praising *Macmillan's Magazine*, applauding the *Cambridge, Globe* and *Golden Treasury* series, the sensible contribution of the junior partner, George Lillie Craik, even the appearance of the books themselves. The piece is not signed, it has the light style of a Thomas Hughes or a Henry Kingsley, but by 1867 Alexander Macmillan had a large circle of admirers and would-be authors, any one of whom might have been supplementing their income by writing for the American press. It is a striking piece to illustrate the regard in which the man was now held, as a publisher and as a leading member of London literary circles. Nevertheless, being well-regarded in the American press was of little benefit when the book trade between America and the United Kingdom was fraught with difficulty.

The problem stemmed from the American refusal to accept British copyright law. British authors and publishers saw their works pirated and sold widely in American markets at knock-down prices and there was nothing they could do about it. Furthermore, the Americans imposed import duties on books, which by 1864 had reached 25 per cent of the cover price, fuelled by evidence that British manufacturing costs were lower. This was particularly frustrating for publishers such as Macmillan, as the American market was three times the size of the British, and its public was more literate. Across the Atlantic in Europe there was a growing movement to protect copyright, but the Americans were having none of it – even though some of the more perspicacious American authors could see that the flood of cheap British reprints were damaging the home-grown literary scene, preventing a domestic identity from forming. Adding insult to injury, American authors could protect their copyright in Britain by taking a trip over the border to Canada, a British dominion from 1867, to prove they were resident on the day of publication, to register title.

The rush to snap up British bestsellers, reprint them in cheap editions and launch them into the American market had led to price wars which put many smaller publishers out of business, until the adoption by the larger firms of a set of voluntary rules known as 'trade courtesy'. If an American firm could negotiate with a foreign publisher to obtain advance proofs and then announced its intention to print the work in the trade magazines, it could secure a monopoly position. In return, the British publisher could at least obtain a fee or commission to share with his author, usually a 10 per cent royalty. Slowly, with progress hindered by the disruption of the Civil War, British and American firms began to negotiate a way to work together. Macmillan chose to partner with Lippincott in Philadelphia, with Scribner and with Pott and Amery in New York, and with Ticknor and Fields in Boston. Letters passed back and forth teasing his contacts with forthcoming publications, trying to tempt advance offers out of them. Juggling these different relationships with different firms, all of whom wanted assurances that they were dealing with Macmillan on favoured terms, and all of whom used the excuse of 'proofs not arriving in time' to avoid paying agreed licence fees, caused Alexander huge frustration. Even when a deal was secured, it sometimes felt as if the technical problems were only beginning. How to get the full text into the American dealer's hands fast enough for the book to hold its value?

There were three options available – the least cost-effective option being to send boxes of books, heavy to transport and attracting the maximum import duty. The benefit was that it gave Macmillan absolute confidence that the quality of his product, and hence the reputation of his brand, would be protected. The risk was that a pirate edition would be marketed before the books could get there and damage his sales. He could send flat printed sheets to be bound in America, and risk losing some control of the quality, or quickest of all he could send an advance proof to be reset and printed by an American firm, at which point he had no influence on the typeface, the illustrations, the paper or the binding.

There were already a handful of British publishers who had tried to get more control over the process by opening offices in the States, Routledge and Cassell being two notable examples. Their aim was to protect the market by achieving simultaneous publication on both sides of the Atlantic. George Routledge had managed to turn the tables to great effect; his business had been more or less founded on cheap reprints in England of American texts, and in 1852 he sold 600,000 copies of *Uncle Tom's Cabin*. It was unlikely that the Macmillans would have attempted anything as ambitious as an American branch while cautious Daniel was still alive, and the short interval between the latter's death and the start of the American Civil War had seen Alexander fully occupied with his London project and the launch of *Macmillan's Magazine*. By the end of the 1850s he had begun to work with American partners, developing relationships that would need to be both cordial and robust to withstand the prickliness of Anglo-American relations during the Civil War.

Alexander may have met James T. Fields, of Ticknor and Fields, as early as 1852 when the Boston publisher visited Europe. The two men had much in common, born just a year apart and rising through a similar career path. Fields, who lost his father at a very early age, had started work as a shop assistant in a bookstore aged fourteen. He then joined Allen & Ticknor as a clerk and had worked his way up to partner. Renowned for his ability to befriend and encourage some of the great writers of the age, including Hawthorne, Longfellow, and Emerson, he was also a great admirer of English literature, and publisher in America of Dickens and Thackeray. In 1859 he and his wife Annie visited England together, and Alexander felt that the time they spent together then, with wives in tow, had forged a strong personal bond. The firm of Ticknor and Fields was a useful conduit for Macmillan's titles, its network extending well beyond Boston, doing over 70 per cent of its business across the continent, and happy to pay royalties to English publishers. A deal was struck for Fields to reprint selected articles and fiction from *Macmillan's Magazine*, sometimes within Fields' own publication, *The Atlantic*, and sometimes Macmillan reciprocated with articles from the American magazine.

James Fields had struggled with the difficulties of running a publishing house during a war, when people only wanted to read newspapers. He sadly told Macmillan that much as he loved the poetry of the likes of Tennyson, no one would buy it during the war. And the difficulties with transport intensified: a letter of 7 May 1862: 'up to this date only about half of Ravenshoe has appeared . . . You are publishing capital books . . . my wife and I were talking yesterday of our Cambridge visit and how greatly we enjoyed it. That row on the river! How pleasant it all was.'[2] As early as 1865, as the dust of the Civil War settled, Alexander began to plan a trip to America, but it was not until the summer of 1867 that he was ready to go, with family difficulties behind him and confident that the business was in safe hands.

He wrote to his friend and author James Fraser: 'I hardly anticipate doing much actual business, but only to gain a more accurate idea of what can be done in the future. It will be much to get the goodwill of gentlemen engaged in educational work and to let them know what books we already have published, and also what we propose publishing in future.'[3] In particular, Alexander wanted to make sure that his firm's strength in high-quality textbooks and academic works, supplemented by his Oxford University Press agency, was as well known in America as some of his fiction and lighter publishing. In June 1867 he wrote to Kitchin, the Secretary to the Board of Delegates 'I think of going to America on Aug 10. Would the Delegates authorise me to deal with their books according to my discretion always providing that I sold nothing without some profit, say 10 per cent on cost per copy? Also would they be disposed to pay £50 towards my expenses? Their decision on these two points would in some measure aid my own. I go solely on business and would be back by the end of October.'[4] His request was granted.

Macmillan's enthusiasm for America may have been slightly dented during the war, but to him it still remained a country of enormous political, and economic, promise.

America! The land of life, of liberty, the hope of the world, inheritor of our greatness, our light, our freedom, alas! Inheritor to too great a degree of our arrogance, money-worship and faithlessness to high calling and gifts of God, but which on the whole she is shaking off nobly in spite of our imbecile arrogance and silly sneers – our . . . unpatriotic pirates and worshippers of slave-holding aristocrats! . . . what right have we to talk slightingly of the land that produced Peabody, and produces hundreds like him, men whose aim is not to 'found families' but to help forward God's cause in the world! . . . Of course, the Yankees have their faults, and when I see them I don't hesitate to tell them in very plain words what I think of their faults. But have we none like them? Where did they get their brag from? Their love of money? Their contempt of other people? . . . Look at our contempt of the Irish, of France, of Germany, of America . . . of everybody and every race but our vain-glorious selves, on whom God had bestowed so much, and to whose cause, as a nation and in the mass, we have rendered back so little.[5]

It was not the first time Alexander had crossed the Atlantic: but travelling first class on Cunard's RMS *Scotia* was a very different experience from his rarely mentioned voyage as a young deckhand in the 1830s. The *Scotia* was the second largest ship in the world at that time, the star of Cunard's steamship fleet and holding the Blue Riband for the fastest Atlantic crossing. It was a paddle steamer, with no steerage quarters, designed for the rapid transport of first-class passengers. Alexander travelled in great comfort – enjoying two glass-windowed saloons, dining space for three hundred passengers, a bakery, a butcher and an icehouse on board. He was delighted to discover a couple of English lords among his fellow passengers. The ship arrived on 20 August, after a trouble-free ten-day voyage, Alexander whiling away his time reading the poetry of James Russell Lowell, Goldwin Smith's *Lectures* and, for a little light relief, or 'vacuous excitement' as he called it, the popular bestseller *Lady Audley's Secret*. Over the next six weeks, Alexander visited Illinois, Toronto, Niagara, Montreal, Philadelphia, Long Island, Washington, and Boston. It was a trip of a lifetime and never repeated. His experiences, and the people he met, made such an impression that he wrote it up as a lecture, 'A Night with the Yankees', delivered in Cambridge Town Hall in March 1868 and then printed for private distribution. Harvard Library's copy is personally signed by Alexander for Senator Charles Sumner.

As always, Alexander was careful in his analysis to avoid sweeping generalizations or to pretend that one six-week journey could entitle him to pontificate upon a continent of thirty-four million people:

> I will endeavour to confine myself strictly to stating things I actually saw . . . The craving which seems to haunt so many persons, both readers and writers, for complete rounded judgements of men and classes and nations, seems to me one of the most unhealthy in its nature, and injurious in its consequences, that can infect the mind and narrow the heart of man.[6]

The RMS *Scotia* docked at Jersey City, and from there Macmillan took a ferry into New York, booking into the Fifth Avenue Hotel.

> I here first made the acquaintance with the hotel clerk – a type of American gentleman that for serene lofty demeanour is, I think, unequalled by any of the *genus homo* I ever met . . . a dignified self-confidence and repose, with not a touch of what you would call rudeness, that seemed to me inimitable. But I found it in all other hotels I went to: it was the manner of the class – the repose that stamps the cast of Vere de Vere[7] could not be finer. Once at Buffalo I had a slight touch of sauciness, which I was able to snub, but it was only momentary and the man soon recovered his armour.[8]

Two nights aboard a sleeper train brought him to Chicago, where he spent two days.

> The whole place had a raw, unsettled look, the pavement dry mud on the carriageway and planking on the footpath. It is the great corn market for Illinois and the great lake district. But the

whole place had an unsettled feeling, as if one were on a sea
of mud or sand, and gave one an experience as of mental sea-
sickness. Yet I met some really pleasant cultivated men there;
and this unsettledness is natural in a place which has grown so
rapidly . . . I spent little time in that city . . . so distressed by the
heat, choked and blinded with the dust, and annoyed by the
snarling hum of the mosquito, that my frame of mind was not
favourable to much study of the place . . . Besides there are a
good many Irish. I saw gigantic placards on the walls summon-
ing Fenian meetings for the overthrow of England.[9]

His purpose in visiting Chicago, apart from spending time with
a bookseller there, was to visit his sister and brother-in-law, Margaret
and Robert Bowes, who lived on the prairie about a hundred miles
outside the city, in Waltham, La Salle. The pair had left Arran in the
late 1840s, joining a small group of other Scottish emigrants scraping a living on Illinois farmland. Even here, in relative backwoods
country, Alexander was impressed by the emphasis on education,
with school buildings noticeable every few miles, and the farming
folk eager to discuss politics and literature: 'I met farmers in the
prairies who had read and understood Carlyle, Mill, Buckle, Ruskin,
Lecky and authors of that class.'[10] And 'in every house I visited there
was a good library, and books like Macaulay's England and Hallam's
works were not infrequent . . . Unquestionably, I think the general
intelligence of these simple men and maidens was up to the level of
our ordinary middle class.' He wrote to his wife on 29 August, 'Life
is exceedingly simple here, not unlike that of our old Arran friends,
but with more tidiness in most respects and very much more plenty.
The house where Margaret lives is about as large as the Glen Sannox
manse.'[11]

From Illinois he travelled to Canada, where he stayed with
Daniel Wilson, and saw Niagara Falls, sailed down Lake Ontario
and into Montreal 'greatly changed since I saw it thirty years ago'.
By mid-September he was staying with the publisher Lippincott in

Philadelphia, then on to New York where he spent a weekend on Long Island with an amateur but highly respected Shakespearean scholar, Richard Grant White.[12] In the city itself he dined with the founder and editor of the *New York Tribune*, Horace Greeley, and then spent a night in Washington where he visited the Capitol and was introduced to the President and to the head of the Smithsonian Institution, Joseph Henry. His support for the winning side in the war opened doors that may not have been available to some of his competitors. His final journey was to Boston, to stay with Fields, and then with Andrew White, founding Principal of Cornell University.

One of the main delights of his trip, as far as Alexander was concerned, was the munificence and philanthropy of the wealthy American, even from the young and newly minted, and his talks with White led him to tell the tale: 'A Mr Cornell, who twenty-five years ago was a working mechanic, and who has made a large fortune by some discovery connected with the laying of telegraph wires, has just given half a million dollars to found a University in the upper part of New York State.'[13] He was impressed by the assumption that money should be spread across the community like this, and that the notion of leaving it all to the children was discouraged. He was equally impressed by the number of working men who owned their own homes or farmed their own plots. This, he believed, would surely lead to a more settled political climate: 'Poverty, social degradation, want of a stake in the country – that is the fuel which kindles into fury and destruction at their fires. All old States in Europe will have to look to that disease', wrote Alexander Macmillan, just three years before the Paris Commune.[14]

During his week in Cambridge, Massachusetts, Fields took him to a dinner of the Atlantic Club, where he met Longfellow, Oliver Wendell Holmes, James Russell Lowell, Charles Sumner and Wendell Phillips: the Boston Set, the root and centre of the abolitionist movement beloved of Macmillan and his Christian Socialist friends. 'They are unquestionably New America. No great idea that works through the States but has its birthplace, or at least its cradle, there.'[15]

Longfellow invited him to lunch at his house. He heard Emerson lecture to an audience of two thousand on 'Eloquence': he had been given a platform ticket and took delight in the audience's bright faces. At the other end of the scale he was taken to see a boys' reformatory on board the Boston School Ship as a guest of Judge Russell, former host of Charles Dickens.

'One of the main objects I had set before myself in going to America was to see and learn something of the collegiate and higher education going on there.'[16] In New York, Alexander visited one of the state-supported schools, which offered free education in English, maths, history, geography, classics and languages, and even if not legally compulsory, but was 'practically compulsory by the habits and opinions of society.'[17] The school had more than a thousand pupils and he was greatly struck by the discipline and good behaviour of all the students.

Throughout his travels, Alexander was delighted with how proud the people he met were of their country and their political institutions: 'I found no one who did not at once, and strongly, express his confidence in the soundness of the Republican Government, and its ultimate power to carry their nation to great and permanent wellbeing.'[18] He was more determined than ever to assume the role of peacemaker between two nations that should be friends, and to work to repair the damage that had been done to transatlantic relations by the War.

However, the principal purpose of his voyage was to scout out supporters and allies in his ventures to increase book sales in such an educated and booming literary market. On his journey home, he sketched out his thoughts in a long letter to James MacLehose.

The high tariff is a terrible drawback, undoubtedly, and in case of an international copyright taking place, if the tariff continued American publishers would reap the benefit. But if we had a house there and an able man to manage it, this might be met. The true idea would be to have a printing office either of one's own or connected with one you could depend on, so as to be prepared to publish there and here at the same time. A great international publishing house is possible, and could be a grand idea to be realized . . .[19]

Alexander was not the first British publisher to have this thought, but as stated in the papers of the Bibliographical Society of America, 'Only one house—Macmillan, in Britain—was truly successful in transplanting itself across the ocean.'[20]

The search was on for the right person to send, and it was not until July 1869 that Alexander was able to tell the Delegates of the Oxford University Press, who supported his scheme, that the right man had been found. George Edward Brett was a man of forty, born near Rochester in Kent, who had entered the book trade as a clerk at Simpkin & Marshall, the place that had frightened Daniel Macmillan off in 1833 with its long hours and exhausting work. Brett left to join Macmillan at the end of 1868, having reached a senior position in the counting-house. In less than a year Alexander decided that this was the man he could rely on abroad, giving precedence to loyalty over local knowledge, but as with George Lillie Craik, Alexander trusted his instincts, and his choice proved highly successful. In June 1869, Macmillan wrote to William Amery, of Pott and Amery in New York, explaining why he was opening his own branch office rather than appointing one of his existing partners on an exclusive basis.

Our desire that our name & publications should stand clear before the American public so that what is ours should be at all times clear . . . however might be interfered with, if another name were attached to it. And then when we sought hereafter to stand alone there might be difficulty in arranging matters so as to prevent in the public mind some idea of alienation as the course of separation. We have been much tempted by the very kind offer you make to calm us of so much anxiety & assurance at starting. But it seems to me that if we are to go into it at all we had better face it fully. If we fail – tho' I have no fear – we cannot lose a great deal, and we can blame no one but ourselves.[21]

This is very reminiscent of Daniel's sentiments when they first opened their own shop twenty-five years before. If it all went wrong, there was no one to blame but themselves.[22]

TO THE TRADE.

MESSRS. MACMILLAN & CO., of London, beg to inform the trade that they have opened an Agency in New York under the management of Mr. GEO. E. BRETT, by whom all their Publications, and those of the Oxford University Press, including the well-known Clarendon Press Series of Educational Works, will in future be supplied.

Catalogues (to be ready in a few days) will be mailed free on application.

The official histories of the New York office pay tribute to the extreme hard work and diligence of George Brett, who sailed to New York with his wife and children, and with Alexander's power of attorney, and set up an office in Manhattan at 63 Bleecker Street, in August 1869. His task was certainly formidable; but he was given early support by Ticknor and Fields, who made over the lease of their office to him, and by the partners at Pott and Amery. Some twelve hundred pounds' worth of stock was transferred to him from Scribner's warehouse, and London began shipping to him directly, mostly textbooks, educational works on history and geography. Early titles included Huxley's *Lessons in Elementary Physiology*, and Bryce's *Holy Roman Empire*. The agency also became the sole supplier of Oxford University's Clarendon Press schoolbook series.

Not all of Macmillan's old trading partners were pleased to see this interloper: Lippincott and Van Nostrand in particular complained about unfair competition. Furthermore, the post-Civil War protectionist backlash created huge headaches for importers. The New York Customs House drove Brett mad by impounding the imported books for weeks on end and challenging him on the stated values and taxes owing. One ten-month battle resulted in a fine of nearly three hundred dollars (worth sixty pounds at that time). Brett wrote weekly to George Lillie Craik, his main contact, his handwriting neat and careful, filling every corner of the paper, arguing about pricing, and complaining about the hostile attitude of the US book trade: 'It is abundantly clear that the American publishers look upon this market as solely their own, and if an English publisher chooses or dares to come and sell his own books, every impediment must be placed in his way and every effort made to oust him.'[23] The rules of trade courtesy, requiring advance proofs and an advertisement, were particularly hard to work with when Brett was trying to market Macmillan's periodicals, which by 1869 included not just the *Magazine*, but also the newly launched *Nature* and *The Practitioner*. Brett tried to get round this by having small parcels of these titles sent directly to academic customers as 'samples' that would not ring alarm bells as they went through Customs.

The business was very slow at first and back in London, Macmillan and Craik were rattled. Brett pressed for higher discounts, especially on bulk orders, and lower, more flexible pricing structures. Although Macmillan had initially determined to do things his own way, independent of American financial support, there exists in the archives of Macmillan Publishers in Basingstoke a deed dated July 1870 which admitted William Amery of New York into the Macmillan & Co. partnership. William Amery agreed to pay Alexander £1,500 (being 3/20ths of the goodwill) for three shares in the business, such that the ownership of the firm was thirteen shares to Alexander, four to George Lillie Craik and three to the new partner. The deed allowed that Amery could continue to operate as a bookseller in New York, but if he ceased to do so, Alexander would transfer to him one more share valued at a twentieth of the goodwill of the business at that date. In addition, Amery had to contribute towards the existing capital of the business, on a pro rata basis, to match the £12,000 assumed to have been invested to date by Alexander and Craik. This development was not at all in line with the original business plan, and no one was more surprised, or aggrieved, than George Edward Brett.

20 August 1870

To Messrs. Macmillan & Co.

Dear Sirs

I think it right to mention that a report has reached this country through Mr Dutton, Broadway, of Mr Amery being now a Partner in the firm of Macmillan & Co. In an ordinary way this is no affair of mine and it would be unbecoming in me to notice it but under the peculiar circumstances of Mr Amery being also a partner in a firm in this City it will be at once seen how highly important it is to me to know if there exists any arrangement with Mr Amery or with Messrs Potts and Amery whereby the position of this agency will be affected. I think I have some claim for this information. Reposing the most perfect confidence in Messrs Macmillan & Co. I broke up my home, severed lifelong connections with relatives and friends, gave up everything in fact with the object of promoting the interests of the Firm in this country, have worked on for months upon an insufficient salary in the full belief that the thing would pay by and by and now after all this the Agency it seems is to be abandoned. I shall be glad to hear from you fully on this matter by an early mail and remain dear Sir, yours ever George E Brett[24]

I would love to see how Alexander answered this. Sadly, the files do not contain his reply to the unhappy George, but it must have been swiftly and privately dealt with as no further mention is made in the letters he wrote in the following month, which are fully occupied with the distribution of the newly launched *Nature* and how best to secure American copyright for *Through the Looking-Glass and*

What Alice Found There, due out the following year, in what would be a cut-throat American market. Ill-health forced William Amery to leave the partnership just one year later, and his £1,500 was repaid in instalments, with Alexander and Craik taking back his shares.

Brett remained nervous about his position. In the spring of 1871 Alexander sent his eldest nephew Fred, aged twenty, to join Brett in New York, a sign of increased confidence in the operation, or perhaps of nervousness. Brett's letter to Alexander in May regarding this posting is a masterpiece of tactful probing to understand what this might mean for his own situation: he promises to give Fred 'all the attention and regard his position entitles him to, that no effort shall be wanting on my own or my wife's part to render his stay here whether of short or long duration a pleasant one – it cannot help but prove to be a profitable one as regards business experiences. In a word he will receive from us all the most cordial welcome and from myself also be the power as you suggest of our taking occasional journeys should such seem desirable.'[25]

Brett had been asking for some time for Alexander to invest in a commercial traveller for the business, rather than depending on Pott and Amery's salesman; now he felt confident that he and Fred could cover the east coast between them, and take on their own employee for 'further afield', terminating the P&A arrangement. The letter ends with a plea for an increase in salary – the offer that he had thought very generous when he was in London had proved extremely disappointing when faced with New York expenses, with his wife reduced to domestic drudgery, as he put it, barely able to clothe his daughters. Although this sounds like the letter of a man becoming more certain of his position, the next letter in the file to Craik asks very nervously how a recent visit from Mr Pott had been received in London and whether the progress of his agency had been discussed. The accounts at the end of 1871 showed that sales had reached £15,000, but Macmillan and Craik were still far from comfortable with their investment.

– 14 –

TAKING STOCK

(1867–69)

THE

GOLDEN TREASURY

OF THE BEST SONGS AND LYRICAL POEMS
IN THE ENGLISH LANGUAGE

SELECTED AND ARRANGED WITH NOTES BY
FRANCIS TURNER PALGRAVE
FELLOW OF EXETER COLLEGE OXFORD

Cambridge
MACMILLAN AND CO.
AND 23 HENRIETTA STREET COVENT GARDEN
London
1861

Golden Treasury, *1861 title page*

'Blessed is the man who has the gift of making friends; for it is one of God's best gifts. It involves many things, but above all, the power of going out of oneself, and seeing and appreciating whatever is noble and living in another man.'

Thomas Hughes

ALEXANDER RETURNED TO Tooting from New York at the end of
October 1867 to be greeted warmly with a family celebration. The
house was lit up with lamps in every window, there was a great bon-
fire burning in the paddock, and Malcolm 'as head pyrotechnist' had
prepared a small firework display. 'The excitement was pleasant to
me, and the home love and the home dinner and even dog Piper's
embraces of my legs', as Macmillan wrote to MacLehose.[1] Of course
after more than ten weeks away, there was plenty to catch up on, and
the voyage had given him time to reflect.

It was ten years since Daniel had died. In the intervening years,
Alexander had lost a baby son and a dearly loved sister-in-law, but
gained a new business partner in George Lillie Craik. Waiting for his
return was a crucial court case. Fanny Macmillan had died intestate
and her brother William Orridge had been appointed to administer
her affairs and as guardian of her children. With no other instruction, her assets, which were estimated at an amount approaching
£12,000 (a not inconsiderable £1.4 million at today's values) should
have been held in trust to be divided equally among her offspring as
and when they came of age, the principal asset being her share in
the London partnership. The problem was that although a deed of
partnership had been agreed, it had never been completed, and the
family needed guidance on how to settle the matter. There was a
lot of money at stake, and Craik's position was vulnerable with no
deed in place.

At the end of November 1867, Alexander's friend Thomas
Hughes launched a suit in the Court of Chancery, effectively to
uphold the unsigned partnership deed, which was otherwise not
legally binding. There is no suggestion that there was any hostility in the case: Hughes, as barrister, acted for Fanny's three male
children with James MacLehose standing as their 'Friend' in court,

in an action against William Orridge, Alexander, Craik, and Fanny's twelve-year-old daughter Kate. The documents lodged at court in November 1867 tell the sad story. Until July 1865 Fanny and Alexander were assumed to be equal partners in the business but without any legal deed. That was the month when Craik had joined the partnership, and although a balance sheet was struck and the assets were valued, no agreement was signed, an error, probably just caused by the pressure of work, that would cost the partners much heartache. In August 1865, Macmillan had asked his lawyer George Burges to call in to discuss such an agreement, but it was not until early June the following year that a draft was finally drawn up: prompted, one assumes, by the state of Fanny's health and her recent suicide attempt. However, although the court was told that Fanny had seen and approved the document, she never signed it. The deed allotted five shares in the business, or fifty per cent, to Alexander, three to Fanny and two to Craik.

It is clear from the agreement that as far as all three of the partners were concerned, this was a Macmillan family business and should remain so for as long as possible. Provisions were expressly made for both Alexander and Fanny to pass their shares in the business to their sons, when adult – but there was no such provision for Craik. Indeed, the drafting seems to go out of its way to reassure a distressed and unhappy Fanny that her sons would be entitled to join the business, with an unusual provision to protect their interests in the case of her death. Unfortunately, Fanny was never well enough to draw up the will which would have made provision for Kate.

The key clause in the suit lodged in Chancery said that the plaintiffs, being Fred, Maurice, and Arthur, 'claim to be entitled to all the share and interest of their mother in the business of the said partnership of Macmillan and Company to the exclusion of their sister Katherine'. Even though Fanny had been an active and appreciated partner in the business, she had not considered that her daughter would want to take an interest, but nor had she made any other provision. The lawyers acting for Katherine claimed that as the boys were all still minors and not capable of becoming partners at this date, it might be fairer for Fanny's share in the partnership to be sold or liquidated and the proceeds divided equally among the four children. Alexander and George Lillie Craik were equally defendants of this suit with Katherine, and proposed that they would continue in the partnership and would buy out the children's share, with a loan which would be retained in the business. This would have given the girl her fair share of the money but would also give them sole control of the business, until the next generation came of age.

The case ran for several years, with regular trips back to court for fresh instructions. The court ruled that Fanny's shares in the partnership should be divided equally between the four children, and Alexander and Craik 'bought' these shares for £6,669 (valuing the London firm at £22,230 or £2.6 million today). However, the money was retained within the business, initially as an unsecured loan, with the two partners paying generous interest on it into court for the benefit of the children. Fanny's share in the Cambridge business, in which Fanny and Alexander had partnered with Robert Bowes but not with Craik, was also turned into cash for the children to share. In 1870 they all went back to court so that Alexander and his wife could assume the guardianship of the four children from Orridge, and be reimbursed out of Fanny's estate for past and future maintenance and education costs. The final settlement was that all of Katherine's inheritance was held in court for her, amounting to more than £2,500, but a large proportion of the boys' inheritance, some £1,700 each out of the total, was kept in the business to be used for paying up their capital if and when they decided to join the partnership.

After the shocks of losing William and Fanny, Alexander felt compelled to improve his home–life balance: business dinners were held at home in Tooting as often as at the Garrick (although the pressure of constant entertaining was not helping Caroline's health). Her weekly letters to young George at Summer Fields are full of descriptions of dinner parties, alternating with mysterious spells of ill-health and recuperative visits to her sisters in Cambridge. In early

February 1868 Caroline was full of pride at a dinner she and Alexander had hosted at The Elms, attended by Tennyson and Kingsley among others, and on 1 April Alexander hosted his favourite event of the year, the All Fools' Dinner. He still travelled to town six days a week, but Sunday in Tooting was his family day, marked, as his daughter Margaret tells us, with special clothing, 'a very brilliant scarlet coat and later on a brown velvet coat and hat, which were very becoming to him, and he came down with a peculiarly happy and serene expression.' The family walked along the road to Holy Trinity church for 'the usual long service of those days' then went for a stroll before the family dinner at three. The rest of the day was given over to visitors from London, either sitting under the trees enjoying the garden, or divided between the library 'thick with the smoke of many pipes' and the drawing room, before they reassembled round the dining table for family tea. Caroline would read aloud to the little ones from improving books, and once the musical governess Louisa Cassell had arrived, there was singing. Margaret says that her father had many faults in his untrained voice 'but there was character in it, and a very special attention to the words, and his singing of Scottish songs, when his voice was still strong, was really enjoyable.'[2]

Meanwhile the children were growing up fast. Fred, who was sixteen and now taller than Alexander, had finished at Uppingham in the summer of 1867 and had started working in the firm, living in Cambridge with his cousin Robert Bowes. By all accounts he had settled down happily, described as 'very pleasant and . . . very nice manners'.[3] Maurice was still at Uppingham and turning into a fine scholar; Malcolm was living at home, attending King's College School as a day boy; and George, much to Alexander's great pride, was on his way to winning a scholarship at Eton. Little Arthur, Fanny's youngest boy, had just gone to join his cousin George at Summer Fields in Oxford. The relationship with the Maclarens at Summer Fields continued to strengthen – after little William's death in 1866, the Maclaren family had taken Arthur and George away with their own daughter to the Isle of Wight for the whole summer holiday, relieving some of the domestic pressure on Caroline and Alexander as they grieved. The girls, Maggie, Olive, and their cousin Kate, were being schooled at home by Louisa Cassell, the governess who since the baby's death had become almost part of the family.

April 1868 saw a particularly happy family event in Cambridge, where Alexander's nephew Robert Bowes was marrying Caroline's half-sister Fanny. The couple were thirty-two and thirty-six years old respectively, and had known each other for many years. Fanny had been living the typical life of a Victorian spinster in the Brimley family home in Park Terrace, looking after her elderly aunts Mary and Anne, and now Robert would move in there too. Maggie, Olive and Katie were bridesmaids with their cousin Fanny Johnson. Caroline also wrote to George with great amusement of a day in May when she hosted a coach party of twenty-six girls from a London orphanage – they had given them tea, showed them round the garden and organized a paperchase in a neighbour's hayfield, Caroline laughing that some of them had never seen a cabbage growing before. There was yet more activity in July when Alexander hosted Longfellow at a dinner to meet Charles Kingsley, F. D. Maurice, Thomas Huxley and Matthew Arnold. Longfellow, with whom Macmillan had spent some time while in New England, was being feted and entertained all over the country – there was a formal banquet held in central London in his honour just the night before to which Macmillan had not been invited, so he was extremely proud that the famous poet had been happy to accept a more intimate invitation.

In the summer of 1868, the family assembled for a much-needed six-week holiday at the little Welsh seaside resort of Penmaenmawr, made fashionable by Gladstone. Alexander may have been hoping for a glimpse of his hero paddling in the sea, but only managed to get away for three weeks to join them there. It was a time for celebration – George had won a scholarship to Eton, which made Alexander extremely proud, dropping it into all his correspondence over the summer. Caroline's letters to her boy at the time are full of earnest advice and loving concern about the temptations that would face him at his new school: 'Let it be understood by any companions you have that you mean to make work the chief object and amusements may be left to take care of themselves . . . honest work will keep you from the peculiar temptations of Eton . . . try and get help in daily prayer and attending upon God's word, the daily psalm and gospel.' She wrote faithfully every week, apologizing if she had missed a post because of her increasing ill-health: George preserved every letter.[4]

Across his own business, the fruits of his investments in new titles and series were paying off, and Macmillan was building a small but dedicated support network of readers and editors to help with the volume of submissions and publications. In 1867 the firm published eighty-one titles from a list of authors that had more than doubled in the ten years since Daniel died. Twenty-five of these earned reprints or further editions. In addition that year the firm reissued forty other earlier works. The new books alone ran to nearly nineteen thousand pages (as opposed to just over six thousand in 1857 plus a dozen reprints). This was a business of significant scale, which was also publishing a monthly periodical, *Macmillan's Magazine*, the annual *Statesman's Year-Book*, and a learned journal, *The Journal of Anatomy and Physiology*, which had launched the previous year.[5]

It is hard to tell how Macmillan & Co. compared in size with the other publishing giants: John Murray, Longmans, William Blackwood and Smith, Elder had the advantage of longer back catalogues and stronger balance sheets, but Macmillan's reputation for quality and innovation was firmly established. Other Victorian publishing houses came and went, they ran out of capital, made unwise investments, partners fell out with partners and names changed with rapidity, but Macmillan & Co. stood out as a beacon of stability and steady growth.

Macmillan's Magazine had a settled circulation, occasionally boosted by one-off scandals such as the debate between Kingsley and Newman, or Arnold's review of Colenso. Thomas Carlyle's final piece of journalism on contemporary politics, 'Shooting Niagara', had run in the *Magazine* the previous year, to widespread horror among the liberal readership. As his biographer Simon Heffer writes, 'The bile that characterises this masterpiece of reaction was fed by an onset of dyspepsia.'[6] Appalled by what he saw as the Conservative Party's betrayal of principles in its support for widening democracy, Carlyle likened the proposed electoral reform to 'shooting Niagara'. 'Everybody shall start free, and everywhere, "under enlightened popular suffrage" the race shall be to the swift, and the high office shall fall to him who is ablest if not to do it, at least to get elected for doing it.' When reprinted as a pamphlet, the article sold 4,000 copies in three weeks. As the sentiments contained are so far removed from the Gladstonian liberalism of the proprietor, Alexander must have shuddered to see it: but Carlyle was Carlyle and Macmillan would defend his right to speak his mind even though the sentiments hurt.

The difficulties that Alexander had experienced in 1866 in dealing with the likes of Mrs Norton were exacerbated by the fact that the *Magazine*'s editor, David Masson, was no longer living in London. Since 1865 he had been combining the role with the Chair of English Literature in Edinburgh, and the tensions were becoming more noticeable. At first, Alexander acted as deputy editor, and when the workload became too much he appointed Edward Dicey to take the London role. However, Dicey's tendency to disappear on foreign correspondent adventures caused increasing frustration. As Alexander wrote to Masson, 'Distance, though it may lend enchantment to some views, does not seem to lend clearness to others.'[7] He next appointed a new literary associate, George Grove, as deputy, but again Grove's attendance was only sporadic, and by the time Alexander returned from America he was deeply concerned about the confusion and delay that was upsetting contributors.

At the end of 1867 Macmillan very reluctantly accepted Masson's resignation. 'The idea of your connection with the *Magazine* ceasing is very painful to me.'[8] Masson was retained as 'consulting editor' until Grove, now the editor, felt well established, and the first few numbers of 1868 were mostly filled by Macmillan's oldest and most trusted contributors. Macmillan was deeply concerned about the survival of the periodical, but Grove wrote to him: 'Cheer up old Man, we shall beat the *Spectator*, and all the other 'ators, and get up to 20,000 a month yet, and that by fair means.'[9] Macmillan agreed to pay Grove £250 per annum. Over time, the new man changed the character of the *Magazine*, making it less radical, less political, and no longer a mouthpiece for the Christian Socialists, who were in any case running out of steam. Some of the main players, such as Kingsley, had moved to the right: Hughes and Ludlow were focusing on electoral and trade union politics, which did not make good copy for a light-hearted periodical aimed at the middle classes.

If Macmillan had been asked to identify his beliefs at that time, he would have described himself first and foremost as an Anglican, and secondly as a Gladstonian Liberal. This alignment was reflected in the catalogue: the firm commissioned several collections of essays on controversial topics such as political reform and education, with contributors including Henry Sidgwick, John Seeley, Lord Houghton, Leslie Stephen, Goldwin Smith, and James Bryce. Alexander was becoming more interested in national than local politics and had taken a particularly proprietorial interest in the 1865 General Election, when Tom Hughes, Henry Fawcett, George Trevelyan, all 'his authors', had been elected to Parliament alongside John Stuart Mill. He wrote to Trevelyan, congratulating him: 'Isn't it glorious to see such an access of strong clear-headed Liberals as Mill, Fawcett, Hughes and yourself? The sky has been clearer to me ever since.'[10] Many of his old Cambridge friends were now of an age to achieve positions of power in the Civil Service, the Church, the Bar and the Government. His pride in these connections, added to his enjoyable correspondence with Gladstone during the launch of *Ecce Homo*, allowed Alexander to feel that he was beginning to have more insight into current affairs, and possibly more influence, than his brother could ever have imagined.

Of particular pleasure and pride to him had been the election of F. D. Maurice in 1866 to the Chair of Moral Philosophy in Cambridge – it seemed a fair reward for his decade in the wilderness after his dismissal from King's College London. Alexander wrote happily to the man he called The Prophet: 'Old links seem renewed and very precious memories relive themselves: the sense that things passing are yet knit to things Permanent, and that much that seemed gone is here, come on me. Of course I am glad, so are many others: am I entitled to claim a right to be a little extra glad?'[11] Being Alexander, even with his sentimental hat on, the chance to be commercial did not pass him by: he told Maurice that he was planning to advertise all his works to coincide with the appointment.

Highlights of the firm's book catalogue in 1867 include Matthew Arnold's *New Poems*, John Morley's *Edmund Burke*, Maudsley's *Physiology and Pathology of the Mind* and William Rossetti's *Fine Art*. The *Sermons* of Bishop Cotton of Calcutta, who had died the previous year, are worth noting: George Cotton had been dearly loved for his work in India, where he had lived and worked since 1858, but he was one of Alexander's particular friends, a member of the Trinity, Cambridge set, and had contributed numerous published sermon collections, as well as articles to the *Magazine*. Once in India, he called on his previous experience as a master at Rugby and headmaster of Marlborough to found numerous educational establishments for Indian and Eurasian children that survive to this day. One of his pastoral concerns was to ensure that the children were properly dressed, including socks, which he had imported in bulk from England and 'blessed' on arrival. Over time, Cotton's socks became 'cotton socks'. George Cotton drowned in 1866 crossing a river on the way to bless a new cemetery, washed away and never seen again, at which point, so the legend goes, the Archbishop of Canterbury was asked, 'Now who will bless his cotton socks?'

The firm's prestigious arrangement with Oxford University Press seemed to be bedding down, although not without frustrations on his part and suspicions on theirs. The Delegates had finally begun to focus on what they had meant the Clarendon Press schoolbook series to be: Alexander still thought they were being too slow, missing opportunities and paying authors far too much. Always the perfectionist, he was fighting a losing battle in trying to get them to apply consistent quality standards across their catalogue. Earlier in 1867 he had felt obliged to write to Kitchin, Secretary to the Delegates: 'I don't like to say it, and I have refrained from saying it in hopes that I might change my mind. But I have not, after repeated trials. My feeling is that your *First Reading Book* is very poor – very . . . I say all this with the utmost reluctance, but with the darkest convictions, that people who see it will say "Is it possible that the University of Oxford really recommends this stuff as the foundation of learning and culture for the rising generation?" . . . Were the book mine, I would pay the author and suppress it.'[12] This type of frank language did little to endear the publisher to his client and it is unlikely that they took any immediate action.

The slightly sticky relationship with Oxford University Press persisted, and at one point Macmillan threatened to walk away, 'If I can't defend my position I will retire from it gracefully';[13] but just ten days later he can be seen angling, unsuccessfully, for a partnership at the Press. He dealt with the continued pressure from the Delegates to open a shop in Oxford (as he had committed to in 1863) by firmly putting the onus onto the Press managers. 'You should if possible have the place more or less fixed before I come. A shop of about 50 feet by 20, and one or two smaller back rooms, is about my idea.'[14] Nothing more was heard on the subject and eventually the Press opened their own shop.

The two thousand-odd pages of outgoing correspondence in the Macmillan archives for 1868 are increasingly written in Craik's barely legible scrawl – Alexander's partner was the man paying the bills and chasing the creditors, leaving the founder free to build his network, to think creatively and explore new ideas. Alongside the *Golden Treasury* series, and the *Globe* editions, in 1868 Macmillan launched the *Sunday Library*, a series of Christian works suitable for families to read. A letter he wrote to François Guizot, a historian and educationalist who had once been Prime Minister of France, explains the background to this series, which was edited by Miss Yonge working with Frances Martin, the friend of Dinah Craik. It also speaks volumes of the life of the young Alexander.

> On being thrown on my own resources at so early an age in a large town away from all home restraint, I lost many of the convictions and mental habits of my early life . . . I no longer felt it wrong to permit more freedom to myself in what I should read that [Sabbath] day, nor have I restrained my children strictly on this matter. But of late years, as my boys are growing up and acquiring a taste for reading themselves, [I have] felt my mind recurring to the old influences of sabbath on my own mental and moral habits and on those of my nation. I cannot avoid the conviction that much of the steadfastness and thoughtfulness of the Scotch has arisen from having their minds when young turned for one day to the contemplation of noble lives and interests of a permanent, eternal kind. The increased activity during our working day lives, the bustle and distraction of secular interests seem to me very injurious to depth and strength of character.[15]

The eventual list of more than a dozen books in the series included new works by Mrs Oliphant, Annie Keary, Mrs Craik, Charles Kingsley, Miss Yonge, and Tom Hughes, and to secure a book from an author as prestigious as Guizot, Macmillan was prepared to offer £350 to £400. This series, according to Margaret Macmillan, was not a great success with the public, although it apparently was with the children in The Elms. It caused enormous difficulties for the publisher, as Miss Yonge had High Church leanings, which Frances Martin, the joint editor and disciple of F. D. Maurice, found increasingly irritating and offensive, with both women constantly appealing to Alexander for support.

If Alexander had been asked for his publishing highlight of 1868, he would have pointed to a poem that featured in May's *Macmillan's Magazine*: the lengthy poem entitled *Lucretius*. Grove negotiated a rather complicated deal to allow Tennyson to publish simultaneously in America with J. T. Fields. A charge often levelled against Macmillan by literary critics was that it was he who had requested the omission of four rather racy lines describing naked nymphs, which nevertheless made it into the American version of the poem and were later restored by the poet when he published it in a volume of collected verse: in fact it seems to be Grove, and also Masson, when consulted in Edinburgh, who asked the poet for the amendment, more on the grounds of poetic fluency than of prudishness. Alexander wrote to Tennyson, 'Grove seemed to prefer the shorter description of the Oreads [nymphs]. On the whole the balance of taste seems in favour of it. You shall see both and I will leave you and Grove to decide.'[16]

Business was booming, and Alexander was still an assiduous networker. He was a founder member of the Savile Club, established in 1868 as the New Club, and renamed when it moved to premises in Savile Row in 1871. Another all-male preserve, it was particularly designed to suit the needs of the literary men of London; from 1871 to 1873, Macmillan served on the committee. The club offered billiards and cards, but its principal defining character was the sociable half-crown fixed-menu lunch and dinner, served communally on two long tables, for the express purpose of encouraging conversation. This was a place to meet and talk, not a place to hide away.

There was one particular unsolicited manuscript that arrived in the summer of 1868 that Alexander spent enormous time over, which had come from a young unknown in Dorset called Thomas Hardy. The novel arrived on Macmillan's desk in the last week of July, when Alexander was already under enormous pressure to clear his desk and join his family in Wales. As he had once written to a friend, 'getting away is worse than having one's leg cut off.'[17] Nevertheless, his reply was written within the fortnight, in among the many other business letters he had to clear off his desk before he could get away.

This densely written, four-page response to Hardy's *The Poor Man and the Lady* is famous among literary critics for the care that Macmillan took with it, and for proof that the publisher had indeed spotted extraordinary talent and wished only to advise and encourage the author. Macmillan found Hardy's bitterness against the upper classes just too difficult to stomach, although he admitted to recognizing much truth in the story as well. His comments are interesting for what they say about his own life at that point.

> I have read through the novel you were so good as to send me with care and with much interest and admiration, but feeling at the same time that it has what seem to me fatal drawbacks to its success, and what I think, judging the writer from the book itself you would feel even more strongly – its truthfulness and justice.
>
> Your description of country life among working men is admirable, and though I can only judge of it from the corresponding life in Scotland which I knew well when young, palpably truthful. Your pictures of character among Londoners, and especially the upper classes, are sharp, clear, incisive and in many respects true, but they are wholly dark – not a ray of light visible to relieve the darkness, and therefore exaggerated and untrue in their result. Their frivolity, heartlessness, selfishness are great and terrible, but there are other sides . . . The utter heedlessness of all the conversation you give in drawing-rooms and ball-rooms about the working classes, has some ground of truth, I fear, and might justly be scourged, as you aim at doing, but your chastisement would fall harmless from its very excess . . . My own experience of fashionables is very small, and probably the nature of my business brings me into contact with the best of the class when I do meet them. But it is inconceivable to me that any considerable number of human beings – God's creatures – should be so bad without going to utter wreck in a week . . .

There follow several more paragraphs of detailed comment on plot and character, but his final words are:

> You see I am writing to you as to a writer who seems to me, at least potentially, of considerable mark, of power and purpose. If this is your first book I think you ought to go on.[18]

This letter meant a great deal to Hardy, who preserved the original, even though the manuscript of the novel has been lost: when an excerpt of the letter was published in Graves' *Life and Letters of Alexander Macmillan* in 1910, Hardy took the trouble to write to George Macmillan correcting some mistakes in the text.[19] Hardy also sent his next manuscript to Macmillan, but there was some confusion about the response he received, and it was not until 1887 that the firm published *The Woodlanders* and began an intermittent but cordial partnership. Hardy himself became a friend of the family, visiting Tooting and asking Alexander to introduce him to membership of the Savile Club.

The autumn of 1869 found Alexander plunged into massive controversy when he took an article from *The Atlantic Monthly* in Boston. Fields was away on holiday, and the acting editor, William Dean Howells, was sent a piece written by Harriet Beecher Stowe. It has to be said that Stowe was not quite the pull she had been before the war, and in the era of Reconstruction she was struggling to sell her work. However, during the glory days of her tour round England on the back of *Uncle Tom's Cabin*, she had met and become friends with Lady Byron, whom the poet had abandoned when he left England with bankruptcy and scandal at his heels. Lady Byron had whispered to Harriet some of the true nature of her husband's behaviour and of his cruelty to herself and her daughter, much of which had been brushed under the carpet or left secret in the Byromania which engulfed the world after his death fighting for Greek independence in 1824. Lady Byron, and her daughter Ada Lovelace, were now dead, and in 1869, one of his mistresses, Theresa, Countess

Guiccioli, published a book which idolized the poet and blamed his wife's coldness and frigidity for driving him out of England. Stowe was incensed, particularly as she was becoming agitated by the oppression of women and the denial of their rights. She took up arms in the article which did not just defend her friend, but in barely disguised language accused Byron of incest with his half-sister, Augusta Leigh. The article was published simultaneously on both sides of the Atlantic, appearing in September's *Macmillan's Magazine*, and all hell broke loose.

In America, the reading public was shocked and appalled, not so much by Byron's behaviour, but by the impropriety of Stowe naming it, particularly as she was a woman, and by a respected monthly like the *Atlantic* for printing it. Readers cancelled their subscriptions by the tens of thousands, and for a while it appeared that the magazine might fail. In England, the Leigh family solicitors issued a furious rebuttal which was printed in all the papers. Macmillan, on a family holiday in Torquay, remained resolute. He had never approved of Byron and was delighted to be the instrument which would reveal the true horror of the poet's moral delinquency. He wrote to Stowe: 'I cannot doubt that, in spite of the present ferment the article will do much good permanently, and though the public may hug its fallen idol, the idol will fall.'[20] However, there is no doubt that the row spoiled his vacation. He wrote under some pressure to MacLehose defending his decision. 'There is a strong tendency at present in the press at large to a theory that genius is an excuse for any excess . . . I hope that in the end [this controversy] will help to destroy this damnable doctrine and bring home to the public mind and also to men of all sorts of genius that they have no more right to misuse their brains than a navvy has a right to misuse his muscles.'[21] MacLehose warned him that his subscriptions might drop as they had in the States, but Alexander was determined: 'what you tell me of the probable consequences to the magazine and myself, though I cannot pretend to be indifferent to either, affects me less than the greater question of my own right or wrongdoing.' He understood that the story would have come out at some point, as Stowe was not the only person that Lady Byron had told, and it was better to have come out in a respected periodical in a serious piece of writing than 'in any more sensational magazine.'[22]

Back in London, Macmillan as ever consulted the men whose opinion he most trusted, including Tom Hughes and Matthew Arnold, and decided to maintain absolute silence and let the affair blow over. If we view the controversy through the lens of our own time, then Macmillan stood fair and square on the side of the women in the story – that the abused and oppressed woman should be believed, even though she accused a great and adored public hero, and that Stowe, though a woman, had as much right to tell the tale as any man. Of course, partisans of both Lord and Lady Byron rushed to buy the *Magazine*, which according to the *Volunteer Service Gazette and Military Dispatch* of 11 September went into four editions. However, when the following year Stowe doubled down, by publishing her account as a full-length book, Macmillan declined the honour of issuing it in London. Stowe's reputation did not recover until after her death in 1896, although the *Atlantic* bounced back strongly.

There was, however, another woman writer and campaigner for Macmillan to take under his wing: the wife of his great friend Henry Fawcett. In 1867 Fawcett had married Millicent Garrett, the twenty-year-old younger sister of the famous campaigner for a woman's right to practise as a doctor: Elizabeth Garrett Anderson. As a teenager Millicent was taken to hear F. D. Maurice preach, and she rapidly became part of the wider circle of his Christian Socialist supporters. By 1866 she had also become familiar with the political philosophy of John Stuart Mill and his wife Harriet Taylor, and was inspired to join their campaign for the right of women to have the vote on the same terms as men. In her memoirs, Millicent described Alexander Macmillan as one of her most valued friends. It was he who had encouraged her to start writing, and he published her first article in *Macmillan's Magazine* in 1868: 'The Education of Women of the Middle and Upper Classes'. Her argument was that women should be able to take University degrees and that more professions should be made open to them. She was paid seven pounds for the article, which she donated towards John Stuart Mill's election expenses that year. This article marked the start of her life as a public campaigner, and the fact that it was written and published in the same year that she gave birth to her only child, Philippa, suggests that she would never let domestic duties deflect her from her mission in life.

The following year, 1869, Millicent began a career of speaking in public, and in 1870 Macmillan published her book *Political Economy for Beginners*, which ran through seven editions over the next twenty years. It was aimed at encouraging the teaching of economics to schoolchildren, and the chapters ended with questions and puzzles. Each edition was carefully revised to account for new theories as they had arisen, and facts and figures were taken from another Macmillan publication, *The Statesman's Year-Book*. In 1872, husband and wife co-authored *Essays and Lectures on Social and Political Subjects*, which included Millicent's lecture 'Why Women Require the Suffrage'.

Millicent never forgot the publisher who had first given her a pulpit from which to preach. Her fondness for Alexander Macmillan shines through her memoir: 'On one occasion, after a great talk on all things in heaven and earth, Mr Macmillan, who had the Scot's turn for metaphysics and philosophy as well as the Scot's eye for the main chance, exclaimed, "I often ask myself, Why am I here?" whereupon my husband at once rejoined "Why, to publish Barnard Smith's arithmetic, of course." This friendly chaff Mr Macmillan took in very good part. He was a real friend to both of us.'[23]

As the catalogue grew and print runs increased, Alexander became ambitious to tap into the growing numbers of English-speaking readers overseas. The trip to America had given him an insight into the largest of these markets, but there were dominions and colonies to tackle, as the growing populations of Canada, South Africa, Australia, and India became more accessible and better educated. From the start of the partnership, the brothers had carefully exploited their network of overseas academics, priests, and missionaries. This was a two-way street – the Cambridge men who found themselves isolated and feared they were forgotten in far-flung corners of the Empire were delighted to receive long gossipy letters from Alexander with news of Cambridge and Church politics. In return, they provided him with material to publish, and with information about the literary markets. As early as 1860 he was quizzing his old friends about the possibility of an agency in India, and in April 1863 he was writing to George Trevelyan: 'We are increasing our business with India both in schoolbooks and in the supply of Libraries and Book Clubs and private persons and we could do more if it came our way. What strides education must be making among the natives! We sell considerable numbers of our mathematical books, even high ones, every year to India. I should be glad to know something about these same scientific natives. Please write me a longer letter when you next write.'[24]

His appointment as publisher to Oxford University gave a further boost to this export trade, the prestigious name giving him access to networks which he could exploit to his own ends. As English-speaking schools and universities spread across the world, the demand for textbooks grew exponentially. Macmillan began to prepare for a significant shift in focus – sermons were no longer required, the New World was as hungry as the Victorian middle classes were for science, and discoveries were proceeding apace. Books could no longer keep up, something more immediate was required, and Alexander Macmillan was working on the answer. He was already commissioning work from the most highly regarded mathematicians, scientists, geologists, and naturalists in the British Isles and publishing schoolbooks and textbooks at the cutting edge of knowledge. In 1869 he published Alfred Russel Wallace's *The Malay Archipelago*, a key text in the development of evolutionary thought, and launched *Nature*: his place as the pre-eminent publisher of scientific research would be assured.

15

THE BIRTH OF *NATURE*

(1869)

Nature cover, 4 November 1869

'Sit down before fact as a little child, be prepared to give up every preconceived notion, follow humbly wherever and to whatever abysses nature leads, or you shall learn nothing.'

T. H. Huxley

OF ALL ALEXANDER Macmillan's contributions to posterity, surely the launch, and long-term financial support, of a loss-making weekly publication called *Nature* is the most laudable. *Nature* survives to this day as one of the most highly respected scientific publications in the world, with an international online readership of over thirty-eight million. Alexander's money and determination allowed this periodical to succeed where so many had failed, and his inspired appointment of thirty-three-year-old Norman Lockyer as editor gave *Nature* an ambition and curiosity that enabled it to develop an international reputation for inclusivity and objectivity. So much depends on chance, and if an Italian revolutionary, Count Orsini, had not attempted to blow up the Emperor Louis Napoleon with a bomb that was manufactured in Birmingham, Lockyer, a career civil servant and amateur astronomer from Wimbledon, might never have fallen into Macmillan's orbit.

It was in 1859, while Macmillan was still living in Cambridge, that England became gripped by the terror of an imminent invasion – Louis Napoleon was extremely unhappy about the Orsini plot and made it clear that the British government was not reacting strongly enough to stamp out international terrorism. Might France turn against its recent ally and attack Britain? A decision was taken that an armed militia should be formed for self-defence – the Volunteer Rifle Corps. Obviously no one in authority was enthusiastic about the idea of arming the working classes so soon after 1848, so the call went out to the professional middle classes, the men who could afford to buy their own arms and equipment. Tennyson wrote a poem that was published in *The Times* in May 1859: 'Riflemen, Riflemen, Riflemen form!'. Alexander even joined up, encouraged by his favourite poet.

The Volunteer movement is the thing that occupies most space in the public mind here. Drilling and parade constantly going on. We had a grand display of the whole force – numbering over 500 men – in King's the other day. It appeared to me they were as likely to stand bullet or bayonet as any 500 men that could be found anywhere. This rifle Volunteer movement is a piece of serious earnest in the country whether it ever be needed or not. I hope it never will – for I am one myself![1]

Not surprisingly, one of Alexander's friends was an even greater enthusiast for the movement – Thomas Hughes, the boxing barrister, who enrolled with his friend John Ludlow in the Wimbledon company. There they met an enthusiastic civil servant, Norman Lockyer. Lockyer had to be at his desk in the War Office by ten in the morning, so he drilled on Wimbledon Common between six and seven every day, returned home for breakfast and then set off to work by train, where he would bump into Tom Hughes again, off to the Inns of Court. In the evenings he attended the village club, where Hughes and Ludlow were on the committee. Thrown together in this way a friendship developed, despite very different backgrounds. Lockyer's father was a surgeon-apothecary with an interest in science, but he died when Lockyer was nineteen. Norman was educated at Kenilworth Grammar School and began a career as a teacher but his abilities were spotted by the local landowner who recommended him for an appointment in the Civil Service. He moved to London and joined the War Office just as it needed to reorganize after the near disaster of the Crimean War. Hughes and Ludlow, delighted with their new young friend, introduced him into the Christian Socialist circle and at some point he met Macmillan.

Meanwhile at the Wimbledon Village Club, Lockyer had made friends with an amateur astronomer who owned a telescope in his back garden, and by 1861 Lockyer had installed his own instrument and was joining the ranks of the self-educated amateur scientists who achieved so much in Victorian Britain. There was precious little formal scientific training to be had at this time, and when he was not required for drill practice or at his desk, Lockyer could be found devouring the latest texts at the British Library Reading Rooms. Hughes and Ludlow became increasingly impressed by his wide-ranging knowledge, particularly when he began to contribute short observations and essays to periodicals. Ludlow was still sulking that Macmillan had not offered him the editorship of *Macmillan's Magazine* and became convinced that the chosen one, Masson, was trying to muzzle him. Macmillan wrote placatory but increasingly impatient letters denying that this was the case, but to no avail. Ludlow persuaded Hughes that they should set up a weekly periodical of their own, which would be less constrained from discussing some of the more controversial subjects of the day. The paper would also be free to review any or all books, something which posed a problem for Masson and Macmillan, who were nervous about being seen to 'puff' the Macmillan catalogue, or to criticize rivals.

In January 1863 the friends launched the *Reader*, issued weekly and containing 'free uninhibited discussion of science, religion and the arts', with Ludlow as editor. Lockyer was asked to contribute on topics of astronomy, and eventually to be the scientific editor. Ludlow gave up after just three months (which rather suggests that Macmillan had been right to distrust his stamina), and the prolific David Masson took over this magazine as well, bringing in other contributors from Macmillan's circle such as Kingsley, William Rossetti, and Tom Taylor. Macmillan was relaxed about the competition, probably predicting that the *Reader* would not succeed commercially. In 1864 Hughes and Ludlow handed control to a new group of investors who had a very different end in view: to fill the huge gap in the market for an up-to-date and professionally authored scientific journal. These men were the leading scientists of the decade, led by Thomas Huxley, Darwin, Galton, Spencer, Lubbock, Spottiswoode, and Tyndall: a grouping calling itself the X-Club, who met monthly over dinner. They ran the magazine for a year, increasingly dependent on Lockyer's contributions, but they could not sustain the losses and in 1865 they sold it on again. By 1866 it had perished.

Over the preceding two decades there had been several attempts to create a solid basis for specialist scientific publishing. Huxley had contributed to John Chapman's *Westminster Review* in the 1850s and took the role of editor of the *Natural History Review* in the early 1860s but resigned through pressure of all his other commitments: it failed shortly afterwards. Macmillan & Co., on the other hand, was already an established publisher of periodicals. Back in the 1840s the brothers had taken on the *Cambridge and Dublin Mathematical Journal*, which ran until 1854, and by 1869 Alexander had ten years' experience of publishing the monthly *Macmillan's Magazine*. In 1866 Alexander had agreed to publish *The Journal of Anatomy and Physiology*, edited by J. W. Clark, a Fellow of Trinity College, Cambridge. This journal, which was published perhaps two or three times a year at first and was warmly supported by the likes of Huxley, survives to this day as the *Journal of Anatomy*, now published by Wiley. In 1868 he founded *The Practitioner*, a monthly journal of practical medicine, edited by Francis Anstie, which also continues to this day.

Throughout the 1860s, Macmillan commissioned a series of science textbooks for schools which he was determined should be written by acknowledged experts in the subject. In 1866 he was particularly delighted to publish a pair of ground-breaking titles by Roscoe and Huxley, containing 'elementary lessons' on chemistry and physiology, respectively. In 1868 he commissioned Norman Lockyer to write *Elementary Lessons in Astronomy*. Lockyer used to tell the story that when he sent in the manuscript for the book, Macmillan replied, 'This is not the book I expected at all . . . (long pause), it is something much better', for which he was happy to double the fee.[2] Macmillan referred to Lockyer as his 'consulting physician in regard to scientific books and schemes', a gap he felt needed filling and which despite his best efforts he had been unable to persuade the ridiculously busy Huxley to take. 'You are waking an appetite for food which no one can supply so well as yourself.'[3] It was on the back of these conversations that Lockyer approached Macmillan with a proposal for a scientific journal. His career at the War Office was floundering but his scientific credentials had been established by his work in discovering helium in the corona of the Sun, earning him election to the Royal Society. Macmillan was, as ever, driven by two motives: an earnest desire to improve the quality of scientific publishing in Britain and beyond by only commissioning work from acknowledged experts in the field; and a hearty appreciation of the first-mover advantage in a market that would increase exponentially as schools and universities around the world grasped the necessity of teaching science.

Nature entered an increasingly crowded market – according to some estimates the number of scientific periodicals published in England had risen from five in 1815 to eighty in 1895. In addition, many of the general literary periodicals, such as the *Athenaeum*, carried scientific articles and reviews. Macmillan and Lockyer planned to produce a popular science magazine that could be read by both scientists and laymen: they agreed that it was unlikely that the market of serious scientists could be large enough to support a purely technical publication. Lockyer was very clear when he wrote to contributors that he and his proprietor had two rather ambitious aims.

> First, to place before the general public the grand results of Scientific Work and Scientific Discovery, and to urge the claims of Science to a more general recognition in Education and Daily Life; and
>
> Secondly, to aid Scientific men themselves, by giving early information of all advances made in any branch of Natural Knowledge throughout the world, and by affording them an opportunity of discussing the various Scientific questions which arise from time to time.[4]

Lockyer began commissioning pieces from the contributors who had featured in the *Reader*: his core supporters would be Huxley and the X-Club crew, who despised the popular science articles peddled by journalists and amateurs which were filling the press. Macmillan wrote to the great and the good of the scientific world to gather endorsements, although he did not always meet with encouragement. Joseph Hooker, Director of the Royal Botanical Gardens at Kew, sent his best wishes but expressed doubts that *Nature* could succeed, its brief being too wide-ranging for any one editor: 'I do not see how a really scientific man can find the time to conduct a periodical scientifically, or brains to go over the mass of trash.'[5] In Lockyer, however, Macmillan had found just such a man.

While Lockyer gathered supporters for the new publication, Macmillan decided on the title, much to Huxley's delight. 'Macmillan told me yesterday that he had nailed his colours to the mast – and was going in for *"Nature"*, pure and simple.'[6] The journal was aiming at an international audience, carrying reviews of the latest scientific papers from across Europe and the United States, reports of meetings, articles on recent experiments, editorial and, crucially, a correspondence column, which allowed scientists to exchange ideas across the world on a weekly basis. The subject matter ranged widely, from astronomy to zoology. Lockyer had a completely free hand, and much of his time was spent refereeing disputes between some of the big beasts of the scientific world, which he did tactfully and firmly. He thrived on controversy and his biographer says he often lost the argument, but he had the energy and self-confidence of youth on his side and was never daunted.

Macmillan took a huge financial risk, pricing the weekly at only four pence a copy, when most weeklies were six pence. The first edition launched on Thursday 4 November 1869: '*Nature: A Weekly Illustrated Journal of Science*'. Its masthead showed the Earth rising above the clouds and a quotation from Wordsworth, 'To the solid ground of Nature trusts the mind which builds for aye.' The astute would remark that in the original it had been Mind which was capitalized rather than Nature; a sign perhaps that there would be little theology or respect for a Deity within the pages that followed. (The

masthead would remain unchanged until the 1950s.) The editorial of
the first edition was pulled together rather grandiosely by Huxley
based on aphorisms he had translated from Goethe: 'Nature! We are
surrounded and embraced by her; powerless to separate ourselves
from her and powerless to penetrate beyond her.' As was becoming
his custom, Alexander chose to mark the launch with a grand dinner
of scientists at the Garrick Club.

The first issue contained, as well as Huxley's editorial address,
illustrated articles on plant fertilization and on the recent eclipse of
the Sun, an editorial on teaching science in British schools, an obituary of a Scottish chemist, reports from recent meetings in Paris and
Philadelphia, and news of exciting discoveries. Over the next few
decades, all under Lockyer's editorship, *Nature* published articles
which celebrated the scientific advances of the era: the invention
of the typewriter and the bathometer and the application of electri-
city to lighting. One of the most significant original contributions,
according to *Nature*'s website, was a letter in 1880 documenting the
use of fingerprints to catch criminals. Throughout the periodical
campaigned for better scientific education and a career structure for
scientists.

Despite Lockyer's and Macmillan's best intentions, it soon
became clear that much of the material was well above the head of
the enthusiastic lay reader. Charles Kingsley had contributed a book
review to an early issue – but by 1872 he was writing to Lockyer, 'I
have the highest respect for [*Nature*], and I wish I were wise enough
to understand more of it. But I fear its circulation must be more
limited than you would wish.'[7] Lockyer's contributors had proved
more interested in debating with each other than in trying to educate
the general public, and the content had become more specialist and
technical. *Nature* had become the embodiment of the scientific elite's
determination to professionalize science in Britain. The next generation of British scientists saw *Nature* as the ideal forum for spreading
word of their discoveries and for establishing their credentials. Getting an article published in an authoritative scientific journal became

a recognized route to establishing a scientific career, at a time when there was little formal scientific education at degree level or beyond.

However, none of this would make *Nature* a profitable enterprise, and Alexander Macmillan's public-spirited determination to continue to support a loss-making enterprise for many years tells us much about the man. It is not easy to get at the facts, but when Charles Morgan wrote his history of the house of Macmillan, he claimed that it did not pay its way until the mid-1890s. At the time of its centenary, *Nature* produced a series of articles reflecting on its history and success, and the author Roy McLeod estimated that the periodical had cost well over £2,000 to produce annually, and was funded predominantly by advertisements rather than counter sales or subscriptions, which remained in the hundreds rather than the thousands until the twentieth century. The figures are not conclusive, the losses not enormous, and the justification for the claim that Alexander bore the losses resolutely for many years comes from the letter that Craik wrote to the editor in 1899: 'I am glad that your diligence and tenacity has been at last rewarded by money besides all the honour that *Nature* has brought you. We have waited many years.'[8] It is worth remembering that Craik was ever the pessimist when it came to financial performance.

Lockyer was the editor of *Nature* for fifty years, and his relationship with Macmillan remained strong throughout; he named one of his sons Alexander. When he suffered from strain and overwork in the 1870s, Macmillan sent him a cheque to pay for a holiday.

Why did *Nature* succeed where others had failed? Certainly, having an ambitious and energetic editor who approached it as a full-time job gave it a head start. Journals that relied on the few hours a week that the likes of Huxley could spare were doomed to fail. Secondly, it was a weekly publication that prided itself on being absolutely up to date. It specified 2.30 p.m. on Thursdays as the point of publication, distributed by Saturday. Consequently the articles were short and the turnaround very rapid, essential in such a fast-moving field. Thirdly, it was independent of any of the learned societies and unique in its spread of interests. Even more importantly, according to John Maddox, the editor at the time of the centenary celebrations in 1969, 'it was a splendid piece of journalism'. He went on to say: 'at its best, journalism is a way of creating a sense of community among people who would otherwise be isolated from each other. This is what Lockyer's journal did from the start.'[9] Overriding all of this was Alexander Macmillan's determination, and financial ability, to support it.

16

TEAMWORK

(1870)

John, Viscount Morley

'No one can read with profit that which he cannot learn to read with pleasure.'

Thomas Hardy

THE DAWNING OF a new decade was marked by the passing of a piece of legislation that would illustrate how perceptive Alexander had been in choosing to concentrate on schoolbooks and textbooks. The 1870 Elementary Education Act was sponsored by William Edward Forster. He was well known to Macmillan and the old Christian Socialist set; indeed, he had been a contributor on the subject of the American Civil War in one of the earliest issues of *Macmillan's Magazine*. Forster's views on education had been shaped by his father-in-law, Dr Arnold, and by his brother-in-law Matthew Arnold's experiences as a school inspector. Demand that something be done to improve education in England had been growing for the past decade. The 1861 census revealed that of the four million children of primary school age, some were in state-aided voluntary schools, some were in Church schools, but nearly half were receiving no education at all. The 1867 Reform Act which had widened the franchise had brought calls for better schooling, so that the newly enfranchised voters might be educated men. 'We [the legislators] must not delay . . . now that we have given them political power we must not wait any longer to give them education.'[1] This coincided with a concern from industrialists that Britain needed a better-educated workforce if it was to compete internationally.

The Act provided for the establishment of school boards, to be elected by the ratepayers, both male and female. Where there was agreed to be inadequate provision in a particular location, the boards were instructed to establish schools for the education of children between the ages of five and thirteen. However, attendance would not become compulsory until the Mundella Act of 1880, and even then, only between the ages of five and ten. Parents still had to pay school fees, although school boards were able to assist the poorest children. Schooling would not be free until 1891. The additional funding required over and above parental fees was collected via the rates, and the schools were subject to regular inspection. Much of the Act was contentious – there was unhappiness about the provision of religious education in schools which had to be non-denominational in the board schools, and parents had the right to withdraw their children from religious instruction if it was against their particular faith. In most places in England, nothing changed overnight, but this was a significant milestone and indicated a direction of travel. Over the next decade, several thousand new schools were built, millions more children entered education and many thousand teachers were trained and recruited, mostly women. Textbooks rolled off the presses and Macmillan's strategy for his own business and for the Oxford University Press paid significant dividends.

In 1870 the Macmillan family had a summer holiday on the west coast of Scotland, Alexander claiming it was the longest he had enjoyed for years. They took a house in Dunoon, and travelled by steamer to Irvine, where he was greeted, to his surprise, by a delegation from the Provost. Irvine awarded him the freedom of the town, 'as a mark of esteem and respect for the distinguished and honourable position and reputation he has through his own successful enterprise achieved for himself in connection with Literature and Art, and in appreciation of his worth and admiration of those virtues which adorn his character.'[2] He accepted the honour with great pride, a rare honour in a life that saw few public awards, and was delighted that it brought him back into correspondence with old friends who remembered his schooldays. As reported in the local press, he was proud of his roots, saying 'the stability of the future in no small degree depended on reverence for the past.'[3]

However, 1870 also brought a pressing problem much closer to home: what to do with his eldest son, Malcolm. That summer the young man finished his education at King's College School in

London, garlanded with prizes for literature, and his father sent him to live in Cambridge, as his cousin Frederick had done before, to stay with cousin Robert Bowes and learn the book trade. Malcolm's last year at King's was full of literature and drama, and all the previous problems he had with schooling seemed to have been overcome. Banishment to Cambridge backfired badly, however, as Malcolm had other ambitions – it must have been heart-breaking for him to walk the streets every day among boys he had been at school with, and watch them disappear into colleges and halls, while he went to stand behind a counter and learn double-entry bookkeeping. By October it had become insupportable, and he wrote to his father expressing a desire to go on to university, specifically to Cambridge. Alexander replied to Malcolm's request with a letter which the family carefully preserved, setting out the advantages and disadvantages of both positions, and ending in a blatant appeal to Malcolm's conscience to think of his father's health.

> It has been to no small degree a disadvantage to me that I did not enter a business career till I was 21. The study and the practice of the laws which lead to success in business is a very serious study and practice, and if undertaken in a spirit of thorough integrity may be a very ennobling one. Promptitude in executing orders, quickness in understanding them, intelligence in suggesting to young men what books will enable them best to master and study, accuracy and care in accounts, all these things and many others which will suggest themselves to you as you go along in business with Cousin Robert are admirable training for all your faculties. Temper and courtesy to customers and to servants, the habits of command and of obedience, all these are to be learnt in a retail business. Political Economy, Logic, Moral and Mental Science are here in their practical elements. Your private reading will supply you with the speculations of others, your private thinking will realise them for yourself. You need not cease to be a student, because you are a

shopkeeper. There are mean half-thoughted students, I assure you, as there are mean half-thoughted shopkeepers. Baseness in morals, poverty in thought attach themselves necessarily to no line of legitimate human effort, they are damages from which no line of human effort is free.

You remind me in your thoughtful letter that I have sometimes set no great store on circumstances as determining human character or action. In a certain sense, everything depends on circumstances. I am a certain circumstance to you, the words I am writing are circumstances, they are not you. They come to you from outside your proper self. They influence you in some way, whether you reject or accept them. But you have the power of discrimination, choice, judgment.

I am now putting before you two possible sets of circumstances which are to be chosen by our joint judgment, one or other, as best fitted to aid you in fulfilling your life's work. But what I have always sought to call your attention to as that which concerns you most is yourself, the being who is in the midst of the circumstances. No one can afford to overlook circumstances. The wise man makes the best of them and regulates his life accordingly. In this part of my letter I am very anxious to direct your attention to the whole circumstances of your present position and ask you to weigh them well and see whether my judgment of the best course you are now to follow is not the right one, and whether it may not be possible for you to carry out the really high ideal of life which I most gladly recognise in your letter without abandoning the course you have now entered on – whether the study of life in business is wholly or even to a serious extent incompatible with study of books and thought.

I think then that to lose the three years of study of business which you would do in going to college would be a serious disadvantage which you should not incur for a merely possible gain. The possible disadvantage is one which I speak of with some reluctance, as it may savour of selfishness. But I think I may candidly put it before you, trusting to your generous interpretation. Besides it really does concern you and your prospects. I am no longer a young man, my life has been a long strain. I hope I may live to dandle your children on a strong enough knee. But I sometimes feel very weary and would gladly see you, whom I have always looked forward to as the one to take my place in the business, getting into shape and mood for so doing. Now, however great the advantage to your own mental discipline a college course might be it would not fit you for this. The training you already have had will fit you for such a part far better than I am fitted by culture or education . . . The best businessman almost I know is Mr John Evans of the firm of Dickinsons, the great paper makers.[4] He is a Fellow of the Royal Society, and a most distinguished Naturalist and Antiquarian. He never was at college.

I told you that your mother and Mr Maclear [his headmaster] took the same view of your letter as I do. You know what that is. I must repeat your letter, though I don't agree with it wholly, gave me great pleasure: and I shall gladly hear from you again. In the meantime I am sure that you will see that your course is to work as hard as you can with cousin Robert and do everything you possibly can to help him in the business.[5]

It is a thoughtful letter, which Alexander had clearly taken great pains over, but it must have been deeply frustrating for Malcolm, who could see that there were two other young men, his brother and his cousin, quite capable of taking his place in the business, alongside Fred who was already in harness and about to leave for the States. Alexander gained his point at the time, but Malcolm did not take to the work, although Caroline wrote to George in February 1871 that his brother had settled down in Cambridge, had joined the Volunteers run by his Uncle Robert and was learning to drill, attending lectures, studying French and talking politics.

When the family were not dealing with Malcolm, their social calendar remained as exhausting as ever, especially for the ailing Caroline and the over-worked Alexander. Caroline's letters to George remain full of tales of dinner parties of a dozen guests or more, overnight visitors, and male-only evenings at the Garrick. In February Alexander visited Edinburgh and Glasgow for ten days – labelled as a holiday but packed with meetings. Caroline wrote to George: 'Papa saw everyone of any note in Edinburgh and went to large parties, and at Glasgow where he stayed with MacLehose. I have not seen him in such good spirits for two years, it is quite a relief to me, for a long time he seemed weighed down by anxiety.'[6] The All Fools' Dinner of 1871 was held at The Elms, although as all the trees had blown down in a storm the family was considering renaming their house 'The Stumps'. In May, Caroline organized a major redecoration of the downstairs rooms, which had to be celebrated with yet another large party, where guests included Professor Henry Fawcett and his wife Millicent.

Macmillan, like any Victorian entrepreneur, assumed that the firm he and his brother had founded would be carried on by his sons and his nephews. He held Daniel's share in the business in precious emotional trust for Daniel's three boys, Fred, Maurice, and Arthur. But while he waited for them to be old enough to take possession, he came to rely on three other men, all of exceptional talent and ambition. Two of these we have already met: Norman Lockyer and George, later Sir George, Grove. The other was John Morley, later Viscount Morley. His relationship with these three men is indicative of the changing nature of the intellectual in England in the second half of the century. All three came from the less affluent end of the middle classes: Morley's father was a provincial doctor, Lockyer's father just one step down from this, a surgeon-apothecary, and Grove's father was a fishmonger and dealer in game. Of the three, only Morley went to university, and that was because Oxford had just introduced the open scholarship exam, and his parents were able to scrape together enough money to send an obviously bright lad to Cheltenham College for three years to be prepped.

For the first twenty years of his publishing career, Macmillan had relied on the Oxbridge-educated wealthy middle and upper classes to supply authors worth publishing – and most of those came from landed gentry, who wrote either as a personal hobby, like Hughes, or to supplement the dwindling income of a parish living, like Kingsley. Now a new intellectual elite was forming, Thomas Huxley being the most obvious example, comprising men who chose to make a living from their pens, and who relied on their first-class brains and specialist knowledge to claw their way to the top of a whole new profession: the man of letters. These individuals were a breath of fresh air in Victorian Britain, and to Alexander personally. He was no longer just a tradesman, commissioned by his 'superiors' to turn their pet projects into books – he was an equal, a publisher and entrepreneur whom these men of letters would respect for his business success, with whom they could collaborate on significant and ground-breaking projects such as *Nature*, *Grove's Dictionary of Music*, and the *English Men of Letters* series of biographies, which Morley would edit.

John Morley was born in 1838, the son of a surgeon practising in Blackburn, Lancashire. From Cheltenham College, where he won prizes in history and Greek, Morley went to Lincoln College, Oxford, in preparation for ordination, but fell under the spell of a fellow student, Cotter Morison, who introduced him to the writings of Carlyle, Emerson, and the Positivists. All thoughts of a career in holy orders were abandoned and, cast adrift financially by his devout and angry father, Morley set off to London to make a career as a journalist. This he recognized as precarious and risky, but as he wrote in his memoirs, his life was made significantly less precarious when he was introduced to Alexander Macmillan. The passage is worth quoting at length, as it is written by one of the acknowledged great minds of the late Victorian and Edwardian eras.

Aptly has it been said by one of the most brilliant writers of
our day, that the great publisher is a sort of Minister of Letters
and is not to be without the qualities of a statesman. Extravagant as it may sound to the unthinking, more than one passage
in chronicles of the writing and selling of books confirms
the view. The head of the house of Macmillan when I came
to London – it had been founded at Cambridge by an elder
brother then deceased – had these qualities in the full sense and
measure proper for his task. He had the very first of them to
begin with: he was sincerely interested in the drift and matter of
good books in serious spheres. The worst of statesmen is that
they sometime rather feign than feel this sort of interest. With
him it was genuine. He went about his work with active conscience and high standards, he had the blessing, both attractive
and useful, of imagination, added to shrewd sense and zeal for
the best workmanship. His eye for the various movements in
his time of knowledge and thought, literary, scientific and religious, showed extraordinarily acute insight. He knew his world:
it comprised the most enlightened of our social strata, and he
gathered a body of men around him with many vigorous tal-
ents, with his own strict exaction in way of competency, and
his own honourable sense of public responsibility. His energy,
tranquil persistence, and view of his calling reminded one of
Perthes, the famous publisher who did so much for his trade in
Germany in the earlier years of the nineteenth century.

It was no secret between us two how very materially, as he
said, my way of looking at men and the world differed from
his own. He bore the light opinion I held of some favourite teachers and apostles of his without the least impatience,
consoling himself by the retaliatory guess that "Mill and the
Comtists are not quite at the centre of truth and would speed-
ily pass their day." Fortunately for me this made no difference
either in his constant and zealous goodwill to me as a friend,
or his indulgent confidence for many years in my professional

utilities, though my advice like most advice was sometimes bad if sometimes good.[7]

The 1860s were exceedingly hard-going for Morley until in 1867 he was appointed editor of a new publication, the *Fortnightly Review*, and began acting as a paid reader for Macmillan. From then until he entered politics as an MP in 1883 he was very much Alexander's right-hand man when it came to literary decisions. His unconventional family life does not seem to have bothered Macmillan at all: in May 1870, shortly after the death of his mother, John Morley married Mary Rose Ayling, a woman with whom he had already been living openly, and who had had two children, possibly out of wedlock by an apparently unknown partner.[8]

George Grove came from even humbler stock. He attended a small weekly boarding school on Clapham Common, which he left at the age of sixteen to qualify as an engineer. For five years in the 1840s he lived and worked as an engineer in the West Indies, and then returned to work on the Britannia Bridge over the Menai Strait in Wales. Here he was noticed by some of the great engineers of the day, including Brunel and Robert Stephenson, who sent him to London where he was appointed Secretary to the Society of Arts, at a period of crucial activity in preparation for the Great Exhibition of 1851. When the Exhibition closed and the elaborate glasshouse which housed it was dismantled and moved to Sydenham, Grove was appointed Secretary to this, the Crystal Palace, and was at last able to indulge his real passion for classical and choral music, putting on a series of concerts for which he wrote all the programme notes. 'I wish it to be distinctly understood that I have always been a mere amateur in music. I wrote about the symphonies and concertos because I wished to try to make them clear to myself and to discover the secret of the things that charmed me so; and from that sprang a wish to make other amateurs see it in the same way.'[9]

His great friend from preparatory school, met when he was only eight years old, was George Granville Bradley, later Headmaster of

Marlborough and Dean of Westminster, and in 1851 Grove married Bradley's sister Harriet. In his spare time, he and his wife began visiting the Holy Land and worked on a dictionary of the Bible and a concordance of biblical place names. Grove's essay 'Nabloos and the Samaritans' was included in one of Macmillan's *Vacation Tourist* volumes. He was in the same mould as Lockyer, a self-taught enthusiast who could turn his hard-won knowledge into clear and easily accessible prose for the general public – and in 1867 he began to assist Masson with editing *Macmillan's Magazine*, and then took over as editor. By 1874, Macmillan was paying Grove £300 per annum for this role and another £600 for general management of the literary department of the business. This probably involved reading manuscripts and shepherding them through the press: Alexander remained the final arbiter of what was to be published. But at last he had a capable team to work with: if it was a technical or scientific subject, he would enquire of Huxley, or of Norman Lockyer. If it was literary, he turned to John Morley or George Grove. The literary side of the firm was no longer such a one-man band, and its output increased in range and quality.

17

CAROLINE AND EMMA

Winnington Hall

'Yet if you should forget me for a while
And afterwards remember, do not grieve:
For if the darkness and corruption leave
A vestige of the thoughts that once I had,
Better by far you should forget and smile
Than that you should remember and be sad.'

Christina Rossetti

IN THE SPRING of 1871, Caroline Macmillan took to her bed for the last time. She was dying of the heart disease that had plagued her with periods of ill-health for a decade or more. In the two months before she died the failure of the heart to pump properly led to swelling and oedema, and although doctors had begun to understand the causes of the illness, there was little they could do before the invention of diuretics except to administer digitalis, and syphon off the excess fluid that collected in the legs. No expense was spared in treating her – for several years before she died her physician was Dr William Gull of Guy's Hospital, who was awarded a baronetcy by the Queen in 1872 for his success in treating the Prince of Wales's typhoid fever. Caroline was moved into the shady front bedroom at The Elms, previously the nursery, where she had a view of the trees, the 'murderous elms' which kept 'shying branches down on people', as Alexander had written in happier times. Her final illness lasted some twelve weeks, and her daughter Margaret remembers it as a time when the family took it in turns to sit with her reading to her from the newspapers, lurid tales from the siege of Paris and gossip from the first trial of the Tichborne Claimant. 'My father would come in from town and, having set aside all thoughts of business, sit and chat quietly to my mother as if he had not a care in the world. For a man of his strong feeling he had an extraordinary power of self-control.'[1]

Considering that Caroline bore Alexander five children before she died aged only forty-eight, and was married to him for almost twenty years, she figures very little in the family or company archives. She is scarcely mentioned in Graves's biography of her husband that her children commissioned, not even meriting an entry in the index, and there are no known surviving portraits. When her eldest daughter, Margaret, wrote her own memories of her childhood, she remembered that on Sundays her mother would lead Bible readings: 'She had the art of teaching the Bible stories so that they were, to say the least, as interesting to us as any other stories. My eldest brother, whose memory went further back and in everything concerning her was vivid, thought that her gifts in this way were remarkable.'[2] It is not much to go on, and disappointing that her children had so little else to say on the subject; even within the usual polite, unemotional confines of Victorian biography this is a meagre tribute. Her death in July 1871 was notified to the registrar by Mary Ann Coxall, the faithful maidservant and nanny who had been with the family for twenty years already and who was 'present at the death'.

Caroline was buried in the same grave as her little son William, in West Norwood Cemetery. The stone is a simple cross, just marking her name and dates, 'the wife of Alexander Macmillan', and the legend 'Then shall I know even as I am also known.' There is no gushing tribute to a beloved wife or mother. George Macmillan wrote that her death 'deprived [Alexander] of a companion whose unfailing sympathy and keen intelligence had been of priceless value for just twenty years of strenuous effort and whose loving wisdom had been his stay in all family relations.'[3] But he then proceeds, scarcely drawing breath, to announce that within fifteen months of this loss, Alexander had remarried. Caroline's gravestone itself seems to bear witness to the speed with which the family moved on – it was clearly bought and erected with the intention that the names of Alexander and other family members would be added in later years: in fact, below Caroline's name there is only eighteen inches of smooth stone.

The correspondence files at the British Library tell us little of the effect on the family, as they are mostly concerned with business and not with how Alexander coped with this loss. There are two brief passages in letters which Alexander sent to his old friend Alexander Campbell Fraser later that year: the Macmillan headed paper is now black-bordered, and he wrote that he had spent the summer in Tooting, commuting daily to work, and then took the children and their governess to Brighton for three weeks: 'We have all been the better for the change.' Then in January 1872 he wrote again: 'We were very happy on the whole this Christmas. My nephew Robert Bowes from Cambridge and his wife – my wife's sister as you may remember – and their two babies came. These and one old friend who has dined with us every Christmas for many years made our circle. The children are all wonderfully well, except my nephew Arthur, who suffered so much from the effects of the rheumatic fever. I can hardly foresee what I will be able to do in the spring. If I do come to Edinburgh I am engaged to stay with my friend Geikie, whom I will have to console for the recent infliction of a very charming wife whom he met at my house. For all I hear he is not greatly the worse or unhappier for it.'[4] The wife in question was born Alice Pignatel, and Alexander would be calling her his sister-in-law before the year was out.

Emma Pignatel, Alice's sister, was twenty-nine in 1872, one of four daughters of a French father and English mother. Her father, Eugene, was born in Lyon around 1818, making him an exact contemporary of Alexander, into a well-to-do family that owned one of the silk-trading businesses prominent in the area. Eugene began travelling for the firm, arriving in Dover for the first time in January 1838 and settling in Mosley Street, Manchester. On Christmas Day 1839 he married eighteen-year-old Priscilla Bundy Browne, the daughter of a tobacconist in Manchester, and together they moved to Livorno in Italy, where they lived for the next ten years and started a family. Their first daughter, Lucy, was born in 1840, followed by Emma in 1843, Mary in 1845, Victor in 1846, and Charles in 1848. Emma's early life was one of relative prosperity, combined with constant upheaval and uncertainty. In 1848 revolution broke out in Tuscany, and Eugene became a member of the liberal provincial government that took control of Livorno, moving his family back to Lyon as he was appointed consul to Tuscany. When more conservative forces came to power in 1851, Eugene took his family to his wife's home town of Manchester, a journey that Emma remembered as 'long and tiresome'.

After a comfortable life in Tuscany and Lyon, damp and dirty Manchester must have been a terrible shock. The couple's last child, Alice, was born there in 1851, and the three elder girls, all under the age of eleven, were packed off to boarding school at Cheadle Hall, then to another establishment in Paris. They were lovely and attractive girls, speaking three languages, artistic and musical, especially the oldest, Lucy, who trained on the piano with Charles Halle. But financial disaster struck in the mid-1850s with the outbreak of silkworm disease in Europe, and Eugene's firm failed. With six children to support, drastic decisions had to be taken. The whole family moved back to France, this time to Chatou on the Seine, in the outskirts of Paris, and then to a smaller furnished house in Avranches on the coast. In the autumn of 1857, all four girls were sent to a boarding school in Lymm, Cheshire, where their father visited them to say goodbye – he was moving to Japan to try to restart his silk business. They never saw him again. Emma wrote: 'I suppose the terms must have been made possible. We were kindly done by there. Lucy and I both took to drawing and water colour painting and a kind governess lent us books and read poetry. There were old fashioned servants who taught us laundry.'[5] Their mother Priscilla had stayed behind in France, in a quiet country cottage, looking after the two boys until they were old enough to join their father in Nagasaki. Emma appears to say that her mother had a breakdown and it is possible that the marriage effectively ended, with Eugene later starting a new family with a Japanese woman.

In March 1859, Emma, aged sixteen, and her older sister Lucy, eighteen, began working as teaching assistants at Winnington Hall School in Cheshire, where their pay enabled their younger sisters Mary and Alice to board as pupils. There they met and became friends with a regular visitor, John Ruskin. This slightly odd story was only documented when a large cache of letters came to light in the 1950s, and is chronicled in *The Winnington Hall Letters*, edited by

Van Akin Burd. The school was originally founded in Manchester by Miss Margaret Bell, daughter of a Wesleyan Methodist preacher, and from him she inherited her strong and forceful personality. However in the 1840s she abandoned his faith to follow the Broad Church teachings of F. D. Maurice and Julius Hare. In 1851 she took the tenancy of Winnington Hall, just outside Northwich in Cheshire, from the Stanley family – a beautiful stately home with grounds and a lake. She took girls from as young as six until eighteen, and in the 1861 census there were seven teachers, ten servants, and only twenty-three boarding pupils – which may explain the financial difficulties under which Miss Bell laboured. Attracting the attention of the wealthy and famous John Ruskin seemed to be the answer to her prayers, and it was achieved by taking some of her girls to hear him lecture, expressing interest in his collection of artwork by J. M. W. Turner, and engineering an invitation to visit the Ruskin home in Denmark Hill in London, followed by a reciprocal offer. At the time, Ruskin was pining for Rose la Touche, the girl he had been obsessed with since he had met her the previous year, when she was just nine years old. Unable to progress this relationship, he transferred his attentions to the bevy of beauties at Winnington.

For seven years, Ruskin often stayed at the school and wrote regularly to Miss Bell and her pupils. He called the girls his 'birds', helped them with their drawing lessons, taught Bible studies alongside geology, played hide and seek, croquet, and cricket with them, watched their country dancing and choral evenings, stayed in the best room, and had the use of a private study. He wrote to Miss Bell that he had 'fallen in love with all thirty-five young ladies at once', and the cheques began to follow, a couple of hundred pounds at a time, much to the disapproval of his father, who clearly thought Miss Bell was a woman on the make.[6] By 1867 Ruskin had lent Miss Bell over a thousand pounds (multiply that by one hundred for today's values).

Among the names mentioned in the letters from Ruskin to Miss Bell are Emma and Lucy Pignatel. Emma's memoirs tell the story.

It was on 13 March 1859, just after we had settled in, that Ruskin paid the school his first visit, having been interested in what he had heard of Miss Bell's endeavour to carry out the teachings of his 'Elements of Drawing' . . . that evening he arrived in a travelling coach which was laden, I am sure, with the precious treasures he always carried about. That first evening we, in white dresses, assembled in the octagonal drawing room (a room for which the silk wallpaper had been made in China) and he shewed us Turners and made friends with us.

The next day he encouraged them to practise drawing from nature.

By some, for me wonderful chance, he sat down in my place and painted the bit of bark I still possess. In the course of time he encouraged me about my feeling for colour and in such odds and ends of time as came to me I learnt to copy William [Holman] Hunt and various bits of Ruskin's own work. He liked the dancing Miss Bell had instituted – a classical sort unknown to many people at that time, and then it was he wrote the verses *Awake Awake* which he gave to Aunt Lucy on her birthday and suggested that she and Mary Leadbeater (afterwards the wife of Canon Capes) should find a tune to make it into a dance . . . As he came a good many times he became a kind personal friend to some of us. He was particularly kind to Marie, who in her shyness had very sweet ways and when she grew ill in 1865 (she took cold after measles and in six months died of consumption) he wrote her many little notes to cheer the dreary times she went through.[7]

Yale University archives hold the proof sheets of Ruskin's *Praeterita*, and in among the notes Ruskin prepared for a theatrical performance he lists Emma as 'a great cricketer, perfect dancer, and entirely unselfish and clear-sighted counsellor'.[8] When Miss Bell fell ill in 1866, Ruskin wrote to another girl, 'I've always had great faith in Emma Pignatel', which suggests that she had assumed some seniority during Miss Bell's occasional lapses of concentration.⁹ Emma wrote: 'Miss Bell's teaching was sometimes very good indeed, and at other times things were irregular and uncomfortable, but we owed her so much in many ways that I don't want to refer to shortcomings.' The school fell increasingly into financial difficulties and within a few years Miss Bell had moved on to Weston-super-Mare. By 1873, Ruskin was regretting ever having met her or lent her any money: 'Damn Miss Bell'.¹⁰

In 1865, Emma's younger sister Mary fell terminally ill. There must have been financial support from somewhere, perhaps from the wealthy relations in Lyon who kept close to the girls and invited them to stay in the family chateau or took them sketching in Switzerland. Lucy took lodgings in London trying to find help for Mary, where they employed a nurse and found a kindly doctor, and Emma came to stay as well until Mary died. The sisters initially returned to Winnington, but Emma left in 1868 and Lucy the following year, by which time they had taken lodgings in Balham and were able to bring their mother over from France to live with them. In 1870 they took a lease on a smart little house, 20 Kensington Park Road, but that was where news reached them that their father had died of apoplexy in Nagasaki.

Macmillan family history relates that Emma was a friend of Louisa Cassell, as they had been teaching at the same school in Cheshire. This must have been Winnington Hall, although there is no mention of Louisa's name in any of Ruskin's letters. At some point around the time of their father's death, the girls re-established contact with Louisa, who was living in Tooting with the Macmillan family. They started to attend services at the Vere Street Chapel to hear F. D. Maurice preach, and were invited to visit The Elms by Caroline Macmillan. Emma wrote: 'I was shy about making any new acquaintances and feared to intrude when Mrs Macmillan very kindly pressed me to go and see them. Knapdale appealed to me; the kindness of the family, the old house and the book shelves a bit like Winnington.'[11] Caroline had often mentioned in her letters to George that the Miss Pignatels were coming to spend an evening, sometimes with their mother, and that they would all enjoy their musical talent.

The friendships between the Pignatel and Macmillan households were entwined more closely when Alice, the youngest of Emma's sisters, met and fell in love with one of Alexander's favourite authors, the geologist Archibald Geikie. Geikie, whom Alexander referred to as 'the man of stones', was thirty-five, Alice not quite nineteen when they married at St George's, Campden Hill, Kensington, in August 1871. Geikie had known Alexander for more than a decade, introduced to him by George Wilson in Edinburgh. The friendship between the two men flourished, as they shared an interest in science, a passion for the Arran landscape, and a love of Scottish songs. Once Geikie began to spend more time in the south to further his career, he was a regular guest in Cambridge, then at Henrietta Street and in Tooting, only struggling with the dense tobacco smoke that surrounded the publisher and affected his eyes. He was well loved by the Macmillan children, having given them a microscope and taught them how to use specimen slides.

Incidentally, the two officiating ministers at Alice's wedding were men who had married two sisters who also taught at Winnington Hall. William Wolfe Capes had married Mary Leadbeater in 1870, and her sister Joan had married his great friend Robert Henniker. Capes had met Mary at Winnington – he was an Oxford don, lured to the Hall in the early 1860s by Miss Bell and introduced by her to Ruskin. He was now rector of a little parish on the Surrey/Hampshire border called Bramshott, a place that would loom large in the Macmillan family's future.

Emma and Alexander were married on 24 October 1872 by licence, with Canon Kingsley officiating, at the same church where her sister Alice had married Geikie the year before, the newly built St George's in Campden Hill. There is a certain reticence visible in the arrangements made – a marriage by licence avoided the need for banns to be read at the parish church in Tooting – was Alexander hoping to avoid local gossip? The ages of bride and groom are not specified, the form just says 'Both of full age'. In fact, he was fifty-four and she was twenty-nine. Alexander describes his father Duncan as 'Gentleman, deceased', which was true in one sense, but not the usual sense. The witnesses were Emma's sister Lucy, and a mysterious Mr (or Mrs?) Whiteford. None of his family signed the register, but that may be because none of them were over the age of twenty-one. A brief notice was placed in *The Times* and the *Morning Advertiser* a few days afterwards, and the news was picked up in the gossip columns of the *Daily Mail*. The honeymoon was brief, just a few days in Torquay, as Alexander was still struggling with the sciatica that had laid him low all summer.

Alexander clearly felt in some way nervous about the reaction of his friends: it was not until February 1873, in response to an enquiry from Alexander Campbell Fraser, that he confessed:

My dear Fraser

I have been blaming myself over and over again for not having long ago written to two such friends as you and Mrs Fraser about all my own affairs and the changes that have taken place in them. But it is very hard to sit down deliberately and do this, although I have done it over and over again at shorter and greater length during the last few months. I did not want to write hurriedly to you, I am afraid that now I write you as I must at once, it cannot seem otherwise than hurried.

But I am glad to be able to tell you from my own mouth what you have heard from others that I am exceedingly happily settled in my home again, after many months of serious trouble. I do hope you will be able to come and see us . . .[12]

There are several letters of this type, none of which actually use the word 'wedding', or mention anything about his bride. Alexander seems to have chosen to present it to friends and clients as a convenient domestic arrangement. Was it the speed of the re-marriage or the twenty-five-year age gap that made him slightly nervous or embarrassed?

For Emma, approaching thirty, who had just lost her father and may have had a difficult relationship with the mother who sent her away for much of her childhood, the offer of marriage from wealthy Alexander would have been tempting whatever she felt about the older man. He was in fact attractive, according to Emma, 'a tall broad-shouldered man whose face inspired confidence, not only in his clear-sighted way of looking at things and firmness in dealing with them, but with always a kindly and patient outlook . . . I wonder if by saying "he was a rock to stand by" I can explain what a centre of his family he had become.'[13] For Alexander, grieving the loss of his first wife, yet overwhelmed by the responsibility of managing eight teenagers, three of them girls, the marriage must have been an enormous relief. When in 1878 his old friend Leslie Stephen similarly remarried after being widowed, Macmillan wrote to him: 'I may venture to congratulate you on following my example in restoring a shattered home with a new sweet centre of woman life. Whatever their wrongs and rights, they are very essential to our home life – these same women.'[14]

– 18 –

NEW HORIZONS

Knapdale House

'The wheels of life stand never idle, but go always round.'

Matthew Arnold

THERE WAS A new mistress at The Elms, soon to be renamed Knapdale, but little changed. Emma must have been glad of her experience of managing a large domestic staff at Winnington Hall when she arrived back from honeymoon in the autumn of 1872. The first Mrs Macmillan had managed a full complement of six servants, all of whom had come from the Cambridge area and three of whom had been with the family for more than ten years. According to Emma, some of Alexander's relations advised her to dismiss them all and hire her own staff, but Alexander 'kindly advised me to take my time and gratefully I remember how right he was in letting me trust their loyalty and devotion.'[1] For a man whose professional life and social life were so tightly intertwined, the ability to host his friends and authors at home among his family was an essential tool in his belt, and he was hoping for as little disruption as possible. Alexander was delighted that Emma slipped so easily into the life in Tooting, offering the same warm hospitality to others that had once been offered to her.

The cook was Sarah Porter, a large, confident woman who taught Emma how to entertain on the grand scale that Alexander now expected. Charlotte Wright, in her mid-forties, was the house-maid, also according to Emma 'a fine figure and very impressive. No one took liberties with her, or her notions about house linen.' Then there was Emma Pettit, also in her forties, who acted as parlour maid – 'a dear, and spoiled everybody within limits. She did not see why afternoon tea should be served – kettledrum it was called in those days – as well as the tea tray brought in after dinner into the drawing room, but she gave in; she was wonderfully patient with the "boys" when they ordered meals at odd times. She wore the neatest close cap tied under the chin, which she made herself on a never-changing pattern.' In her reminiscences, the new Mrs Macmillan told the story of when her husband had asked for coffee for a guest, to which Pettit replied that they had no coffee. Alexander fixed her with a firm stare: 'I did not ask you Emma if you had any coffee, I said bring coffee.' From then on, Pettit ensured that there was always coffee as well as tea for any guest. Pettit stayed with the family until she could work no longer and was then looked after by Alexander in the country for the rest of her days.

However, it was Mary Ann Coxall, known as 'Mamie', who was, according to Emma, the real 'ruler' in the house. Now forty years old, she had lived with the Macmillans since she was seventeen, starting straight from Sunday school, and doted on both Fanny and Caroline's family, having nursed them all as babies, especially poor little Willie who died so young. When Emma was expecting her first baby and asked Coxall if they should hire a nursery nurse, Coxall replied, 'Do you think there could be a baby in this house and me not caring for it?' The corner front room, where Caroline had died, reverted to being Mamie's domain with a night nursery next door, then on the other side of Maggie and Olive's bedrooms, further along, what had been the old schoolroom became a spare bedroom for overnight guests, of whom there were many, and a little school-room was created downstairs near the back door.

There was still nearly a full complement of Macmillan children based at home. The girls had started to attend a local day school and were studying for exams. Maurice had moved from Uppingham School to Christ's College, Cambridge, at Michaelmas 1871 with a scholarship. Arthur had followed Maurice to Summer Fields but was already struggling with the tuberculosis that would kill him before his twentieth birthday. In early 1873 he set sail for India, hoping that the heat might improve his health, but to no avail and within a few months he was home again. Emma became very fond of the young man, and they sat and read the Bible together, Arthur draped in one of Emma's grey woollen shawls.

Alexander's increasing wealth, combined with the changing lifestyles of the younger generation who comprised the majority of residents, including his new young wife, led to greater evidence of prosperity. 1873 saw the arrival of one horse then two, a carriage and a coachman called Stribling, a pony carriage and pony. The young people made friends with their neighbours: across the street in Stapleton House lived the Lucas family with ten children of similar ages, and nearby, the Erichsen family, Danish in origin, with talented, artistic daughters Alice and Nelly. Cousins from Cambridge added to the fun: the Johnson and Bowes children mixed with the MacLehoses from Glasgow and the children of Sir Frederick Maurice, F. D. Maurice's son. Croquet, tennis, and bowls became regular amusements, as well as concerts and performances devised by Malcolm. Large garden parties were held throughout the summer, including the 'wayzgoose' to entertain all the firm and its friends, male and female. This was an all-day event, according to Emma, with 'Lunch, cricket and bowls and the tea and recitations, and "Uncle Alex" called on to recite Little Billie, and Auld Lang Syne was a very real jollification to end with.'[2] Evening parties consisted of dances for the 'quality', as Emma liked to call them. The old guard were disappearing: F. D. Maurice died in 1872 and the constantly harassed and over-worked Kingsley followed him to the grave in 1875, much to Alexander's distress as they were of the same age, just fifty-six. But there were new regulars: friends from Cambridge such as Aldis Wright (the great Shakespeare scholar and polymath, known to his friends as Always Right); John Green the historian and his lovely Irish wife Alice Stopford Green; and Henry and Millicent Fawcett. Alice Green wrote:

The persistent hospitality of Knapdale can never be forgotten. No friend, so long as he lived, was I think ever set aside or allowed to fall out of the circle. If he was sick or solitary, so much more the reason for drawing him into the family group, and the welcome had always the same freshness and heartiness, which won even the most recalcitrant to good humour and contentment. Certainly Mr Macmillan had an unfailing tenderness and sympathy behind his cheerful welcome: the warmth of his kindness drew together all the diverse elements of his group. I have known no house since Mr Macmillan's where there was so single-minded a desire to welcome men absolutely on their own merits, whatever might be their work or their persuasion or their position.

She painted a vivid portrait of the man.

Mr Macmillan preserved a perpetual youth of character and heart . . . he was extremely vivacious at times in discussion, when the subject moved him, and with his hands on the arms of his chair would lift himself half out of it while he denounced an adversary's views. But his ardour was so evidently for the subject in hand, and so little against his opponent, that as far as I remember it only gave animation to the talk but did not silence it. He made no effort to lead the conversation, being in general more desirous to hear others than to speak, and his vivid and obvious interest in all that was said certainly stimulated discussion. He was more than a host in the ordinary material sense: he was a host also, whose presence was never forgotten nor negligible, in the intellectual entertainment of his guests.[3]

A particular favourite with the teenagers was a cleric called Alfred Ainger, a graduate of Trinity College, Cambridge, and since 1866, a Reader at the Temple. Ainger seems to have been an extraordinary personality, tall and slim, good looking with startling blue eyes. A friend said of him, 'When he left us, we always felt as if we had been at a wedding: we did not know what to do for the rest of the day.'[4] He had first written for *Macmillan's Magazine* in its early days of 1859, but when he found himself driven to increase his income by the necessity of providing for his many orphaned nephews and nieces he began to contribute regularly, and was a particular friend of George Grove. He loved to act and could recite reams of Shakespeare. Emma remembered him singing to Lucy Pignatel's piano accompaniment and reading Chaucer to a little company of Tooting neighbours.

In January 1873 Emma was pregnant – J. R. Green wrote to a mutual friend, the historian Edward Freeman, mentioning rumours of 'a small Macmillanides, or Mac-Mac-millan', but she suffered a miscarriage, and was in need of a complete change of scene.[5] This led to the beginning of Alexander's travels on the Continent. His daughter Maggie wrote, 'We had known very little of foreigners or foreign travel. My father had once been to Paris and constantly declared that nothing could induce him ever to leave England again. It is quite characteristic of him that after this vehement assertion he was persuaded, the year following his second marriage, to make his first journey to Italy, humorously professing himself subject to the irresistible will of another . . . he came back full of talk about all they had seen and done.'[6] This was a second honeymoon for the couple, as their week in Torquay following the wedding had been more of a rest cure for the groom than a honeymoon. Alexander was certainly a nervous and reluctant traveller; he wrote to Charles Dodgson: 'Alas! And Hurrah! Are both in my mind when I think of it. I want and shall enjoy the rest and the trip, but I feel reluctant to leave my work.'[7]

The journey began in Paris where Alexander re-acquainted himself with Lowell the abolitionist, whom he had met in Boston. In Lyon they stayed with Emma's French relatives the Pignatel family, and were taken driving in 'Cousin Victor's fine open carriage with his £300 pair of beautiful English horses'.[8] They then travelled to Marseilles and took the slow train along the coast to Menton in company with an Austrian baron, who helped Alexander to pick a branch from an olive tree at a wayside station to send home to his daughter Olive. Menton enchanted Alexander, as he wrote to Craik, looking out from his hotel bedroom at 'the sun-spangled blue of the Mediterranean stretching before me . . . It is only ten and I have been up three hours, had coffee in our bedroom, been out in the garden in front of the sea, smoked my pipe and read Saturday's Daily News, and now my wife is dressing and we are chatting of our plans, which become a little perplexing from the richness we feel before us. What we have seen is enough to last one's life for its glorious beauty.' However lovely the surroundings, or the pleasure of Emma's company, Alexander found it hard to shake off his work worries. 'Of course I will come back at an hour's notice for anything really important.'[9]

They stopped in Genoa, where Emma introduced Alexander to her friends from Winnington, the Capes, and then on to Pisa, to Livorno (or Leghorn as they knew it) and Montenero. In Rome they stayed near the Pantheon, then on to Naples and Capri, where they met John Green, at that point still a bachelor. By the middle of April they were in Venice, staying at the Alberga Europa, having a very romantic time taking moonlit excursions around the lagoon in a gondola. 'It is clear that I am rapidly becoming demoralised by this holiday-making, as I have had no letter from the business for ten days and only one from Malcolm from home, and yet I am not in the very least worrying about anything.'[10] They travelled home with Green, bringing jewellery, Venetian glass, and innumerable photographs.

That summer of 1873 Alexander was happy to cross the Channel again, this time with his daughters as well as Emma. He deposited them in Boulogne in a typical French house with an ivy-covered courtyard and a sunny walled garden, overlooking the ramparts and away from the fashionable areas – or 'above the swells and smells', as he wrote to Kingsley.[11] The family drove round the picturesque fishing villages, and walked in the forests, while Alexander went back to London, feeling under pressure at work as always. He returned in early September to take them all to Paris, which Maggie described as 'an episode of perfectly unclouded delight', visiting the Louvre, Versailles, and Saint-Cloud, still black and ruined from the recent Franco-Prussian War.

While Alexander and Emma were enjoying their new life together, Frederick was in New York, where the fledgling business was absorbing capital at an alarming rate and struggling to produce a return. There were still difficulties with the New York Customs

House, and even with Fred on the ground, Craik found it hard to understand the accounts. In December 1871 the partners had received an approach from Charles Welford, Scribner's man in England. The Scribner publishing house in New York had been founded in 1846, and in 1870 it launched a monthly magazine much like *Macmillan's*. Following the death of the founder in 1871 the firm was re-organizing its capital structure and Welford, as he set sail for the States, casually suggested that they might come to some arrangement or cooperation with Macmillan in New York. Alexander and Craik leapt on this as a possible solution to their difficulties and wrote to Fred. Welford had flattered Alexander by saying they could retain the name 'Macmillan' as of great value. Alexander instructed Fred: 'get them to make the offer, the notion comes from them'.[12] It is possible that Welford had no authority for the suggestion he had made, for nothing happened while he was in New York. The partners waited anxiously for Welford to return to England, hoping he would bring a proposal with him. Fred's first stab at the 1871 accounts arrived and Craik was horrified to see that annual expenses were running at 20 per cent of sales – at that rate, he argued, some of their authors would have done better to deal directly with the American publishers. Alexander wrote to Fred saying that if they decided to close the New York office completely, and could do so without financial loss, Fred could return home with valuable knowledge of the American market, and they could feel that they had achieved a great deal to raise awareness of English authors abroad. This, said Alexander, had been one of his motives for opening there, but would hardly have been of much comfort to Brett, who had settled his wife and children in Manhattan.

Craik was keen that if Welford did come back to London with a proposal, he should be able to communicate very rapidly with Fred and Brett, and he described in a letter a series of coded telegram messages to be sent, depending on whether the offer was of any interest. By 14 March Welford, who had suffered an accident on board ship and was laid up in lodgings, had still not visited Bedford

Street, so Craik, resignedly, told Fred to renew the Bleeker Street lease for one more year. Welford never did make an offer, and the partners had to reluctantly continue to pour money into New York, and at additional cost: to smooth Brett's ruffled feathers, Alexander wrote offering to add to his salary of £450 per annum with a five per cent profit share – 'the sooner this rises to a large sum, the better for all concerned.'[13] It should also have encouraged Brett to reduce costs, as Craik required.

Frederick settled into New York life, and now he met and fell in love with an American woman, Georgiana Warrin, some five years his senior. Her parents were English: Thomas Warrin had been born in Redditch, Worcestershire, and Elizabeth Lord in Cheshire, but they had emigrated to America in their youth, and Georgie, as she was known, was their eldest child, born in Queens, New York, in 1846. Thomas had become a successful businessman, the manufacturer of 'Warrin's Needles', a trade he had learnt in his home town, and had married well: Elizabeth's father, Samuel Lord, had made a great fortune in the dry goods business and had retired to England, leaving Thomas to manage his estates around Newtown, Long Island. In January 1874 Fred wrote home with the announcement that he was engaged to be married, and asking if he could have an advance from his capital of £150 for the necessary expenses of the marriage and to furnish a home for his bride. Unfortunately, this happy news launched a bombshell – within three weeks a letter arrived from George Brett tendering his resignation, on the basis that Fred's marriage was likely to lead to his settling permanently in America, to the detriment of Brett's position. Alexander and Craik were appalled and the correspondence shows them scrambling to recover the ground. They seem to have forgotten that just two years earlier they were talking about merging or closing the office completely.

On 17 February, Alexander wrote in shocked terms to Brett: 'In answer to your letter I must first say that Mr Frederick's marriage is not likely to lead to his settling finally in America more than if he had remained unmarried, but rather have a contrary result with he and his future wife having the strongest preference for living in England as she has relations and friends here who would make a home in this country pleasant to her.' He pointed out that Fred would now be a very useful asset to them in London, with so much American expertise under his belt. 'It is impossible for us to realise in what way your mind has come to feel as you do on this matter and it would cause us the deepest regret if anything in our conduct justified the feeling you express and it will be very much indeed against our wish if you leave. Would it not have been well if you had spoken to Mr Frederick before writing to us.' Alexander implored Brett to sit down with Fred and ended: 'I am sending Fred your letter and asking him to talk to you.'[14] Even Craik, whose many letters to Brett over the last five years had never been remotely cordial, now back-pedalled. 'I have said before and I wish to repeat how much we value your faithful conduct of the business.'

Ten days later Alexander, deeply frustrated by the difficulties in communication, wrote at length to Fred discussing their options if Brett did not change his mind. Could they find someone else to take his place or would that also be fraught with danger? Could Fred and his wife be persuaded to stay in the States after all? The firm might benefit from the appearance of Fred settling down with an American wife. Financially, Fred need not worry, Alexander tried to reassure him. Taking an average of the last four years' profits, Fred's share including the interest on his capital would not be less than £600 a year and with his salary added his income would be £900 (around £110,000 in today's money). Alexander then dangled a carrot that if Fred could make a success of the New York business, they could adjust the relative partnership shares to give Fred a larger stake in America and a smaller stake in London. Fred had suggested that he might sail home with his new wife after the marriage in April to discuss the problem, but Alexander was very unwilling to agree to that – it would be expensive, and 'my wife will about that time have an engagement of a very pressing kind which will quite prevent the possibility of her expressing hospitality for a month or more.' With Emma's mother and sister likely to be around as well, 'I don't think we can even offer a bed'.[15] Luckily by the end of March, Alexander was heartily relieved to hear that Brett had withdrawn his resignation.

Later that year, Brett brought his son George Platt Brett into the business, a man who would become one of the great American publishers. The business flourished. In 1876 Frederick returned to London, but remained closely watchful over the progress Brett was making. A branch office was established in Chicago and the New York office began to look for American writers to publish, hoping to find the next Henry James. The business began to import stereotype plates and contract directly with American printers, turning from a retailer and agency into a publishing house, creating its own recognizable American style. When the Chace Act of 1891 finally introduced some measure of copyright protection in America, the ability of the New York branch to access this network of printers allowed the firm to obtain rapid copyright protection in America for bestsellers such as Kipling, James, and Tennyson, way ahead of many of its competitors. The financial performance of the firm on both sides of the Atlantic improved dramatically, and the success of the venture gave Macmillan & Co. the confidence to expand its reach across the English-speaking world.

The summer of 1874 did indeed see 'an engagement of a very pressing kind', the arrival of a daughter, Mary, for Alexander and Emma, and holidays were confined to England: the family went to Whitby on the North Yorkshire coast, an area that would become very dear to them all. They rented a house that looked straight across the water to the ruins of St Hilda's Abbey. Macmillan wrote to his old friend James MacLehose, 'I am here with wife and new daughter, our two older girls Maggie and Olive, and Arthur and Katie. I have also a friend staying with me, the Rev J. R. Green, whose name will be known to you soon as the writer of the best History of England for College and Higher School Use.' Macmillan was anxious to show Green a bit of Scotland but asked MacLehose to telegraph the state of the weather, as Green did not have the constitution for a typical Scottish summer: 'He has been wintering in Italy till last year for several years and though better is still delicate in the chest.'[16] Alexander would wander down to the harbour to watch the fishing boats coming in: it must have sparked many memories of his youth in Irvine. But even here, with his new wife and baby daughter, Alexander never shook off the cares of the business. The family could not start on an expedition until the post had come, and he often hurried them all back in case something important arrived in the evening.

Alexander's character was hardening, as his seventh decade approached, and unsurprisingly it was his children, turning from biddable infants into educated and opinionated adults, who bore the brunt. He never ceased to remind them that however comfortable their lives were now, they came from humble beginnings. The parental pressure he put on Malcolm, and that could be seen in the letters Caroline had written weekly to little George, must have been formative, to say the least. To quote from Maggie's memoirs:

Vehement in loves and admirations, he was also vehement in his aversions (though these were less deep and lasting). A little phrase occurs in my mother's journal, some time before her engagement: "AM in a fine frenzy". The "fine frenzy" was a frequent condition, a great glow of enthusiasm, expressing itself in speech that came with a certain difficulty and in a face that lighted up or shadowed with the mood of the moment. Never in the nursery days do I remember having the slightest fear of him, and he must always have been gentle to us as little children. Later on there was a certain fierceness in his treatment of remarks that he did not approve of which made some of us rather frightened of speaking at all. Yet he did not understand and even resented anyone's being afraid of him. A young relative who always got on with him acutely remarked: "he doesn't mean half he says and he thinks you ought to understand that".[17]

Emma wrote that in trifles he was careful and economical, deploring 'all waste in matches and soap. But if it was a question of giving, he could bear no niggardly ways. If away from home, he always put gold in the church collection, saying "we expect to find what we like and what helps us, and how mean not to recognise it in a practical way."' He was full of homilies and advice for his family, with regularly repeated sayings:

> Take time when you have a decision to make, but when you have made it, never look back; it is only a waste of time and energy. Take pains to find out who you may trust; once trusted, go on trusting. A liberal heart deviseth liberal things.[18]

Religion remained his principal guide to life, the cornerstone of his private belief system and his business ethics, and although he often seems overly deferential to authority in his correspondence with titled or noble authors, at home he ruled the roost. William Benham was an old friend, a Macmillan author who wrote as Peter Lombard in the *Church Times*.

> I have more than once said that Alexander Macmillan was the best, the holiest layman I have ever known. Conscientious and loyal Churchman as he became, under the influence of Maurice, his Scotch blood never lost its colour. Let who would be visiting in his house, Bishop or other, I very much doubt whether he would have relinquished the leadership of the morning family prayers to anyone.[19]

– 19 –

MAKING HISTORY

John Richard Green

'Whatever the worth of the present work may be, I have striven throughout that it should never sink into a "drum and trumpet history."'

J. R. Green

THE 1870s WAS the decade when the next generation of Macmillan men came of age, and there was an exponential increase in the firm's output. In January 1874, George Macmillan left Eton and obediently joined his father in the business in London, learning the ropes, meeting the authors, and dealing with correspondence. There had been some discussion of whether he might go on to Cambridge, including a very supportive letter from George Grove urging the advantages of a university education, but for whatever reason, as he wrote somewhat wistfully many years later: 'circumstances prevented my following his advice.'[1] His cousin Maurice was finishing his degree at Cambridge and managed to avoid being pulled into the firm: in 1875 he joined the staff of St Paul's School in the City of London to teach Classics. It is not clear why Alexander would not support George in what he had allowed Daniel's son to do. Meanwhile Malcolm, having spent four years in the business, was still agitating to be allowed to go to college, and passed the summer of 1874 at Kirby Lodge, Little Shelford, being coached for entrance examinations, perhaps hoping to win a scholarship.

The pace of work never slowed. The firm had grown out of its second London premises in Bedford Street and moved down the road to the double unit of Numbers Twenty-nine and Thirty. The investment of money and effort continued apace, both into the New York office, and in support of loss-making *Nature*, but the financial success of other new titles made for decent enough balance sheets and dividends. If the highlight of 1872 was Carroll's *Through the Looking-Glass* (twelve editions and reprints in fifteen years), 1873 saw Walter Pater's ground-breaking and controversial *Studies in the History of the Renaissance*, a collection of essays he had previously written on art which appeared to endorse amorality and hedonism, and which were roundly condemned by some of Macmillan's established authors, including Mrs Oliphant, who called it 'rococo epicureanism'.[2] However, 1874 brought even more success with John (J. R.) Green's *Short History of the English People*.

Alexander took a personal interest in all his principal authors, hosting them at his house or his club, introducing them to family and to other friends, travelling with them, and guiding and encouraging their writing careers; but there was one individual with whom the friendship would become particularly intimate. John Richard Green was one of Macmillan's young proteges, an author with an unconventional pedigree, on whom the publisher was prepared to take a risk because the young man's passion for his subject, and his ambitious programme for communication of that passion, matched Alexander's own ideas of what publishing should be about. Leslie Stephen, one of Green's close friends, said that he had written 'the first history of England which would enable his countrymen to gain a vivid and continuous perception of the great processes by which the nation had been built up.'[3] For the Victorians of the 1870s, more conscious than any previous generation of the might and glory of their country and of the British Empire, this was the history they most wanted to read.

Green was born in Oxford in 1837, the son of a skilled tailor, the maker of academic silk gowns. He was educated at Magdalen College School until the death of his father, when he was fourteen, and thereafter he was tutored privately and successfully, winning one of the first open scholarships to Jesus College, Oxford, when he was eighteen. However, despite this promising start, he was very unhappy at Jesus, only managing a pass degree. Disliking some of the more academic historians of the day, he fell instead under the spell of Arthur Stanley, then a Fellow at Christ Church, and was thus introduced to the gospel of F. D. Maurice. Inspired by Christian Socialist philosophy, and lacking any professional alternatives, he took orders in the Church of England, in what he later referred to as a 'fit of enthusiasm'. His first curacy was in the East End of London, a very poor parish, where he lived in the house of the Ward family (one of the Ward sons, Humphry, who became his good friend, later married Mary Arnold, niece of the poet, and better known as the popular novelist Mrs Humphry Ward).

From 1861 to 1869 he struggled with increasingly poor health, eking out a living as a parish priest in Hoxton by writing articles for the *Saturday Review*, and gradually building a reputation as a talented historian. He was by all accounts an exemplary parish priest, a successful preacher who filled his church on Sundays with sermons that appealed to the particular needs of his parishioners. When not preaching to them, he campaigned for improvements in their living conditions, writing many articles lamenting the poverty of the East End. He often said that it was this exposure to human life at its most desperate and honest that coloured his ability to write meaningful social history. He was first introduced to Macmillan by a mutual friend, the geologist Boyd Dawkins, in 1862. He had written to Dawkins when the latter joined the Geological Society, 'Pray introduce me to Macmillan when you arrive, if such a thing be possible. You never made a better hit. Among the Stanley and Kingsley set Macmillan is the "pet publisher of the day".'[4] The brilliance of Green's conversation, his encyclopaedic knowledge of so many topics and his ability to bring them all to play in torrents of wit and erudition soon made him a regular guest and dining companion in Tooting, loved equally by publisher and the family. A photograph taken in Florence in 1869 shows a young man with terrific sideburns but a smooth, domed forehead and intense stare. Among the Macmillan set, who were impressed by his endeavours in the East End, he was generally known as 'Bethnal Green'.

By 1869 he was contributing to *Macmillan's Magazine*, and developing his ideas for a comprehensive, easily readable history of England, aimed at the general reader and the senior school student. This was something he had been thinking about since 1862, yet had found no time to write, struggling as he was with terrible health and the need to supplement his income with regular *Review* pieces. However, 1869 was the year when it became clear that this way of living was not sustainable, and an eminent physician diagnosed terminal lung disease. This grim prognosis forced him to make a change if he wanted to prolong his life – after all he was only thirty-two. He resigned his parish, taking an unpaid post as Senior Librarian at Lambeth Palace, and Macmillan took him under his wing. The two men sat up late into the night on several occasions, discussing a range of projects from a history of France to a *Historical Review* journal, to school primers, to a series on Men of History.

Alexander invited him to spend Christmas of 1869 at Tooting, but Green declined, as his doctor had forbidden him to leave home. Instead, he sent a detailed proposal to his preferred publisher.

> I propose to condense into a volume of 600 pages the history of the English People which I contemplated undertaking on a far larger scale. The work would serve as a school-manual for the higher forms and as a handbook for the universities, which in a more general sense it might I think supply a great want in our literature – that of a book in which the great line of our history should be fixed with precision, and which might serve as an introduction to its more detailed study. The book would be strictly a history of <u>England</u> in which foreign wars and outer events would occupy a far more subordinate position than they generally do, and in which the main attention would be directed to the growth, political, social, religious, intellectual of the people itself. Thus men like Aidan and Bede would claim more space than the wars of the Anglo-Saxon Kingdoms, and Spenser and Shakespeare and Bacon would stand as prominently forward as the defeat of the Armada or the death of Strafford. The style of such a book . . . ought to be more picturesque in the true sense of the term, than if it were on a larger scale . . . If such a work is worth anything to you it is of course worth a good deal, and for myself I must consider it as representing not merely a 'pass' good work but the result of ten years' reading and thought. I do not think £450 an excessive

sum for the copyright, but of this of course you are a better judge than I, and I am sure, my dear Macmillan, that there will be no disappointment on my part if you feel yourself unable to pursue the negotiation any further. I will only say frankly that I would rather publish the book with you than any other London house.[5]

Macmillan loved the idea, although he negotiated the fee to be paid in advance down to £350, with another £100 payable if sales broke 2,000 copies in the first six months.[6] But the *Short History*, eventually published at the end of 1874, would be unlike any of the 'drum and trumpet history' of other writers. At first Green found it hard to break away from the style of his *Review* articles, feeling that his book was just a series of essays, and he had to contend with patronizing advice from friendly historians like Edward Freeman who felt there were not enough facts or dates. Leslie Stephen felt it must have taken extraordinary courage and energy to persevere with so little support. But Macmillan, who was developing a pitch-perfect sense of what the market wanted, unwaveringly backed him and his authorial decisions.

The necessity to travel extensively every winter for months at a time, to San Remo, Menton, or Capri, meant that his hours of library time were limited, and his task was not aided by the absence of many primary documents. The result was that his conclusions leapt far in advance of the facts at his disposal and when the first edition finally emerged at the end of 1874 it was not perfect. Nevertheless, as the distinguished historian Bryce wrote in his obituary of Green, 'The success of the *Short History* was rapid and overwhelming. Everybody read it. It was philosophical enough for scholars, and popular enough for schoolboys. No historical book since Macaulay's has made its way so fast or been read with such avidity. And Green was under disadvantages which his great predecessor escaped from. Macaulay's name was famous . . .'[7] After 8,000 copies had been sold, Alexander sent for the contract in which Green had assigned his copyright, tore it up and, according to Charles Morgan, 'substituted for it a royalty agreement greatly and continuously to the advantage of the author and his heirs. Thirty-five thousand copies were sold in the first year.'[8] Over the next six years the whole book was completely revised and gradually extended into a four-volume work. Throughout Green remained determined to stick to his easy, conversational style: 'I give English History in the only way in which it is intelligible or interesting to me.'[9] In his Preface he insisted that this was 'a history not of English Kings or of English conquests but of the English people'.[10]

In 1877 Green found a true helpmate in his labours when he married Alice Stopford, a highly educated and strongly opinionated Irish woman, daughter of the Archdeacon of Meath, who in later years became a historian in her own right, and a campaigner for Home Rule and Women's Suffrage. For six years Alice worked alongside her husband as amanuensis and researcher, and he trained her in his methods. He continued to take on more work for Macmillan, acting as a reader of manuscripts. But his health deteriorated dramatically, and although he said that he only hoped to live to be with Alice, his 'little wifie', he died in March 1883, at the age of forty-six.

One of Green's lasting legacies was a series of school primers in History and Literature that he commissioned and edited for Macmillan. They followed the pattern of the successful *Science Primers* which had begun in March 1872 with Professor Henry Roscoe's chemistry primer, for which an accompanying case of chemical apparatus could be bought. This volume alone went through five reprints until 1877, when 'Questions' were added, and eleven more reprints were required by the time that the *Macmillan Bibliographical Catalogue* was compiled in 1889. Macmillan and his editors firmly believed that the only people who could be trusted to write the most basic of textbooks for children were the authorities on the subject, hence Geikie wrote physical geography and on geology (with a box of geological specimens available to complement the text), Hooker wrote botany,

Jevons tackled political economy and Lockyer, astronomy. Huxley himself wrote a general introduction to the series in 1880.

When the baton was handed on to Green to produce lists for history and literature, he secured some of the greatest historians and classicists of the day: Mandell Creighton wrote on Rome, Edward Freeman on Europe, Charlotte Yonge on France, Mahaffy on Greece, and Gladstone himself wrote the primer on Homer, much to Macmillan's incredulous delight. Alexander had taken responsibility for the wooing of Gladstone, explaining that though the usual fee for a primer was £50 on publication of 10,000 copies, and 2d per copy sold over 10,000, he would offer the Grand Old Man £100 in advance.

The Primers were designed, as Alexander told Gladstone, for 'boys and girls, and the general intelligent reader'.[11] However, Macmillan's ambitions had now stretched well beyond the Victorian schoolroom, and a major new entrant to his catalogue in 1875 was Roper Lethbridge, with his 'series of textbooks for Indian Schools'. From 1813 onwards the education of the native population had been a responsibility of the East India Company, which was empowered to fund education in both literature and technical subjects out of its profits. There was fierce debate about whether all education should be conducted in English, but from 1854, linked to Lord Macaulay's Report on the education of the Indian Civil Service, it was agreed that the vernacular languages could be used to teach the majority of children, and that education should not be confined to those able to learn English. Decisions on which textbooks should be bought and used in schools were haphazard, sometimes at the discretion of the master, sometimes decided by local committee, but all agreed that the quality on offer was extremely variable, and many British publishers were trying to sell books that were generally unsuitable for the local market, or were being dumped as unsaleable at home.

In 1873, Macmillan was introduced via Charles Kingsley to Roper Lethbridge, a career civil servant, secretary of the Bengal textbook committee and a Fellow at the University of Calcutta. Between them they devised a plan which would follow the pattern of Macmillan's Primers in England – Macmillan would commission the original authors of the primers, or similarly eminent authorities in those fields, to adapt their work specifically for the Bengali market. The series was launched in 1875 and four newly written volumes were issued that year: *An Easy Introduction to the History of India*, accompanied by similar texts on *Bengal*, on *England*, and on *The World*, and these did well, but the bestsellers were six reading books which had originally been prepared by a Bengali academic, Peary Churn Sircar, who began to publish them in 1850. Macmillan and Lethbridge seized upon this series of elementary readers as material that could easily be adapted and updated for launch, and 1875 also saw them published under the Macmillan banner, to great success. According to Morgan, writing in 1943, over five million copies of Sircar's readers were sold, but sadly Sircar would never know of this success: he died of gangrene contracted from a cut on his thumb sustained while teaching gardening classes at a local school. Sircar was a campaigning force in Indian education, especially for girls, and for the application of scientific methods to agriculture. Alexander would definitely have approved of this man.

Unsurprisingly considering the distances involved and the problems of communication, there was some initial difficulty in the commercial arrangements with the Indian distributors, and Lethbridge and Craik were often at daggers drawn over the state of the stocktake and the inaccuracy of accounts. It was not until Maurice Macmillan took over the imperial export trade in the 1880s that the business was able to expand into the sub-continent beyond Bengal. Macmillan was not the only British publishing house to tackle the Indian market, but it was certainly one of the most successful. These textbooks created both brand awareness and a distribution network which would form the bridgehead for the launch of the hugely profitable Macmillan Colonial Library, also under Maurice Macmillan's direction in the 1880s. By the beginning of the twentieth century, the Company was sufficiently established to open branch offices in

Bombay and Calcutta. This pattern of expansion mirrored the original growth of the firm: by being prepared to invest in resources for education, to combine socially responsible initiatives with profit-making opportunity, Macmillan was able to build a strong foundation for a wider business.

– 20 –

FAMILY PRESSURES,
FAMILY SADNESSES
(1874–78)

Sannox on the Isle of Arran

'Against the long years when family bonds make up all that is happiest in life, there must always be reckoned those moments of agitation and revolution, during which the bosom of a family is the most unrestful and disturbing place in existence.'

Mrs Oliphant

IN 1874, THE increasingly confident Macmillan, who thought any literary project, however ambitious, worth exploring, flirted with the notion of taking on the largest publishing project in the English-speaking world: the dictionary. The idea of creating a proper etymological dictionary of the English language, to supersede Johnson's famous volumes of the previous century, had been around since 1858, proposed by Richard Chenevix Trench, the President of the Philological Society (and a prolific author for Macmillan). He suggested that an army of volunteers would read every available English printed text and submit words with appropriately sourced quotations to an editor appointed by the Society. The first editor appointed by the Society, Herbert Coleridge, confidently predicted he would be able to go to press within two years, but the deluge of paper from enthusiastic volunteers submerged him and he died before the two years were up. The task was then taken over by another old acquaintance of the Macmillan brothers from Cambridge, Frederick Furnivall. Furnivall has been described as an eccentric charlatan – 'living proof of the mad foolhardiness of the whole enterprise'.[1] He was an untypical Victorian, being a teetotal, non-smoking, left-wing vegetarian who offended most of his friends by marrying a lady's maid and then abandoning her. Not surprisingly the project began to run out of steam, as Furnivall was a man of many enthusiasms but not endowed with the concentration or dedication required for this particular task.

While Furnivall struggled, the New York publishing house of Harper's approached Macmillan with a proposal for collaboration on an English dictionary, and Alexander suggested approaching the Philological Society to see what progress had been made. Negotiations began, but Furnivall's relationship with Macmillan was never easy, and the closer they got to agreeing a contract for the dictionary, the more fraught it became. Macmillan wanted to confine it to four volumes, Furnivall said it would take at least ten. Furnivall would not countenance it being called 'Macmillan's Dictionary'; Alexander would not share profits with the Society. Conversations became heated between two men who 'held strong views and could express them strongly.'[2] Eventually the project passed to the Oxford University Press, which finally managed, under James Murray's editorship, to get a first volume into the market in 1884. As George Macmillan later wrote, 'I do not think we had any reason to regret that the enterprise passed out of our hands into those of the Clarendon Press. And we certainly do not grudge the University either the honour or the expense that it has brought upon them.'[3]

However, the project caused Alexander to think seriously about the risks, financial and reputational, of spreading his business too thin. The partnership at that time comprised twenty shares of which Alexander held thirteen (65%), George Lillie Craik had five (25%) and Frederick had two (10%), for which he had paid £1,200, funded from part of his inheritance from his mother which had been left in the business as a loan. In March 1875 Craik wrote to Fred in New York: 'There is the prospect of our getting the help and the entire time of William Jack, and we seriously think of getting him to edit the great Dictionary we have so often spoken of . . . If we float this big book it will take up capital and attention.'[4] He wrote again six months later (nothing moved fast in regards to the dictionary project), 'Jack will join, he proposes starting very soon with the Dictionary.'[5]

William Jack was a renowned mathematician, born in Irvine in 1834 and schooled at the Academy where Alexander had spent some of his youth. He went on to study mathematics first at the University of Glasgow, and then in Cambridge, graduating in 1859. For five years he worked as one of Her Majesty's Inspectors of Schools for Scotland, until he was approached to become Professor of Natural Philosophy (Physics) at Owens College in Manchester. He held this position until 1870 and then returned to Scotland as editor of the *Glasgow Herald*. In 1875 he was elected a Fellow of the Royal Society of Edinburgh, proposed by, among others, the eminent pair of scientists William Thomson, later Lord Kelvin, and Peter Guthrie Tait, both friends of Alexander.

Jack's dual career as academic and author made him an asset to the firm of Macmillan as a technical adviser, particularly when the Irvine connection was identified, and Alexander tempted him with a partnership, something which does not seem to have been offered to his other editors. It may be that his provenance was a deciding factor, but he also had the advantage of some family wealth, as the price had gone up: in December 1875 Jack paid £700 to each of Macmillan and Craik to buy two shares in the business, valuing the company at £14,000, or £1.3 million at today's values, and had to find the equivalent of £130,000 to invest. This would have been well beyond the purses of cash-strapped Morley, Grove, or Lockyer.

Alexander and Craik continued to pursue this addition to the partnership, even after the dictionary project had stalled: it brought relief to Alexander, under pressure from his young wife to take life more easily, but it also reflected an underlying disappointment that his eldest son Malcolm, now twenty-two, was not able or willing to take up his place in the business. The difficulties between father and son were exacerbated by Malcolm's 'incapacity for method and punctuality.' Many years later Emma tactfully wrote 'Malcolm, who was a good deal at home, the children loved. He had a kind of genius which made him very interesting to his able friends and from early childhood his father had built great hopes on him, but his health made him uncertain.'[6] Alexander had confided to one of his friends that he found his eldest son 'a queer, wayward boy, with very much good in him and plenty of brains, only not always duly administered'.[7] In 1875, Malcolm entered Balliol College, Oxford, 'where, as his brother says and this writer can confirm, he formed many valuable friendships' wrote Graves, his father's biographer.[8] But even now Malcolm struggled to fit in – he was five years older than the other undergraduates, and rather overweight and unfit. One of his contemporaries, George Leveson Gower (later Sir George, KBE), remembered an incident from his student days:

> The new Hall [at Balliol] was only approaching completion at the beginning of the Michaelmas Term of 1876. A long ladder was left standing reaching right up to the roof. Malcolm Macmillan accepted a challenge to climb it. He was of stout build, and to our delight, in his descent a projecting nail tore his trousers from Dan even to Beersheba, so that one trouser leg flapped to and fro like a sail torn from the yard arm. The exposure of so large a surface of his portly figure in such a conspicuous position was naturally a source of general jubilation.[9]

Hardly a respectful or even kind memory to share.

In early 1875 Alexander and Emma went again to Italy, travelling with his teenage daughters Maggie and Olive and with John Green. The family stayed at the Palazzo Vendramin in Venice, an impressive villa on the Grand Canal, then travelled to Pompeii, where excavations were progressing on a systematic basis, and still uncovering the voids left by decayed corpses, as Alexander explained to George. Then they headed to Rome but as the summer began they decided to avoid the Riviera and go straight home via Emma's family in Lyon. 'Don't think I am hurrying home,' Alexander reassured George, 'I am sure we have seen enough for two years' digestion.'[10]

But by September all the benefit of the holiday had worn off, as the workaholic publisher fell victim both to his old enemy, sciatica, and to bronchitis, confining him to bed for several weeks. He lay flat on his back with poultices for the pain, while Emma took dictation.

Possibly prompted by this health scare, and the feeling that the man was working too hard, in January 1876 the fifty-seven-year-old Alexander was presented with a bronze statuette of himself made by the fashionable sculptor Joseph Boehm, accompanied by an 'Address' written by his old friend Dinah Mulock Craik.

Dear Mr Macmillan,

It is not easy for us, the undersigned, friends of all ranks, and associated with you in all manner of ways, to express the feeling which has prompted us to offer you this statuette. We do it, first out of strong personal regard; next to show our respect for a self-made and absolutely stainless name; for sincerity and probity in business; for faithfulness in friendship; for a largeness of heart and high sense of honour which have exalted the work of your life, and won attachment after a very rare fashion. In your success many of us share; and your warm sympathy helps us to enjoy it. That your own enjoyment of well-earned prosperity may be long and full, is our earnest and affectionate wish.[11]

There were nearly seventy names attached to this address, including his partners Craik and Jack, his editors Grove and Lockyer, and his loyal staff including George Coxall, who had been in the London office since it opened in 1858. By this stage, Macmillan & Co. was a business with significant and long-standing trading relationships; the other names on the list give an indication of the quality of these suppliers, men with whom he had been working since the business first began. His printers include Clays of Bungay, Constables of Edinburgh, and William Clowes in London. Charles Henry Jeens had been engraving illustrations for Alexander since 1860. James Burn and Harvey Orrinsmith were both partners in Macmillan's bookbinders, and family friends. Sir John Evans of Dickinsons the paper-makers, the father of Arthur Evans the archaeologist, was another close relationship, being the man that Alexander had quoted to Malcolm as his example of a successful self-made man who had not been to university.

That same year, someone in the Bedford Street office acquired a book with plain papers and a blue cloth binding, on which was embossed in gold type 'Macmillan & Co., At Home'. The happy-go-lucky Tobacco Parliaments of seventeen years earlier had become more formal affairs, and both the numbers and the status of the attendees were on a different scale, worthy of careful note. The first event in the book was held on Valentine's Day 1876 and the guests were an eclectic but entirely male collection of authors, literary critics, scientists, lawyers, and engineers. Nearly all had already featured in the Macmillan catalogue, such as the Christian Scientist John Llewellyn Davies, first published by the firm in 1856. Some were, or would be, appointed editors of its learned periodicals, *The Practitioner*, the *Journal of Physiology*, and to be launched in 1878, *Brain*. There are more than twenty such soirees recorded in the book, ending in June 1881, with some notable gaps when the book may have been mislaid (!) for the whole of 1877. They were held every two or four weeks in the spring months only, and regulars include Henry James, Leslie Stephen, Alfred Russel Wallace, Richard Garnett, and Oscar Wilde.[12]

Not everything was happy at home, however. In July 1876 Alexander's nephew Arthur Macmillan died, just nineteen years old, and was buried near his aunt Caroline in West Norwood Cemetery. As always, Mamie was with him to the last – 'as long as the boy breathes I shall not leave him for a moment.'[13] Malcolm, who was at Oxford, wrote to a friend:

I had news of the death of a cousin of mine, of whom I was very fond, soon after you left. He was a talented, bright, affectionate fellow, with more insight and sympathy than most people twice his age. He had long been an invalid, and bearing up bravely against fearful disorders; we hoped he was going to get better. I'm sure he is a loss to the world, and still more to all who were or would have been his friends. He was almost the life of our home; and his death seems to take a great piece out of my life. He had one of the most wonderful gifts of effective sarcasm of all shades of bitterness, which he often vented on me, and very justly; but the last time I saw him, we agreed very well in our general view of things, and he showed nothing but his sweeter side.[14]

Frederick and his American wife Georgie had just returned to England and soon began to host their own parties at their house in St John's Wood: Henry James in particular became a friend, and later described them as 'the flourishing and convivial young Frederick, who has a pretty, dressy, worldly little American wife and a very charming and hospitable house'.[15] The sadness in their life was that no children came, but at some point in the early 1880s they adopted Georgie's American niece Betty, the third child of her brother Samuel Warrin. Betty was born in 1881 and by the age of five was living in England with Fred and Georgie as their daughter.

While Malcolm studied at Oxford and dreamed of becoming a poet or a literary critic, his younger brother George was off on an adventure that he surely would have envied. In March 1877 George was invited to accompany John Pentland Mahaffy (Professor of Ancient History at Trinity College, Dublin) and two other young men to study the ruins of Greece. This short trip filled George with inspiration, and led to the founding of the Society for the Promotion of Hellenic Studies, with George, still in his early twenties, as a driving force in its creation, becoming Honorary Secretary. The Society survives to this day and some of George's letters home to family are preserved within its archives. His letter to his father from Genoa describes his two young companions.

Young Goulding whom you all abused so but who turns out to be a right good fellow in his way, very full of spirits – delightfully innocent of what we call culture, but still thoroughly entering into the delight of what we see – whether scenery, pictures, palaces etc. In fact he is a good downright honest wild Irishman, with no end of fun in him and no particular harm, quite

an entertaining companion, and a very good contrast to the last
man of the party – for we are four. This last who joined us at
Charing X just as we were starting is an old pupil of Mahaffy's
and a scholar of Magdalen Oxford by name Oscar Wilde. He is
a very nice fellow whose line lies decidedly in the direction of
culture as Goulding's lies away from it. He is aesthetic to the
last degree, passionately fond of secondary colours, low tones,
Morris papers, and capable of talking a good deal of nonsense
thereupon but for all that a very sensible well-informed and
charming man.[16]

Wilde kept in touch with the House of Macmillan over the years,
attending their social gatherings, and in 1889 they published one of
his essays in the English Illustrated Magazine, but they turned down
Dorian Gray 'on the ground that it contained unpleasant elements'.[17]

George returned home from Athens after ten days of rough
riding through the interior of the Peloponnese ('we met but few
brigands and those for the most part disposed to be friendly') just
in time to celebrate the birth of a new half-brother, John Victor,
named after Emma's father and brother, and christened the following month by Alfred Ainger, who had taken Kingsley's place as chief
celebrant at Macmillan family ceremonies. Even though he was now
spending more time at home with his young family, Alexander could
not change the habits of a lifetime. Emma remembered that he still
stayed up late into the early hours reading and did much of his thinking on the corner sofa in the library.

In August 1877 a large family party of Macmillans and Bowes set
off for Arran, leaving Frederick and George in charge of the London
office. Alexander and Emma, Olive, Maggie and Maurice, the babies
and their nurse Mamie all crowded into the Corrie Inn, just a mile
from the croft where Daniel was born. The Bowes family from Cambridge were staying nearby, as was Robert's mother, Margaret Bowes.
Alexander's only surviving sibling, she had been recently widowed
and returned home from Illinois. She was living in Cambridge with

her son, but anxious to revisit the scenes of her childhood. Maggie wrote of her to George: 'She strikes me as being a very uncommon and interesting character, with a great deal of intellect. She is not at all demonstrative, but seems to draw people to her in a quiet sort of way and she notices character a great deal. I think like all old people she lives mostly in the past and I think it gives her a great deal of pleasure to talk to some of the old people here about old times.'[18]

The next generation of the MacLehose family arrived to join in some of the strenuous hiking expeditions on the island. Alexander wrote to George: 'Robert and James came down on Friday night and started off on Saturday morning on the bus that leaves here for Brodick at 6 am. From there they had walked up Goatfell and went along the ridge to Glen Sannox, reaching the Bowes' cottage at half-past four in the afternoon. Olive, Cousin Robert [Bowes] and Maurice were with them and they seem to have enjoyed themselves greatly. The MacLehoses went off again at 6 this morning. Maurice and Maggie went over to breakfast at Sannox, meeting with Cousin Robert and Hatty and George Johnson to do Feargus, but it is a dull morning and I doubt they will manage it.'[19] Alexander never stopped thinking of work – he sent letters instructing Fred to publish an advertisement for the works of F. D. Maurice, Kingsley's sermons, and Macleod Campbell's books, as they were being discussed in *The Spectator*, and 'Craik is coming tomorrow to discuss Morley'. He wrote to George, 'you must a little put up with my anxiety seeing that it is an inherited characteristic and indeed is not without its uses'.[20]

Meanwhile, Malcolm was staying at Abernyte Manse in Perthshire, being tutored by Allan Menzies, a clergyman and academic, later joining the party on Arran. He wrote to his younger brother George to tease him about reading poetry in the garden with an unnamed party. George was indeed courting and in October that year became engaged to Margaret Lucas, the very beautiful daughter of neighbours in Tooting. She was only just twenty and the wedding did not take place until July 1879, presided over by Ainger and Mahaffy, with witnesses including George's friend from Eton, Herbert Ryle, later Dean of Westminster. October 1877 also brought Alexander's fifty-ninth birthday, celebrated with old friends Aldis Wright and William Jack, and newer friends Norman Lockyer and the Craiks. Margaret Macmillan wrote of Wright and Jack: 'with these friends whom he had known in their undergraduate days and who in those days had been constantly in and out of the house at Trinity Street, my father was perhaps more absolutely himself than with any later friends. One gets glimpses in recalling his intercourse with them, of the great part that the University life at Cambridge had played in his young growing days and his interest in Cambridge never ceased.' These visits 'were to the very end of his life the greatest source of pleasure to him and always seemed to make him young again . . . My father . . . was not fluent in conversation, but when he was in the vein, and in the company most congenial to him, he came out in a very happy way.'[21]

However, in among these happy events, the family was once again rocked by unexpected sadness: firstly, as John Green wrote to his friend Freeman in January 1878, whatever was making Malcolm unhappy and unsettled came to a head: 'The boy is now under medical treatment. I have never seen his father so shaken.'[22] There was never any suggestion that Malcolm suffered from physical illnesses so this must have been a case of severe depression or a nervous breakdown. Then, according to Green, just as Malcolm began to recover, Daniel's daughter Kate fell catastrophically ill. On 25 July 1878, a patient recorded as 'Kath C Macmillan' was admitted as a private patient to Normansfield, an asylum in Hampton Wick near Teddington owned and managed by Dr John Langdon Down (after whom Down's syndrome was named). Kate would have been twenty-two at the time and had been a perfectly happy and intelligent child. When she was about five, Alexander wrote to her godmother, George Wilson's sister, 'Katherine is growing quite a companionable young lady. She is bright, healthy and well-grown, and very sharp – cleverer I think than either of her elder brothers and as good as good withal.

So you need not be ashamed of your godchild.'[23] By 1877, of course, she had lost both her parents and had watched her younger brother Arthur die of the same disease that had killed her father. Her oldest brother, Fred, who had been away for many years, now had his own household and wife, and Maurice was busy working as a classics master at St Paul's School. She may have suffered from depression, or I think it likely that her withdrawal from society into medical care may have been triggered by the onset of an organic illness such as epilepsy, which had struck once she reached her teens. The first mention of her suffering from any illness is in early 1873, while Alexander and Emma were touring Italy, when the Freeman family had looked after her, but Alexander had been certain that she would get better.

The Normansfield asylum took up to a hundred and sixty private patients at £200 per annum, a considerable amount of money, and catered for the offspring of well-off families who suffered from physical or learning disabilities or epilepsy. Dr Langdon Down and his wife Mary had purchased a large mansion set in five acres of grounds in Teddington, and the intention was to treat the patients as humanely as possible, teaching them life skills, taking part in daily exercise sessions including roller-skating, riding, tennis, and swimming, and by 1877, helping out at a small farm. They had some success treating epileptic patients with bromide. Kate was there for nearly a year, not leaving until June 1879, in time to attend George's wedding. Unfortunately, the recovery was not permanent. All Emma would later say on the subject was 'Katie, his niece, affectionate and wayward, very lovable, but not easy. She was often away.' This seems to suggest that it was more than just epilepsy, but may be the resultant psychological damage, which led to the prolonged stays under medical supervision over the next thirty years.

– 21 –

OF MUSIC

and

MEN OF LETTERS

Sir George Grove

'Books worth reading once are worth reading twice; and what is most important of all, the masterpieces of literature are worth reading a thousand times.'

John Morley

1878 SAW THE launch of two major contributors to the firm's success for the next decade and beyond: *Grove's Dictionary of Music and Musicians* and the *English Men of Letters* series. For nearly a decade now, Macmillan had been putting his faith in George Grove and John Morley as men who understood his purpose and his ethics, and they in turn delivered projects that added greatly to the reputation and international standing of the business. Grove, a workaholic like Alexander, had been the editor of *Macmillan's Magazine* for ten years, while continuing to hold the Secretaryship of the Crystal Palace, and travelling and writing extensively on European music. The magazine flourished under his hand, due in no small part to his warm personality: as one contributor put it, 'I felt drawn to him irresistibly by the delightful cordiality and grace of his manner, the brightness of his intelligence and the goodness of his heart . . . the most delightful editor I have ever known.'[1] Under his control, and with Alexander increasingly happy to let him take that control, his list of regular contributors included Fawcett, Huxley, Tennyson, Freeman, Hughes, Arnold, Stanley, and J. R. Green. New names introduced during his time in charge included George Meredith, Walter Pater, George Eliot, Robert Louis Stevenson, Mrs Humphry Ward, Hubert Parry, Andrew Lang, and Gladstone himself. In 1873 he resigned his post at the 'C.P.' to devote himself to the duties of the firm. J. R. Green wrote to congratulate him.

> I am immensely glad of your deliverance from the C.P., both
> for your own sake and for Macmillan's. What a fine fellow Mac
> is, when one comes to know and understand him. It was one
> of my fixed fancies in life that I never could like a Scotchman;
> but I have got very fond of Macmillan in spite of it. It is just the
> work you can do better than almost any man; and I have an odd

notion that just as we have got to learn what the capacities of
Literature are as a profession, we have still to realize what Publishing may be, and what an immense power a Publisher might
wield for good without the least neglect of business consider-
ations. But it seems to me that all the good things in the world
lie in a future I shall never see.[2]

The prospectus for the musical *Dictionary*, to be edited by Grove,
was released by Macmillan in January 1874.

There is no book in English from which an intelligent inquirer
can learn, in small compass and in language which he can
understand, what is meant by a Symphony or Sonata, a Fugue,
a Stretto, a Coda or any other of the technical terms which
necessarily occur in every description or analysis of a concert
or a piece of music . . . Such questions are now constantly
occurring to those who five-and-twenty years ago would never
have thought of them. Within that period music in England
has made immense progress and the number of persons who
attend concerts and practise music has very largely increased. It
is no longer regarded as a mere idle amusement, but has taken,
or is taking, its right place beside the other arts as an object of
study and investigation.[3]

In other words, Macmillan and his trusted literary adviser
had spotted yet another gap in the market, and one in which the
increasingly curious and ambitious middle classes had a particular
interest – they wanted to go to concerts and to understand what was
happening, without being patronized. Grove rapidly assembled a
troupe of willing contributors: his great friend Arthur Sullivan, John
Hullah, Hubert Parry, William Chappell the sheet music publisher,
and many European authorities. He had at hand all the well-
researched and carefully written programme notes for the concerts
he had organized at Crystal Palace. He shared an office in Bedford

Street with George Macmillan around this time, and this had a lasting impact on the young man: 'Some of the keenest pleasures I have since enjoyed, especially in the fields of music and literature, owe their origin or encouragement to his infectious enthusiasm.'[4] George Macmillan would later be Honorary Secretary and a generous donor to the Royal College of Music (founded in 1883 with Grove as its first Director). But it wasn't all hard work – apparently Grove regularly tempted George out to a local pastry-cook to sample the three-cornered jam tarts for which he had a weakness. When George married, Grove bought the couple the complete set of Schubert's Songs as a wedding present.

The production of the *Dictionary*, not surprisingly, turned out to be a significantly more complex and time-consuming job than either Macmillan or Grove had envisaged when the project began. As Grove explained, 'To drive a team of contributors half of whom are amateurs, and half can get three times the pay we can give them elsewhere, takes a frightful amount of goading and coaxing and correspondence: and the editing and correcting and checking and completing – as I feel bound to do it – is a matter of great labour and incessant thought and occupation.'[5] The problem was exacerbated by Grove's previous undertaking also to produce a textbook on geography for Macmillan's *Classbook* series – by 1877 it was agreed that something had to give, and Craik offered to find someone else to take on the textbook. Grove wrote 'I was in a terrible dilemma between Dictionary and Geography. On the one hand my duty to my family and to the Firm urged me to the Geography; on the other hand I felt myself so far committed that I could not give up the Dictionary. I must now work like a steam engine and try to finish it within the dates named.' Regarding the geography project: 'I hope you won't attribute it to vanity if I say I don't think anyone could do it quite as well as I. Because I have such a very strong feeling of my own shortcomings and ignorance. I know what I do not know, and that must be, as a rule, what most ordinary people do not know: and then I set myself to work to find it out and to tell it to others just as it has struck me.'[6] The Macmillan archives hold a note in Grove's hand dated 31 July 1877.

> After careful calculation Mr Grove sees his way to complete the
> Dictionary of Music for publication by Dec 31, 1880, and in the
> event which he believes extremely improbable of its not being
> then completed, he engages to complete it, with all possible
> despatch without Messrs Macmillan & Co. making any further
> payment to him in respect of it. Messrs Macmillan agree to
> postpone the *Classbook* of Geography and they do not ask him
> to attend in Bedford Street except during such times as may be
> necessary or convenient for him to enable him to conduct the
> *Magazine* and the *Dictionary*.[7]

Volume I of the *Dictionary* was issued in December 1877, weighing in at 768 pages. The original scheme had been for just two volumes, but the work continued to grow, and Craik, ever the bad cop in the Macmillan partnership, began to nag that it was turning into a liability. Grove got the hint, and replied in his usual friendly way:

16 May 1879

Dear Craik

I am much delighted by your kind and full letter. I quite see your position and can only say that I hope sincerely that the firm may make some money out of the Dictionary, to repay them for their large outlay. If the book does not succeed it is not, and shall not be, for want of effort on my part.

Yours ever G Grove[8]

In 1880, Volume II hit the press, but the project was still only half complete. Alexander remained totally supportive of his editor:

June 1880

My dear Macmillan

I have your letters of 11th and 16th offering to pay me £800 on the completion of the Dictionary over above the existing arrangement which terminates this year and to increase my salary as Editor of the Mag from £300 to £500. These proposals are very generous and I gladly and gratefully accept them . . . The copyright of the Dictionary is yours. I was distressed to find, from the light thrown upon the subject on Tuesday, that the work is not likely to be remunerative to you. I had always hoped that it would turn out a very good profit to you, and the prospect of the reverse is to me a bitter disappointment. However if care and pains on my part can alter this, you will not have to complain of me.[9]

Volume III was published in 1883 and Volume IV in 1889. Grove need not have worried, the *Dictionary* became yet another pillar in the temple of Macmillan's publishing empire. The work has since been constantly updated and revised, with supplements for American music, for Jazz and for Musical Instruments. Its fame was such that when the second edition began to be published in 1904, it was renamed as *Grove's Dictionary*. Owned now by Oxford University Press, it is fully digitized and world-famous, running, in print, to twenty volumes.

Morley's *English Men of Letters* series had a similar purpose – to provide a guide to the newly literate masses on what they should be reading and how they should understand it. The commentariat of the late Victorian age was becoming nervous that with the explosion of mass literacy and the new channels for mass distribution of literature, a beast had been unleashed that needed careful control, if it was to be a force for good and not for evil or political unrest. Every town, every railway station, had a W. H. Smith kiosk selling cheap novels and penny papers, which were also retailed through stationers, tobacconists, sweetshops, and toyshops. In particular, Macmillan and Morley would have been only too aware of the massive circulation around the Fleet Street area of the 'penny dreadfuls', weekly instalments of trashy and sensationalist stories specifically marketed to the thirty per cent of London's male population who comprised 'boy labour' – errand boys, office clerks, and factory workers. The Newsagents' Publishing Company, which specialized in these 'dreadfuls', was selling 30,000 copies weekly. For the first time ever, popularity had become problematic: the people, particularly the young, were reading too much trash and it was as bad for the health of the nation as untreated water or sugary sweets.

Macmillan and Morley agreed that the moral and cultural life of Britain could be improved if only the population were properly educated and given guidance to seek out the best that English literature could offer them. In 1876 John Morley addressed an audience in the Midlands, committing himself to a project through which the fruits of high culture could be made available to the workers, even the 'roughest-handed man or woman in Birmingham'. He believed it was imperative for the good of the nation that access to inspiring and uplifting education should be made available to all: 'What we see every day with increasing clearness is that not only the wellbeing of the many, but the chances of exceptional genius, moral or intellectual, in the gifted few, are highest in a society where the average interest, curiosity, capacity, are all highest.'[10]

Morley sketched out to Macmillan his idea for a series of books covering the lives of the great voices in English literature, from Chaucer to the present day. The influence of Carlyle's notion of the 'Great Man of Literature' led to this idea taking shape as a series of biographies, rather than a chronological treatment, and brought a particular slant to the series – that the works would always be seen within the prism of the writer's upstanding moral character and his adherence to the Victorian trope of working to achieve respectability. Thus, for example, Trollope seemed to equate Thackeray's claim to fame with his financial achievement rather than his literary merit.

The title for the series, *English Men of Letters*, was only decided upon after much debate, with Macmillan triumphant: Morley had wanted to call it 'Short Books on English Authors'. He was asked to commission the series from writers of 'the highest respectability and the highest capacity', which he considered quite a challenge, but 'I accept your doctrine, all the same.'[11] What he achieved was remarkable; the first series under his editorship produced thirty-nine volumes over fifteen years, kicking off with Leslie Stephen writing on Johnson, followed by Swift and Pope, and included Huxley writing on Hume, Henry James on Hawthorne (the only American in the list), Froude on Bunyan, Symonds on Shelley and Sidney, and Edmund Gosse on Gray. Mrs Oliphant was allowed to tackle Sheridan, but no women were included in the subject list, as Austen, Burney, Gaskell, and the Brontës were considered by Morley and his friends to be writers of domestic fiction, which 'gave little but pleasure at the best; at the worst [was] simply scandal idealized.'[12] (Eventually a second series, begun in 1902, included Austen and George Eliot.) The selection included poets, dramatists, philosophers, and essayists, but relatively few novelists, as the novel was also seen as second-class literature in comparison even to poetry. The guides were particularly critical of coarseness and sexual humour, and many of the traits of the eighteenth-century novelist came in for heavy criticism, as did over-emphasis on political point-scoring, with Dickens and Thackeray both falling foul on this count. The authors preferred their texts clear, manly (to appeal to all the boys otherwise tempted by sensationalism), and uplifting, while priding themselves on being unprejudiced by 'accidents of time and place'.

The correspondence between Morley and Macmillan about who would accept which commission took up many months and much anxiety. First Matthew Arnold and then George Eliot were approached to write on Shakespeare but both turned it down despite entreaties: the task had to wait for the next century. However, many of Macmillan's old friends responded eagerly: Goldwin Smith, Alfred Ainger, David Masson. The series was an immediate success and was treated as an authoritative survey from the first, accorded semi-official status. Each volume was printed at 3,000 copies, and some of the better-known titles were reprinted frequently; Leslie Stephen's *Johnson* was reprinted seven times in its first ten years.

It was important for the business that Macmillan was able to create intellectual property of this type under its own name. Alexander's relationship with the Delegates of the Oxford University Press had never been easy, there was often friction about the costs being incurred and the strategies that Macmillan employed to market the Press's books. He found them frustrating to deal with from the very beginning: in 1866 he wrote to his good friend Alexander Campbell Fraser, whose work on Bishop Berkeley was in the Press 'I am sorry to say they are not bright there and it is needful to be very explicit with them.'[13] From 1868, Macmillan found his freedom of movement even more tightly circumscribed following the appointment of Professor Bartholomew Price as Secretary to the Delegates, with executive authority to transact on their behalf. Price was a strong personality, a mathematician by training and a professor of Natural Philosophy, an active committee man and politician with a small 'p'. Known to his friends, including to his pupil Charles Dodgson, as 'Bat Price', he had fingers in many pies: 'Twinkle twinkle little bat, how I wonder what you're at.'[14]

Given the job of managing the Press, Price dedicated himself to the task at hand and Alexander found himself under increasing pressure. Where Macmillan as publisher was interested in the content of the books themselves and their capacity to change lives, Price preferred rules and routines, and went into the numbers in great detail. Early in 1875, Macmillan saw the first sign of real trouble ahead, when Price requested an end to the firm's exclusive right to market the Press's books. Alexander capitulated nervously but on the understanding that he would always have the first option to buy books on whatever terms were being offered to other booksellers.

> I am quite willing to agree to what you ask, namely the deletion of the clause that confines your sales to us; trusting to the Delegates with full confidence that they would do nothing

detrimental to our interests; only there is one region and you name it, America, where I think it would be very probable that any action you might take would certainly injure us, unless we clearly knew and agreed what you did. We have, as you know, developed a quite new market there, sunk a good deal of money in stock and spent a good deal in advertising, presentation copies, travelling and the like. If any American house bought copies on the same terms that we do, or even approximately on the same terms, they get all the advantages of our operation without the cost . . . When people come to New York from County Schools and Universities they go to our house in Aster Place to see what is new from Oxford. You have seen the result, which has not been inconsiderable.[15]

However, this was just the beginning of the crisis. In December 1875 Alexander wrote at length and bitterly to Fred in the States, with very worrying news.

I am afraid that I must tell you that the Delegates of the Clarendon Press mean to be their own publishers and that at midsummer next we shall cease to hold the position we have held now for twelve years. They have a fancy that they have got all the knowledge and help they can get from us, and think that they can do their own work themselves. I suspect Professor Price has had this in his mind for some time . . . that it is in any sense a wrong to us they will in no way consider. As Prof Price said to me years ago 'The Delegates acting for the University will never allow themselves to be influenced by what you have done for them, but only by what they think you can do in future.' It is the old story . . . so it is no use our making any complaint about it.

I am writing to you to go into the question seriously and consider whether it might be well to close the agency in New York, so far as keeping a staff and stock and paying rent is concerned and for you to come and live here and work our American trade from this side . . . As regards our own work at home I think we have as much to do as will give us all full employment and even I think leave us freer to develop our own business when we have not the care of theirs, which has certainly not been without its worry and anxiety.[16]

In fact Alexander was able to negotiate a new contract but on greatly reduced terms: his commission was cut from ten to seven and a half per cent, his bond was increased from £4,000 to £10,000, and he had to settle his accounts three times a year. Sir John Evans, the paper merchant and family friend, was prepared to help by putting up the increased security (over £500,000 at today's values). Contract negotiations were finally concluded in April 1876, but only for a five-year term. The writing was on the wall.

By the end of the decade, Macmillan & Co. was firmly established as one of the leading quality and academic publishers in the world. The publisher's list for 1879 was one hundred and fifty items long, studded with small gems such as Henry James' *Daisy Miller* and *Roderick Hudson*, and with novels by Mrs Molesworth, Frances Hodgson Burnett, and Charlotte Yonge, but principally driven by academic texts, from school primers to learned editions of Greek classics, Maudsley's *Pathology of the Mind* and Alfred Marshall's *The Economics of Industry*. As the frontiers of knowledge expanded, so did the Macmillan catalogue. It would need to be capable of standing alone without the addition of the titles from the Oxford University Press, as 1880 finally saw the relationship, in England at least, come to an end.

– 22 –

THE CHANGING
OF THE GUARD

(1879–83)

Alexander Macmillan

'He had long decided that abundant laughter should be the embellishment of the remainder of his days.'

Henry James

Malcolm Macmillan's studies had seemed to be making some slow progress, but in the summer of 1879, while still at Oxford and working on unsuccessful attempts to win the Newdigate Prize for Poetry, he was involved in an appalling accident, which not surprisingly knocked him further off course. On the River Thames at Oxford is the Sandford Lasher, or weir, on the left bank upstream of Sandford Lock. The pool below the weir has been notorious since the nineteenth century because of the number of individuals who have drowned there. Weirs, like the Sandford Lasher, generate powerful currents that can trap and hold a victim (and often attempted rescuers) underwater at the base of the structure; hence their reputation as 'drowning machines'. One afternoon in June, Malcolm and another student, a boy of eighteen called Clarence Collier, were rowing above the weir, when their boat overturned and both they and the boat were carried by the current over the weir and into the lasher pool. Malcolm escaped 'and swimming hard to avoid the current, managed to reach the shore. [Collier] was on the other side of the mountain-like eddy and was whirled around in it all night till by mere chance his body was thrown up in the morning and so recovered . . . You could not conceive anything more touching than the funeral of the poor boy – the white coffin, with white wreaths in the chapel, Jowett's own voice breaking as he read the service.'[1] Several months later, the horror, and the grief, was still sinking in. Malcolm was travelling in Europe, mostly in Germany, Leipzig and Dresden, listening to opera and hoping to improve his German. He wrote to another friend from Balliol, the young American Louis Dyer: 'I suffered a fearful loss by the death of Collier. I was as fond of him as I could be. My acquaintance with him (not formed when I last wrote) seems like a beautiful bright dream, full of perfect sympathy and a constant soft-rippling stream of happy intellectual communion and affectionate hope.'[2]

In 1880 Malcolm's time at Oxford was at an end but he had still to pass his German examination if he wanted to take a degree. This would take him until 1883, but at some point before then he suffered a second nervous breakdown. In the 1881 census he is recorded as staying in private lodgings at 1 Claremont Crescent, Weston-super-Mare, with a Dr Edwin Fox and described as 'Lunatic', which sounds extreme but was at that time a term generally used to classify someone 'not of sound mind'. Fox was a descendant of the well-known Bristol-based psychiatrist Dr Edward Long Fox, who like the staff at the York Retreat believed in the humane treatment of the mentally disturbed. Malcolm wrote to his sister Maggie at the beginning of April describing the scenery and the walking he was doing. The language is lovely: 'It is the brown, sulky, saline barrenness of colour which charms me. It is a note in the landscape of the Kentish coast, and there as here stains easily, under any deepening of light, into something richly sombre; and over its greyness and flatness the sunsets have the fullest and warmest field.'[3] As he was not confined or restrained, it suggests that his condition was a recurrence of the depression or nervous exhaustion which had interrupted his studies at Oxford in 1876, and which recurred occasionally throughout the next decade. Interspersed as they were with periods of energetic activity, extravagant foreign travel and episodes of irritability, it is possible that he was a victim of some form of bipolar disorder.

Alexander had become resigned to the fact that Malcolm would not be joining the family business. In March 1880 he wrote to one of his old friends, Alexander Maclaren.

I am in my sixty second year and yet it does not appear as if my work was quite done, nor, am I glad to say, my power of work. I have excellent helpers in Craik, my nephew Fred and my son George, who, I think, could carry it on if I were obliged to give up, but they don't seem to want to get rid of me – I hardly want to go. But oh! The tempting vision of retirement to Glen Sannox or High Corrie with a few friends to meditate and discuss on all that has been, and may be, and is – each with its perplexities and its consolations too, thank God.[4]

It is certainly the case that, whether from pressure of ill health or increasing age, or from the joy of his new family, the 1880s saw Alexander loosening the reins at Bedford Street. The outgoing letters in his hand become fewer, the European travels more extensive. In the few letters that survive, it is clear that he was never able to shake off the deference of the Irvine schoolboy:

To the Right Hon W E Gladstone, 17 August 1880

It was a most pleasant sight to me to receive a letter from you
in your own handwriting, when we were watching day by day
the bulletins about your health, which had been causing so much
affectionate anxiety to the millions who look on you as their leader
in high and noble, national and human endeavour; and stirred
feelings only vaguely suspected by themselves, perhaps, in many
whose aims and ideas are different from yours and ours. Indeed it is
a matter of large and deep thankfulness to the world at large, and
our prayers in many forms and in many languages will go forth for
the completion of your recovery . . .[5]

In 1880 the relationship with Oxford University Press came to an end, but the New York office continued to act as the Press's American agent for another fifteen years. The termination notice was served at the end of 1879 and Alexander was determined to complete the severance with dignity and to remind the Delegates how much he had achieved on their behalf. He wrote to Price: 'I shall look back to the seventeen years during which I have occupied the position with satisfaction. That your organisation is now in such a state that you can do for yourselves what I have hitherto done, has for me its consoling side.'[6] There seemed to be an unnecessarily long wait for his service to be recognized, but in March 1881 the Dean of Christ Church, Henry Liddell, wrote to say that the University proposed to confer an Honorary Degree of Master of Arts on Macmillan. He replied: 'The kind words you personally add enhance greatly the value of this public recognition. That I had to do in some efficient way in tending the twig which is now a prosperous and fruitful tree and that you and those who have the best means of judging recognise this is specially pleasant to me.'[7] If there is a hint of archness in this reply, did the Dean notice? This and the Freedom of Irvine were the only honours Alexander ever received. The intellectual snobbery and distrust which seems to have haunted the relationship between Delegates and publisher has its final word in the twentieth-century appointment of Alexander's great-nephew, Harold, to the position of University Chancellor, which he held for twenty-seven years.

As a sign of how fast times were changing, 1880 saw Olive, Macmillan's twenty-one-year-old daughter, enrolled at Newnham College, Cambridge, to take a degree in moral sciences. The year before she had travelled to America with her cousin Fred and his wife Georgie, and her brother Maurice. They had stayed on Long Island with Georgie's family, and then toured Niagara, Toronto, and down the St Lawrence River. Olive was not the only daughter with academic credentials; that year her older sister Margaret had translated from the Italian a *Guide to the Study of Political Economy* by Luigi Cossa, which Macmillan had published with a preface by W. Stanley Jevons, the well-regarded economist. Jevons wrote: 'The work of translation has been carried out by a former lady student in one of the excellent classes of Political Economy, conducted under the superintendence of the Cambridge Society for the Extension of University Teaching.'

Many of the names linked to the foundation of the women's colleges at Cambridge, and to Newnham in particular, are so closely associated with the Macmillan set and his catalogue that it is not surprising that Alexander was happy to let his daughter Olive enrol.

Throughout the 1840s, '50s, and '60s, efforts were made to offer better levels of education to women – whether it was the foundation of Queen's College for Women by F. D. Maurice in 1843, or the University Extension lectures held in London which were attended by Margaret Macmillan. In 1869 a Cambridge Examination for Women was established to allow women wishing to become teachers to obtain a qualification. In the following year, 'Lectures for Ladies' was established in Cambridge, set up by a group which included F. D. Maurice and Henry Sidgwick meeting at the house of Henry and Millicent Fawcett. (Sidgwick had first been commissioned by Macmillan to write an essay when he was a Fellow at Trinity in 1867, and in 1874 Macmillan would publish his greatest work, *Methods in Ethics*.)

In 1871 Sidgwick rented a house in Regent Street, just along from Llandaff House where Alexander's brother-in-law William Farthing Johnson kept a school. Bedrooms were offered to women from outside Cambridge who wished to attend the lectures and take examinations, and Sidgwick persuaded Anne Jemima Clough, sister of Arthur Hugh Clough (a poet published by Macmillan), to supervise the house and the women's education. This was the origin of Newnham College – and by the time Olive Macmillan attended in 1880 the women were living in a purpose-built hall designed by Basil Champneys. This gave students their own rooms, a dining hall, a library, and common rooms arranged over four floors. They had permission to attend some of the university lectures. Alexander would also have been impressed and comforted by the fact that Helen Gladstone, the Grand Old Man's youngest daughter, had studied there from 1877 and stayed on as secretary to Miss Clough. By 1881 the University had granted women general permission to sit its examinations, although they would not be granted degrees until 1948. Olive took her exams in 1883, obtaining a second class. In Newnham College records her cousin Alice Johnson wrote of her: 'She thoroughly enjoyed the College life. She had great social gifts and, from very early years, a singular power of attraction, exercised quite unconsciously, and she delighted in making friends. Political Economy was one of her favourite subjects, because of its direct bearing on social problems, for her bent was essentially practical.'[8]

In 1881 the pre-Raphaelite artist Frederick Sandys was staying in Tooting and drew in coloured chalks a touching portrait of Alexander holding his little son, John. The boy is not quite four years old, and both he and his father are dressed in velvet jackets. Alexander's face is tender, smiling, and proud, his long straight nose still prominent, his wavy silver hair parted in the middle and curling gently about his ears, his whiskers neatly trimmed around the edge of his face, leaving his chin clean-shaven. He wears a waistcoat, and a fob watch chain into which John has slipped his finger. John's blond hair is straight, and his brown eyes have the same intense gaze as his father. Alexander wears a signet ring on the little finger of his right hand, a stud in his shirt front, and a soft, silky bow tie. John's outfit is topped off with a wide lace collar and a pale ribbon tie. His arm is round his father's neck.

Sandys was undertaking a great commission for Macmillan. A late entrant to the pre-Raphaelites, he had begun life in Norwich as an illustrator and in the 1860s had had brief fame as a painter in oils, but by the 1870s his large florid paintings were going out of fashion. It appears that he was supporting two mistresses and fourteen children as well as a gambling habit, and so unsurprisingly was struggling for money; he was declared bankrupt twice. Luckily, in the 1870s he became closely involved with a group of prosperous merchants in the South London area, such as Henry Doulton and the Flower family, and through them he was introduced to Alexander Macmillan who commissioned a sketch of Emma and her little daughter, Mary. Sandys had always sketched his oils first in coloured chalks, and these now became his preferred and more commercial medium. Alexander was delighted with the outcome: Emma looks truly beautiful, with large dark eyes, a broad forehead, and pretty snub nose. She smiles at the artist. Her hair is brown and smoothed back with a centre parting under a lace cap. On her lap sits little Mary, equally interested in the artist, clutching a rag doll and a picture book, her bare arm resting on her mother's wrist. Emma's workbasket is on the table behind, knitting needles poking out. Macmillan commissioned Sandys to make a series of portraits of some of his favourite and most eminent authors. They were conceived as large bust-length portraits in coloured chalk on blue paper, which could then be used as engravings for frontispieces of Macmillan's works. The subjects included John Morley, Matthew Arnold, Goldwin Smith, J. Henry Shorthouse, and, of course, Alfred, Lord Tennyson. Craik decided to commission a few of his own: Robert Browning and Mrs Oliphant. In 1886 Sandys returned to draw George's two little boys, William and Alister, and later again the teenage Mary and John.

That summer of 1881, Emma persuaded Alexander to take a holiday in France, leaving George and Frederick in charge of the business. They rented a chateau in Samer, in the Pas de Calais region, and took with them the Bowes family, Mamie to look after little John and Mary, and Stribling the coachman. They hired a cook there and according to Emma, 'had mighty doings and excursions to the seacoast and the forest with the one conveyance of the place – an old landau – and a cart loaded with hay for the rest of us. Alexander read Sir Walter Scott, volume after volume as was his summer habit, in a quiet corner of the garden.' Staying nearby were Emma's mother and her sister Lucy, who lived together, but Emma said, 'Lucy's finely strung temperament and my mother's worn nerves made it not always easy'.[9]

There was still much going on in London, particularly with the planned launch of a new magazine, which had no name as yet, and Alexander found it hard to leave the young men to get on with it. On 13 August he wrote to George from Samer: 'why should I not run over on Monday, when the boat leaves Boulogne at noon reaching Charing X at 3.40. We could have a consultation with Morley on Tuesday or Wednesday, we could then settle the name. I am sure Craik will agree to whatever we four decide.'[10] There is no evidence in the files that George took him up on this offer, and it is difficult to work out the extent to which Alexander was happy to let go of the reins. George Macmillan wrote that his father stayed fully involved until the end of the decade, but there are so few letters in his hand from this time onwards that the assumption must be that while he remained the lead and consulting partner, he was not the most active going forward.

1882 saw the third and final member of the second generation join the firm. Maurice Macmillan had been teaching classics at St Paul's for six years since leaving Cambridge, where his career had been successful academically, gaining a first in classics, but also in sport, with many prizes for his athletic prowess. At one point there was a suggestion that Maurice might be set up in the bookshop at Eton College, which was for sale, but the terms proposed by the school were very unattractive. With the three young men now stamping their own ideas on the business, changes would be made, which Alexander was happy to support.

One of the first items on the young men's agenda was the publishing of periodicals. *Macmillan's Magazine* was faltering, with sales falling, hit by the launch of a sixpenny periodical from Longmans. It was Craik who drew the short straw of writing to his friend Grove in December 1882.

> There is no use shutting our eyes to the fact that the sale of the *Magazine* does not keep up to the old level; altho' the advertisements are still very good we cannot repose on them if the sale goes on dropping off. Last year's result was a bad one – for while the sale was maintained our payment for editorship was considerably increased – I am satisfied we are not behind others in our rate of payment and I have no feeling that too small payment to authors is at the root of our non-success. The energetic competition of other magazines forces us to consider our position and we feel we must do something to meet it.[11]

The partners were aware that the demands on Grove's time were increasing: he was still working on the *Dictionary of Music* and had just been appointed as the first Director of the Royal College of Music. The plan the partners had come up with was two-pronged, and probably slightly surprising to Grove. They wanted to ask John Morley to take Grove's place at *Macmillan's Magazine*, and to launch a completely new periodical into the market as well, this time with pictures, and a gentle mixture of light fiction, the odd poem, and informative essays. 'It is a sore matter for us all to part with you as our editor, but I know you will not take it as a personal matter on my part who writes this letter.'[12] The name finally decided on by the partners for the new periodical was the *English Illustrated Magazine*, to be edited by Joseph Comyns Carr for an annual salary of £400 on a three-year contract. As with *Macmillan's Magazine*, the partners laid off the risk by taking a contribution of £2,000 from Clay Sons and Taylor, as their favourite printing firm in Cambridge was now called. New staff had to be taken on – a Mr Heighway was employed to sell advertising in *Macmillan's Magazine*, *The Practitioner*, the *Statesman's Year-Book*, and the new magazine.

Further progress was made when, at the end of 1882, the firm finally managed to part company with the increasingly erratic Frederick Martin, and take full control of the *Statesman's Year-Book*. Martin had arrived at the office in a terrible state one day in December 1881 saying that the work was killing him and that in his anxiety he had mislaid a significant portion of that year's manuscript, leaving it on a train. It was George who met him and hastily wrote offering to relieve him of the role as work needed to be completed at speed. The book was due out in January and John Scott Keltie, who worked on *Nature*, was appointed to finish the work. No sooner had this had been agreed than Martin erupted, and a soothing response from Alexander as senior partner was required: 'Your telegram of Saturday took me by surprise, your letter of today surprises me more . . . there has been no "high-handedness" in this transaction, nor any wish other than that the work should be well done.'[13] If Martin wanted the job back of course he could have it. But when the *Year-Book* had still not emerged by the end of February, the partners despaired, offering Martin £450 for the copyright and to buy him out completely.

The dispute dragged on miserably throughout 1882, with Martin pleading for financial help – Alexander had advanced him £100 in January, and in the summer offered to let him have Scott Keltie to work with him again. But Martin was heading towards breakdown and bankruptcy and when the profits for the 1882 edition continued to disappoint, he wrote to George Macmillan: 'Some friends suggest to me that the best thing to be done with the unfortunate *Statesman's Year-Book* will be to throw it into Chancery and have it put up for sale.'[14] Martin's health was failing him, attributed by the *Pall Mall Gazette* to an accident when he had been knocked down by a coach some ten years earlier, and he died on 27 January 1883 at his house in north-west London, at the age of just fifty-three, leaving a widow with a young family. Just the month before, a new agreement was signed which assigned Martin's copyright in the *Statesman's Year-Book* to Macmillan.[15] It later transpired that at his worst moment in 1882 he had attempted to improve his fortunes by selling manuscripts that he had stolen from Thomas Carlyle when he had worked for the great man in the 1850s.

1883 also saw the death of one of Macmillan's favourite authors: the illness that had affected John Green's life for twenty years finally carried him off. His widow Alice wrote of Alexander and Emma's great concern for their friend.

> On hearing how grave the danger was, Mr and Mrs Macmillan left London by the very next train, leaving themselves scarcely an hour for preparations. At Mentone [Alexander] came over every morning from his hotel, and remained practically all day in my sitting room, waiting for any occasion when he might possibly be of use. I was too much occupied to be able to see

him for more than a few moments occasionally, for many days indeed not at all – and I need not tell you how deeply touched I was then, and am now, when I think what it meant to an impatient man to sit thus waiting in gloom. Nothing I suppose could have been more trying to such a temperament as his, so ardent, so impetuous. But not once did the shadow of impatience appear upon him. He had indeed a genius of the heart, a great and unselfish soul. In his admiration for others he was willing to do himself injustice, and I have never seen a more truly generous spirit or one less preoccupied with himself. He earned indeed the warm and undying affection and gratitude of all who knew him well.[16]

Alexander was greatly affected by Green's death: he may have felt that in some way by allowing Green to work so hard, to take on so many projects (not just the *History of England*, but the editing of the Primer Series), that he had contributed to his ill-health and shortened life. He wrote to William Stubbs, the Regius Professor of Modern History at Oxford: 'No man ever lived, I think, who had more the making of a real historian than he had, because he felt keenly, charitably, largely, humanly, man's work and aims.'[17]

The books that were adding to the family fortunes in the early 1880s are not ones that are greatly read, or even heard of, today. *John Inglesant*, by J. Henry Shorthouse, had been going the rounds of publishers since first written in 1876, and having been rejected by all, the unknown author printed a hundred copies privately, one of which made its way into the hands of Mrs Humphry Ward, who passed it on to Alexander. The firm published it in 1881. A historical novel set in the time of the English Civil War, which dealt with questions of faith and Catholicism, it sold 10,000 copies in its first year, and was publicly praised on all sides of Victorian opinion: fans included Huxley and Cardinal Manning. When the author and his wife were invited to meet the Prime Minister, Gladstone, in Downing Street, Alexander and Emma accompanied them to an evening reception where they also met the Prince of Wales and the Crown Prince of Denmark.

If Shorthouse was Alexander's find, it was Frederick Macmillan who cultivated the novelist F. Marion Crawford, a man who commanded substantial royalties and advances, occasionally in excess of the profits accruing to the firm. 1881 also saw the beginning of a string of successful novels from Henry James, Fred's investment in this friendship bearing profitable fruit. That year they published *The Portrait of a Lady* and *Washington Square* – just two years later they produced a fourteen-volume set of James' works.

In September 1883, Macmillan garnered the reward of a lifelong friendship with Tennyson when he was asked to bid to become the Poet Laureate's publisher. This was not the first time Tennyson had changed publisher, but Macmillan was always very circumspect when it came to disrupting existing contracts, and although he had tried on a couple of previous occasions to put himself forward, he had been either too shy or too cautious. However, the previous relationship with Kegan Paul, Malcolm's former tutor, now in publishing, had ended in mistrust and unhappiness. Hallam Tennyson wrote in his biography of his father: 'With none of the publishers into whose hands circumstances had thrown my father, was the connection so uninterruptedly pleasant as with Messrs Macmillan, unless perhaps that with Mr Henry King. Alexander Macmillan's genuine enthusiasm for his authors was especially remarkable.'[18] The contract that Alexander offered was thought by the trade to be excessively generous: a ten-year deal paying a royalty of one third of the advertised price on all books sold, and also a non-refundable advance of £1,500 every year on these royalties; not surprisingly, the long-term security, as well as the price, was highly attractive to the Tennyson family. The sums paid over to the family in fact were well in excess of the advance every year, proving that Macmillan had judged his market well.

A letter Alexander wrote to Lady Tennyson in January 1884 illustrates just how happy he was with this arrangement.

It is just forty-two years since I first read 'Poems by Alfred Tennyson' and got bitten by a healthy mania from which I have not recovered and don't want to recover. I then tried to bite others, with some success. I have now other, I cannot say deeper motives for continuing the process. How much I owe to Alfred Tennyson for the increase of ennobling thought and feeling, no one can tell. Now our closer connection will not lessen my desire to repay the debt.[19]

This last but best relationship of poet and publisher continued for the rest of their lives, and was acknowledged by the Tennyson family when they asked the firm to organize the poet's funeral in Westminster Abbey.

However, before the deal with Tennyson was in the air, it was a slim volume written by Tom Hughes, published in 1882, that was Alexander's pride and joy: a biography of his brother Daniel. The *Memoir of Daniel Macmillan*, according to my 1883 edition, went into 4,000 copies. Alexander distributed them as gifts far and wide, and the grateful letters from family, friends and colleagues poured in. Hughes in his Preface wrote:

> Whoever glances at these pages cannot fail, I think, to admit that there was something in this man's personal qualities and character, apart from his great business ability, which takes him out of the ordinary category – a touch, in fact, of the rare quality which we call heroism. No man who ever sold books for a livelihood was more conscious of a vocation; more impressed with the dignity of his craft, and of its value to humanity; more anxious that it should suffer no shame or diminution through him.[20]

Alexander must have had a happy time distributing the work and enjoying the response. The only complaints were that the drawing at the front did not do justice to Daniel's 'large lustrous eyes that were the ruling power of Johnson's dingy shop when I was an undergraduate' or his 'remarkably expressive mouth'.[21] Senior academics competed for the honour of being the first to have noticed just how remarkable Daniel was. An old friend from London days wrote: 'my admiration of him as a man was akin to my admiration for Carlyle as a writer – but in Daniel there was not the morbid element which I perceived and regretted in Carlyle.'[22] The great promoter of the circulating library, Mudie, called him 'a noble-hearted man working nobly for noble ends.' Matthew Hale, Bishop of Brisbane, wrote: 'No one acquainted with him would have supposed for a moment that in his passage through life he would be contented simply to drift with the stream.' Finally, Alexander would have been touched by this, from W. W. Howard: 'One day he talked about his mother whom he loved and worshipped so profoundly. I have often thought of this talk and it has made clear to me why you two brothers were so different from most of the men that one comes into contact with.'[23]

For Alexander, who felt that he owed everything to Daniel, publishing this tribute marked the culmination of his active career. He lived for thirteen more years, but it would be fair to say that the four junior partners, Fred, George, Maurice, and Craik, increasingly took the weight off the older man's shoulders. The work divided quite neatly between them: George pursued the classics, Fred concentrated on the American market he knew so well, Maurice developed the colonial trade, and Craik chased the debtors. Alexander turned his attention away from London, and with failing health and family concerns, the Hampshire hills beckoned.

– 23 –

HEADING FOR THE HILLS

(1884–96)

Bramshott Chase

'However it was, he was exhausted with the struggle, his strength was worn out. That lull of pain which does not mean any cure, or even any beginning of healing, but is merely a sign that the power of the sufferer to endure has come to its limit, gave him a kind of rest.'

Mrs Oliphant

As ALEXANDER'S PRESENCE at Bedford Street became less and less necessary, and as the damage wrought by years of sciatica, lumbago, and bronchitis slowly affected his mobility, he often wondered about a return to Scotland. In the end he settled happily for a landscape which reminded him of his youth, but with a significantly milder climate. He still enjoyed foreign travel, as Emma wrote, 'if he could freely poke about in corners and watch the ways of the people, but he also appreciated pleasant talks at table d'hotes. In those days one sat at long tables.' He was particularly happy if he met with an artist who could record the scene and send him home with a memento of a happy holiday: 'Dear man, how he enjoyed buying a picture.'[1] But travelling abroad in a large family group, with nurses and servants, was not something to be undertaken lightly and some years a quiet holiday in Scotland or by the sea at Torquay or Eastbourne suited Alexander better – less travelling, easier to get back to the office in a crisis. In 1880 he had taken a house in the New Forest at Lyndhurst, where he could enjoy a fortnight's rest but Emma and the little ones could stay for longer. The serenity of the countryside and the beauty of the Hampshire Downs struck a chord, and within four years the family moved to live in the county.

Their original idea was to acquire a small country place that the family could use as a summer home, to make holidays easier. However, in the summer of 1884 Alexander and Emma were invited to visit by Emma's old friends from Winnington Hall, William and Mary Capes. William was rector of a small parish called Bramshott, set on the downs above Haslemere. They rented the rectory at Hasle-merc for six weeks and set out to explore the surrounding area. The fresh air of the gorse-covered hills, which reminded Alexander of Arran, combined with the convenient railway line, made the location highly attractive. There was much to tempt them socially as well:

not just the Capeses, but a whole panoply of well-known writers and literary figures had chosen to move out to these charming and undeveloped Surrey/Hampshire borders. The Tennysons had built a house at Aldworth on Black Down, south of Haslemere, in 1869. Alexander will have remembered that Anne Gilchrist had taken a cottage in nearby Shottermill to finish writing her Blake biography after the death of her husband Alexander, and had entertained George Eliot and Christina Rossetti there at various times. William and Helen Allingham, the poet and his artist wife, lived at Witley, twelve miles along the road to London, and Humphry and Mary Ward rented a farmhouse near them. Frederic Harrison, the Positivist philosopher, rented a house near Black Down, while Sir Frederick Pollock, the jurist, lived in Hindhead and his friend the scientist John Tyndall, who was building a house there at the same time, declared the air to be as pure as that in the Swiss Alps. These were all people known to Macmillan and published by him. As Emma put it, they fell in love with the place.

Capes took Alexander to see his parish at Bramshott, where a large plot of land and a farm called the Chase was up for sale, and on an impulse, Alexander bought it and set to work to create a new house, the aspirational country home of the self-made Victorian family. Emma remarked:

> It was much bigger than anything we had ever thought of, but Alexander took to it and with his habit of not wasting time if a thing was to be done, bought it at once. So the next thing was the building of the dear house we all loved for twenty years; with its well-laid out garden and home farm. There we moved for the summers and [Alexander] got about in a bath chair and enjoyed the woods and wildflowers and we became in a quiet way, very sociable, being on the hill halfway between Liphook and Haslemere. A little circle of neighbours became intimate. It was a haven of rest and place of beauty, and Alexander was

as happy as the peaceful home and the love of his children and friends could make him.[2]

The three-storey red-brick house had several grand reception rooms, fourteen bedrooms, large gardens, two cottages, one for Stribling, the groom, and one for farmworkers. There were greenhouses, paddocks, and stables; everything a grand Victorian family could wish for. A photograph in the MacLehose family archives suggests that it was built in the new Arts and Crafts style, with tile-hung upper storeys, exposed timbers in the eaves, steep sloped roofs, and tall, Tudor-looking chimneys.

PHILOSOPHERS IN RETREAT.

Hind Head, Haslemere, is, the *Daily Telegraph* remarks, fast becoming a favourite retreat of the legal and learned. "It ought to be called Mind Head," a lady observed lately ; "its population is two-thirds savants, and a merely intelligent person feels like a fool in ten minutes." Mr. John Morley is staying at Blackdown Cottage ; Mrs. Ritchie and Miss Edith Sichel are at Sir F. Pollock's cottage ; Dr. Tyndall and Dr. Williamson, F.R.S., are both at their more or less newly-built residences ; Mr. Frederic Harrison has a cottage, Mrs. Humphry Ward is going to build one ; while Mr. Arthur Balfour, M.P., owns forty acres of ground as yet unbuilt upon. Dr. John Hopkinson, F.R.S., possesses a wooden shanty of charming dimensions ; and the whole settlement is bounded at one end by the Poet Laureate and at the other by Mr. Alexander Macmillan, his publisher.

St James's Gazette, 12 June 1889.

The house took two years to build, which meant it was not ready in time for Olive Macmillan's wedding in March 1886, which took place in Tooting. The groom, to Alexander's delight, was the youngest son of his old Glaswegian friend James MacLehose. James had died just the previous year, to Alexander's great sadness, but to see their families joined through this marriage eased the pain. His son's name was Norman and he had trained as a doctor at Glasgow University before coming south to work in Sevenoaks, where he and Olive, who had known each other since they were children, fell in love. After their marriage they moved abroad for a couple of years, living in Berlin, and then settled in Sevenoaks, where Norman specialized in ophthalmology. Their first child, James Alexander, was born in December that year, to be followed by Norman in 1889 and Caroline Barbara in 1893.

In the summer of 1888, Olive and Norman were staying in the Tyrol, from where she wrote at length to her brother George.

> After our long travelling we are actually on our way . . . Malcolm has come up with us for these few days before going south to meet Mr Wills at Perugia which he does on Tuesday. Since M joined us I believe I have sent almost nothing but postcards home, so I will write a little more fully about him now, if you wouldn't mind forwarding my letter to Knapdale. He seems to me wonderfully well, in some ways better than I have seen him for years. I mean he is so very calm, quieter, less excitable and irritable than he ever was at home. Of course the quietness is no doubt to some extent unnatural and he feels it so himself. He asked me if I noticed it. It is the remains of the depression of which one still sees signs every now and then. He spoke to me of the depression, as being really in the main past and the recollection of it is evidently so terrible to him that he has not quite lost the dread of its return. Beyond this – and this has been a few words on two occasions – he has not spoken of his illness nor of the past at all. He seemed very glad and a good deal moved at seeing us, has several times spoken of feeling it very nice to be in a family again. He is a good deal thinner and it has altered his face a good deal, but only for the better. He really is wonderfully handsome. He did not strike either Norman or me as looking very strong when he first came – but he has liked the Tyrol air very much and certainly looks better for it. As one would expect he does not seem to have very much energy, eg he seemed to dread the moving from Mentelberg here – tho' after all I was rather pleased to see him get thro' his packing quite quickly and without any

help. He is pretty late in the morning, but so long as he sleeps Norman thought it was wise to leave him and that the more sleep he has the better. He goes to bed pretty early and always takes a long walk every day.

About the future he doesn't speak much, and he still thinks of Egypt for next winter – but all his plans are I think vague in his head – he seems inclined to leave it so. I have tried to open the subject once or twice but he doesn't take it up, always seems to prefer just time in the present, in which with his reading and his walks he seems very contented. It strikes us that this is all natural, healthy and probably the mental rest his mind needs. We feel very pleased to have had this month with him – he is very happy and Baby evidently enjoys playing with him very much. He always seems disappointed if anything has prevented their daily game. He is reading in German a little now – happily is evidently still keen in his intellectual interests as ever – only there is that sort of almost aggressive restlessness that one used to notice . . . he has talked with great pleasure and interest of the various nice people he has met in Athens and Cyprus – they must have helped him a great deal to throw off the depression.[3]

This is clearly the sort of letter that concerned siblings would share, when discussing a brother who has suffered from prolonged and worrying bouts of mental health problems. In the years between his stay under medical supervision in Weston-super-Mare and 1888 Malcolm had finally managed to complete his Oxford degree, and had enrolled at the Inner Temple to study law, but he never took the time to learn enough, or attend the required dinners, to be called to the Bar. The collection of letters which his brother George had privately printed after his disappearance reveal a man who had deep interests in culture and the arts, particularly a love for poetry and opera, but who struggled to fit in and find a role for himself. At one point while at Oxford he wrote to a friend that he felt, having been named for his godfather Charles Kingsley, that he ought to be a writer or a poet. He had spent much time in the early 1870s, immediately after the death of his mother, working in the business alongside his father, and he still on occasion would read manuscripts, but as often as not the letters suggest that he has mislaid crucial copies, or forgotten his commitments. He was living off an allowance from his father, supplemented by the occasional cheque from his brother George. The family struggled at times to keep track of him: there is a plaintive note from Alexander, on holiday in Whitby, to George in July 1885: 'have you seen anything of Malcolm lately? He has not written once since we came here'.[4]

During the 1880s he began to travel widely, sometimes alone, sometimes with friends from Oxford. These travels took him to Uppsala and Stockholm, to Bayreuth, Munich, and Mürren, and to Italy on several occasions. For several years he worked on the manuscript of a book, to be published anonymously by the firm in 1886, called *Dagonet the Jester*. Any hopes he might have had that this would make his fortune would be dashed, as it sank without trace. Writing to his brother George, his flippancy and carelessness, even about this important subject, suggest his inability to focus on anything: 'I send you some errata for *Dagonet*. As there is never likely to be another edition, would it be unusual to insert a slip in binding any copies that are still unbound? I was rather horrified to find I had passed so many things after spending more than two hours in correcting the proofs.'[5]

Even the copy that Alexander proudly sent to William Gladstone has not survived in the Hawarden Library. In January 1887 Malcolm was back at Knapdale, writing to George that his annual allowance of £100 would scarcely cover his tailor's bills and the books he had bought. The previous year he had gone through £115 in cheques from George alone. The strain on family relationships continued: over the summer Malcolm must have had another relapse, with George picking up the pieces again. His father wrote to him: 'it was a blessed day when you came to us and your continual presence is an unspeakable blessing to me and all of us . . . All you are doing about

Malcolm has my most cordial approval. If you do go to see him, you can tell him how constantly and tenderly we all think of him.'[6]

Later that year Malcolm travelled to the eastern Mediterranean in the company of a friend from Balliol, Louis Dyer, on an indefinite trip which would take him all over Europe. Dyer was the same age as Malcolm, unmarried and from Chicago, the son of a well-known anti-slavery campaigner, Charles Volney Dyer. He had studied classics at Harvard before coming to Balliol. At the start of 1888 Malcolm and Dyer were in Athens, visiting ancient ruins with the great archaeologist Schliemann, then Dyer returned to the States and Malcolm set off again, calling at Cyprus, Alexandria, Giza, Venice, Perugia, and Florence – funded by cheques from George totalling £300. At some point he developed a nasty case of jaundice.

The letters home to George became more alarming in content, as the writer swung between ideas of establishing himself quietly with an income from reading manuscripts and journalism, or perhaps that could wait while he researched and wrote a novel. Perhaps he would return to Boston to stay with Dyer. Then news reached him that Alexander was struggling with his walking and he began to fear that this deterioration was the sign of something more sinister, and perhaps the truth was being kept from him, which he claimed had been the case when his mother was dying. He promised to come home to see his father, once he had completed his long wished for trip to Constantinople. This would be his final voyage and he would come home. Or perhaps he would live in Rome. Nothing was certain, except that he had no plans to marry and settle down, as his brother and cousins had done, and no plan to re-join the business.

Malcolm sailed from Brindisi to Constantinople in June 1889, travelling with Schliemann. He wrote to George from the Hotel Royal: 'I have just arrived here after one of the most delightful voyages in the world, which has thrown me into the most splendid health and appetite.' He had arrived safely 'under the wing of the Embassy' as he described it, trespassing on the kindness of Arthur Hardinge, who was a junior official at the British Embassy, an old friend from Balliol. After ten days he moved on to the cooler district of Therapia, writing to his sister Maggie that he would be home 'by about the 26th July, perhaps earlier. It depends on whether I decide to career about the Black Sea and the Danube.'

Arthur Hardinge, a young career diplomat whose memoirs are decidedly pompous, had only been in Turkey a few months and was keen to take the opportunity to explore the country and learn the language. He and Malcolm decided to set off for Brussa (now known as Bursa), around a hundred miles south of Constantinople, and two days later Malcolm wrote to his father:

> My dearest Father – I shall be home now in a very few weeks; but I have not written to you for a long time, and I thought you might like to have a line from me while I am still in what was once called New Rome . . . on this side of the Strait the upland country towards the Belgrad forest very much resembles the country about Hindhead, where I hope you now are. It is a heath covered with bracken, heather, small Spanish chestnuts and firs in the shrub stage, and the soil is sandy . . . I am very sorry to hear that you have been able to take so little food lately. I am sure that in the air of Bramshott you would be able to take a little more.[7]

It was the last Alexander would ever hear from his son.

This is the tale that Hardinge told about the events of 11 July 1889.

> After spending a couple of nights at Brussa, and inspecting its historic mosques and other sites, we determined to ascend Mount Olympus . . . and to return to Therapia by way of Ismid. Starting on horseback at eight in the morning from Brussa, with a Consular cavass [armed guard] as our guide, we reached the foot of Olympus at midday and resolved to climb the mountain before luncheon and enjoy the view from its highest

peak. There was no single or regular path, and as I myself was both younger and much lighter than my companion, I soon got ahead of Macmillan without realising that I had lost sight of him, and in less than forty minutes I arrived at the top of the mountain, and looked for some times at the magnificent panorama of the Mysian Plain and the distant outlines of the Golden Horn and the Bosphorus. On returning to the spot where I had left our horses and cavass, I found that my companion had not yet returned, and decided to wait till he did so before opening our luncheon basket. As some time passed without his reappearance, I did so and demolished a portion of its contents; but as the afternoon wore on, and no sign of him was visible, I began to wonder if he had taken a wrong path and perhaps lost his way. After waiting till nearly four o-clock, I began to feel a little uneasy, and suggested to our cavass that it might perhaps be prudent to obtain a guide from a small body of Albanian shepherds, who were, so he told me, in charge of the Sultan's large flocks and lived in a few huts which we had passed at a short distance from the point at which we first dismounted. One of these men, a grey-bearded old Albanian, declared himself ready to go with me, and together we explored on horseback and on foot, when the paths were too rugged, the whole of the summit of the mountain.

Towards evening a thick mist came on and we found it rather hard to see our way. I began moreover to fear that Macmillan might have slipped and injured a foot or ankle; but the old shepherd insisted that it was useless and even dangerous to go on searching the summit of Olympus in a dense and deepening fog and that my missing friend had probably returned by some other way to the camping ground occupied by the shepherds. As, on reaching the latter, I was told that he had not yet reappeared, I directed the cavass to return to Brussa, with a request to our Vice-Consul to send me, as early as he could the next day, some Zaptiehs [Turkish police officers] or, if possible, soldiers, not because I then seriously feared that Macmillan had met with foul play on the part of the Albanians, but because I thought that the sight of Turkish uniforms would stimulate their energies and prevent them from slackening in their search.[8]

Hardinge slept that night on the ground in a shepherd's hut, and the following day he and a small detachment of Turkish soldiers combed the area with no success. At that point something happened which made Hardinge, for the first time, suspect foul play: they came across an Albanian Roman Catholic priest with a party of schoolboys who overheard the shepherds planning to rob the Westerners and if necessary kill them. He returned to Brussa to rouse up the local police, and there follows a very strange passage in his memoirs: 'A Turkish *Juge d'instruction* who had been ordered to take my depositions and had probably derived his conceptions of European life from French novels, was evidently of [the] opinion that I had slain Macmillan in a *drame passionel* prompted by jealousy, selecting as a means of evading detection, the silent summit of Olympus.'[9] Luckily the Turkish civil governor thought it was more likely that Malcolm had been killed by a bear. According to Hardinge he and his men spent many days searching the countryside but found no trace of Malcolm.

There is much about Hardinge's story that is hard to read – he was, after all, not just Malcolm's friend and travelling companion, but a member of the consular staff, with a well-connected and wealthy Englishman under his protection. The idea that within just forty minutes he had completely lost sight of Malcolm, and had kept the armed guard with himself rather than assigning him to look after his guest, is shocking. That he thought it appropriate, in the circumstances, to mention that he sat down and ate his lunch before even wondering where Malcolm was, does not make his tale any more sympathetic. He tells the story as if it was just an amusing anecdote, with the mention of murder, or an attack by bear, being treated with less gravity than his own difficulties with a local judge.

Hardinge rounds off his story with an even more improbable set of circumstances – he claims that many years later Sir Maurice de Bunsen heard of a deathbed confession given to a priest by an Albanian Christian, that he had murdered Malcolm to rob him and had 'buried him in a depression on the summit of Olympus'. Hardinge thought it likely that Malcolm would have put up a fight if he was being robbed as he was 'a strong and active man.'[10] But not strong or active enough to keep up with Hardinge in a forty minute ascent? And the grave was so well concealed that no trace of it was found by all those who searched the area?

No one will ever know what happened on the mountain. Malcolm had no money, and no means of making a living, so any romantic notion that he had agreed with Hardinge to escape from the family and financial pressures awaiting him in England by concocting this disappearance and setting off for a secret life somewhere else seems unlikely. He had written to George that he hardly had the money to make it home – the journey to Turkey had cost him £100. Yet it was an extraordinary coincidence that this disappearance happened on the very last day of Malcolm's prolonged absence from England, just as he was meant to start for home and a life that did not really suit his temperament; of course to his family, the news was doubly tragic – the telegrams of his disappearance must have arrived just as they were planning his welcome.

George's great-grandchildren hold several documents that shed a little more light on the story, and throw some doubt on Hardinge's version. There is a letter from the British Vice-Consul in Broussa, J. C. Scholar, to the Ambassador, Sir William White, in Therapia, containing news that the search party had found marks made by slipping heels along with a couple of silver coins, which suggested to them that Malcolm had set off toward a different village. Further searches were instituted but again with no result. Scholar also claimed, in contradiction to Hardinge's story, that he had offered the two men an armed guard to accompany them but they had refused, taking only a local guide. White himself wrote to the British Prime Minister, Lord Salisbury, on 17 July, and said that he was awaiting the result of a cross-examination of the shepherds who lived in the hut close to where Malcolm had last been seen. There is no mention in these despatches of the Roman Catholic priest's accusation, as mentioned by Hardinge. In early August, Maurice Macmillan and Norman MacLehose travelled to Turkey but gained no further information. They wrote to White expressing unhappiness at the way the search had been conducted: it seemed to them highly unlikely that there had been any sort of accident, now that they had viewed the location. Murder was by far the most likely explanation and they felt that the shepherds should have been questioned away from the site. They alleged that the local villagers were all afraid of the Albanians and unwilling to search more thoroughly for fear of reprisals: if the shepherds were removed from the mountain, a more conclusive search could be undertaken.

This is where it becomes clear that the local diplomatic staff were simply not prepared to rock the boat to that extent. Maurice and Norman were told that if the Turkish authorities failed to act, the Ambassador would need permission from the Foreign Office to escalate the matter. On 15 August, George Macmillan wrote to Lord Salisbury's staff: 'We feel that we are entitled to claim from the Foreign Office that the suspected murder of a British subject in the Turkish dominions should be regarded as a matter of political interest, which cannot be allowed to pass without the most stringent enquiry directed not only to the detection but to the punishment of the perpetrators.' White's response was to argue that as there was no evidence incriminating the shepherds, nothing further could be done and the family were best advised to appoint a lawyer who could represent them at the enquiry which they hoped would be instituted. The man they chose was Edwin Pears, an English lawyer based in Constantinople, but unfortunately not someone that White thought much of, for reasons that were not clear. When Pears discovered that he would not be allowed to attend the enquiry in person, the British Embassy did nothing to help 'as the demand might give rise to difficulties.' Similarly, when George proposed writing to *The Times* cautioning British tourists against taking risks in the Turkish countryside, the British Embassy leapt into action to discourage him, in a masterpiece of tact:

> Sir William White does not think that criticisms in the British press are likely to have any salutary effect and deprecates the publication of such a statement as you propose in your letter. Lord Salisbury is disposed to agree. (Private: The Turks might possibly reply and with some effect, that startling crimes and mysterious disappearances occurred in other countries, which the Police were unable in any way to trace. But they would be more likely simply to sulk.)[11]

George took the hint, particularly as the newspapers at the time were full of the unsolved crimes of Jack the Ripper.

At the end of August, Hardinge wrote to George Macmillan from Therapia, to report the distressing news that the 'smell of a putrefying body' had been detected, but nothing could be confirmed or retrieved until the weather cleared. As Hardinge, in his memoirs, makes no mention of a body being found, this seems to have been inconclusive or misleading. There are no further mentions of any enquiry being held or coming to any conclusions. In November, Alexander wrote, for the last time, to Gladstone.

> Thank you for your kind allusion to the cloud of personal trouble which has been hanging over our family now for more than four months. In the absence of all news we can scarcely hope now that our anxiety can be relieved. Indeed the result of strenuous enquiries leaves but little doubt as to a fatal termination. The sorrow has been all the heavier that we were beginning to form high hopes of a prosperous career for my

son in literature. I venture to send you a little story he published anonymously a few years ago which has gained the approval of many good judges.[12]

Less than five months after Malcolm's disappearance, Maggie married his good friend Louis Dyer. In the light of what the family was going through, one wonders about this – was Dyer's grief for his friend part of the bond that brought him and Maggie together? Maggie was thirty-two, Dyer thirty-eight. Was there a conscious effort to distract Alexander and give him something else to think about? The very quiet wedding took place at All Souls' Church, Langham Place, presided over by Alfred Ainger, with George, Frederick, and John Victor Macmillan, and Dyer's artist brother Charles, as witnesses. There were no notices in the newspapers, the family wishing to minimize curiosity or disapproval at a time when they might have been in mourning. If Alexander was there, he did not sign the register. The bride was married from the new Macmillan family London home; the previous year Alexander had given up Knapdale, gifting it to the newly created Diocese of Southwark, and, for ease of commuting to Bedford Street, had taken a grand house at 21 Portland Place. Dyer took a job teaching in Oxford, and Alexander gave them the money to buy a house on the Banbury Road.

The preface to the privately printed selection of Malcolm's letters, written one assumes by George, declared that if Malcolm's life had been spared, his knowledge and faculties 'might have resulted in work of permanent value in the field of criticism, if not of creation.'[13] It seems a harsh judgement on a man of nearly forty, to have had so many opportunities and achieved so little. The one thing that is certain is that the mystery, the uncertainty, and the grief were terrible. Alexander never recovered. His daughter Margaret wrote of the 'one great grief and disappointment above all, [which] crushed his spirit and dimmed his eye'.[14] For a man to whom family and legacy had been so much, he must have wondered, and blamed himself, for what had gone so terribly wrong in the life of his first-born son. It was such a tragically different end than he had envisaged when he held the baby in his arms above the shop at Trinity Street, Cambridge. Over the years there had been so many difficulties: from Malcolm's failure to thrive at Marlborough, to the battle of wills when he had wanted to go to university rather than join the business, his inability to settle down, and his descent into depression and breakdown.

From this time on, Alexander fades from view, becoming the man in the bathchair, being wheeled around the grounds of Bramshott, visited by old friends on his birthday, enjoying the odd game of whist, or if he was strong enough, croquet. The letters kept by Craik show an increasingly shaky hand, and a corresponding increase in sentimentality. 'My dear Craik, you will hardly want a word from me but I feel I should like to say that the balance sheet is a great comfort to us all. Thank you, dear Craik, and my good boys, for all you do for me.'[15] We see a glimpse of him from Henrietta Huxley, widow of the great scientist: 'The last time I saw him was at his house on Portland Place, oh with his silky white hair falling over the collar of his black velvet coat. He insisted upon coming downstairs with me, much to my distress, and in spite of my appeal to his wife.'[16]

The decline was slow but continual, and it was seven years later, in January 1896, that he died in his bed at 21 Portland Place. He did not live to see the partnership become a limited company, in the month after his death, or the move from Bedford Street to St Martin's Street, but these were both developments for which he had laid the foundations. The death certificate states the cause of death as 'senile dyspepsia' and according to Graves, his mental faculties were intact until the end. 'Only a few hours before his death, Mrs Macmillan was reading to him the last chapter of *The Pilgrim's Progress* and when she came to the words "My Sword I give to him that shall succeed me in my Pilgrimage, and my Courage and Skill to him that can get it" he smiled and repeated the words, adding "to him that can *use* it."'[17]

THE BROTHERS' LEGACY

Mary MacLehose

'It was a life so completely fulfilled in all that hope and endeavour set out to accomplish that all there is to regret is the absolutely inevitable end that awaits us all.'

Frederick Greenwood, writing of Alexander Macmillan

THE PROBATE COPY of Alexander Macmillan's will can be seen today, preserved in the files of Maxwell, Batley & Co., Solicitors, in the London Metropolitan Archives. It is a complex document, five very large sheets of thick parchment covered in copperplate writing, difficult to spread flat or to read – three pages of the original document, five codicils. Its length contrasts tellingly with Daniel's will of the 1850s, which consisted of just a few lines leaving what little he had to his widow. Time and the business had moved on dramatically. Alexander's estate was valued at just under £180,000 (or £19 million today).

The will was dated 1 July 1889, drawn up while Malcolm was still travelling, but the detail says much about Alexander's strained relationship with his oldest son. Emma was to receive an immediate payment of £1,000. She had the use of Bramshott Chase for the rest of her widowhood, unless she remarried, together with an annuity of £1,500 and her choice of books, art, furniture, carriages, and horses. If she married again, she would receive a final lump sum of £2,000. Provisions were made for each of the children to choose personal items, and to George went one of Alexander's shares in the business. However, to Malcolm, a man approaching forty years of age, Alexander left £20,000, tied up in a trust, giving his son no access to the capital itself, only an annuity worth £1,000 (around £100,000 today). George, Malcolm's younger brother, would be one of the trustees of this settlement. The clear implication is that Malcolm could not be trusted with the money. There is no suggestion that he was a gambler or drinker, he certainly was no fool – but maybe this is evidence of the unstable behaviour that had coloured his adult life, and that he could not be trusted not to waste it all on wild projects or extravagant living.

In October 1889, a codicil was added amending the will to

recognize the possibility that Malcolm would never return, but holding out the hope that some evidence of him being alive might be found:

> Whereas my son Malcolm Kingsley Macmillan has not been heard of for some time past and it is doubtful whether he is now alive or dead: Now I hereby declare that if by the first day of January 1892 no evidence shall have been obtained by me or by my Executors that my son be living it shall for all the purposes of my said Will be assumed and considered that my said Son died in my lifetime. I hereby express my wish but not so as to legally bind my Executors or any person claiming any interest in my estate under my said Will that if at any time after the said first day of January 1892 it shall be found that my said son Malcolm Kingsley Macmillan is living arrangements shall be made for giving him such an interest in my estate as he would have had under my said Will had not this Codicil been made.

Subsequent codicils recorded the settlement made on Margaret's marriage to Louis Dyer; and appointing his wife Emma as a trustee. Alexander left small amounts to his most trusted servants: an annuity to Mamie Coxall, who had been with him for more than thirty years, and lump sums to Stribling his coachman, Clark his gardener, and Cresswell his bailiff. All his other domestic servants received the sum of £2 for every completed year of service. The premises at 1 Trinity Street, Cambridge went to Robert Bowes. The remainder of Alexander's estate, less one or two small legacies to Daniel's descendants, was put into a trust, with the income to be shared between all his children equally. This trust effectively tied the Macmillan family into the continuation of the publishing house for the next hundred years, preserving their connection with the source of all the wealth and prestige they enjoyed.

Emma lived on for nearly forty years and never remarried, whatever Alexander may have hoped or feared. On his death, she gave up Portland Place and moved back to Bramshott with her daughter Mary. The death of her father was a terrible loss to Mary, and she turned for comfort to James John MacLehose, the austere-looking Glasgow publisher and son of her father's oldest friend, already her brother-in-law through Olive's marriage to Norman. The wedding may have been quiet, as the family were still in mourning, but *The Hants and Sussex News* of 7 October 1896 reported that Bramshott church was decked in flowers and palm leaves, and her brother George walked her up the aisle, accompanied by seven little brides-maids and pages. As she left the church, she and Emma laid flowers on her father's grave. James and Mary MacLehose made their home in a lovely house, the Old Rectory at Lamington near Glasgow, where they brought up their four children. For Emma, her son-in-law James 'has been to me unceasingly a blessing'. This branch of the MacLehose family continues in publishing to this day and holds its own valuable family archive which they kindly allowed me to consult.

In 1906 the Chase was sold and Emma spent her last thirty years in London, living near the Thames, at 32 Grosvenor Road (later renamed 32 Millbank and long gone). This was four doors down from Alice Stopford Green, widow of their old friend John. One of her great-granddaughters, now in her nineties, remembers visiting her there. Emma died of pneumonia, the old lady's friend, in May 1935 at the grand old age of ninety-two. Her last years appear to have been happy, doted on by her son John Victor, who was on his way to being appointed Bishop of Guildford. Emma wrote: 'John's never failing care and the happiness I have had in his career have coloured my life with many beautiful things'. His marriage in July 1906 ranks high among the events that would have swollen his father's heart with pride: his bride was Annie Maurice, the granddaughter of the man Alexander and Daniel called The Prophet, F. D. Maurice. The wedding, presided over by Randall Davidson, Archbishop of Canterbury, was held at St Peter's Church in Vere Street, where Maurice himself had been the incumbent from 1860 for nine years, and in the presence of the two surviving members of the Christian Socialist movement, both well into their eighties, John Ludlow and Lowes Cato Dickinson. There would be grander Macmillan marriages in the years to come, but none would have given Alexander more pleasure, or seemed such a fitting tribute to what he had achieved.

Alexander's other surviving children, Margaret, Olive, and George, began to spend more time away from London, enjoying the comfort of country residences and small estates. George and his wife Maggie were increasingly drawn to the home they built near Whitby, Botton Hall. They lost one son, Alister, when he was just ten, but they had two other children, William and Helen, and William's grandchildren Janet, David, and Catherine hold many touching and affectionate family letters and portraits. George remained an active partner in the firm, taking responsibility for academic, archaeological, and music books, not only *Grove's Dictionary* but the *Cambridge Natural History* and Frazer's *The Golden Bough*, of which the first edition in two volumes was published in 1890. He had a busy interior life, with other passions, for music and the classical world, which may have compensated him for any disappointment he felt in not having gone from Eton to Cambridge. He remained the Secretary of the Hellenic Society for forty years, and in 1898 was elected to the prestigious and select gentlemen's club The Society of Dilettanti, becoming Secretary in 1911. He held the role of Chairman of Stainer and Bell, the music publishers, and served on the Council of the Royal College of Music. Alexander would have been particularly proud that in 1911 he was made an Honorary Fellow of Lincoln College, Oxford, for his services to Hellenic scholarship.

Margaret and her husband Louis Dyer settled in Oxford on the Banbury Road and had three children. Louis worked as an academic at the university, occasionally lecturing in the States at Princeton and Cornell, in both classics and political economy. In 1893 Macmillan published a revised edition of Cossa's economics text which Margaret had originally translated in 1880. This time, her husband took the credit. But he died in his fifties, leaving Margaret a widow, who lived on alone until her death in 1935. Her younger sister Olive died in 1926, having been crippled with rheumatoid arthritis for many years. In 1902 Olive and husband Norman built a house on the common above Berkhamsted, where she brought up two sons and a daughter.

What of Daniel's children, Fred, Maurice, and Kate? On Alexander's death Frederick Orridge Macmillan became Chairman of the newly incorporated company. He became one of the most distinguished figures in British publishing, the pioneer of the Net Book Agreement which tried once and for all to settle the issue of discounting by retailers which had irritated Alexander for so many years. In 1890 Fred wrote a letter to *The Bookseller* deploring the random discounting of books by retailers which threatened the survival of many smaller bookshops – a cause which his uncle had taken up with Gladstone himself in 1868. Fred wrote, 'A well-stocked bookshop is a centre of mental culture': his uncle had written, 'an intelligent bookseller in every town of any importance in the kingdom would be almost as valuable as an intelligent schoolmaster or parson. How can you get that if you don't pay him for his work and thought?'[1] The Macmillan-led campaign slowly gathered pace, resulting in the Net Book Agreement of 1899, which regulated the publishing industry until the 1990s.

Fred enjoyed fox-hunting and the life of the clubs in Pall Mall where he could enjoy a good cigar. He was a plump man, with rosy cheeks and twinkly eyes, four times President of the Publishers' Association. He had one other significant interest in his life, which earned him his knighthood in 1909 – The National Hospital for the Paralysed and Epileptic, as it was then known, in Queen Square, where he chaired the board for many years. He was knighted by King Edward VII during a royal visit to the hospital, the King borrowing a sword from one of his attendants for the purpose. It is interesting to speculate why this cause was so close to Fred's heart, and whether it was linked to the continued decline of his sister Kate. She had been experiencing prolonged stays in specialist institutions since the 1880s, alternating with time at home with her family. At the time of

the 1891 census she was one of a dozen so-called 'lunatics' living at
The Grove, a women-only asylum in Hendon. It may well be that
she had in fact developed epilepsy as a teenager, which was poorly
understood and could only be treated with bromide at that time. If
left untreated, the deterioration can be severe. It can also be linked
with depression and psychosis. By 1901 Kate was under the full-time
residential care of a Dr Bisdee, initially living as the only boarder at
his home in Hoddesdon, Hertfordshire (close to Frederick's country retreat at Temple Dinsley), and then moving with the Bisdee
family to Weston-super-Mare. In 1911, Kate fell from a fourth-storey
window in the doctor's house and died within hours. The newspaper
reports of the inquest made no mention of her famous family, and
a verdict of accidental death was recorded, although reading the evidence, suicide would also seem a plausible conclusion.

Fanny, Daniel Macmillan's widow, and her daughter Kate were
the grandmother and aunt, respectively, of Harold Macmillan, later
Prime Minister, but their stories were buried with them. Kate has
been completely airbrushed out of the biographies of her brothers
and nephew, and it was a chance find in the archives at the University
of Reading of a letter from the son of her physician that led me to
discover the circumstances of her death.[2] If Frederick and Maurice,
Fanny's two elder sons, were kept in the dark about their mother's
illness, they certainly would have known what had happened to their
sister Kate. Her death occurred when Maurice's son Harold, the
future Prime Minister, was sixteen years old, and his mother Nellie
would have been well aware of the horror, and of the history of
mental illness and suicidal tendencies in Daniel's family.

Maurice Macmillan took responsibility for the firm's colonial
business, initiating the opening of offices in Bombay in 1901, and
for its educational series. He, like his brother, married an American
wife, a pretty young widow known as Nellie. Her full name was
Helen Artie Tarleton Belles, and like Maurice she had had a tragic
childhood, losing her mother and four siblings by the time she was
six. She married in 1874 at the age of eighteen, but within six months

her husband Jack Hill had also died. She fled to Europe and while she was studying art in Paris in 1883 she met Maurice. They were married the following year, from the Craiks' house in Beckenham, Kent. The bride was given away by James Russell Lowell, the poet, at that point living in England as the American Ambassador. Maurice and Helen, known as Nellie, went on to have three sons, Daniel, Arthur, and perhaps the best-known member of the family, Harold.

Unsurprisingly, Nellie Macmillan was a clinging, possessive mother. Her second son Arthur suffered from epilepsy, which again suggests that this is what had affected Kate, and was never strong, choosing a career in law, and quietly marrying a Macmillan from the Isle of Arran, a distant cousin. After Daniel also made a marriage that Nellie considered less than fortunate, she centred all her ambition onto her youngest boy, Harold. Her ambition seemed to be paying off when in April 1920 he married Lady Dorothy Cavendish, the daughter of the Duke of Devonshire, at St Margaret's, Westminster. They had met when he was attached to the Duke's staff while he was Governor-General of Canada. The power of the Macmillan publishing house was on full display at the wedding: Nellie had insisted on issuing invitations to all the best-known authors on the firm's list. The congregation included John, now Lord, Morley, Thomas Hardy, and Rudyard Kipling, all holders of that most prestigious honour, the Order of Merit. Morley, weighing up the guests on the other side of the aisle, is said to have whispered to Hardy, 'Which weighs most, three OMs or one Duke'.[3]

However, the marriage was soon known to be less than perfect, and although Harold's political career started well, with him elected as a Conservative MP for Stockton in 1924, by 1929 he had lost his seat and his wife was having an affair with his friend Bob Boothby. Knowing, as his mother would have done, the history of mental instability that had killed both his grandmother and his aunt Kate, and had affected his cousin Malcolm, Nellie became watchful and protective. In 1931 Harold appears to have had a nervous breakdown, struggling under the continual misery of war wounds, the lull in his political career, and his wife's infidelity. There were even rumours of a suicide attempt. Nellie took control and, perhaps remembering Fanny and Kate, despatched him to a sanatorium in Bavaria to be nursed back to health.

The First World War had cut a swathe through the young Macmillan men. John Victor Macmillan, Alexander's youngest child, had already taken holy orders and served as a military chaplain. Harold was badly wounded, but three of Alexander's grandsons were killed and one badly maimed. Only George's son William came through relatively unscathed, having served as a captain in the Scottish Rifles and then on the General Staff. The first to die was Olive's son, Norman Crawford MacLehose, killed in Flanders in 1915, just two months after arriving at the front. He had been a distinguished scholar at Rugby School and Balliol College, Oxford, and had worked for a while at Toynbee Hall, an educational settlement among the poor in the East End of London where he would have rubbed shoulders with William Beveridge and Clement Attlee. Cecil Dyer, Margaret's son, was killed in April 1915 at Ypres at the age of twenty-one. His cousin James Colin MacLehose, Mary's boy, died at Ypres in 1917, aged just nineteen. Olive's oldest boy, James, lost a foot. Maurice's other son Daniel was invalided out.

The firm offered a refuge to the men of the next generation who survived the war, principally to Maurice's sons Daniel and Harold, and George's son William. George, Maurice, and Frederick, the three senior partners in the business, died within a few months of each other in 1936, by which time the business was being capably managed by this next generation. The deaths of all three partners in one year and the subsequent death duties payable put a great strain on the business: George's only surviving son Will, who had just lost his wife suddenly to meningitis, chose to sell his shares to Daniel and Harold, and this ended the active participation of Alexander's descendants in the firm. However, these two continued to hold their shares in both the British and the American companies for several decades.

At the time of Alexander's death, the New York business, with sales approaching $500,000, was being separated into an independent company, The Macmillan Company of New York. George Platt Brett Senior, the son of the man whom Alexander had sent to New York in 1869, was made president and was able to acquire a ten per cent shareholding. The Macmillan family retained a controlling interest in the business until the 1950s when they sold their majority shareholding to George Platt Brett Junior. By this time, the American branch had become 'considerably larger and more powerful than its London counterpart.'[4] As Alexander had predicted and planned back in 1867: 'A great international publishing house is possible, and could be a grand idea to be realized.' The brave choices Alexander had made, by backing his own judgement, and his own man, had created the opportunity to 'change the course of the company by transforming it into one of the first truly internationally based publishing firms in the world.'[5]

George Edward Brett, in his last days, wrote to Frederick Macmillan about Alexander.

You will remember, Mr. Frederick that it was he [Alexander] who found me – wandering in the wilderness as we may say – put me in the way of using my trade in his service, and above all put it in my powers to cultivate my intellect. The very highest earthly good; and beyond all this which indeed alone rendered all that possible, exercised such kind generous forbearance towards me in the early days of the Agency which I feel I could not have deserved but for which my gratitude will be endless. What do I not owe him.[6]

Alexander had made enough money to set up all his children and his nephews and niece in comfort for the rest of their days. But Brett was not the only person to feel gratitude – many, many other people outside the family profited enormously from the success of the company, and from the generosity with which the first partners, Daniel and Alexander, conducted their business. As Charles Graves wrote, 'Alexander Macmillan never professed to regard publishing as a charitable or philanthropic undertaking, but it is right to say that the instances of his liberality and generosity are not confined to those recorded [in Graves's book], that he always advised authors not to part with their copyrights, and that no writer of note ever transferred his allegiance to another firm.'[7]

One of the last letters in Alexander's own hand in the letterbooks, dated February 1887, is his note to Mrs Todhunter, widow of Isaac, the great mathematician. It accompanied a cheque for £4,590, being that year's royalties on Isaac's many textbooks, worth over £700,000 in today's money.[8] Todhunter was a man from the most meagre of circumstances but with extraordinary mathematical skills; the son of a Congregationalist minister, he had worked his way up from assistant master at a school in Peckham to St John's College, Cambridge. In 1848 he was the Senior Wrangler, and crucially, met the Macmillan brothers. They published his *Treatise on Differential Calculus* in 1852, which went through five editions in twenty years, and was reprinted every three years thereafter. This was just the first of twenty-four titles that would be published under his name and sent around the world. His wealth at probate in 1884 was £81,000, or £1.4 million in today's values.

When Graves' *The Life and Letters of Alexander Macmillan* was published in 1910, his son George sent presentation copies to many of his old Scottish friends, and to his staff and servants. Among the many grateful replies, full of reverence for an old friend or master, came one from Frank Clark, whose father George had been gardener at Knapdale.

Dear Sir,

I'm afraid I cannot adequately thank you for the splendid book you have sent me, the Life and Letters of my dear master . . . How often I have longed for this, I felt sure it would be published and often wondered who would write it. It is the grandest book in

every respect I have ever had, and it arrived on his birthday Oct
3rd, a day when my mind has always naturally turned to some of
the happiest and best times of my life, those days at Knapdale and
Bramshott Chase. Some of my earliest recollections are associated
with the garden at Knapdale, where I generally spent my holidays.
For years I quite thought it was my father's garden, and I can
remember now the name and position of every tree and shrub. Later
in life I was privileged to live in the House, and wait on the master,
I was awfully awkward and nervous, but he quickly helped me to
overcome that and it was not long before I looked for the time to
come when he came in from Bedford St. He taught me everything
I know about books, and gave me Tom Brown at Oxford to read
aloud to the maids in the hall. It was a red letter day to me when
shortly after this Mr Hughes himself came to dinner, and I had the
pleasure of hearing him talk. I had seen him once before, when he
planted the mulberry tree in Knapdale gardens. I often think over
the scenes in the picture gallery of my memory, associated with my
life of ten years under your father's roof, and feel very grateful that
I had such a fine introduction into life. He shewed me how to look
for the best and highest in everything, and instilled into my young
mind the very finest principles and ideals, anything of real worth in
my character, I can now trace back to those memorable days and I
feel I owe your family a big debt that I can never hope to repay.[9]

It is hard to imagine a better epitaph.

Acknowledgements

This book could not have been written without the encouragement and support of the Macmillan family, particularly Lord Stockton and David Macmillan, Janet and Robert Stevens, Catherine Macmillan, Christopher and David Maclehose, Christine McCrum, Elizabeth Frayling-Cork, and Peter Young, all of whom have either talked to me or shared family papers and photographs, or both. Thanks also to David Faber and Georgiana Lebus for looking. Kathy Cowell, a descendant of the Geikie family, gave permission for us to use the photo of Emma Macmillan.

I am also very grateful to Professor Jane Ridley for her wisdom and guidance and to my fellow MA students at the University of Buckingham, especially Caroline, Chris, Henry and Tuli, who have always been enthusiasts for this project and have supported me at every point. At various stages of the project I have enjoyed useful conversations, if only online, with Robert Douglas-Fairhurst, Karen Bourrier (the biographer of Mrs Craik) and Etta Madden.

There are many archivists, current and retired, that I need to thank for all their help and patience, starting with those at Macmillan & Co. in Basingstoke: John Handford, Alysoun Sanders and Elly Crooks, especially Alysoun for sharing her photos of Achog croft and both John and Alysoun for reading my manuscript, correcting my errors and making helpful additions. I have spent many, many hours at The British Library, and would particularly mention Elizabeth James, Catherine Angerson and all the helpful staff in the Manuscripts Reading Room.

I should also thank Nicky Monroe at the University of Reading, Special Collections; Rosalind Grooms and Frank Bowles at Cambridge University Archives; Yaye Tang at the Cambridgeshire Archives; Margaret Wright and Karen Barbour at Arran Museum; Valerie Gaskin at Liphook Heritage Centre; John Childs at Grayshott Heritage; Moira Goff at the Garrick Club; Robert Harding at the Savile Club; Julie Carrington at the Royal Geographic Society; Becky Loughead at The Society of Antiquaries; Dr Nicholas Melia at the Borthwick Institute in York; Lowri Jones at the Royal College of Physicians for answering questions on TB and sciatica; Witold Szczyglowski at the Working Men's College; Martin Maw at Oxford University Press Archives; Eileen Hori at St Andrew's Street Baptist Church, Cambridge, for sharing the archives of the Church and of Llandaff House School; John McCrory at the University of Manchester Archives for facilitating an online viewing of the Freeman papers; Kristina Krasny at Indiana University Bloomington for James Eldridge's notes on Nellie Macmillan; Hazel Menzies at North Ayrshire Heritage Centre for identifying the grave of Duncan and Catherine Crawford Macmillan; J. P. Rudman at Uppingham School; Alexander Foulds at The Gladstone Library, Harwarden; Frieda Midgley at Newnham College, Cambridge; Dr Robin Darwall-Smith, archivist at Jesus College, Oxford for the papers of J. R. Green; Lucy Inglis at King's College School; Victoria Perrin, who shared her dissertation on 1 Trinity Street; Simon Humphries for discussing his work on Christina Rossetti; Brian Talbot for his knowledge of the Scottish Baptist movement; Nigel Richardson, who was fascinating on the subject of Edward Thring; Father William Hebborn, who showed me round Knapdale in Tooting; Dame Helen Stokes-Lampard for talking to me about tuberculosis; Jill Dudman at the Friends of West Norwood Cemetery, who pointed me in the direction of Caroline's grave; Gordon Nicoll at Abernyte; Philip Wray of Preston, Hertfordshire for his help with Sir Frederick Macmillan; and Alys Blakeway, the Chair of the Charlotte Yonge Fellowship. A special mention goes to Claire Jarvis, an excellent freelance researcher at the National Archives who helped me find the papers relating to the 1869 Chancery case. I am grateful to the helpful staff at the Harriet Martineau archive at the University of Birmingham, the London Metropolitan Archives, The National Archives, the Senate House Library at the University of London, and the New York Public Library, which houses the Berg Collection.

I am enormously grateful to my friends: to Therese who has always been an enthusiast for the book, to Kate who read my manuscript for me with a city-trained eye for typos, and gave me lots of things to think about, and especially to Judith who helped me understand the Chancery papers and the impact they had on Alexander Macmillan's family and his business. In 2021 the proposal for this book won the Tony Lothian Award from the Biographers' Club, and this early support was incredibly welcome, so I thank the judges and organizers. I couldn't have been luckier than to have Caroline Dawnay as my agent, with Kat Aitken ever helpful, and the team at Pan Macmillan, especially my editor Ingrid Connell, her assistant Lydia Ramah, and copy-editor Nicholas Blake.

My children have been a constant source of interest, enthusiasm and good-natured teasing, but above all I can hardly express how much I owe to my beloved husband Peter, who has encouraged and pushed me every step of the way, driven me round Scotland and Cambridgeshire in the footsteps of Daniel and Alexander, who has read every page and listened for hours, and who genuinely seems to have enjoyed the whole process as much as I have. His love and support mean the world to me.

Bibliography

ARCHIVES

Cadbury Research Library, University of Birmingham, Harriet Martineau Papers

Cambridgeshire Archives Service, Cambridge, St Mary the Great Overseers: Poor Rate and Account Books 1844–88

Garrick Club Archive, Membership Records 1864

Jesus College, Oxford, The Private Papers of John Richard Green

London, The British Library

—, The Macmillan Archive, Add MS 54786–56035 and Editions Book

—, The Gladstone Papers, Add MS 44246

—, The Layard Papers, Add MS 38986–9

London Metropolitan Archives

MacLehose Family Archives: privately held

The National Archives

—, *Census Returns of England and Wales*, 1841, 1851, 1861, 1871, 1881, 1891

—, Chancery Records

—, Foreign Office Papers

National Library of Scotland (NLS), Manuscript Collections, Dep. 208 Professor A Campbell Fraser DCL LL.D, Boxes 12 and 16

New York, New York Public Library

—, Astor, Lenox and Tilden Foundations, Henry W. and Albert A. Berg Collection of English and American Literature:

—, Dinah Maria Mulock Craik Manuscript Material, Pforz MS

—, Alexander and Anne Gilchrist Collection of Papers, 1859–1863, uncatalogued

—, Thomas Hughes Collection of Papers 1856–1889, Berg Coll MSS Hughes, T

—, Dante Gabriel Rossetti Collection of Papers, 1855–1941, Berg Coll MSS Rossetti

Oxford University Press Archives

Senate House Library Archives, University of London: The Papers of Sir John Robert Seeley

Stevens Family Archives: privately held

University of Cambridge, Special Collections, The John Malcolm Forbes Ludlow
    Papers
University of Manchester, Special Collections, Edward Freeman Papers
University of Reading, Special Collections,
—, Bowes and Bowes (Cambridge) Archive
—, Macmillan & Co. Archive
Uppingham School Archives
York, Borthwick Institute for Archives, University of York, The Retreat Archive
    1792–2000

WORKS CONCERNING THE MACMILLAN FAMILY AND

THEIR PUBLISHING COMPANY

Anon., *Selected Letters of Malcolm Kingsley Macmillan* (Printed for Private
    Circulation, 1893)
Davenport-Hines, Richard, *The Macmillans* (London: Heinemann, 1992)
Dyer, Margaret, *Reminiscences of Alexander Macmillan*, unpublished document
    held by the family
Graves, C. L., *Life and Letters of Alexander Macmillan* (London: Macmillan, 1910)
Hertz, Alan L., 'Macmillan's Magazine under David Masson: 1859–1867'
    (unpublished doctoral thesis, University of Cambridge, 1982)
Horne, Alistair, *Macmillan*, 2 vols (London: Macmillan, 1988)
Hughes, Thomas, *Memoir of Daniel Macmillan* (London: Macmillan, 1883)
James, Elizabeth, ed., *Macmillan: A Publishing Tradition* (Houndmills: Palgrave
    Macmillan, 2002)
Macmillan, George A., ed., *Letters of Alexander Macmillan* (Printed for Private
    Circulation, 1908)
Morgan, C., *The House of Macmillan (1843–1943)* (London: Macmillan, 1944)
Nowell-Smith, Simon, ed., *Letters to Macmillan* (London: Macmillan, 1967)
Thorpe, D. R., *Supermac: The Life of Harold Macmillan* (London: Chatto &
    Windus, 2010)

SECONDARY SOURCES

(INCLUDING ACADEMIC JOURNALS AND THESES)

Altick, Richard D., *The English Common Reader: A Social History of the Mass
    Reading Public 1800–1900* (Chicago and London: Phoenix Books, 1957)
Anon., *A Bibliographical Catalogue of Macmillan and Co.'s Publications from 1843 to
    1889* (London: Macmillan, 1891)
Ashton, Rosemary, *One Hot Summer: Dickens, Darwin, Disraeli and the Great Stink
    of 1858* (New Haven and London: Yale University Press 2017)
—, *Thomas and Jane Carlyle: Portrait of a Marriage* (London: Pimlico, 2003)

—, *Victorian Bloomsbury* (New Haven and London: Yale University Press, 2012)

Atkinson, Diane, *Love and Dirt: The Marriage of Arthur Munby and Hannah Cullwick* (London: Macmillan, 2003)

Bain, J. S., *A Bookseller Looks Back* (London: Macmillan, 1940)

Baker, Samuel, *The Albert N'Yanza: Great Basin of the Nile* (London: Macmillan, 1866)

Barton, Ruth, ' "Huxley, Lubbock, and Half a Dozen Others": Professionals and Gentlemen in the Formation of the X Club, 1851–1864', *Isis*, 89:3 (1998)

Batchelor, John, *Tennyson: To Strive, To Seek, To Find* (London: Vintage, 2014)

Benzie, William, *Dr F. J. Furnivall: Victorian Scholar Adventurer* (Norman, Oklahoma: Pilgrim Books, 1983)

Blake-Hill, Philip V., 'The Macmillan Archive', *The British Museum Quarterly*, 36 (1972)

Bourrier, Karen, *Victorian Bestseller: The Life of Dinah Craik* (Ann Arbor: University of Michigan, 2019)

Briggs, Asa, *Victorian People* (London: Penguin, 1955)

Broomfield, Andrea, 'Towards a More Tolerant Society: *"Macmillan's Magazine"* and the Women's Suffrage Question', *Victorian Periodicals Review*, 23 (1990), 120–26

Broomfield, Andrea L., 'Much More than an Anti-feminist: Eliza Lynn Linton's Contribution to the Rise of Victorian Popular Journalism', *Victorian Literature and Culture*, 29 (2001)

Burd, Van Akin, *The Winnington Letters: John Ruskin's Correspondence with Margaret Alexis Bell and the Children at Winnington Hall* (Cambridge, MA.: Harvard University Press, 2014)

Cannon, Walter F., 'Scientists and Broad Churchmen: An Early Victorian Intellectual Network', *Journal of British Studies*, 4:1 (1964)

Carpenter, Humphrey, *The Seven Lives of John Murray: The Story of a Publishing Dynasty 1768–2002* (London: John Murray, 2008)

—, *Secret Gardens: A Study of the Golden Age of Children's Literature* (London: Faber and Faber, 2012)

Catton, Bruce, *The Civil War* (Boston and New York: Houghton Mifflin, First Mariner Books Edition, 2004)

Chainey, Graham, *A Literary History of Cambridge* (Cambridge: The Pevensey Press, 1985)

Chilston, Viscount, *WH Smith* (London: Routledge & Kegan Paul, 1965)

Chitty, Susan, *The Beast and the Monk: A Life of Charles Kingsley* (London: Hodder & Stoughton, 1974)

Coghill, Mrs Harry, ed., *The Autobiography of Mrs Oliphant* (Chicago: University of Chicago Press, 1988)

Cohen, Morton N. and Anita Gandolfo, eds, *Lewis Carroll and the House of Macmillan* (Cambridge: Cambridge University Press, 1987)

Colloms, Brenda, *Charles Kingsley: The Lion of Eversley* (London: Constable, 1975)
—, *Victorian Visionaries* (London: Constable, 1982)
Colls, Robert, *This Sporting Life: Sport and Liberty in England 1760–1960* (Oxford: Oxford University Press, 2020)
Cruse, Amy, *The Victorians and Their Books* (London: George Allen & Unwin, 1935)
David, Deirdre, ed., *The Cambridge Companion to the Victorian Novel* (Cambridge: Cambridge University Press, 2001)
DeBlock, Elizabeth, 'Macmillan & Co. in New York: Transatlantic Publishing in the Late Nineteenth Century' (Unpublished M.Phil. thesis, University of St Andrews, 2017)
Desmond, Adrian, *Huxley: From Devil's Disciple to Evolution's High Priest* (Reading, Massachusetts: Perseus, 1994)
Dickerson, Vanessa D., 'Thomas Carlyle: Case Study of a Dark Victorian', in *Dark Victorians* (Urbana, IL: University of Illinois Press, 2008)
Easley, Alexis, 'George Eliot and "Macmillan's Magazine"', *George Eliot – George Henry Lewes Studies*, 60/61 (2011)
Ehnes, Caley, 'The New Shilling Monthlies: Macmillan's Magazine and The Cornhill', *Victorian Poetry and the Poetics of the Literary Periodical*, 2019
Eliot, Simon, ed., *The History of Oxford University Press* (Oxford: Oxford University Press, 2013)
Ellman, Richard, *Oscar Wilde* (London: Hamish Hamilton, 1987)
Ewan, Christopher, 'The Emancipation Proclamation and British Public Opinion', *The Historian*, 67:1 (2005)
Fawcett, Millicent Garrett, *What I Remember* (London: Fisher Unwin, 1924)
Feather, John, *A History of British Publishing*, 2nd edn (London: Routledge, 2006)
Flanders, Judith, *Consuming Passions: Leisure and Pleasure in Victorian Britain* (London: Harper Perennial, 2007)
Foreman, Amanda, *A World on Fire: An Epic History of Two Nations Divided* (London: Penguin, 2011)
Fredeman, William E., 'The Bibliographical Significance of a Publisher's Archive: The Macmillan Papers', *Studies in Bibliography*, 23 (1970)
Gettmann, Royal A., *A Victorian Publisher: A Study of the Bentley Papers* (Cambridge: Cambridge University Press, 1960)
Glynn, Jenifer, *Prince of Publishers: A Biography of George Smith* (London: Allison & Busby, 1986)
Graves, Charles L., *The Life and Letters of Sir George Grove, C. B.* (London: Macmillan, 1903)
Griest, Guinevere L., *Mudie's Circulating Library and the Victorian Novel* (Bloomington: Indiana University Press, 1970)
Grigson, Geoffrey, ed., *William Allingham's Diary 1847–1889* (London: Centaur Press, 1967)

Gross, John, *The Rise and Fall of the Man of Letters: Aspects of English Literary Life since 1800* (London: Weidenfeld & Nicolson, 1969)

Gower, Sir George Leveson KBE, *Years of Content* (London: John Murray, 1940)

Gurr, A. J., *'Macmillan's Magazine'*, A Review of English Literature, 6 (1965)

Hagen, June Steffensen, *Tennyson and His Publishers* (London: Macmillan, 1979)

Hale, Piers J., 'Monkeys into Men and Men into Monkeys: Chance and Contingency in the Evolution of Man, Mind and Morals in Charles Kingsley's "Water Babies"', *Journal of the History of Biology*, 46:4 (2013)

Hardinge, Sir Arthur, *A Diplomatist in the East* (London: Jonathan Cape, 1928)

Hare, J. C., *Guesses at Truth by Two Brothers* (London: Macmillan, 1867)

Harrison, Anthony H., ed., *The Letters of Christina Rossetti* (Virginia: University Press of Virginia, 1997)

Harrison, J. F. C., *A History of the Working Men's College 1854–1954* (London: Routledge & Kegan Paul, 1954)

Heffer, Simon, *High Minds: The Victorians and the Birth of Modern Britain* (London: Windmill Books, 2014)

—, *Moral Desperado: A Life of Thomas Carlyle* (London: Phoenix, 1996)

Hesketh, I., *Victorian Jesus: J. R. Seeley, Religion, and the Cultural Significance of Anonymity* (Toronto: University of Toronto Press, 2017)

Hort, Arthur F., ed., *The Life and Letters of Fenton J. A. Hort* (London: Macmillan, 1896)

Houghton, Walter E., *The Victorian Frame of Mind, 1830–1870* (New Haven and London: Yale University Press, 1957)

—, 'Victorian Periodical Literature and the Articulate Classes', *Victorian Studies*, 22 (1979)

Hudson, Derek, *Munby: Man of Two Worlds: The Life and Diaries of Arthur J. Munby 1828–1910* (London: John Murray, 1972)

Hutchings, Richard J. and Brian Hutton, ed., *The Farringford Journal of Emily Tennyson* (Isle of Wight: County, 1986)

Huxley, Leonard, *Life and Letters of Thomas Henry Huxley by His Son* (London: Macmillan, 1900)

Irvine, William, *Apes, Angels and Victorians: The Story of Darwin, Huxley, and Evolution* (New York: TIME Reading Program Special Edition, 1963)

Joseph, Marrisa Dominique, 'Literary Businesses: The British Publishing Industry and its Business Practices 1843–1900' (Unpublished doctoral thesis: Queen Mary University of London, 2016)

Kingsley, Charles, *The Gospel of the Pentateuch, A Set of Parish Sermons* (London: Macmillan, 1863)

—, *Alton Locke, Tailor and Poet. An Autobiography* (London, Macmillan, 1876)

Kingsley, F., ed., *Charles Kingsley: His Letters and Memories of His Life* (London: Chapman & Hall, 1852)

Leary, Patrick, *The Punch Brotherhood: Table Talk and Print Culture in Mid-Victorian London* (London: The British Library, 2010)

Lockhart, J. G., *Memoirs of the Life of Sir Walter Scott, Bart* (Edinburgh, Robert Cadell, 1845)

Ludlow, John, *John Ludlow: The Autobiography of a Christian Socialist*, ed. by A. D. Murray (London: Frank Cass, 1981)

Mack, Edward C., and W. H. G. Armytage, *Thomas Hughes: The Life of the Author of Tom Brown's School Days* (London: Ernest Benn, 1952)

McKitterick, David, *A History of Cambridge University Press*, 2 vols (Cambridge: Cambridge University Press, 1998)

MacLeod, Roy M., 'The X-Club: A Social Network of Science in Late-Victorian England', *Notes and Records of the Royal Society of London*, 24:2 (1970)

Marsh, Jan, *Christina Rossetti: A Literary Biography* (London: Jonathan Cape, 1994)

—, *Dante Gabriel Rossetti: Painter and Poet* (London: Weidenfeld & Nicolson, 1999)

Masterman, N. C., *J. M. Ludlow: Builder of Christian Socialism* (Cambridge: Cambridge University Press, 2008)

Maurice, Frederick, ed., *Life of Frederick Denison Maurice: Chiefly Told in His Own Letters*, 2 vols (London: Macmillan, 1884)

Meadows, A. J., *Science and Controversy: A Biography of Sir Norman Lockyer* (Massachusetts: The MIT Press, 1972)

Morley, John, *Critical Miscellanies* (London: Macmillan, 1886)

—, *Recollections* (London: Macmillan, 1917)

Munro, J. J., *Frederick James Furnivall: A Volume of Personal Record* (Oxford: Oxford University Press, 1911)

Murray, Nicholas, *A Life of Matthew Arnold* (London: Hodder & Stoughton, 1996)

Packer, Lona Mosk, ed., *The Rossetti–Macmillan Letters: Some 133 Unpublished Letters Written to Alexander Macmillan, F. S. Ellis, and Others, by Dante Gabriel, Christina, and William Michael Rossetti, 1861–1889* (Cambridge: Cambridge University Press, 1963)

Parry, Ann, 'Theories of Formation: *"Macmillan's Magazine"*: Vol. 1, November 1859 Monthly', *Victorian Periodicals Review*, 26:2 (1993)

Phegley, Jennifer, 'Clearing Away "The Briars and Brambles": The Education and Professionalisation of the Cornhill Magazine's Women Readers 1860–65', *Victorian Periodicals Review*, 33 (2000)

Phillips, Melanie, *The Ascent of Woman: A History of the Suffragette Movement and the Ideas Behind It* (London: Abacus, 2004)

Reader, W. J., *The Rise of the Professional Classes in Nineteenth-Century England* (London: Weidenfeld & Nicolson, 1966)

Sanders, Valerie, *The Tragi-Comedy of Victorian Fatherhood* (Cambridge: Cambridge University Press, 2009)

Schmidt, Barbara Quinn, 'Novelists, Publishers, and Fiction in Middle-Class Magazines: 1860–1880', *Victorian Periodicals Review*, 17:4 (1984)

Secord, James A., 'How Scientific Conversation Became Shop Talk', *Transactions of the Royal Historical Society*, 17 (2007)

Shaen, Margaret Josephine, *Memorials of Two Sisters, Susanna and Catherine Winkworth* (London: Longmans, 1908)

Shattock, Joanne, 'Professional Networking, Masculine and Feminine', *Victorian Periodicals Review*, 44:2 (2011)

Sichel, Edith, *The Life and Letters of Alfred Ainger* (London, Constable, 1906)

Smiles, Samuel, *A Publisher and His Friends: Memoir and Correspondence of the Late John Murray* (London: John Murray, 1891)

Spencer, Herbert, 'The Morals of Trade', *The Westminster Review*, 71 (Jan to Apr 1859)

Stephen, Leslie, *Life of Henry Fawcett* (London: Smith, Elder, 1885)

—, *Letters of John Richard Green* (London: Macmillan, 1901)

Stowe, Harriet Beecher, *Uncle Tom's Cabin; or, Life among the Lowly* (Boston, MA: John P. Jewett, 1852)

Sutcliffe, Peter H., *The Oxford University Press: An Informal History* (Oxford: Clarendon, 1978)

Sutherland, John, *Mrs Humphry Ward: Eminent Victorian, Pre-eminent Edwardian* (Oxford: Clarendon Press, 1990)

—, *The Stanford Companion to Victorian Fiction* (Stanford: Stanford University Press, 1989)

—, *Victorian Fiction: Writers, Publishers, Readers* (New York: St Martin's Press, 1995)

—, *Victorian Novelists and Publishers* (Chicago: University of Chicago Press, 1976)

Tennyson, Hallam, *Alfred Lord Tennyson: A Memoir* (London: Macmillan, 1897)

Thirlwell, Angela, *William and Lucy: The Other Rossettis* (New Haven and London: Yale University Press, 2003)

Thwaite, Ann, *Emily Tennyson: The Poet's Wife* (London: Faber & Faber, 1996)

Tosh, John, 'Gentlemanly Politeness and Manly Simplicity in Victorian England', *Transactions of the Royal Historical Society*, 12 (2002)

Trevelyan, Laura, *A Very British Family: The Trevelyans and Their World* (London: I. B. Tauris, 2006)

Tucker, Herbert F., ed., *A Companion to Victorian Literature and Culture* (Oxford: Blackwell, 1999)

Uffelman, Larry, and Patrick Scott, 'Kingsley's Serial Novels, II: "The Water-Babies"', *Victorian Periodicals Review*, 19:4 (1986)

VanArsdel, Rosemary T. '"Macmillan's Magazine" and the Fair Sex: 1859–1874 (Part One)', *Victorian Periodicals Review*, 33:4 (2000)

—, '"Macmillan's Magazine" and the Fair Sex: 1859–1874 (Part Two)', *Victorian Periodicals Review*, 34:1 (2001)

Vance, Norman, *The Sinews of the Spirit: The Ideal of Christian Manliness in Victorian Literature and Religious Thought* (Cambridge: Cambridge University Press, 1985)

Van Remoortel, Marianne, 'Christina Rossetti and the Economics of Publication: "Macmillan's Magazine", "A Birthday," and Beyond', *Victorian Literature and Culture*, 41:4 (2013)

Vidler, Alec R., *F. D. Maurice and Company* (London: SCM Press, 1966)

Waller, John O., 'Charles Kingsley and the American Civil War', *Studies in Philology*, 60 (1963)

Webb, Beatrice, *My Apprenticeship* (London, Longmans, 1926)

Wharton, Philip and Grace, *The Wits and Beaux of Society*, 2nd Edition (London, James Hogg, 1861)

White, Jerry, *London in the Nineteenth Century* (London: Jonathan Cape, 2007)

Wilson, A. N., *The Victorians* (London: Arrow Books, 2003)

Wilson, Charles, *First with the News: The History of WH Smith 1792–1972* (London: Jonathan Cape, 1985)

Woolner, Amy, *Thomas Woolner, RA, Sculptor and Poet: His Life in Letters* (London: Chapman & Hall, 1917)

Worth, George J., *Macmillan's Magazine, 1859–1907: 'No Flippancy or Abuse Allowed'* (Aldershot: Ashgate Publishing, 2003)

—, 'Alexander Macmillan and his Magazine I', *Victorian Periodicals Review*, 26:2 2 (1993)

—, 'Alexander Macmillan and his Magazine II', *Victorian Periodicals Review*, 26:3 (1993)

—, 'Macmillan's Magazine and The American Civil War: A Reconsideration', *Victorian Periodicals Review*, 26 (1993)

Yeo, Richard, 'Science and Intellectual Authority in Mid-Nineteenth Century Britain: Robert Chambers and *"Vestiges of the Natural History of Creation"'*, *Victorian Studies*, 28 (1984)

Young, Percy M., *George Grove: A Biography* (London: Macmillan, 1980)

Zacharias, Greg W. et al., ed., *The Complete Letters of Henry James 1884–1886 Volume 2* (Lincoln, NE: University of Nebraska Press, 2021)

Online Resources

British History Online, https://www.british-history.ac.uk

British Newspaper Archive, https://www.britishnewspaperarchive.co.uk

Carlyle, Thomas and Jane Welsh Carlyle, The Carlyle Letters Online, ed. Brent E. Kinser, XII (Duke University Press 2007–2016), https://carlyleletters.dukeupress.edu/home

Darwin Correspondence Project, https://www.darwinproject.ac.uk/letter/DCP-LETT-3206.xml

Digital Dinah Craik Project, http://www.tapasproject.org/node/443

Education in England: The History of our Schools, http://www.educationengland.org.uk/index.html

Oxford Dictionary of National Biography, https://www.oxforddnb.com

University of Michigan Health, https://www.uofmhealth.org/health-library/d03960a1

A Series of Series: Twentieth Century Publishers, https://sites.owu.edu/seriesofseries/globe-edition

The Wellesley Index to Victorian Periodicals 1824–1900, http://wellesley.chadwyck.co.uk/marketing/index.jsp

Letters of Charlotte Mary Yonge, https://c21ch.newcastle.edu.au/yonge

Notes

BL: British Library
UCL: Senate House Library Archives, University of London
NLS: National Library of Scotland
Reading: University of Reading, Special Collections
All calculations of monetary items into today's value are taken from the Bank of England's Inflation Calculator https://www.bankofengland.co.uk/monetary-policy/inflation/inflation-calculator

INTRODUCTION

1. Charles L. Graves, *Life and Letters of Alexander Macmillan*, p. 235.
2. Charles Morgan, *The House of Macmillan (1843–1943)*, p. viii.

1: THE BROTHERS (1813–33)

1. Charles L. Graves, *Life and Letters of Alexander Macmillan*, p. 3.
2. Thomas Hughes, *Memoir of Daniel Macmillan*, p. 2.
3. Ibid., p. 182.
4. Ibid., p. 183.
5. Graves, *Life and Letters of Alexander Macmillan*, p. 6.
6. Emma Pignatel Macmillan's Recollections, MacLehose Family Papers.
7. Hughes, *Memoir of Daniel Macmillan*, p. 183.
8. Ibid., p. 5.
9. Ibid., p. 7.
10. Ibid., p. 11.
11. Ibid., p. 11.
12. Ibid., p. 15.
13. Ibid., pp. 16–17.
14. Ibid., p. 49.
15. Quoted in Simon Heffer, *Moral Desperado: A Life of Thomas Carlyle*, p. 75.

16. Hughes, *Memoir of Daniel Macmillan*, p. 39.
17. Ibid., p. 44.
18. Graves, *Life and Letters of Alexander Macmillan*, p. 8.
19. Ibid., p. 255.
20. George A. Macmillan, *Letters of Alexander Macmillan*, p. xvii.
21. Ibid., p. x.
22. Hughes, *Memoir of Daniel Macmillan*, p. 185.
23. Graves, *Life and Letters of Alexander Macmillan*, p. 20.

2: The Publishing Industry

1. John Feather, *A History of British Publishing*, p. 61.

3: The Founding of the Partnership (1833–43)

1. Thomas Hughes, *Memoir of Daniel Macmillan*, p. 47.
2. Ibid., p. 47.
3. Ibid., p. 50.
4. Ibid., p. 51.
5. Ibid., p. 55.
6. Ibid., p. 59.
7. Charles L. Graves, *Life and Letters of Alexander Macmillan*, p. 19.
8. George A. Macmillan, *Letters of Alexander Macmillan*, p. xv.
9. Hughes, *Memoir of Daniel Macmillan*, p. 65.
10. Ibid., p. 70.
11. https://carlyleletters.dukeupress.edu/volume/12/lt-18400117-TC-RWE-01.
12. Hughes, *Memoir of Daniel Macmillan*, p. 71.
13. Ibid., p. 79.
14. Ibid., p. 116.
15. J. C. Hare, *Guesses at Truth*, p.xiii.
16. Hughes, *Memoir of Daniel Macmillan*, p. 118.
17. Ibid., p. 120.
18. Ibid., p. 122.
19. BL, Macmillan, Add MS 55109, DM to J. C. Hare, 25 July 1842.
20. Hughes, *Memoir of Daniel Macmillan*, p. 143.
21. BL, Macmillan, Add MS 55108.
22. Hughes, *Memoir of Daniel Macmillan*, p. 103.
23. Ibid., p. 145.
24. Ibid., p. 146.

4: 'This small seed' (1843–45)

1. BL, Macmillan, Add MS 55108, DM to D Watt, 31 August 1842.
2. Ibid., 29 April 1843.
3. Thomas Hughes, *Memoir of Daniel Macmillan*, p. 78.
4. BL, Macmillan, Add MS 55109, J. C. Hare to DM, 22 August 1843.
5. Ibid., DM to Hare, 24 August 1843.
6. Ibid., Hare to DM, 28 August 1843.
7. Ibid., DM to Hare, 6 October 1843.
8. Ibid., AM to Hare, 21 February 1844.
9. Ibid., Hare to DM, 23 February 1844.
10. Ibid., DM to Hare, 27 February 1844.
11. BL, Macmillan, Add MS 55089, DM to George Wilson, 29 May 1843.
12. Ibid., DM to GW, 10 April 1844.
13. BL, Macmillan, Add MS 55109, DM to Hare, 21 June 1844.
14. Hughes, *Memoir of Daniel Macmillan*, p. 108.
15. BL, Add MS 55108, DM to D. Watt, 15 November 1844.
16. Hughes, *Memoir of Daniel Macmillan*, p. 208.
17. Reading, Bowes and Bowes (Cambridge), BAB 17, Trinity Street lease.

5: Building a Network(1845–53)

1. C. Morgan, *The House of Macmillan (1843–1943)*, p. 30.
2. Thomas Hughes, *Memoir of Daniel Macmillan*, p. 211.
3. Charles L. Graves, *Life and Letters of Alexander Macmillan*, p. 114.
4. Hughes, *Memoir of Daniel Macmillan*, pp. 234–5.
5. Morgan, *The House of Macmillan*, pp. 33–4.
6. Hughes, *Memoir of Daniel Macmillan*, p. 229.
7. Graves, *Life and Letters of Alexander Macmillan*, p. 44.
8. Ibid., pp. 48–9.
9. *The Christian Socialist*, Volume II, pp. 79–80.
10. BL, Add MS 55108, DM to D. Watt, 21 December 1848.
11. Hughes, *Memoir of Daniel Macmillan*, p. 236.
12. Arthur F. Hort, *The Life and Letters of Fenton J. A. Hort*, vol. I, pp. 154–6.
13. *The Cambridge Chronicle*, 1 November 1851.
14. Graves, *Life and Letters of Alexander Macmillan*, p. 42.
15. Graves, *Life and Letters of Alexander Macmillan*, p. 42.
16. Hughes, *Memoir of Daniel Macmillan*, pp. 188–9.
17. Graves, *Life and Letters of Alexander Macmillan*, p. 34.
18. George A. Macmillan, *Brief Memoir of Alexander Macmillan* (printed privately, 1908), p. xxix.
19. Stevens Family Papers.

20. Ibid.
21. BL, Add MS 55109, DM to JCH, 4 April 1851.
22. BL, Add MS 55108, DM to Llewellyn Davies, 25 May 1852.
23. Ibid.
24. Morgan, p. 40.
25. BL, Macmillan, Add MS 55109, DM to JCH, 25 June 1853.
26. Hughes, *Memoir of Daniel Macmillan*, p. 251.
27. Graves, *Life and Letters of Alexander Macmillan*, p. 55.
28. BL, Add MS 55108, DM to D. Watt, 2 October 1855.
29. Graves, *Life and Letters of Alexander Macmillan*, p. 316.

6: WESTWARD HO! AND TOM BROWN'S
SCHOOL DAYS (1854–57)

1. Simon Heffer, *High Minds*, p. 6.
2. F. Kingsley, ed., *Charles Kingsley: His Letters and Memories of His Life*, pp. 123–5.
3. Charles Kingsley, *Alton Locke*, p. 30.
4. Charles L. Graves, *Life and Letters of Alexander Macmillan*, p. 43.
5. BL, Macmillan, Add MS 54911, CK to AM, 26 July 1851.
6. Simon Nowell-Smith, ed., *Letters to Macmillan*, p. 37.
7. Thomas Hughes, *Memoir of Daniel Macmillan*, p. 252.
8. Graves, *Life and Letters of Alexander Macmillan*, p. 58.
9. BL, Macmillan, Add MS 54911, Charles Kingsley to AM, 22 July 1854; 12 August 1854.
10. Ibid., 17 April 1855.
11. Ibid., 26 May 1855.
12. Graves, *Life and Letters of Alexander Macmillan*, p. 68.
13. BL, Macmillan, Add MS 55108, DM to D. Watt, 2 October 1855.
14. C. Morgan, *The House of Macmillan (1843–1943)*, quoted in the dedication.
15. Quoted in J. F. C. Harrison, *A History of the Working Men's College, 1854–1954*, p. 25.
16. Graves, *Life and Letters of Alexander Macmillan*, p. 90.
17. Joseph Bickersteth Mayor (1828–1916), Professor of English and classical scholar, father of Flora Macdonald Mayor, who wrote *The Rector's Daughter*.
18. BL, Macmillan, Add MS 54917, DM to Hughes, 16 October 1856.
19. Ibid., DM to TH, 5 November 1856.
20. BL, Macmillan, Add MS 54918, TH to DM, 11 October 1856.
21. Ibid., TH to DM, 15 December 1856.
22. Nowell-Smith, p. 31.
23. Asa Briggs, *Victorian People*, p. 162.
24. BL, Macmillan, Add MS 54918, TH to AM, 6 August 1857.

25. Edward C. Mack and W. H. G. Armytage, *Thomas Hughes: The Life of the Author of Tom Brown's Schooldays*, p. 89.
26. BL, Macmillan, Add MS 55089, DM to George Wilson, 17 May 1854.
27. BL, Macmillan, Add MS 54918, TH to DM 7 June 1857.
28. Hughes, *Memoir of Daniel Macmillan*, p. 302.
29. Ibid., pp. viii–ix.
30. Ibid., pp. 262–3.

7: ALEXANDER ALONE: (1858–59)

1. George A. Macmillan, *Letters of Alexander Macmillan*, p. xxviii.
2. Charles L. Graves, *Life and Letters of Alexander Macmillan*, p. 70.
3. Herbert Spencer, 'The Morals of Trade', *The Westminster Review*, 71, p. 385.
4. Photograph taken by O. G. Rejlander between 1860 and 1870, in Graves, *Life and Letters of Alexander Macmillan*, frontispiece.
5. Ibid., p. 186.
6. Thomas Hughes, *Memoir of Daniel Macmillan*, p. 247.
7. Graves, *Life and Letters of Alexander Macmillan*, p. 91.
8. Ibid., p. 113.
9. Ibid., p. 91.
10. BL, Layard, Add MS 38986, TH to Layard, 7 May 1858.
11. Mack and Armytage, *Thomas Hughes* p. 107.
12. BL, Macmillan, Add 54792, D Masson to AM, 1 July 1857.
13. Macmillan, *Letters*, p. 38.

8: MACMILLAN'S MAGAZINE AND THE WATER BABIES: (1860–63)

1. Charles L. Graves, *Life and Letters of Alexander Macmillan*, p. 135.
2. Ibid., p. 136.
3. Macmillan by now felt sufficiently confident of his relationship with Tennyson to write a letter of introduction for his friend Alexander Campbell Fraser who was visiting the Isle of Wight. He advised Fraser to call before lunch, which was at 1 p.m., to join the poet for 'a glass of ale and a bit of bread and cheese'. NLS, Fraser, Dep 208, Box 16: AM to Alexander Campbell Fraser, 27 June 1860.
4. Leonard Huxley, *Life and Letters of Thomas Henry Huxley by His Son*, I, 199.
5. T. H. Huxley, 'Time and Life: Mr Darwin's "Origin of Species"', *Macmillan's Magazine*, I, p. 146.
6. Graves, *Life and Letters of Alexander Macmillan*, p. 140.
7. Ibid., p. 147.
8. NLS, Fraser, Dep 208, Box 16: AM to Alexander Campbell Fraser, 1 December 1859.

9. BL, Macmillan, Add MS 55837, AM to Sebastian Evans, 16 November 1859.

10. BL, Macmillan, Add MS 55837, AM to Fenton Hort, 20 March 1860.

11. Ibid., AM to Vansittart, 14 April 1860.

12. BL, Add MS 55838, AM to Huxley, 30 April 1860, 12 June 1860.

13. Leslie Stephen, *Life of Henry Fawcett*, p. 116.

14. Ibid., p. 204.

15. Charles Kingsley to Charles Darwin, 18 November 1859, Darwin Correspondence Project, https://www.darwinproject.ac.uk/letter/DCP-LETT-2534.xml.

16. Adrian Desmond, *Huxley: From Devil's Disciple to Evolution's High Priest*, p. 263.

17. Ibid., pp. 288–9.

18. Graves, *Life and Letters of Alexander Macmillan*, p. 189.

19. Margaret Dyer, *Reminiscences of Alexander Macmillan* – unpublished document. Stevens Family Papers.

20. Humphrey Carpenter, *Secret Gardens: A Study of the Golden Age of Children's Literature* (London: Faber and Faber, 2012), p. 30.

21. F. Kingsley, ed., *Charles Kingsley: His Letters and Memories of His Life*, II, p. 127.

22. BL, Macmillan, Add MS 55841, AM to Elizabeth Gaskell, 18 January 1862.

23. BL, Macmillan, Add MS 55839, AM to Dr George Kingsley, 4 December 1860.

24. George A. Macmillan, *Letters*, p. 87.

25. Ibid., p. 89.

26. Ibid., p. 100.

27. Thomas Hughes, 'Opinion on American Affairs', *Macmillan's Magazine*, IV (1861), pp. 414–16.

28. BL, Macmillan, Add MS 55841, AM to Elizabeth Gaskell, 18 January 1862.

29. Ibid., AM to Edward Dicey, 11 December 1861.

30. Alan L. Hertz, 'Macmillan's Magazine under David Masson: 1859–1867' (unpublished doctoral thesis, University of Cambridge, 1982), p. 101.

31. E. Dicey, 'The New England States', *Macmillan's Magazine* (August 1862), VI (1862), p. 297.

32. W. M. Rossetti, 'English Opinion on the American War', *Atlantic Monthly*, 17 (1866), p. 141.

33. To be translated as 'The American Iliad in a Nutshell'.

34. Thomas Carlyle, 'Ilias (Americana) in Nuce', *Macmillan's Magazine*, VIII (1863), 301.

35. BL, Macmillan, Add MS 55253, John Ludlow to AM, 29 July 1863.

36. BL, Macmillan, Add MS 55381, AM to Ludlow, 29 July 1863.

37. BL, Macmillan, Add MS 55253, Ludlow to AM, 1 August 1863.

38. Graves, *Life and Letters of Alexander Macmillan*, p. 213.

39. Charles Kingsley, *The Gospel of the Pentateuch, A Set of Parish Sermons*, p. 90.

40. Henry Kingsley, 'Eyre, The South-Australian Explorer', *Macmillan's Magazine*, XII (1867), pp. 499–510.

41. Dyer, *Reminiscences of Alexander Macmillan*, p. 4.

9: Building the Brand (1860–63)

1. BL, Macmillan, Add MS 55839, AM to Daniel Wilson, 22 January 1861.
2. Ibid., AM to Daniel Wilson, 22 January 1861.
3. Jan Marsh, *Christina Rossetti: A Literary Biography* (London: Jonathan Cape, 1994), pp. 267–8.
4. Lona Mosk Packer, ed., *The Rossetti–Macmillan Letters*, p. 5.
5. *Cambridge Independent Press*, 6 October 1855.
6. Charles L. Graves, *Life and Letters of Alexander Macmillan*, p. 181.
7. Macmillan Editions Book, f. 218. The figures are confirmed in a letter of 19 November 1861 to Palgrave from Macmillan (BL, Macmillan, Add MS 55841).
8. BL, Macmillan, Add MS 55840, AM to James Burn, 18 June 1861.
9. https://sites.owu.edu/seriesofseries/globe-edition/
10. Karen Bourrier, *Victorian Bestseller: The Life of Dinah Craik*, p. 111.
11. Graves, *Life and Letters of Alexander Macmillan*, p. 122.
12. George A. Macmillan, *Letters*, p. 164.
13. Ibid., p. xxxi.
14. MacLehose Family Papers.
15. Dyer, *Reminiscences*.
16. Ibid.
17. BL, Macmillan, Add MS 55382, AM to Tom Taylor, 8 January 1864.
18. Christopher Stray, 'Educational Publishing', in *The History of Oxford University Press*, pp. 473–510 (p. 477).
19. BL, Macmillan, Add MS 54917, Bond dated 20 June 1864.
20. BL, Macmillan, Add MS 55326, AM to Professor Price, 18 November 1865.

10: Controversies and Partnerships (1862–67)

1. BL, Macmillan, Add MS 55836, AM to Charles Kingsley, 7 December 1858.
2. Ibid., AM to Jebb, 19 March 1859.
3. Ibid., AM to Clay, 4 June 1859.
4. Ibid., AM to Charles Kingsley, 5 July 1859.
5. BL, Macmillan, Add MS 55841, AM to Colenso, 4 March 1862.
6. BL, Macmillan, Add MS 55380 2, AM to Vaughan, 1 December 1862.
7. Ibid., AM to Colenso, 20 December 1862.
8. Ibid., AM to M Arnold, 27 December 1862.
9. Ibid., AM to Colenso, 1 January 1863.
10. Susan Chitty, *The Beast and the Monk: A Life of Charles Kingsley*, p. 229.
11. BL, Macmillan, Add MS 55382, AM to FD Maurice, 5 January 1864 (wrongly dated).
12. Graves, *Life and Letters of Alexander Macmillan*, pp. 162–3.
13. Ibid., pp. 235–7.

14. https://tapasproject.org/digitaldinahcraik/files/letter-dinah-mulock-craik-ben-mulock-14%E2%80%9323-october-1860 and https://tapasproject.org/digitaldinahcraik/files/letter-dinah-mulock-craik-benjamin-mulock-2-5-july-1861

15. The Carlyle Letters Online, Jane Carlyle to Thomas Carlyle, 30 July 1865.

16. C. Morgan, *The House of Macmillan (1843–1943)*, p. 69.

17. BL, Macmillan, Add MS 55042, FM to AM, 27 February 1864.

18. Ibid., FM to AM, 25 February 1865.

19. Ibid., 15 April 1869.

20. Ibid., 20 April 1870.

21. Ibid., 26 and 27 November 1870.

22. Ibid., 7 September 1875.

23. UCL, Sir John Robert Seeley, GB 96 MS 903, JRS to Ann Seeley, 25 November 1865 (or 1866).

24. Ibid., WE Gladstone to AM, 25 December 1865.

25. BL, Gladstone Papers, Add MS 44246, AM to WEG, 29 December 1865.

26. Ibid., AM to WEG, 3 March 1866.

27. UCL, Seeley, JRS to JB Mayor, 26 November 1866.

28. Graves, *Life and Letters of Alexander Macmillan*, p. 253.

29. BL, Macmillan, Add MS 55841, AM to Arnold, 21 January 1862.

30. John Sutherland, *The Stanford Companion to Victorian Fiction*, p. 596.

31. BL, Macmillan, Add MS 55384, AM to Mrs Oliphant, 12 April 1865.

32. BL, Macmillan, Add MS 54964, AM to Caroline Norton, 24 April 1866.

33. Ibid., Norton to AM, 24 April 1866.

34. BL, Macmillan, Add MS 55842, AM to Caroline Norton, 12 June 1866.

35. George A. Macmillan, *Letters*, p. 191.

11: Alice in Wonderland and Other Surprising Adventures

1. BL, Macmillan, Add MS 55383 2, AM to Charles Dodgson, 19 October 1864.

2. BL, Macmillan, Add MS 55384 1, AM to CD, 10 February 1865.

3. Ibid., AM to CD, 9 May 1865.

4. BL, Macmillan, Add MS 55386 1, AM to CD, 30 April 1866.

5. BL, Macmillan, Add MS 55390 2, AM to CD, 2 February 1870.

6. BL, Macmillan, Add MS 55391 1, AM to CD, 6 November 1871.

7. Unpublished pamphlet by C. L. Dodgson, 'The Profits of Authorship'.

8. Samuel White Baker, *Great Basin of the Nile and Explorations of the Nile Sources*, pp. vii–viii.

9. BL, Macmillan, Add MS 55386 1, AM to Baker, 4 May 1866.

10. Samuel Baker, *The Albert N'Yanza*, II, pp. 357–8.

11. BL, Macmillan, Add MS 55842, AM to Baker, 11 March 1867.

12: DEATH COMES TO THE ELMS

1. BL, Macmillan, Add MS 55381 2, AM to Roland Hamilton, 17 August 1863.
2. BL, Macmillan, Add MS 55840, AM to Dinah Mulock, 2 August 1861.
3. Ibid., AM to Henry Kingsley, 8 October 1863.
4. W. J. Reader, *The Rise of the Professional Classes in Nineteenth-Century England*, p. 105.
5. Uppingham School Archives, AM to Edward Thring, 25 February 1861.
6. BL, Macmillan, Add MS 55380 1, AM to ET, 25 June 1862.
7. Karen Bourrier, *Victorian Bestseller*, p. 116.
8. BL, Macmillan, Add MS 55382, AM to Bradley, 18 February 1864.
9. Anon., *Selected Letters of Malcolm Kingsley Macmillan*, pp. 1–3.
10. Uppingham School Archives, AM to Edward Thring, 3 April 1867.
11. Archibald Maclaren, 'Girls' Schools', *Macmillan's Magazine*, 10 (1864), pp. 409–16.
12. Charles L. Graves, *Life and Letters of Alexander Macmillan*, p. 297.
13. Ibid., pp. 254–5.
14. Ibid., p 254.
15. BL, Macmillan, Add MS 55386 1, AM to Samuel Baker, 26 June 1866.
16. George A. Macmillan, *Letters*, pp. 337–41.
17. Graves, *Life and Letters of Alexander Macmillan*, p. 262.
18. *York Herald*, 26 January 1867, p. 10; *Yorkshire Gazette*, 26 January 1867, p. 4.
19. Borthwick Institute for Archives, University of York, The Retreat Archive, RET/1/5/1/69, ff. 776–7.
20. *Morning Post*, 24 January 1867, p. 2.
21. Uppingham School Archives, AM to Edward Thring, 3 April 1867.
22. BL, Macmillan, Add MS 55839, AM to Mulock, 5 December 1860.
23. BL, Macmillan, Add MSS 55386, AM to CM Yonge, 18 February 1867.

13: MACMILLAN CROSSES THE ATLANTIC (1876)

1. *The Tennessean* (Nashville, Tennessee), 30 May 1867.
2. BL, Macmillan, Add MS 54891, Fields to AM, 7 May 1862.
3. George A. Macmillan, *Letters*, p. 230.
4. BL, Macmillan, Add MS 55842, AM to Kitchin, 25 June 1867.
5. Macmillan, *Letters*, p. 201.
6. 'A Night with the Yankees', ibid., pp 342–72.
7. Tennyson's definition of an aristocrat, in his poem *Lady Clara Vere de Vere*, 1842.
8. Macmillan, *Letters*, p. 351.
9. Ibid., p. 360.
10. Charles L. Graves, *Life and Letters of Alexander Macmillan*, p. 275.
11. Ibid., p. 273.

12. Father of Stanford White the architect, famously murdered in 1906 at the Madison Square Theatre by a jealous husband.
13. Macmillan, *Letters*, p. 353.
14. Ibid., p. 355.
15. Ibid., p. 357.
16. Ibid., p. 355.
17. Ibid., p. 364.
18. Ibid., p. 366.
19. Graves, *Life and Letters of Alexander Macmillan*, p. 275.
20. https://www.jstor.org/stable/24303059.
21. BL, Macmillan, Add MS 55842, AM to William Amery, 9 June 1869, quoted in Elizabeth DeBlock, *Macmillan & Co in New York*.
22. *American Literary Gazette and Publishers' Circular*, 16 August 1869, 238.
23. BL, Macmillan, Add MS 54797, George Brett to George Lillie Craik, 22 March 1870, quoted in DeBlock.
24. Ibid., GE Brett to AM, 20 August 1870.
25. Ibid., GE Brett to AM, 26 May 1871.

14: TAKING STOCK (1867–69)

1. Charles L. Graves, *Life and Letters of Alexander Macmillan*, p. 276.
2. Dyer, *Reminiscences*.
3. J. S. Bain, *A Bookseller Looks Back*, p. 61.
4. Stevens Family Papers.
5. *A Bibliographical Catalogue of Macmillan and Co.'s Publications from 1843 to 1889* (London: Macmillan, 1891), pp. 43–8 and 154–66.
6. Simon Heffer, *Moral Desperado: A Life of Thomas Carlyle*, p. 358.
7. BL, Macmillan, Add MS 55386 AM to David Masson, 21 August 1866.
8. BL, Macmillan, Add MS 55842, AM to David Masson, 20 December 1867.
9. BL, Macmillan, Add MS 54793, Grove to AM, undated 1868.
10. BL, Macmillan, Add MS 55384 2, AM to George Trevelyan, [11] July 1865.
11. BL, Macmillan, Add MS 55386 2, AM to F. D. Maurice, 26 October 1866.
12. BL, Macmillan, Add MS 55326, AM to Kitchin, 7 February 1867.
13. BL, Macmillan, Add MS 55388, AM to Price, 8 May 1868.
14. Ibid., 26 June 1868.
15. BL, Macmillan, Add MS 55842, AM to Guizot, undated 1867.
16. Ibid., AM to Tennyson, 27 February 1868.
17. NLS, Fraser, Dep 208, Box 16: AM to Alexander Campbell Fraser, 2 September 1865.
18. BL, Macmillan, Add MS 55388 AM to Hardy, 10 August 1868.
19. Stevens Family Papers.
20. Graves, *Life and Letters of Alexander Macmillan*, p. 299.

21. Ibid., p. 300.
22. Ibid., p. 301.
23. Millicent Garrett Fawcett, *What I Remember*, p. 86.
24. George A. Macmillan, *Letters*, pp. 136–8.

15: THE BIRTH OF NATURE (1869)

1. George A. Macmillan, *Letters*, pp. 43–4.
2. Charles L. Graves, *Life and Letters of Alexander Macmillan*, p. 262.
3. BL, Macmillan, Add MS 55388, AM to Thomas Huxley, 3 March 1868.
4. A. J. Meadows, *Science and Controversy: A Biography of Sir Norman Lockyer*, p. 28.
5. Ibid., p. 25.
6. Ibid., p. 26.
7. Ibid., p. 28.
8. Quoted in 'Securing the Foundations', *Nature*, 224, 1 November 1969.
9. John Maddox and Harold Macmillan, 'The *Nature* Centenary Dinner', *Notes and Records of the Royal Society of London*, 25, 1 (June 1970), pp. 9–15.

16: TEAMWORK (1870)

1. Quoted in Simon Heffer, *High Minds: The Victorians and the Birth of Modern Britain*, p. 439.
2. Charles L. Graves, *Life and Letters of Alexander Macmillan*, p. 306.
3. *The Ardrossan and Saltcoats Herald*, 10 September 1870.
4. Father of Sir Arthur Evans, archaeologist of Knossos, and brother of Sebastian Evans, Alexander's great friend.
5. Graves, *Life and Letters of Alexander Macmillan*, pp. 306–9.
6. Stevens Family Papers.
7. John Morley, *Recollections*, I, pp. 34–5.
8. Morley apparently told Mrs Asquith that he did not know who the father was. The *Spectator* in 1952 claimed that she had fled from an abusive husband and they could not marry until the husband died.
9. Charles L. Graves, *The Life and Letters of Sir George Grove*, p. 52.

17: CAROLINE AND EMMA

1. Charles L. Graves, *The Life and Letters of Sir George Grove*, p. 310.
2. Ibid., p. 258.
3. George A. Macmillan, *Letters*, p. xiii.
4. NLS, Fraser, Dep 208, Box 16: AM to AC Fraser, 19 October 1871 and 3 January 1872.
5. Emma Pignatel Macmillan's Recollections, MacLehose Family Papers.

6. Van Akin Burd, ed., *The Winnington Letters*, p. 32.
7. E. P. Macmillan.
8. Burd, *The Winnington Letters*, p. 130.
9. Ibid., p. 589.
10. Ibid., p. 675.
11. E. P. Macmillan.
12. NLS, Fraser, Dep 208, Box 16: AM to AC Fraser, 19 February 1873.
13. E. P. Macmillan.
14. Macmillan, *Letters*, p. 301.

18: New Horizons

1. E. P. Macmillan.
2. E. P. Macmillan.
3. Charles L. Graves, *Life and Letters of Alexander Macmillan*, pp. 368–70.
4. Edith Sichel, *The Life and Letters of Alfred Ainger*, p. 87.
5. J. R. Green Archives, Jesus College, Oxford, PP. Green/6, JRG to EAF, 18 January 1873.
6. Margaret Dyer, *Reminiscences of Alexander Macmillan*.
7. BL, Macmillan, Add MS 55393 2, AM to CD, 13 March 1873.
8. BL, Supplementary Macmillan Papers, Add MS 61896, AM to GLC, 18 March 1873.
9. Ibid., AM to GLC, 24 March 1873.
10. Ibid., AM to GLC, 19 April 1873.
11. BL, Macmillan, Add MS 55394. AM to Charles Kingsley, 15 August 1873.
12. BL, Macmillan, Add MS 55842, AM to FM, 14 December 1871.
13. Ibid., AM to GB, 17 February 1872.
14. BL, Macmillan, Add MS 55842, AM to GB, 17 February 1874.
15. Ibid., AM to FM, 26 February 1874.
16. Graves, *Life and Letters of Alexander Macmillan*, p. 327.
17. Dyer, *Reminiscences*.
18. E. P. Macmillan.
19. Quoted in *The Globe*, 1 February 1896.

19: Making History

1. Charles L. Graves, *The Life and Letters of Sir George Grove*, p. 229.
2. *Blackwood's Magazine*, November 1873.
3. Leslie Stephen, ed., *Letters of John Richard Green*, p. 211.
4. Charles L. Graves, *Life and Letters of Alexander Macmillan*, p. 184.
5. BL, Macmillan, Add MS 55058, JRG to AM, December 1869.

6. BL, Macmillan, Add MS 55058 contains an agreement dated 14 July 1875: £300 for copyright, and 18d per copy royalty beyond 8,000 copies, and half as much for copies sold in the US.
7. *Macmillan's Magazine*, May 1883, 48, p. 62.
8. C. Morgan, *The House of Macmillan*, p. 107.
9. Stephen, *Letters of John Richard Green*, p. 358.
10. J. R. Green, *A Short History of the English People*, p. v.
11. BL, Gladstone, Add MS 44246, AM to WE Gladstone, September 1877.

20: FAMILY PRESSURES, FAMILY SADNESSES (1874–78)

1. Peter H. Sutcliffe, *The Oxford University Press: An Informal History*, p. 54.
2. J. J. Munro, *Frederick James Furnivall: A Volume of Personal Record*, p. 105.
3. Ibid., p. 105.
4. BL, Macmillan, Add MS 55842, GLC to FM, 30 March 1875.
5. Ibid., 13 September 1875.
6. E. P. Macmillan.
7. Charles L. Graves, *Life and Letters of Alexander Macmillan*, p. 314.
8. Ibid., p. 314.
9. Sir George Leveson Gower KBE, *Years of Content 1858–86*, pp. 101–2.
10. Stevens Family Papers.
11. Graves, *Life and Letters of Alexander Macmillan*, pp. 334–5.
12. BL, Macmillan, Box L135.
13. E. P. Macmillan.
14. Anon., *Selected Letters of Malcolm Kingsley Macmillan*, pp. 12–13.
15. Greg W. Zacharias, Katie Sommer, Michael Anesko, eds, *The Complete Letters of Henry James, 1884–1886*, 2, p. 135.
16. Taken from the website of The Hellenic Society.
17. Richard Ellman, *Oscar Wilde*, p. 304.
18. Stevens Family Papers.
19. BL, Macmillan, Add MS 54788, AM to FM, 14 August 1877.
20. BL, Macmillan, Add MS 54789, AM to GAM, 2 August 1877.
21. Dyer, *Reminiscences*.
22. J. R. Green Archives, Jesus College Oxford, PP. Green/6, JRG to EA Freeman, 22 January 1878.
23. BL, Macmillan, Add MS 55838, AM to Jessie Wilson, 4 June 1860.

21: OF MUSIC AND MEN OF LETTERS

1. Sir Wemyss Reid, quoted in Graves, *Life of Sir George Grove*, p. 159.
2. Ibid., p. 203.
3. Ibid., p. 205.

4. Ibid., p. 229.
5. Percy M. Young, *George Grove: A Biography*, p. 141.
6. Ibid., pp. 141–2.
7. BL, Macmillan, Add MS 54793, Note from Grove, 31 July 1877.
8. Ibid., GG to GLC, 16 May 1879.
9. Ibid., June 1880.
10. John Morley, Reprinted in *Critical Miscellanies*, III.
11. BL, Macmillan, Add MS 55055, JM to AM, 5 October 1877.
12. R. H. Hutton, *Sir Walter Scott*, English Men of Letters Series, p. 104.
13. NLS, Fraser, Dep 208, Box 16: AM to Alexander Campbell Fraser, 29 August 1866.
14. Lewis Carroll, *Alice's Adventures in Wonderland*, illustrated by Chris Riddell (London: Macmillan Children's Books, 2020), p. 164.
15. BL, Macmillan, Add MS 55842, AM to Professor Price, 16 February 1875.
16. Ibid., AM to FM, 11 December 1875.

22: The Changing of the Guard (1879–83)

1. Anon., *Selected Letters of Malcolm Kingsley Macmillan*, pp. 20–1.
2. Ibid., p. 23.
3. Ibid., p. 29.
4. Charles L. Graves, *Life and Letters of Alexander Macmillan*, p. 305.
5. George Macmillan, *Letters*, p. 307.
6. BL, Macmillan, Add MS 55843, AM to Professor Price, 25 November 1879.
7. Ibid., AM to Dean Liddell, 30 June 1880.
8. Obituary, Newnham College Roll Letter, 1926.
9. E. P. Macmillan.
10. BL, Macmillan, Add MS 54789, AM to GAM, 13 August 1882.
11. BL, Macmillan, Add MS 55843, GLC to Grove, 8 December 1882.
12. Ibid.
13. Ibid., AM to Martin, 28 December 1881.
14. BL, Macmillan, Add MS 55042, Martin to AM, 27 November 1882.
15. Original agreement held in the Macmillan Archive, Basingstoke.
16. Graves, *Life and Letters of Alexander Macmillan*, pp. 369–70.
17. Macmillan, *Letters*, p. 322.
18. Hallam Tennyson, *Alfred Lord Tennyson: A Memoir*, 2, p. 383.
19. June Steffensen Hagen, *Tennyson and His Publishers*, p. 160.
20. Thomas Hughes, *Memoir of Daniel Macmillan*, p. viii.
21. BL, Macmillan, Add MS 55256, D Stewart to AM, 2 August 1882; Add MS 55257, WW Howard to AM, 4 January 1883.
22. BL, Macmillan, Add MS 55256, W Budden to AM, 22 June 1882.
23. BL, Macmillan, Add MS 55257, WW Howard to AM, 4 January 1883.

23: Heading for the Hills (1884–96)

1. E. P. Macmillan.
2. Ibid.
3. Stevens Family Papers.
4. Ibid.
5. BL, Macmillan, Add MS 54789, MKM to GAM, 19 October 1885.
6. Stevens Family Papers.
7. All these quotations are taken from the anonymous *Selected Letters of Malcolm Kingsley Macmillan*, pp. 267–87.
8. Sir Arthur H. Hardinge, *A Diplomatist in the East*, pp. 21–3.
9. Ibid., p. 24.
10. Ibid., pp. 25–6.
11. National Archives, FO 78/4206 etc.
12. BL, Gladstone, Add MS 44246, 19 November 1889.
13. Anon., *Selected Letters of MKM*, preface.
14. Dyer, *Reminiscences*.
15. BL, Supplementary Papers Macmillan, Add MS 61896, AM to GLC 14 November 1890.
16. Stevens Family Papers.
17. Graves, *Life and Letters of Alexander Macmillan*, p. 386.

24: The Brothers' Legacy

1. George Macmillan, *Letters*, p. 243.
2. Reading, Macmillan & Co., MAC BIS, undated letter from AG Bisdee to Sir Frederick Macmillan.
3. Richard Davenport-Hines, *The Macmillans*, p. 175.
4. DeBlock, 'Macmillan & Co. in New York: Transatlantic Publishing in the Late Nineteenth Century', p. 117.
5. Ibid., p. 50.
6. BL, Macmillan, Add MS 54800, George Brett to Frederick Macmillan, 26 March 1890.
7. Charles L. Graves, *Life and Letters of Alexander Macmillan*, p. 390.
8. BL, Macmillan, Add MS 55843, 3 February 1887.
9. Stevens Family Papers.

Index